T5-CAH-545

# Restoring Fiscal Discipline for Poverty Reduction in Peru

*A Public Expenditure Review*

**THE WORLD BANK**
*Washington, D.C.*

**THE INTER-AMERICAN DEVELOPMENT BANK**
*Washington, D.C.*

ISBN: 0-8213-5447-7
eISBN: 0-8213-5448-5
ISSN: 0253-2123

Cover Art: Fernando De Szyslo (Peru, 1925), Duino-Nueve (Orrantia/92), 1992, oil on canvas, 99.06 cm × 99.06 cm, Inter-American Development Bank Art Collection, Washington, DC, courtesy of the IDB Photo Library Unit. Photo of art: Gregory R. Staley Photography.

**Library of Congress Cataloging-in-Publication Data**

Restoring fiscal discipline for poverty reduction in Peru: a public expenditure review.
    p. cm. — (A World Bank country study)
Includes bibliographical references.
ISBN 0-8213-5447-7
  1. Government spending policy—Peru. 2. Economic assistance, Domestic—Peru. 3. Poverty—Government policy—Peru. I. World Bank. II. Series.

HJ7742.R48 2003
336.3'9'0985—dc21
                                            2003050056

# Contents

Abstract . . . . . . . . . . . . . . . . . . . . . . . . . . . . . . . . . . . . . . . . . . . . . . . . . . . .xi

Acknowledgments . . . . . . . . . . . . . . . . . . . . . . . . . . . . . . . . . . . . . . . . . .xiii

Abbreviations and Acronyms . . . . . . . . . . . . . . . . . . . . . . . . . . . . . . . . .xv

I.  Executive Summary . . . . . . . . . . . . . . . . . . . . . . . . . . . . . . . . . . . . . . .1
    Rationale and Organization . . . . . . . . . . . . . . . . . . . . . . . . . . . . . .1
    Main Findings and Recommendations. . . . . . . . . . . . . . . . . . . . . .2

II.  Peru's Fiscal Challenges and Vulnerabilities . . . . . . . . . . . . . . . . . . . . . . . .15
    Long-Run Fiscal Trends . . . . . . . . . . . . . . . . . . . . . . . . . . . . . . . . .15
    The Current Fiscal Disequilibria, 1999–2001 . . . . . . . . . . . . . . . . .20
    The Macroeconomic Consistent Expenditure Envelope, 2002–03 . . . . . . .23
    The Fiscal Adjustment Effort. . . . . . . . . . . . . . . . . . . . . . . . . . . . .30
    Revamping the Fiscal Rules . . . . . . . . . . . . . . . . . . . . . . . . . . . . . .34

III.  Reorienting the Budget Toward Pro-Poor Expenditure . . . . . . . . . . . . . . . . .41
    Modernizing Financial Management . . . . . . . . . . . . . . . . . . . . . . .42
    Upgrading the Budget Management System . . . . . . . . . . . . . . . . . .46
    Building a Medium-Term Expenditure Framework . . . . . . . . . . . . . . . .53
    Protecting the Budget as a Medium-Term Social Policy . . . . . . . . . .57
    Budget Transparency . . . . . . . . . . . . . . . . . . . . . . . . . . . . . . . . . . .60

IV.  Improving the Efficiency of Public Expenditure . . . . . . . . . . . . . . . . . . . . . .65
    Does Higher Government Expenditure Buy Better Results in
    Education and Health Care? . . . . . . . . . . . . . . . . . . . . . . . . . . . . . .66
    Tracing Leakages of Public Funds in Peru—
    A Public Expenditure Tracking Survey . . . . . . . . . . . . . . . . . . . . . .70
    Enhancing Targeting of Social Programs . . . . . . . . . . . . . . . . . . . . .88

V.  Addressing the Promises and Risks of Decentralization . . . . . . . . . . . . . . . . .95
    The Decision to Decentralize: Promises and Risks . . . . . . . . . . . . . . . . .96
    The Deconcentration of Central Government Spending and
    Transfers to the Municipalities: Intergovernmental Fiscal Relations . . . . .98
    The Emerging Legal Framework for Decentralization in Peru . . . . . . . . . .102
    Entering a Decentralization Path . . . . . . . . . . . . . . . . . . . . . . . . . . .104
    Decentralization in the Education Sector . . . . . . . . . . . . . . . . . . . .107
    Decentralization in the Health Sector . . . . . . . . . . . . . . . . . . . . . .110

VI.  Upgrading the Civil Service . . . . . . . . . . . . . . . . . . . . . . . . . . . . . . . . . .115
    The Size and Employment Conditions of the Public Sector . . . . . . . . . .116
    Reforming the Legal and Institutional Framework . . . . . . . . . . . . . .123
    Additional Measures for Improving Human Resource Administration . . . . . .127
    The Education Sector . . . . . . . . . . . . . . . . . . . . . . . . . . . . . . . . . .127

VII.   **Improving Governance and Reducing Corruption** ........................**133**
        The Costs of Weak Governance and Corruption ............................138
        Impact on Public Service Delivery ....................................139
        A Policy Agenda for Improving Governance ..............................141
VIII.  **Fine-Tuning Fiscal and Environmental Mining Policies** ...................**147**
        Background ........................................................148
        The Peruvian Taxation Regime ......................................148
        Comparison of Peru's Tax System to Minerals Tax Systems in Selected Countries .....148
        Improving Mining Environment Management ..........................165
**Annex A.  A Public Debt Sustainability Analysis for Peru** .......................**169**
**Annex B.  The Fiscal Effort Required for a Sustained Structural Deficit** ..........**193**
**Annex C.  Questionnaire on Public Financial Management** .....................**199**
**Annex D.  A Public Expenditure Tracking Survey: Methodological Issues** .........**207**
**Annex E.  Public Enterprise Reform in Peru: Introducing Management
            Contracts at FONAFE** .............................................**217**
**Annex F.  A Methodology for Functional Reviews and for
            Analyzing Functional Prospects** ...................................**221**
**Annex G.  List of Background Papers** .........................................**223**
**Statistical Appendix** ........................................................**225**
**Bibliography** ..............................................................**281**
**Map of Peru** ..............................................................**285**

## LIST OF TABLES

2.1     Key Macroeconomic Variables, 1969–89 ....................................17
2.2     Elasticity to GDP, 1970–2000 ...........................................18
2.3     Elasticities and Growth Volatilities for Peru, 1990–2000 .....................20
2.4     Key Economic Indicators ...............................................24
2.5     Recommendations for Tax Reform ......................................27
2.6     Social Expenditures are Pro- or Countercyclical ...........................35
3.1     Peru: Status of Budget Management Benchmarks .........................48
3.2     Composition of CG Budget Sources .....................................50
3.3     Revised Projection of the 2002 Budget ..................................52
3.4     Composition of Social Expenditure 1999–02 .............................55
3.5     Comparing Multiyear Budgets by Sector ................................56
3.6     Budget for Protected Social Programs ..................................58
3.7     Budget Transparency Ratings .........................................61
4.1.a   Regression Results for Education Indicators: Linear Regressions .............67
4.1.b   Regression Results for Health Indicators: Log-Log Regressions .............68
4.2     Peru: Efficiency of Public Expenditure in Reaching Social Outcomes, 1990–98 .....69
4.3     Per Capita Transfers to Municipalities in 2001 ...........................75

4.4     Municipalities that Do Not Know the Arrival Day of the Transfer . . . . . . . . . . . . . . . .76
4.5     Municipalities that Are Subject to CG Supervision . . . . . . . . . . . . . . . . . . . . . . . . . .77
4.6     Leakages in FONCOMUN and Canon Minero . . . . . . . . . . . . . . . . . . . . . . . . .77
4.7     Fraction of Transfers Used for Current Expenditure . . . . . . . . . . . . . . . . . . . . . . . . . .78
4.8     Beneficiary Households that Received Training/Information . . . . . . . . . . . . . . . . . . . .80
4.9     VDL Transfer Schedule . . . . . . . . . . . . . . . . . . . . . . . . . . . . . . . . . . . . . . . . . . . . . .81
4.10    Leakage Stage 3: Municipality to Local Committees . . . . . . . . . . . . . . . . . . . . . . . . .82
4.11    Worst Offenders, Leakage Stage 3 . . . . . . . . . . . . . . . . . . . . . . . . . . . . . . . . . . . . .83
4.12    Leakage Stage 4: Vaso de Leche Program (at household level, in percent) . . . . . . . . .85
4.13    Leakage Stage 5: Vaso de Leche Program (at beneficiary household level) . . . . . . . .86
4.14    Vaso de Leche Leakages (in percent) . . . . . . . . . . . . . . . . . . . . . . . . . . . . . . . . . . .87
4.15    Correlation Expenditure and Poverty by Department . . . . . . . . . . . . . . . . . . . . . . . .89
4.16    Household Access to Social Programs by Poverty Level, 2000 . . . . . . . . . . . . . . . . .90
4.17    Targeting by Food Assistance, Health, and Education Programs, 2000 . . . . . . . . . . .92
5.1     Budgeted Expenditure for the Public Sector for FY02 . . . . . . . . . . . . . . . . . . . . . . .99
5.2     Expenditure Coefficients by CTAR, 2001 . . . . . . . . . . . . . . . . . . . . . . . . . . . . . . .100
5.3     Expenditure by Department, 2000 . . . . . . . . . . . . . . . . . . . . . . . . . . . . . . . . . . . . .101
6.1     Number of Employees and the Average Monthly Wage Bill . . . . . . . . . . . . . . . . . .118
6.2     Urban Public and Private Sector Employment and
        Average Monthly Earnings, 1997–2001 . . . . . . . . . . . . . . . . . . . . . . . . . . . . . . . . .120
6.3     Dispersion of Salaries Charged to the PUP by
        Occupational Group and Salary Grade . . . . . . . . . . . . . . . . . . . . . . . . . . . . . . . . . .122
6.4     Maximum, Average and Minimum Earnings by
        Occupational Group and Regimen . . . . . . . . . . . . . . . . . . . . . . . . . . . . . . . . . . . . .123
6.5     Hourly Earnings by Occupational Groups and Areas,
        Third Quarter, 1997 (Nuevos Soles) . . . . . . . . . . . . . . . . . . . . . . . . . . . . . . . . . . . .129
8.1     Mineral Taxes in Peru and Other Countries . . . . . . . . . . . . . . . . . . . . . . . . . . . . .152
8.2     Comparative Measures of Profitability and Effective Tax Rate for a
        Model Base Metal Mine in Selected Jurisdictions . . . . . . . . . . . . . . . . . . . . . . . . . .153
8.3     Comparative Economic Measures for a Model Gold Metal Mine in
        Selected Jurisdictions . . . . . . . . . . . . . . . . . . . . . . . . . . . . . . . . . . . . . . . . . . . . . . .154
8.4     Copper Model: Peru's Tax System Sensitivity to Price and Cost Changes . . . . . . . . .154
8.5     Availability of Tax Stability in Selected Jurisdictions . . . . . . . . . . . . . . . . . . . . . . . .155
8.6     Tax System Sensitivity to Income Tax Rate . . . . . . . . . . . . . . . . . . . . . . . . . . . . . . .156
8.7     Income Tax Rates Applied to Mining Projects in Selected Jurisdictions . . . . . . . . . .157
8.8     Depreciation Applied to Typical Mining Equipment in Selected Jurisdictions . . . . . .158
8.9     Tax Sensitivity to Building Depreciation Rates . . . . . . . . . . . . . . . . . . . . . . . . . . . .158
8.10    Loss Carry Forward/Back Policy in Selected Jurisdictions . . . . . . . . . . . . . . . . . . . .159
8.11    Tax Sensitivity to Loss Carry Forward Time Limit . . . . . . . . . . . . . . . . . . . . . . . . .159
8.12    Tax Sensitivity to Annual Allowed Closure Deduction Over the Mine Life . . . . . . . .160
8.13    Tax Sensitivity to Reinvestment Allowance . . . . . . . . . . . . . . . . . . . . . . . . . . . . . .161

| | | |
|---|---|---|
| 8.14 | Presence of Mineral Royalty Tax Systems in Selected Jurisdictions | 162 |
| 8.15 | Tax System Sensitivity to a Royalty Tax | 163 |
| 8.16 | Tax System Sensitivity to Import Duty | 163 |
| 8.17 | Tax Sensitivity to Eliminating Import Duty and Imposing a Royalty | 164 |
| A.1 | Current Macroeconomic and Financial Trends | 171 |
| A.2 | Debt Dynamics Non-Financial Public Sector: Scenario With No External Shocks | 172 |
| A.3 | Scenario Without Shocks (Scenario A) | 176 |
| A.4 | Scenario With No Shocks (Scenario B) | 178 |
| A.5 | Scenario With No Shocks (Scenario C) | 180 |
| A.6 | Real Exchange Rate Adjustment in the Event of a "Sudden Stop" | 182 |
| A.7 | Public Sector Debt Sustainability With and With No Shocks | 185 |
| A.8 | Scenarios With Shocks (10% depreciation in real exchange rate and adjustment for contingent liabilities) (Scenario A) | 186 |
| A.9 | Scenarios With Shocks (10% depreciation in real exchange rate and adjustment for contingent liabilities) (Scenario B) | 188 |
| A.10 | Scenarios With Shocks (10% depreciation in real exchange rate and adjustment for contingent liabilities) (Scenario C) | 190 |
| B.1 | Required Fiscal Effort for Debt Sustainability | 196 |
| D.1 | Total Transfers to Municipalities in 2001 | 210 |
| D.2 | Volatility of Transfers to Municipalities | 211 |
| E.1 | Public Enterprises Target Indicators | 218 |
| SA.1 | Peru: Combined Public Sector Operations (millions of nuevo soles) | 226 |
| SA.2 | Peru: Combined Public Sector Operations (percent of GDP) | 227 |
| SA.3 | Peru: Combined Public Sector Operations (millions of 1994 soles) | 228 |
| SA.4 | Peru: Central Government Operations (millions of nuevo soles) | 229 |
| SA.5 | Peru: Central Government Operations (percent of GDP) | 231 |
| SA.6 | Peru: Central Government Operations (millions of 1994 soles) | 233 |
| SA.7a | Peru: Structure of Central Government's Fixed Capital Formation (millions of nuevo soles) | 235 |
| SA.7b | Peru: Structure of Central Government's Fixed Capital Formation (percent of total) | 236 |
| SA.8a | Peru: Operations of the Non-Financial Public Sector (millions of nuevo soles) | 237 |
| SA.8b | Peru: Operations of the Non-Financial Public Sector (percent of GDP) | 238 |
| SA.8c | Peru: Operations of the Non-Financial Public Sector (millions of 1994 soles) | 239 |
| SA.9 | Peru: Local Government Operations | 240 |
| SA.10 | Peru: Operations of the Non-Financial State Enterprises (millions of nuevo soles) | 241 |
| SA.11 | Peru: Operations of the Rest of the Central Government (millions of nuevo soles) | 242 |
| SA.12a | Peru: Functional Classification of Central Government Budget Expenditures (millions of nuevo soles) | 243 |
| SA.12b | Peru: Functional Classification of Central Government Budget Expenditures (percent of GDP) | 244 |
| SA.13 | Peru: Central Government Spending by Ministry or Institution | 245 |

SA.14    Peru: Social Spending by Type . . . . . . . . . . . . . . . . . . . . . . . . . . . . . . .246

SA.15    Peru: Composition of Social Expenditures (millions of nuevo soles) . . . . . . . . . . .247

SA.16    Peru: PESEM: Projected Social Spending by Institution, 2002–06 . . . . . . . . . . .249

SA.17    Peru: Pledges at the 2002 Consultative Group for Peru . . . . . . . . . . . . . . . . . .250

SA.18    Peru: Privatizations and Concessions, 2001–04 . . . . . . . . . . . . . . . . . . . .251

SA.19    Peru: Current Revenues by Awarded Concessions (millions of US$) . . . . . . . . . . .252

SA.20    Peru: Comparative Performance in Social Indicators . . . . . . . . . . . . . . . . . .252

SA.21    Peru: Main Tax Breaks . . . . . . . . . . . . . . . . . . . . . . . . . . . . . . . . . . .253

SA.22    Peru: Alternative Measures for Tax Reform by Sector or Region . . . . . . . . . . . . . .253

SA.23a   Latin America General Government's Tax Revenues, 1998 (percent of GDP) . . . . .254

SA.23b   Latin American Economies: Outline of Fiscal Policy Rules . . . . . . . . . . . . . . . .255

SA.24    Peru: Elasticities of Social Spending to Total Spending of the
         Consolidated Public Sector in Peru (1997–2002) . . . . . . . . . . . . . . . . . . . . . .256

SA.25    Peru: Degree of Transparency in the Publication of
         Institutional Information . . . . . . . . . . . . . . . . . . . . . . . . . . . . . . . . . .257

SA.26    Peru: Published Information of the Budget in 2002 . . . . . . . . . . . . . . . . . . . .257

SA.27    Peru: Composite Governance Indicators, International Comparisons, 1998 . . . . . .258

SA.28    Volatility in Latin America . . . . . . . . . . . . . . . . . . . . . . . . . . . . . . . . . .259

SA.29    Economic Distribution of General Government Revenue and Expenditure,
         Selected Countries . . . . . . . . . . . . . . . . . . . . . . . . . . . . . . . . . . . . . .260

SA.30    Peru: Distribution of Social Investment by Different Social Programs
         and by Decile of Poverty Severity . . . . . . . . . . . . . . . . . . . . . . . . . . . . . .261

SA.31a   Peru: Average Monthly Per Capital Income of Households, 2000 (US$) . . . . . . . .262

SA.31b   Peru: Household Access to Social Programs by Income Per Capita Deciles,
         2000 (percent of total) . . . . . . . . . . . . . . . . . . . . . . . . . . . . . . . . . . . .262

SA.31c   Peru: Household Access to Social Programs by Income Per Capita Deciles,
         2000 (percent of subtotal) . . . . . . . . . . . . . . . . . . . . . . . . . . . . . . . . . .262

SA.32    Peru: Mistargeting by Types of Food Assistance, 2000 . . . . . . . . . . . . . . . . . .263

SA.33    Peru: Mistargeting by Types of Health Programs, 2000 . . . . . . . . . . . . . . . . . .263

SA.34    Peru: Mistargeting by Types of Education Programs, 2000 . . . . . . . . . . . . . . . . .264

SA.35    Peru: Evolution of Household Access to Social Programs, 1998–2000 . . . . . . . . . .264

SA.36    Peru: Annual Private Expenditure on Education by
         Per Capita Income Decile, 2000 . . . . . . . . . . . . . . . . . . . . . . . . . . . . . . .265

SA.37    Peru: Annual Expenditure on Health by Per Capita Income Decile . . . . . . . . . . . .266

SA.38    Peru: Definitions of the Consolidated Public Sector (CPS) . . . . . . . . . . . . . . . .266

SA.39    Peru: Central Government National and Regional Budget Composition, 2002 . . . .267

SA.40    Peru: Main Revenue Sources for Municipalites, 2002 . . . . . . . . . . . . . . . . . . .268

SA.41    Peru: Departmental Budget–Education and Health by
         Expenditure Category, 2002 . . . . . . . . . . . . . . . . . . . . . . . . . . . . . . . . .269

SA.42    Peru Indexes on Corruption . . . . . . . . . . . . . . . . . . . . . . . . . . . . . . . . .270

SA.43    Peru: Corruption in the Judiciary, National and Municipal Agencies . . . . . . . . . . .272

SA.44    Peru: Expenditure by Department, 2001 . . . . . . . . . . . . . . . . . . . . . . . . . .274

SA.45    Peru: Expenditure Coefficients by Department, 2001 . . . . . . . . . . . . . . . . . . . . . .275

SA.46    Peru: Decentralization in LAC  . . . . . . . . . . . . . . . . . . . . . . . . . . . . . . . . . . . . . .276

SA.47    Peru: Principal Revenue Sources of Subnational Governments . . . . . . . . . . . . . . .276

SA.48    Peru: Summary of Mining Taxation Authority for Selected Taxes and Fees . . . . . . .277

SA.49    Peru: Mining Fiscal Methods and their Amenability to
         Fiscal Decentralization  . . . . . . . . . . . . . . . . . . . . . . . . . . . . . . . . . . . . . . . . . . . .279

SA.50    Total Transfers in Soles  . . . . . . . . . . . . . . . . . . . . . . . . . . . . . . . . . . . . . . . . . . . .279

## LIST OF FIGURES

2.1     NFPS Fiscal and Primary Balances . . . . . . . . . . . . . . . . . . . . . . . . . . . . . . . . . . . .16

2.2     Tax Revenue Composition, 1970–2001  . . . . . . . . . . . . . . . . . . . . . . . . . . . . . . . .16

2.3     Procyclical Fiscal Stance . . . . . . . . . . . . . . . . . . . . . . . . . . . . . . . . . . . . . . . . . . . .19

2.4     Volatility in Fiscal Variables  . . . . . . . . . . . . . . . . . . . . . . . . . . . . . . . . . . . . . . . . .19

2.5     Fiscal Trend Over Time . . . . . . . . . . . . . . . . . . . . . . . . . . . . . . . . . . . . . . . . . . . .21

2.6     LAC: VAT Effectiveness  . . . . . . . . . . . . . . . . . . . . . . . . . . . . . . . . . . . . . . . . . . .30

2.7     Central Government's Expenditure Composition  . . . . . . . . . . . . . . . . . . . . . . . . .31

2.8     LAC: Capital Expenditure (1998) . . . . . . . . . . . . . . . . . . . . . . . . . . . . . . . . . . . .32

2.9     Structure of Central Government's Fixed Capital Formation  . . . . . . . . . . . . . . . .32

2.10    Social and Public Spending  . . . . . . . . . . . . . . . . . . . . . . . . . . . . . . . . . . . . . . . . .34

2.11    Growth Rates in Social and Public Spending . . . . . . . . . . . . . . . . . . . . . . . . . . . .35

2.12    Actual and Potential Output  . . . . . . . . . . . . . . . . . . . . . . . . . . . . . . . . . . . . . . . .38

2.13    Actual Primary Balance (% of GDP) and Structural Primary Balance
        (% of potential GDP) . . . . . . . . . . . . . . . . . . . . . . . . . . . . . . . . . . . . . . . . . . . . . .38

3.1     Comparison of Central Government and NFPS Balance . . . . . . . . . . . . . . . . . . . .53

3.2     Share of Social Expenditures to GDP  . . . . . . . . . . . . . . . . . . . . . . . . . . . . . . . . .54

3.3     Sectoral Budget Allocations . . . . . . . . . . . . . . . . . . . . . . . . . . . . . . . . . . . . . . . . .54

3.4     Index of Budget Transparency . . . . . . . . . . . . . . . . . . . . . . . . . . . . . . . . . . . . . . .62

3.5     Percent of Government Entities Publishing Information . . . . . . . . . . . . . . . . . . . .63

4.1     Lorenz Curves for Intergovernmental Transfers  . . . . . . . . . . . . . . . . . . . . . . . . .74

4.2     How the Milk Disappears in the Vaso de Leche Program  . . . . . . . . . . . . . . . . . .86

4.3     Lorenz Curves in Selected Social Programs . . . . . . . . . . . . . . . . . . . . . . . . . . . . .90

4.4     Lorenz Curves for Health Expenditure . . . . . . . . . . . . . . . . . . . . . . . . . . . . . . . .91

4.5     Lorenz Curves for Education Expenditure . . . . . . . . . . . . . . . . . . . . . . . . . . . . . .91

4.6     Access to Social Programs, 2000 . . . . . . . . . . . . . . . . . . . . . . . . . . . . . . . . . . . . .92

5.1     Municipal Revenues, 2001  . . . . . . . . . . . . . . . . . . . . . . . . . . . . . . . . . . . . . . . . .102

5.2     Central Government Transfers to Municipals, 2001 . . . . . . . . . . . . . . . . . . . . . . .102

6.1     International Government Employment Comparison . . . . . . . . . . . . . . . . . . . . . .116

6.2     Corruption in Public Services . . . . . . . . . . . . . . . . . . . . . . . . . . . . . . . . . . . . . . .117

6.3     Employment and Average Earnings of the Private and Public Sector . . . . . . . . . . .121

6.4     Permanent and Contractual Average Earnings (Nuevos Soles)  . . . . . . . . . . . . . . .124

7.1    Peru's Governance Indicators, 1998–2001 . . . . . . . . . . . . . . . . . . . . . . . . .134

7.2    Obstacles to Doing Business . . . . . . . . . . . . . . . . . . . . . . . . . . . . . . . . . . . .135

7.3    Perceived Level of Corruption in Selected Agencies . . . . . . . . . . . . . . . . .135

7.4    Bribes by Type of Activity . . . . . . . . . . . . . . . . . . . . . . . . . . . . . . . . . . . . .137

7.5    Corruption in Public Service . . . . . . . . . . . . . . . . . . . . . . . . . . . . . . . . . . .138

7.6    Average Percent of Income Paid in Bribes . . . . . . . . . . . . . . . . . . . . . . . . .139

7.7    Indexes of Service Quality and Bribery . . . . . . . . . . . . . . . . . . . . . . . . . . .140

7.8    Quality of Public Services . . . . . . . . . . . . . . . . . . . . . . . . . . . . . . . . . . . . .140

7.9    Quality of Health and Education Services . . . . . . . . . . . . . . . . . . . . . . . . .141

7.10   Provision of Public Services—Local Governments vs.
Other Government Agencies . . . . . . . . . . . . . . . . . . . . . . . . . . . . . . . . . . . .142

7.11   National and Municipal Agencies Are Ridden by
Different Types of Corruption . . . . . . . . . . . . . . . . . . . . . . . . . . . . . . . . . .142

7.12   Public Official's View on Reforms in Public Sector . . . . . . . . . . . . . . . . . .144

A.1    Scenario with No Shocks . . . . . . . . . . . . . . . . . . . . . . . . . . . . . . . . . . . . . .175

A.2    Scenario with Shocks . . . . . . . . . . . . . . . . . . . . . . . . . . . . . . . . . . . . . . . . .182

A.3    Peru Debt Dynamics: Comparison of Scenarios With and With No Shocks . . . . . . .184

D.1    FONCOMUN Transfer Process . . . . . . . . . . . . . . . . . . . . . . . . . . . . . . . . .212

# LIST OF BOXES

2.1    The Fiscal Prudence and Transparency Law . . . . . . . . . . . . . . . . . . . . . . . . .22

2.2    Tax Regime and Proposed Changes . . . . . . . . . . . . . . . . . . . . . . . . . . . . . . .25

2.3    Peru: Evaluation of the Transparency Law 2000–01 . . . . . . . . . . . . . . . . . . .36

3.1    Main IGR/PEM Issues . . . . . . . . . . . . . . . . . . . . . . . . . . . . . . . . . . . . . . . .42

3.2    The Integrated Financial Management System (SIAF) of Peru . . . . . . . . . . . . . .43

3.3    Introducing the SIAF at the Ministries of Defense and
National Security (Interior) . . . . . . . . . . . . . . . . . . . . . . . . . . . . . . . . . . . . .45

3.4    Peru: Principal Stages of the Budget Formation . . . . . . . . . . . . . . . . . . . . . .47

3.5    Peru: Institutionalizing a Virtual Poverty Fund:
A Look at Best-Practice Uganda . . . . . . . . . . . . . . . . . . . . . . . . . . . . . . . . . .60

4.1    MEXICO: Integrating Social Programs for Improved Efficiency—
The Case of PROGRESA . . . . . . . . . . . . . . . . . . . . . . . . . . . . . . . . . . . . . . .93

5.1    Lessons from Decentralization Experiences in Latin America . . . . . . . . . . . . . .97

5.2    The Decentralization Drive in Education in LAC: Some Cases . . . . . . . . . . . .108

5.3    Decentralization of the Health Sector in LAC . . . . . . . . . . . . . . . . . . . . . . .111

6.1    The Sequencing of Civil Service Reform Measures . . . . . . . . . . . . . . . . . . . .130

7.1    Regulation of Infrastructure in Peru . . . . . . . . . . . . . . . . . . . . . . . . . . . . . .136

7.2    A Multipronged Strategy for Addressing Corruption and
Improving Governance . . . . . . . . . . . . . . . . . . . . . . . . . . . . . . . . . . . . . . .143

8.1    Peru: Description of the Existing Mining Fiscal System . . . . . . . . . . . . . . . . .149

8.2    Creating Mining Stabilization Funds: The Ancash Model . . . . . . . . . . . . . . . .165

# ABSTRACT

Since his inauguration in July 2001, President Toledo has proposed to take actions in the areas of macroeconomic stabilization; reopening of country's access to international financial markets; budget modernization and State decentralization; social policy; revamping of the armed forces, the police, and internal security services; and consolidation of Peru's democracy and social stability through consensus-building and transparent and participatory mechanisms. These are all critical development challenges faced by Peru. The momentum for reform, which was strong in the early 1990s, ran out of steam in the late 1990s, and genuine efforts by the new administration to re-invigorate it are facing great social pressure for short-term, populist measures. There is an urgent need to build momentum for "second-generation" reforms, especially those in public expenditure, which would provide longer-term sustainability to the government's strategy of poverty reduction and growth.

Despite its initial progress, Peru is not likely to meet these development goals in the near term. Achieving success in the medium term will depend on completing a public expenditure management agenda summarized in the seven main themes of this report:

- Restoring fiscal discipline
- Reorienting the budget toward pro-poor expenditure
- Improving the efficiency of public expenditure
- Addressing the promises and risks of decentralization
- Upgrading the civil service
- Improving governance and reducing corruption
- Fine-tuning mining taxation and environmental policies.

How to address these themes is clear. Significant primary surpluses are fundamental to achieving sustainable fiscal and debt-management policies, and are thus a top priority. Shifting expenditure to pro-poor priorities is essential for achieving desired social outcomes in the medium term. Making the most effective use of scarce resources is needed for a country in the midst of fiscal retrenchment. Fiscal discipline also implies resolving fundamental questions of the decentralization process, particularly, what functions must be decentralized, and with what resources, timing, and desired outcomes? An ill-designed decentralization process, especially if developed through brand-new regional governments, has considerable potential for engendering severe fiscal disarray and macroeconomic destabilization. Thus there is a need to proceed very cautiously.

The government of Peru also needs to upgrade its human capital. Such reform would contribute to improving governance and fighting corruption, thus providing more productive and less expensive delivery of public service. Finally, fine-tuning mining taxation and transfers and mining-related environmental policies is needed not only to strengthen the global competitiveness of one of the main exports of Peru through a stable tax regime, but to enhance budgetary transparency and minimize environmental damage.

This report is the product of the analytical work of a large number of experts, both Peruvian and non-Peruvian. They distill critical lessons and challenges that are relevant for policymakers in Peru, in Latin America, and in countries that are embarking on comprehensive public expenditure reform. Thus, it is a major contribution to our knowledge and thinking in this area.

# ACKNOWLEDGMENTS

This report is a joint effort of the World Bank and the Inter-American Development Bank. José R. López-Cálix (WB-LCSPE) and Alberto Melo (IDB-RE3/OD5) are the authors and project managers. The report is an outgrowth of a collective effort including partial contributions and background papers by Osvaldo Schenone (consultant–section on taxation, Chapter II); Carlos Oliva (consultant–section on fiscal patterns, Chapter II); Nelson Shack and Oscar Pajuelo (General Budget Director and Accountant General of Peru–Annex C); Bruno Barletti and Lourdes Cueva (SIAF Coordinator and assistant–section on transparency, Chapter III); Rossana Mostajo (consultant–section on protected programs, Chapter III); Lorena Alcazar, Erik Wachtenheim, Mitchel Seligson (consultants–section on public expenditure tracking survey, Chapter IV and Annex D); Gillette Hall (WB–Box on PROGRESA, Chapter IV), Juvenal Diaz (FONCODES– section on targeting, Chapter IV); Richard Moore (consultant–section on decentralization of social sectors, Chapter V and Annex F); Eduardo Fernandez (consultant–municipal debt, Chapter V); Peter Gregory (consultant–civil service, Chapter VI); Francesca Recanatini and Daniel Kauffman (WB–governance and corruption, Chapter VII); José Luis Guasch (WB–box on regulatory agencies, Chapter VII); James Otto (consultant–mining taxation, Chapter VIII) and Felix Remy (WB–environment, Chapter VIII); Elaine A. Tinsley (WB–Statistical Appendix and thorough analytical and research assistance); Rashmi Shankar (consultant–research assistance on Annexes A and B); and Gabriel Ortiz de Zevallos (consultant–Annex E). Peer reviewers were Ritva Reinikka and William Dorotinsky (both WB), who provided very helpful and detailed input.

The report also received numerous comments from Andrew Wolfe and Mauricio Villafuerte (IMF), Guillermo Perry, Mauricio Carrizosa, Sara Guerschanik Calvo, Yasuhiko Matsuda, Gillette Hall, Pierre Werbrouck, Quentin Wodon, Keta Ruiz, Marianne Fay, Harold Adelman, Norbert Schady, Evangeline Javier, Daniel Cotlear, Livia Benavides (all from the WB), and Gonzalo Afcha, Xavier Comas, Rafael de la Cruz, Gonzalo Deustua, Jaime Fernandez, Amanda Glassman, Susan Kolodin, Jorge Lamas, and Jaime Enrique Vargas (all from the IDB). It also greatly benefited from the field survey work of Instituto Apoyo in Peru, which did a magnificent job. Hazel Vargas provided the main administrative and production support and editorial assistance. Diane Stamm was the principal language editor. Also providing production support at various stages were Silvia Marquina de León, Rosalía Rushton, Marianella Rivadeneira and Patricia Chacón Holt. Ana Maria Arteaga and Ana Maria Angulo provided excellent support to field research in Lima. The report benefited from the active guidance and support of Isabel Guerrero (WB–Director), Ana-Maria Arriagada (WB–LCSHD Sector Director), Mauricio Carrizosa (WB–LCSPE Sector Manager), Ernesto May (WB–LCSPR Director), and Ana Maria Rodriguez (IDB, RE3/OD5 Chief).

The team would like to express its sincere gratitude for the excellent cooperation provided by Peruvian officials throughout the process, especially during the team visits in Peru, and including the main mission in late November 2001. In particular, the team would like to thank Mr. Roberto Dañino, President of the Council of Ministers; Pedro Pablo Kuczynski, Minister; Kurt Burneo, Patricia Teuillet, and Fernando Zavala, Viceministers of Economy and Finance; and Oscar Pajuelo, Accountant General, for their enthusiastic support. Many thanks also go to Veronica Zavala, Nelson Shack, Oscar Blanco, Fernando Lituma, Bruno Barletti, Carlos Ricse, Lourdes Cueva, Waldo Mendoza, Carmen Negron, Javier Abugattas, Lander Aleman, Jorge Estrella, Luis Paz, Pedro Francke, Beatriz Merino and Gustavo Perochena, Gilberto Moncada, and Reynaldo Bringas who provided timely inputs and responded to numerous requests.

The report has been subject to early and multiple consultation and dissemination efforts in Lima, Peru. In December 2001, at the closing of the main mission, draft preliminary conclusions were discussed with Peruvian officials. In March 2002, a detailed proposal on the revamping of the Fiscal Prudence and Transparency Law was presented in a Ministry of Economy and Finance seminar on Fiscal Rules. A month later, a framework for decentralization was submitted in the FONCODES/Presidency joint seminar on the Decentralization of the Social Sectors. Finally, in August 2002, the full draft report was openly discussed with officials, think tanks, the media, donors, the private sector, and civil society representatives in a seminar on Fiscal Discipline, Public Expenditure Efficiency, and Decentralization jointly organized with MEF and IDB. Preliminary findings of this report and background papers have also been instrumental in the elaboration of components of the World Bank's Second Programmatic Social Reform Loan and the Country Assistance Strategy for Peru.

# ABBREVIATIONS AND ACRONYMS

| | |
|---|---|
| 2SLS | Two-stage least squares |
| ACE | Community educational associations |
| ADEs | Areas of Educational Development |
| AEs | Areas of Execution |
| BCRP | Central Bank of Peru |
| BN | Banco de la Nación (Treasury) |
| CEC | Consejos Escolares Consultivos |
| CETICOS | Centers for Export, Transportation, Industry, Commercialization and Services |
| CG | Central Government |
| CIF | Cost, insurance & freight |
| CLAS | Local Committees of Health Administration |
| CONAM | Consejo Nacional del Ambiente (National Environmental Council) |
| CONASEV | Comisión Nacional Supervisora de Empresas y Valores |
| CONITE | National Commission for Foreign Investment and Technology |
| CONSUCODE | Consejo Superior de Contrataciones y Adquisiciones del Estado, (Superior Council of Contractings and Procurements from the State) |
| COOPOP | National Office for Popular Cooperation |
| COPRI | Commission for Promotion of Private Investment |
| CPS | Consolidated public sector |
| CTARs | Transitory Councils of Regional Administration |
| DGAES | Dirección General de Asuntos Económicos y Sociales, (General Office of Economic and Social Affairs) |
| DGFP | General Directorate of Fiscal Policy |
| DGSP | Dirección General de Salud Pública |
| DISAs | Regional Directorates of Health |
| DNPP | Dirección Nacional del Presupuesto Publico (National Directorate of the Public Budget) |
| DREs | Regional Directorates of Education |
| EBFs | Extra-Budgetary Funds |
| EDUCO | Educación Comunitaria |
| EGASA | Empresa de Gas Sociedad Anonima |
| ENAHO | Encuesta Nacional de Hogares (National Household Survey) |
| ESSALUD | Seguro Social de Salud (Health Insurance) |
| ETR | Effective tax rate |
| EUs | Executing Units |
| FEF | Fondo de Estabilización Fiscal |
| FGT2 | Foster, Greer, and Thorbecke 2 |
| FIDE | Intergovernmental Decentralization Fund |
| FLIRB | Front-loaded interest reduction Brady bonds |
| FONAFE | National Fund for Financing Government Enterprise Activity |
| FONAHPU | National Savings Fund |
| FONAVI | Fondo Nacional de Vivienda |
| FONCODES | Fondo Nacional de Compensación y Desarrollo Social |
| FONCOMUN | Fondo de Compensación Municipal |
| FONCOR | Regional Compensation Fund |
| FSF | Fiscal Stabilization Fund |

| | |
|---|---|
| FY | Fiscal year |
| GDE | General Directorate of the Environment |
| GDP | Gross domestic product |
| GFS | Government Financial Statistics |
| GG | General government |
| GOP | Government of Peru |
| HIPCs | Highly indebted poor countries |
| IBRD | International Bank for Reconstruction and Development |
| IDB, IADB | Inter-American Development Bank |
| IES | Extraordinary Solidarity Tax (Impuesto Extraordinario de Solidaridad) |
| IGR | Institutional and Governance Review |
| IGV | Value added tax |
| IMF | International Monetary Fund |
| INA | Iniciativa Nacional Anti-Corrupción |
| INADE | Instituto Nacional de Desarrollo (National Institute for Development) |
| INEI | National Institute for Statistics and Information |
| IRR | Internal rates of return |
| ISC | Selective tax on consumption or excise tax |
| ISPs | Institutos superior pedagógicas |
| JNE | Junta Nacional Electoral |
| LAC | Latin America and the Caribbean |
| LIBOR | London Interbank Offered Rate |
| LPTF | Ley de Prudencia y Transparencia Fiscal |
| MAB | Multiyear Budget |
| MED | Ministry of Education |
| MEF | Ministry of Economy and Finance |
| MEM | Ministry of Energy and Mines |
| MINDEF | Ministry of Defense |
| MINSA | Ministry of Health |
| MMM | Marco Macroeconómico Multianual (Multiyear Macroeconomic Framework) |
| Mt/day | Metric tons per day |
| MTBF | Medium-term budgeting framework |
| MTEF | Medium-term expenditure framework |
| NA | Not applicable |
| NFPS | Non-financial public sector |
| NGOs | Nongovernmental organizations |
| NPS | Nonpersonal services |
| NS | Nuevos Soles |
| ODI | Investment office |
| OECD | Organization for Economic Cooperation and Development |
| OLS | Ordinary least squares |
| ONP | Oficina de Normalización Provisional (Pensions) |
| OSIPTEL | Organismo Superior de Inversión Privada en Telecomunicaciones |
| OSITRAN | Organismo Superior de la Inversión en Infraestructura de Transporte de Uso Publico |
| OUs | Operational Units |
| PAAG | Programa de Administración de Acuerdos de Gestión |
| PAF | Poverty Action Fund |
| PARSALUD | Programa de Apoyo a la Reforma del Sector Salud (Health Sector Reform Program) |
| PCM | Presidencia del Consejo de Ministros (Premier's Office) |

| | |
|---|---|
| PDI | Institutional Development Projects |
| PEAP | Poverty Eradication Action Plan |
| PEM | Public expenditure management |
| PER | Public Expenditure Review |
| PESEM | Plan Estratégico Sectorial Multianual (Multiyear Strategic Sector Plans) |
| PETS | Public Expenditure Tracking Surveys |
| PPP | Purchasing Power Parity |
| PPS | Probability Proportionate to Size |
| PROGRESA | Programa de Educación, Salud y Alimentación |
| PRONAA | Programa Nacional de Asistencia Alimentaria (National Food Assistance Program) |
| PRONAMACHCS | Proyecto Nacional de Mantenimiento de Cuencas Hidrográficas y Conservación de Suelos (National Project for the Management of Water Sheds) |
| PSPs | Protected Social Programs |
| PSRL | Programmatic social reform loan |
| PUP | Planilla Única de Pagos (Unified Payroll) |
| RENIEC | Registro Nacional de Identificación y Estado Civil |
| RER | Real exchange rate |
| SEAL | South-West Electricity Society |
| SEDAPAL | Lima's Water and Sewerage Service |
| SENSICO | National Service for Construction Industry Training |
| SEPs | Sector Strategy Plans |
| SIAFITO | A simplified SIAF |
| SIAF-SP | Sistema Integrado de Administrado Financiera del Sector Publico (Integrated Financial Management System) |
| SIMSIP | Simulations for Social Indicators and Poverty |
| SIS-SMI | Integral and Mother and Child Health Insurances |
| SMI | Seguro Materno-Infantil (Mother and Child Health Insurance) |
| SPC | Sector Publico Consolidado |
| SUNAT | Superintendencia Nacional de Administración Tributaria (Superintendency for Tax Administration) |
| SUR | Seemingly unrelated regression |
| UEs | Unidades Ejecutoras |
| UIT | Unidades de Ingreso Tributario |
| USEs | Unidades de Servicios Educativos (Educational Service Units) |
| USIS | Unidades de Seguro Integral de Salud |
| VAT | Value added tax |
| VDL | Vaso de Leche |

CURRENCY EQUIVALENTS: US$1.00 = NS 3.61 (Nuevo Sol exchange rate as of 1 October 2002)
GOVERNMENT FISCAL YEAR: January 1–December 31
WEIGHTS AND MEASURES: Metric System

I

# EXECUTIVE SUMMARY
## A Comprehensive Reform Agenda of Public Expenditure Management for Peru

*A successful economic policy needs two inputs: sound technical design and strong political support to bring it forward. A common mistake is to believe that both aspects are substitutes rather than complementary one to each other. In practice, this leads to wrongly believe that political power may offset poor technical design permanently.*

Juan Carlos de Pablo
"Cómo Fracasa Rotundamente un Ministro de Economía, 1988"

## Rationale and Organization

For the World Bank and the Inter-American Development Bank (IDB), it is a welcome privilege to provide the incoming Administration of a member country with joint and comprehensive diagnoses and policy recommendations in those areas that contribute most to enhancing the client's development prospects.[1] One of these key areas is public expenditure management, which is the purpose of this report. As the Toledo Administration enters its second year in office, we hope that the contents of this Public Expenditure Review (PER) will be useful for Peru to deal with some of the formidable challenges the country faces in its development agenda.

This chapter presents a synthesis of Peru's public expenditure reform agenda from the Banks' perspective. It is based on, and distills, the thematic chapters that make up this report. Chapters II–IV examine the core functions of public expenditure management: macro fiscal aggregates, resource allocations to strategic sectors, and microeconomic efficiency of public spending. Chapters V–VIII explore selected themes, such as the decentralization of public administration and the social sectors; civil service reform; governance and corruption; and fiscal and environmental mining issues. These chapters are, in turn, supported by 15 topic-specific background papers, including an innovative public expenditure tracking survey on municipal transfers, and numerous and valuable comments provided by Peruvian officials throughout dissemination activities.

---

1. Several sector studies for Peru were published in the last few years by both institutions in the areas of education, health, private sector participation and infrastructure, institutional governance, financial management, procurement, and country strategy. However, the last World Bank Public Expenditure Review was produced in 1994.

We do not attempt to provide full coverage of all areas affected by public expenditure. Expressing the strategic coincidence between the World Bank and the IDB around the idea that poverty reduction is the paramount objective of their assistance efforts, the report deliberately focuses on social sectors spending and leaves aside infrastructure and other sectors, which have been the subject of more specific sector studies in previous years. This report was finalized in June 2002, and discussed with Peruvian officials in mid-August 2002. Policy developments that have taken place after that time are not reflected in it.

## Main Findings and Recommendations

At the onset of the new century, Peru faces substantial development challenges. Significant achievements in terms of growth, poverty reduction, and improvements in social indicators up to 1997 have been partially set back by ensuing persistent slowdowns in economic activity, fiscal indiscipline, political uncertainty, institutional weaknesses, and poor governance. The momentum for reform, which used to be strong in the early 1990s, ran out of steam in the late 1990s, and genuine efforts by the new Peruvian officials to reinvigorate it are facing strong social pressure for short-term, populist measures.[2] Populism might bring palliatives, but is deleterious to the macroeconomic fundamentals of the country and, ultimately, to the standard of living. There is, rather, an urgent need to restore fiscal discipline and build momentum for "second-generation" reforms, including those in public expenditure, which would provide longer-term sustainability to the strategy of poverty reduction.

The new Administration inherited a fiscal system under severe stress. Since 1999, Peru's fiscal stance has been fragile due to a combination of adverse external shocks, expansive fiscal policies, elections, and other unfavorable domestic developments accompanying the transition to the post-Fujimori legacy. Led by a primary deficit that for the first time in more than a decade has become negative since 1999, the combined fiscal deficit significantly increased from 0.4 percent of GDP in 1997 to 3.2 percent of GDP in 2000, only to be slightly reduced to an estimated 2.5 percent of GDP in 2001. Low, volatile, and procyclical tax revenue combined with a rigid public expenditure facing popular demands complicate efforts to finance an ambitious poverty-reduction agenda, while achieving fiscal adjustment. Despite a multiyear pro-poor budgeting framework, social spending remains underfunded, diverted through multiple leakages, and mistargeted. The concentration of budget formulation authority in Lima coupled with discretional and decentralized budget execution through Transitory Councils of Regional Administration (CTARs) reduces the impact of social expenditure and the efficiency of service delivery.

Since his arrival in July 2001, President Toledo has proposed taking action in the areas of macroeconomic stabilization; reopening of country's access to international financial markets; budget modernization and State decentralization; social policy; revamping of the armed forces, police and internal security services; and consolidation of Peru's democracy and social stability through consensus-building and transparent and participatory mechanisms. Despite its initial progress, Peru is not likely to meet these goals in the near term. Achieving success in the medium term will rather depend to a great extent on how quickly it restores fiscal discipline, shifts scarce spending to the government's priorities, and ensures an efficient delivery of public services under a very complex and politically driven decentralization process. We summarize the public expenditure management agenda in seven main messages:

■ Restoring fiscal discipline
■ Reorienting the budget toward pro-poor expenditure
■ Improving the efficiency of public expenditure
■ Addressing the promises and risks of decentralization

---

2. In this report, populism is defined as a conception and practice of economic policy that favors unsustainable expansionary fiscal and monetary polices as the main engine of GDP growth and employment creation. For a discussion of the concept, see Dornbusch and Edwards (1991).

■ Upgrading the civil service
■ Improving governance and reducing corruption
■ Fine-tuning mining taxation and environmental policies.

The storyline behind these seven themes is a bit long to tell, but is simple. First, significant primary surpluses are the inescapable premise for sustainable fiscal and debt-management policies. They are also needed to lay the basis for viable countercyclical fiscal and social policies in the future. Second, shifting expenditure to pro-poor priorities is essential for achieving desired social outcomes in the medium term. Budget reorientation requires not only enhancing transparency of budget cuts and reallocations during implementation, but reviewing inertial and in-year seasonal spending. Improving budget protection mechanisms of priority social programs is useful to consolidate an effective countercyclical social policy. Third, making most effective use of scarce resources is essential for a country in the midst of fiscal retrenchment. This implies reducing anti-poor disparities in regional budget allocations; eliminating duplications in social and basic infrastructure projects; minimizing leaks of public funds, particularly in food supplementary programs and at the bottom level of service delivery and, if feasible, considering their gradual downsizing or replacement by cash-transfer programs; and improving targeting of resources, especially outside Lima, for most social programs, especially those addressing the most vulnerable. Fourth, it is essential promptly to resolve fundamental questions of the decentralization process: in particular, what functions must be decentralized? And with what timing and outcomes in mind? An ill-designed decentralization process, especially if developed through brand-new regional governments, has considerable potential for provoking severe fiscal disarray and macroeconomic destabilization. Thus there is a need to proceed very cautiously. Fifth, the government needs to upgrade its human capital in charge of service delivery. The civil service regime is in total disarray and needs to be overhauled. An accurate and dependable public registry of civil servants must be created. The myriad of salary supplements and benefits in cash and in kind now prevailing must be consolidated and replaced by a more rational salary system. Sixth, improving governance and fighting corruption is essential not only to provide a better and less expensive public service delivery, but to fight income inequality and facilitate business activity and entrepreneurship in Peru. In general, local governments perform much worse than national agencies in the quality of delivery of services. In addition, there are more corruption and governance problems at the local level. Seventh, fine-tuning mining taxation, mining-canon transfers, and mining-related environmental policies is needed not only to strengthen the global competitiveness of one of the main export sources of Peru through a stable tax regime, but to enhance transparency of transfers to local governments and minimize environmental damage. Conflicts between mining companies and the local populations will thereby be minimized, thus contributing to improving the quality of mining investment activities, the transparency of intergovernmental relations, and the relationship between foreign investors and local communities.

Around the seven organizing themes of this report revolves a set of multiple and detailed diagnoses and policy recommendations, with some suggestions for their prioritization. The reader should, however, keep in mind several limitations. First, there is no magic formula for achieving results. What is described here is essentially based on Banks' best-practice experiences elsewhere in Latin America and the rest of the world, and on their informed views of Peru. Second, proposed sequencing of reforms is itself subject to political constraints. The World Bank and the IDB remain ready to assist the Government of Peru in implementing the PER's agenda. Finally, it is important to add that implementing these reforms can be achieved only through a new contract between the government and citizens, which would elevate standards for government accountability, transparency, and civil society participation and oversight.

## Restoring Fiscal Discipline

Fiscal sustainability is perhaps the most important challenge of the current Administration. Peru needs to strengthen its structural fiscal position, not only because failure to do so jeopardizes the macro framework in the medium term, but also because significant contingent liabilities might arise from pensions, the financial sector, and subnational government—registered or nonregistered— debts, and because sudden slowdowns or stops in external financing due to financial contagion from external (or regional) turbulence are not to be excluded in the coming years. Fiscal deficits are explained by a combination of both structural and cyclical factors. On the structural side, they feature procyclical and volatile patterns, mainly determined by the behavior of tax revenue and public expenditure. Over the last 30 years, Peru's non-financial public sector (NFPS) deficit experienced five cycles: 1970–79, 1980–85, 1986–91, 1992–96, and 1997–01, and averaged a high 5.8 percent of GDP. This pattern resulted from long periods of fiscal expansion, followed by increasingly shorter periods of fiscal adjustment, particularly before the early 1990s. The main component of the deficit was the Central Government imbalance, which represented about three fourths of the average NFPS deficit. Most fiscal variables are procyclical: they have significant positive correlation coefficients with the growth rate, and the cyclical components of the fiscal deficit and GDP growth are almost perfectly correlated.

In addition, fiscal variables are extremely volatile, and this goes beyond their close correlation to GDP growth. Peru's growth rate volatility, measured by the standard deviation, is 33 percent higher than the average for Latin American and Caribbean (LAC) countries, which is itself twice as high as the average in industrial economies. The volatility of fiscal variables, though, is much higher than the volatility of GDP growth: almost six times in the case of tax revenues; five times in the case of public salaries and transfers; more than seven times in the case of capital investments (the critical budget adjustment variable); and 11 times in the case of fiscal deficits. Tax revenue volatility is also explained by continuous changes in tax policy and administration, the hyperinflation of the late 1980s, and elections in the late 1990s. Expenditure volatility is explained by erratic policies affecting the public payroll, transfers, and capital investments.

Recent disequilibria are explained by expansive fiscal policies, and correcting them is a priority. Since 1997, trends in CG real revenue and real public expenditure have decreased and increased, respectively. In 2001, the tax ratio fell below 12 percent of GDP, a dismal level by international standards, and among the lowest in Latin America. As a result, primary balances have become negative since 1999, and fiscal deficits have deteriorated. Resulting public debt has increased as a percentage of GDP from 42.7 percent in 1998 to a high 46.5 percent in 2001, even though significant amounts of privatization proceeds have been used to finance expenditure and repay public debt. Although the public debt is mostly long term and owed to external creditors, the domestic and short-term components of it have grown at a rapid pace in the last several years. In this connection, it must be borne in mind that domestic debt is exposed to currency risk and rapidly increasing debt service, which contributes to tightening of scarce resources in a shrinking budget. Had Peru kept government tax revenue and expenditure constant in real terms during 1998–2001, it would have preserved a sound fiscal deficit below 1 percent of GDP.

What needs to be done to achieve fiscal discipline and, hence, macro sustainability? Six main policies are essential. First, and most important, Peru needs a comprehensive tax reform. This reform should aim at improving the tax system's equity, neutrality, simplicity, and revenue-yielding capacity. Reform should mainly be based on a combination of measures to broaden the tax base and enhance tax administration. Proposed measures to broaden the tax base suggest removing key tax exemptions (be it sector- or region-specific, or on interest and capital gains, or the exemption on import duties for Centers for Export, Transportation, Industry, Commercialization and Services [CETICOS]); introducing a presumptive income tax method for the self-employed and a slightly wider three-level income tax rate structure for individuals; and unifying the consumption selective tax for vehicles. By complementing these measures with the introduction of a royalty tax on mining (offset by the elimination of the sector's import duties), and/or eventual modification of workers' participation, and the implementation of a major phased improvement in tax administration, the government could raise additional resources approaching 2 percent of GDP within two to three years. The fact that the set of measures proposed does not modify the present tax structure and does not establish new taxes, except in the case of the royalty tax, makes it easier to gain political consensus for its enactment. The other pillar of tax reform is a marked improvement of tax administration by SUNAT, the collecting agency. In general, any improvement results from a combination of enhanced taxpayer services (with upgraded technology support), better auditing systems that focus on tax evaders, and better human resource staffing.

The second area where a significant effort is required is public expenditure. Because capital investment continues to be the residual adjusting item in the budget, Peru now has one of the lowest capital expenditure ratios in LAC: less than 2.5 percent of GDP in 2001, and decreasing. Hence, expenditure reform should aim at reverting the present trend toward an increased current expenditure and a decreased capital investment. Excessive current spending could be cut in the area of defense and internal security in the short term (0.6 percent of GDP in 2002), and in wages and pensions in the medium term, supported by social security and civil service reform. If the proposed increase in fiscal revenue materializes, then capital investment, especially in the social sectors, should be raised accordingly, thus contributing to filling the present gap that Peru has in social expenditure—1.2 percent of GDP in education and 0.2 percent of GDP in health—with respect to LAC averages.

A third area of policy reform is public debt sustainability. The public debt-to-GDP ratio of 46.5 percent in 2001 is too high for a country the public debt of which is highly exposed to currency risk, and which faces potential contingent liabilities in dollars in the financial sector. Lowering such ratio to more sustainable levels is essential to face potential risks in the next decade. Assuming a conservative baseline scenario combining moderate growth and low inflation, a slight increase in external interest rates, decreasing, but still significant mixed concessional–multilateral financing, and a fiscal correction lowering the NFPS deficit from 2.5 percent of GDP in 2001 to −1.4 percent of GDP in 2010, would bring the public debt-to-GDP ratio to a benchmark 36 percent of GDP at the end of the decade.

A fourth area of policy reform relates to fiscal rules through the revamping of the Law of Fiscal Prudence and Transparency. Because the Law is not a substitute, but a complementary tool to build credibility of a sound fiscal program, a prior condition for its official revamping requires, in the near term, thorough compliance with the benchmarks of the 2002–03 macroeconomic program, supported by an IMF Stand-By. Moreover, we do not expect a significant countercyclical policy as long as growth remains moderate and fiscal revenue is stagnant. So, revamping of the Law should proceed gradually, focusing on early credibility gains; prior institutional strengthening required by the Law's technical redesign and monitoring; consensus-building exercises led by Peruvian officials; virtual monitoring indicators and reporting tools, including those for the Comptroller's and Congress's oversight; and introducing a set of sanctions for noncompliance with numerical benchmarks and procedures. The design of a set of fiscal rules for incoming subnational governments should impose hard budget constraints on them and justifies upgrading the incoming Law to one of fiscal responsibility. In addition, in the medium term an effective countercyclical fiscal policy could be based on a structural primary balance benchmark. Such policy would require making automatic fiscal savings in booms and dis-savings in downturns, measured by the differential between estimated actual and structural balance. Under the baseline scenario described above, achieving a more sustainable public debt-to-GDP ratio by 2004–10 would entail a *structural* primary *surplus* ranging around 1 percent of GDP (roughly equivalent to around a 1 percent of GDO *nonstructural* deficit) during such years. Future savings would strengthen the role of the Fiscal Stabilization Fund.

A fifth area of policy reform concerns contingent fiscal liabilities. Peru must start making transparent budgetary provisions to deal with their eventual materialization, which would make projected restoration of fiscal discipline a more difficult task. This report reviews three main sources of contingent risk: bank loans, pension payments, and municipal debt. The Banks' broad estimates of the potential fiscal exposure to a systemic banking crisis is 4 percent of GDP, which is considered in the lower bound of comparable—mostly double-digit—world standards. Sound macroeconomic policies, close supervision of the financial sector, and reduced exposure to external financial contagion can minimize this risk. In addition, pension reform has generated two nonbanking debts with the private sector, which are actually paid through annual transfers. Official transfers to social security represent 0.6 percent of GDP in 2002, and conservative projections indicate they will increase to about 1.0 percent of GDP per year during 2005–07. Pension reform should minimize this liability. Finally, registered municipal debt is not a threat to macroeconomic stability, but it is significant and explosive, and some local governments will become insolvent and illiquid. These local governments will have severe difficulties assuming additional responsibilities with decentralization due to their financial constraints. Nationwide, total registered debt represents a third of the corresponding national debt (current national liabilities considered as short-term debt). In the short term, identifying nonsolvent municipalities and developing a plan for the gradual repayment of their registered debt, especially on pensions, is essential before these districts assume further responsibilities under the forthcoming decentralization process. In addition, the Fiscal Prudence and Transparency Law should put strict limits on new external and domestic debt, and prohibit subnational governments from acquiring contingent debts.

Finally, a sixth area concerns public debt financing. Peru must complete its deficit-financing plan by meeting its privatization targets in the nearest term, sustaining its prudent external debt management strategy—including enhanced access to international capital markets—and developing a market for long-term domestic public debt, issued in soles and inflation-indexed.

### Reorienting the Budget Toward Pro-Poor Expenditure

The task of putting the economy on a sustainable, rapid, and poverty-reducing growth path must be to be carried out with the help of modern public expenditure management. Promising steps have been taken by Peru over the past few years. They include (a) creation of an Integrated Financial Management System (SIAF) in 1998; (b) strengthening of accounting institutions and procedures, compatible with world standards, applied to the entire public sector since 1999; (c) development of a website *Portal de Transparencia* in 2000, which includes defense and national security spending for the first time starting in 2002; (d) passage of the Law of Fiscal Prudence and Transparency in 1999; (e) introduction of performance management contracts for State-owned enterprises under the National Fund for Financing Government Enterprise Activity (FONAFE) in 1999; (f) adoption of multiple medium-term expenditure frameworks starting in 2000, based on three-year Macroeconomic Frameworks and five-year Multiyear Budget (MAB) plans, and carried out through a participatory methodology for multiyear budgeting formulation starting in 2002; and (g) adoption of budgetary provisions for a set of Protected Social Programs (PSPs) as the main countercyclical social policy starting in 2000.

The trend toward pro-poor spending and enhanced accountability and transparency seems irreversible, but consolidating these achievements in the medium term means solving five critical institutional weaknesses: (a) excessive budget rigidity, (b) an incomplete SIAF, (c) a disconnection between multiyear and annual budgeting, (d) a fragile institutional framework surrounding its countercyclical social policy, and (e) inadequate and un-user-unfriendly budget monitoring and reporting that affects public perceptions about the real degree of budget transparency.

Following a budget tracking test of the status of public expenditure management (PEM) jointly developed by the World Bank and the IMF, Peru scores low in the area of budget formulation, average in the area of budget execution, and high in the area of budget reporting other than external. In the first area, the assessment recommends that budget classification be made fully consistent with the Government Financial Statistics (GFS) definition of General Government, and the quality of budget projections (especially in function and sector composition) be upgraded if social priorities are to be sustained in the medium term. The major constraint for budget formulation, though, is inertial expenditure. Peru ranks high among countries with the most inflexible budget not only in LAC, but worldwide. In addition to Brazil, India, and a few highly indebted poor countries (HIPCs), which have above 90 percent of their total expenditure fixed for particular functions in 2002, Peru has, respectively, 91 percent and 86 percent of ordinary and total budget resources assigned to inertial commitments.

Budget rigidities originate from different sources, including wage and benefits considered by the Constitution as inalienable rights; permanent contracts hidden as nonpersonal services (no less than 40 percent of the total budget is allocated to such services, according to Peruvian officials' estimates); an inertial payroll under artificially prolonged investment projects; earmarked transfers to municipalities and the private sector, such as the *Vaso de Leche* and *Comedores Populares* programs; and an earmarked use of the budget "contingency reserve" to fund the March school bonus, and July and December salary supplements (*aguinaldos*). Peru needs to reverse such a pervasive pattern. PER recommendations in this area include (a) an immediate general hiring freeze under the nonpersonal services category accompanied by strict supervision, on a case-by-case basis, of short-term renewal of existing temporary contracts, upon their prior revision; (b) an urgent review of present policies regarding pension and wage benefits in a comprehensive civil service reform; (c) streamlining of funds assigned to inefficient social programs—like *Vaso de Leche* and *Comedores Populares;* and (d) making fully transparent the use of the contingency reserve, to let it play its true role, which is to fill unpredicted in-year budget needs, thus preventing it from filling recurrent needs.

SIAF core subsystems are incomplete. The lack of a budget module, in particular, is a severe handicap. Contrary to similar systems in Latin America, Peru's SIAF is neither a budget formulation tool nor a budget assignment tool, but fundamentally a virtual payment system. As a result, budget formulation and in-year modifications remain little known externally, centralized and decided at the Ministry of Economy and Finance's (MEF's) discretion, and only known ex post, once they are monthly registered in SIAF. Hence, a user-friendly budget module integrated in SIAF is an urgently needed policy tool to help assess consistency of budget proposals with macroeconomic conditions in early stages; facilitate monitoring of in-year budget modifications, consistent with inter- and intrasector budget priorities in a participatory and transparent way; and allow Congress' legally mandated oversight of the budget. SIAF also requires a multiyear budget submodule too; that is, one with capacity to track Government of Peru (GOP) compliance with multiyear budgeting priorities and facilitate production of mandated biannual reports on compliance with MAB targets. Finally, other critical missing modules are the ones on human resources management, national assets, procurement, the national investment system, contingent liabilities risk, and regional and municipal financial management. The human resource module is essential for civil service reform. The one on national assets should have due registry of state assets. The module on procurement, the starting point for e-government, is critical for anti-corruption efforts, the most vulnerable area of governance. The module on public investment should help prioritize multiyear investment plans. The module on contingent liabilities risk would help register them and make proper budgetary provisions, while the one on municipal management would prepare SIAF support for an accelerated scheme of fiscal decentralization, as future regional and municipal governments require a tailor-made SIAF, the development of which should take many years.

The budget-tracking test also found that multiyear projections are disconnected from annual budget priorities and modifications, their quality requires significant improvement, and their monitoring requires an upgraded and regular reporting system. To such purpose, the creation of a budget module and refinement of the existing set of financial and physical indicators in SIAF should facilitate a user-friendly tracking of pro-poor expenditure and an effective results-based control system in budget execution. Complementary external reporting of budget execution, multiyear budgeting, and audits should be frequent, timely, and comprehensive. Regarding reporting, the SIAF subsystem to track financial and physical performance indicators, now being developed, requires a thorough conceptual review before completion, because it is a critical tool for an outcome-oriented budget, and support from monitoring targets and performance management contracts. The present subsystem has too many useless and outdated indicators, and the use of the indicators is poor.

The development of new SIAF modules requires detailed prioritization and permanent training. Peruvian officials have good reason to consider creating a university degree in the management of SIAF systems. Besides, associated systems could be developed outside the SIAF, like a fiscal cadastre, or eventually be connected to a broader e-government strategy (like e-procurement or a geo-referenced expenditure map at the district level, for targeting purposes).

These shortcomings have not prevented an important shift in the budget toward pro-poor expenditure in Peru. In spite of the recession and resulting fiscal adjustment, the share of social expenditure to GDP grew from 3.9 percent of GDP in 1990 to 7.0 in 1999, and this share has remained steadfast until 2002. The fact that the share of social expenditure to GDP has not declined is a positive outcome in a fiscally retrenched economy where total expenditure decreased from 19 percent of GDP to 17.8 percent of GDP during 1999–2002 (about one seventh in dollar terms). Likewise, significant inter- and intrasectoral pro-poor spending reallocation began to take place between 2000 and 2002. The budget for defense and national security has decreased from 2.9 to 2.1 percent of GDP; the budget for education, health, and social assistance has increased from 5.3 to 5.6 percent of GDP; and the *Seguro Social de Salud* (Health Insurance, ESSALUD) expenditure (nontargeted public health insurance administration) has decreased from 1.5 to 1.3 percent of GDP. In addition, the share of poverty-reduction programs (consisting of both programs with universal coverage spending and programs based on targeted spending) in social expenditure increased from 57 percent in 2000 to 60 percent in 2002. Since 2000, poverty budgeting has also included an innovative effort to protect key social programs (PSPs). This approach has consisted of assigning global budget allocations to nonsalary current and capital spending grouped in 11 programs and distributed among eight social and basic infrastructure sectors. In 2001, budget resources equivalent to 12.7 percent of the ordinary budget and 1.9 percent of GDP were protected and executed.

In 2002, the government decided to change its PSPs policy from merely budget protection when a downturn occurs to sustained spending floors needed to reach millennium development goals. This was accompanied by improvement of their focus and monitoring mechanisms, and full transparency in their execution. The ongoing restructuring of PSPs includes expenditure allocation shifts in broad sector functions—education, health and sanitation, and social assistance; a reduced number (from 11 to 6) of now core PSPs, grouped under three sectors: education (pre-primary, primary, and secondary), health (collective and individual) and social assistance, a reduced budget as the amount of aggregate earmarked expenditure to this revised set of PSP represents 1.2 percent of GDP in 2002, down from the previous 1.9 percent of GDP in 2001 (this reduction of 0.7 percent of GDP makes room for increased budget flexibility); a set of monitoring indicators for specific projects grouped under the selected PSPs; and, in a few projects, definition of some performance management contracts to improve their efficiency (for example, the Integral and Mother and Child Maternal Insurances, SIS-SMI). To introduce further flexibility, the PSP budget also includes escape clauses to make provisions for budget underexecution or a major budgetary shortfall at the sector function level; and internal reallocations from underperforming to overperforming programs or projects, but maintaining global spending floors at the program and project levels. To institutionalize and make its countercyclical social policy more transparent, Peru should enhance its de facto "virtual" protected budget policy following the example of Uganda. An enhanced mechanism would add two major features: the development of a permanent institutional framework in charge of PSPs policy, and the introduction of oversight capacity by subnational governments and civil society organizations, and of transparent monitoring and evaluation indicators, into PSPs implementation.

## Improving the Efficiency of Public Services Delivery
The efficiency of Peruvian public expenditure is below the Latin American average for health, but above average for education, and in relation to world averages, the results are similar. However, these results should be viewed with caution. Indeed, Peru's level of efficiency in reaching health outcomes is below both the Latin American and world averages. This is particularly true in malnutrition–height, under-five mortality, and life expectancy. The range of values found suggests that Peru could and should do much better in health outcomes. And although outcome indicators for Peru's net primary enrollment are on a par with other Latin American countries, and net secondary enrollment is much

above the LAC average, its educational shortcomings are too severe in terms of the low quality of education services and poor teacher qualifications, especially in rural areas.

Two major sources of inefficiencies are leakages of public resources and poor targeting of social programs, which ultimately contribute to poor governance and a corruption-prone management.

A highly decentralized budget execution such as Peru's raises the possibility of significant leakages in the flow of resources, thus reducing the extent to which GOP expenditure is able to produce better outcomes. By applying an innovative Public Expenditure Tracking Survey (PETS), it is possible to show that there are substantial leakages in the resources that municipalities first receive under the *Vaso de Leche* program and later transfer to the ultimate beneficiaries through several intermediaries. The actual amount received by final beneficiaries appears much lower than the initial amount sent from the Central Government (CG): on average only 29 cents of each dollar initially transferred by the CG actually reach the intended beneficiaries! Surprisingly, the survey indicates that the leak is much higher at the bottom levels (*Vaso de Leche* committees and households) than at the top levels (CG and municipalities leaks), which demonstrates not only significant improvements in the official channeling of resources by the SIAF/MEF, but challenges the predominant view that local private organizations are more accountable in managing public resources than official ones. Leakages in municipality-level transfers are compounded by the generalized lack of audit controls, poor transparency, and volatility. Finally, leaks most affect the poorest urban and provincial municipalities, and their level appears similar among districts of different sizes and distances to the province.

Peruvian officials should pursue a twin strategy. In the short term, any effort leading to improving supervision, accountability, and transparency of the flow of resources should be pursued. This includes a regular and user-friendly publication of detailed transfers to municipalities by SIAF, capacity training at the local level in SIAF reporting, proper registration of beneficiaries, and strengthened budget and auditing procedures by the Comptroller's office. A mini-Stabilization Fund for *canon minero* transfers could contribute to minimizing their annual volatility. In the medium term, however, authorities should consider replacing these programs with a voluntarily adopted cash-transfer ("grants") program, following the successful model of the *Programa de Educación, Salud y Alimentación* (PROGRESA) program in Mexico. Under such a scheme, grants would be provided to mothers not only for food supplements, but also for basic education and preventive health, which, following a proper registration of beneficiaries, should also improve targeting of resources on beneficiaries at risk.

Poor targeting is another important shortcoming of the multiplicity of social programs in Peru. The general level of spending on targeted extreme poverty-reduction programs increased from 1.1 percent to 1.7 percent of GDP between 1993 and 1998, but then remained constant until 2002, which appears adequate due to the fiscal situation and program inefficiencies, and despite pressures to increase it. Poor targeting, however, deviates part of these outlays toward the non-poor. Targeting rates in social programs vary tremendously. Past findings indicate that with the exception of the *Fondo Nacional de Compensación y Desarrollo Social* (FONCODES) and the *Programa Nacional de Asistencia Alimentaria* (National Food Assistance Program, PRONAA), which have had about a 50 percent success rate, most targeted social programs have had rates reaching below 40 percent of the intended poorest. More recent findings on the food and nutrition programs confirm this picture. Targeting among the three main national programs—*Desayunos Escolares, Vaso de Leche,* and *Comedores Populares,* also reflects prevailing weaknesses: during 1998–2000, *Desayunos Escolares* had the highest success rate at 70 percent, followed by *Vaso de Leche* and *Comedores Populares,* which had lower rates of 64 and 54 percent, respectively. As a program becomes better targeted, the differential between its rural and urban success rates decreases: *Desayunos Escolares* had a lower range (77 percent compared to 56 percent) than *Vaso de Leche* (77 percent compared to 50 percent) and *Comedores Populares* (72 percent compared to 37 percent). Finally, programs of temporary employment, like *A Trabajar Urbano,* have not started on the right foot, since they offer too high a wage rate to attract workers in the poorest deciles.

Peruvian officials should make intensive use of excellent targeting tools, especially the poverty map, already in their hands. The myriad of multiple social programs in Peru should be ranked, and those with substantial mistargeting should be redesigned, merged, or closed. Fiscal savings generated from such an exercise should be used to increase coverage of more effective programs. Targeting criteria should be made more explicit and focused on extremely poor populations. In the case of *A Trabajar Urbano*, the immediate solution is to decrease the wage rate paid. A similar policy in *A Trabajar Rural* is not possible, since the individual income earned by a rural worker is often shared with other members of his or her community, and so the self-targeting mechanism does not work in the same way as it does with urban workers. In both cases, though, authorities should be aware of the countercyclical and short-term nature of these employment-generation programs: once the economy recovers its dynamism with high rates of growth, their budget resources should be phased out.

### Addressing the Promises and Risks of Decentralization

In the past decade, Peru has made irreversible progress toward redefining the role of the State, but this agenda is unfinished. In the early-to mid-1990s, the size and scope of the public sector were reduced; the nature of government shifted from ownership and intervention to market regulation and provision of social services. However, in the mid-to-late-1990s the State reform process lost steam, and key tasks were not even initiated. Prominent among pending reforms set aside by the authoritarian leadership of the 1990s was the decentralization of the State.

The current government has decided to reinvigorate the State modernization and decentralization agenda. This decision must be seen as part of a broader, positive trend toward democracy in the region. However, State decentralization is pregnant with both potentialities and risks. If appropriately carried out, it can, indeed, increase both the efficiency of the delivery of government services and the responsiveness of government to citizens' needs. Nonetheless, decentralization also entails serious macroeconomic risks. First, CG deficits can worsen if governments are unable to reduce expenditures or increase revenues to make room to accommodate the fiscal cost of additional functions and responsibilities transferred to subnational governments. The government may find itself decentralizing both revenues and expenditures, but unable to reduce existing levels of CG spending in those functions that have been decentralized. Second, attempts to eliminate rising deficits through higher taxes can fail or take longer than expected to materialize. Third, decentralization can also hamper a government's ability to respond to economic shocks because it reduces central control over aggregate public sector revenues and expenditures. Fourth, subnational government debt policies and indebtedness behavior can undermine overall fiscal discipline. Subnational governments may end up borrowing excessively in the expectation that the CG will bail them out.

In sum, decentralization has the potential to be a destabilizing factor for already deteriorated Peruvian public finances and, ultimately, for the country's overall macroeconomic framework. The Latin American experience suggests, moreover, that decentralization should not be carried out without a coherent overall strategy and without prior technical and institutional preparation at the subnational levels of government. In the case of Peru, the fact that municipal governments are heavily dependent on central transfers justifies caution in the transfer of responsibilities to them. Taking into account that the degree of satisfaction in the provision of public services by local governments appears to be low, gradualness in the transfer of functions and a sizeable effort to strengthen the administrative capacity of subnational governments prior to the transfer of responsibilities seem to be necessary conditions of any reasonable decentralization strategy.

Putting the process of decentralization on a sound path is a critical public policy challenge for the Toledo Administration. While Peru's initial efforts toward modernization and decentralization offer substantial promise and, for the most part, are headed in the right direction, the latent risk that fiscal discipline may turn out to be a casualty of the decentralization process will continue to be high until a clear framework for intergovernmental public finances is finally enacted and enforced. The guiding criterion for such a framework has to be the establishment of hard budget constraints for the expenditure and—external and domestic—indebtedness decisions of subnational governments. The immediate agenda includes issues of paramount importance, such as the alternative options for intergovernmental fiscal relations, the budget and indebtedness constraints on subnational governments, the possible functions and competencies to be decentralized, the characteristics and funding sources of the future Regional Compensation Fund and Intergovernmental Fund for Decentralization, and any possible changes to the transfers scheme for municipalities. It is also imperative that the hard budget constraints for regional and local governments here advocated be an integral part of the future revamped Law of Fiscal Prudence and Transparency. Finally, a complete diagnosis of the financial status of municipalities, including its pension liabilities and other registered and non-registered debt, and a plan for both strengthening municipal tax collection and restructuring local government debt, are essential before these are assigned new expenditure powers.

## Upgrading the Civil Service

Civil service reform is the missing link of the outcome- and poverty-reducing-oriented modernization of the state in Peru, and is in desperate need of a major overhaul. The past decade witnessed a severe deterioration of Peru's civil service. Hyperinflation of the late 1980s and the beginning of the 1990s sharply reduced the real earnings of civil servants. A poorly conceived downsizing of the CG work force in the early 1990s, which, in the end, amounted to a very modest reduction in the overall public sector, led, nonetheless, to the departure of the most capable civil servants. There is an inherited disregard for the provisions of the existing civil service law and its associated regulations. Civil servants are employed under a variety of legal regimens with a wide dispersion in salaries for similar tasks. The existing formal salary structure has not been revised in over a decade, so base salaries are increased through resorting to a multiplicity of supplements and benefits in cash and in kind. With the proclamation 10 years ago of a ban on hiring into permanent positions, institutions have resorted to hiring on a contractual basis, a process that is not subject to any required procedures for recruitment and selection, and that has severe fiscal implications.

All these factors have contributed to the existing legacy of a work force that is poorly prepared, poorly trained, poorly supervised, and hence of very low productivity. Consequently, there is an urgent need for a thorough reform to reestablish some semblance of control over the wage bill and to promote the creation of a more efficient government. The current civil service law has major weaknesses that argue for its replacement by a new framework designed to promote a higher level of efficiency in the delivery of government services.

Any initiative designed to improve the performance of government must include a major overhaul in the institutional framework that governs public sector employment and the management of its human resources. Four actions are particularly relevant. First, the creation of a Civil Service Reform Commission should precede the establishment of an autonomous Directorate to administer the civil service. Second, developing an SIAF module on human resource management would greatly simplify registry of public servants and would be instrumental in the task of simplifying the remuneration package from the myriad of present benefits to a cash-equivalent amount. Third, introducing pilot performance contracts in the health sector seems appropriate, given its recent successful experience with *Seguro Materno-Infantil* (Mother and Child Health Insurance, SMI), which makes it a natural candidate for later mainstreaming of such practice in the rest of the public sector. Finally, a new law and *reglamento* should place emphasis on merit and specify determinants for compensation.

The education sector also faces serious problems with its civil service. There is general dissatisfaction with the quality of instruction and with the allocation of faculty resources among schools. The Ministry of Education is taking steps to improve the quality of instruction in the country's schools of pedagogy. However, the profession continues to attract individuals whose test scores rank at the bottom of the distribution of students entering institutions of higher learning. Improvement in the quality of instruction is likely to require a number of reforms. While the current level of salaries appears to be more than adequate to attract a surplus of candidates with minimal qualifications, the level and earnings trajectory over time are inadequate to attract more promising individuals. In addition, both the *Ley Magisterial* and the *Ley General de Educación* are too rigid for most forms of decentralization and should be revised.

Reforms must focus on four aspects. On the institutional side, the current institutional morass in the education sector (financially depending on regional bodies, and normatively depending on sector ministries) should be unified under the decentralization design. On the recruiting policy, new entrants to the profession should be required to qualify by passing a rigorous examination. Successful candidates would be hired at a higher salary not much different from the current entry wage, but should be able to look forward to salary increases similar to those accruing to persons with similar skills and abilities in the private sector as long as performance is evaluated and meets defined standards. On the hiring levels, implementation of a new remuneration policy would be facilitated by moving to a system of contracting of teaching personnel in place of the currently generalized system of permanent tenure upon appointment. This would also have obvious fiscal savings. On the legal side, the new *Ley del Profesorado* and the *Reglamento de la Ley del Profesorado* should be based on teaching performance and effective attendance, rather than on a range of factors such as seniority, number of training courses attended, papers presented at professional meetings, and so forth, none of which necessarily have any impact on the quality of teaching.

## Improving Governance and Reducing Corruption

Peru's picture in matters of governance is mixed. In the World Bank's scoring system for governance indicators, Peru's scores in government effectiveness and regulatory quality have dropped significantly, even as the country moved from an authoritarian regime to one with a more vocal and active opposition. The score in corruption has remained approaching the LAC average. Peru's corruption appears particularly high in procurement contracts of public works. To offset such a gloomy picture, Peru's scores in voice and accountability, political stability, and rule of law have improved, thus reflecting the political opening that is taking place. Significant challenges remain in these areas, however.

Reducing corruption and improving governance requires a multipronged strategy that addresses the various forms of corruption—from *state capture* to *administrative corruption*, enhances political accountability and transparency, promotes a competitive private sector, strengthens institutional restraints, improves public sector management, and embraces civil society participation. It is more than just a matter of law enforcement. The evidence in this report also identified the support of public officials for civil society oversight and merit-based civil service reform as anticorruption mechanisms. Public officials also favor strengthening public administration through simpler administrative procedures. They are also in favor of the introduction of a system of checks and balances and the oversight of public sector activities by the civil society.

The government first needs to build credibility with respect to its intentions to fight corruption. In the survey, there is a significant discrepancy between users and public officials in their perception of the government's commitment to fighting corruption. More than half of users, versus only 20 percent of public officials, reported that the government is not committed at all. This lack of trust is keenly felt among low-income users of public services. Conversely, the fact that a high proportion of public officials report preparedness in the public sector to fight corruption is an encouraging sign. The government needs to make the fight against corruption a top priority. The church and the media should be potential contributors in the fight.

As a complement, the government needs to continue enhancing transparency, especially through SIAF. Transparency is synonymous with openness. Introducing it requires that the government provide the public—civil society organizations, the media, or anyone else who is interested—sufficient information about the budget and project activities, to serve as an effective check on abuses by government and public officials. Enacting a Freedom of Information Law that requires governments to provide information to the public unless there is a valid reason for the information to remain secret (such as a threat to national security) would be welcome.

The government needs to be accountable and reduce the potential gains for "captor" firms and politicians alike. Government officials should consider issuing an Ethics Code Law for public service, with clear prohibitions of conflicts of interest, and effective enforcement of its regulations on both political and civil service positions. This is an essential corruption-deterrence tool. They should also demand transparency of the financing of political parties and campaigns, making clear the links, both explicit and implicit, between politicians and the interests that support them. Mandated and publicized detailed reports of the finances of all political organizations, and identification of contributors and beneficiaries, are tools to reduce the sources of state capture. Another possible measure would include banning the use of State resources for incumbents' political campaigns, limiting the amount that can be spent on political campaigns, providing public funding, and prohibiting certain types of entities from contributing to political campaigns.

The government needs to promote a sound business environment by examining and simplifying the number of regulations and inspections. Clear rules defining when a regulation is appropriate, and sound analysis of the impact of regulations on firms accompanied by a constant dialogue with the business community, should be required to make regulatory reform sustainable.

Finally, a high-level steering committee, supported by a professional secretariat, can help bring together representatives of government bodies, both central and local, to develop the specific action plans to implement the governance strategy. By explicitly including representatives from outside government, such committees can further build credibility while mobilizing an important ally for reducing corruption.

## Fine-Tuning Mining Taxation and Environmental Policies

Given its size in the economy and social network, the mining sector is essential for public finance, structural reform, and governance in Peru. The mining industry generates more than 45 percent of export earnings and contributes to 5 to 7 percent of GDP. It employs over one-quarter million people, and its tax exemptions account for about 0.4 percent of GDP, which is nonnegligible. Key structural and transparency issues have negatively affected the competitiveness and attractiveness of mining activities with foreign investors and local society, particularly with the local communities since the late 1990s. The mining reform brought about the effective opening of the sector to direct foreign investment and the shift of the role of the State from owner–operator to lessor–regulator. This was accomplished by reforming the legal and institutional framework, privatizing the mining state-owned operations, and initiating an environmental management program.

While the first three reforms, legal, institutional, and privatization, have been widely considered successful, the sectoral approach of the environmental reform has proven to be controversial and is considered in need of adjustment. The perception of inadequate environmental control and of widespread conflict between mining companies and local populations is endangering the contribution and stability of a key sector of Peru's economy. In addition, the highly centralized and nontransparent nature of transfers from the CG has created an issue of credibility with the local populations. Although the Mining Law establishes that 40 percent of the income tax generated by the mining operations—the *canon minero*—should go back to the municipalities (20 percent) and the regions (20 percent), and the report's findings show that its overall redistribution has been progressive, there is a widespread perception that the local communities are not benefiting from it. Furthermore, the environmental information that the Ministry of Energy and Mines (MEM) has received from the mining companies has not been adequately released to the public, resulting in a feeling of mistrust against mining activities.

Loss of competitiveness due to the taxation system is also an issue. To the extent that it affects rates of return on investment, the effective tax rate in a given country is a major factor influencing the decision of foreign investors about where to invest their capital. The report shows empirical evidence that supports the view that the current Peruvian mining tax system is among the more globally competitive systems in the world, and provides an appropriate balance between investor needs and government needs. However, there is room for improvement.

Addressing major issues in taxation, environmental regulations, and the transparency of *canon minero* transfers is very important for preserving international competitiveness. Main tax policy changes proposed are (a) introducing a 3-percent royalty tax combined with the elimination of import duties and modifications to worker participation; (b) adjusting by a premium increase of 5 percent all future stability agreements; (c) extending the carry-loss forward time limit beyond five years; (d) enhancing the system to register tax deduction of mine contributions to local communities and infrastructure; and (e) publishing *canon minero* monthly transfers to municipalities in SIAF, while providing training at the local level. Agreements on roles and responsibilities in the environmental provisions are needed, accompanied by a new regulatory framework of environmental management, a new designated national authority with no conflicting interests and integrated with regional and local authorities; and with local participation—nongovernmental organizations (NGOs) included—in local environmental monitoring and consultation mechanisms, to allow them to protect community interests. Given the volatility of fiscal transfers, the creation of small mining stabilization funds to offset temporary declines in fiscal revenue, and simulating the successful experience of the Ancash Model, are not to be excluded.

### Assembling All the Pieces of the Agenda

Peru's policymakers are well aware of the difficult fiscal situation and the need for discipline. The agenda described above is large and requires prioritization and sequencing, possibly starting with tax reform and a modern and institutionalized pro-poor budgeting, followed by efficiency improvements in social programs and civil service reform—both critical inputs to consolidate expenditure management reform—and then completed by the decentralization, governance, and anticorruption programs, and by fine-tuned environment and taxation policies in the mining sector. Short-lived aggregate demand boosts, like those advocated by populism, will only delay needed reforms. Consistent choices have to be made and some efforts will likely have to be postponed. Most of the PER's agenda, however, is feasible provided that there is not only commitment of the Executive, but also support in the Legislature. Peruvian officials are well aware of this. The 2001 budget presentation to Congress broadly covered each of the three aspects of public expenditure performance. It singled out the paramount need to restore fiscal discipline to preserve price stability, to readjust the pattern of expenditures toward priority social areas, and to improve service delivery with efficiency gains. This report argues that for fiscal policy to become a powerful tool for Peru's development, designing an outcome-managed, poverty-oriented, and consensus-built budgeting strategy is necessary. Both the World Bank and the IDB are ready to continue assisting authorities in marshalling such efforts.

# II

# PERU'S FISCAL CHALLENGES AND VULNERABILITIES

*At the onset of the new century, Peru faces daunting fiscal challenges due to a combination of adverse external shocks, expansive fiscal policies, elections, and other unfavorable domestic developments accompanying the transition to the post-Fujimori legacy. During the early-to-mid-1990s, volatile and procyclical expenditure accompanying good times made the country's response to negative shocks more difficult to manage and vulnerable to a prolonged slowdown, like the ones that have occurred since the end of the decade. Since 1998, the fiscal stance has deteriorated, with successive negative primary deficits, in part due to a resilient decline in tax revenue, which reached a decade-low 11.9 percent of GDP in 2001. The ensuing combined fiscal deficit significantly increased from 0.4 percent of GDP in 1997 to 3.2 percent of GDP in 2000, only to be slightly reduced to an estimated 2.5 percent of GDP in 2001. Rigid and expansionary expenditure has also undermined fiscal stability. Ending privatization proceeds and high and dollarized public debt offers limited room for financing deficits in the years to come. The prolonged economic slowdown and political uncertainty resulting from external and domestic factors, including populism, also put additional stress on the fiscal balances. The fiscal rules enshrined in the Fiscal Prudence and Transparency Law of 1999 have not been fully met. In any case, they are no substitute for sound policy, and require thorough revamping before they become a tool for consolidating credibility. This chapter analyzes Peru's main fiscal challenges and vulnerabilities with respect to restoring fiscal discipline, including tax policy measures and new rules to be considered in a revamped Law.*

## Long-Run Fiscal Trends

Long-run trends in Peruvian fiscal policy can be broadly split into two contrasting periods: before and after the 1990s.[1] The average non-financial public sector (NFPS) fiscal deficit was a staggering 5.4 percent of GDP during 1970–90, and a much more moderate 2.4 percent of GDP in the 1990s. Such outcomes resulted from long periods of fiscal expansion, followed by increasingly

---

1. This section mainly draws from Oliva (2002).

15

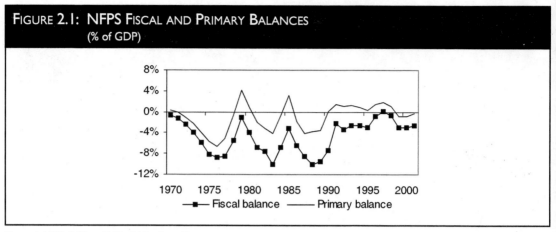

FIGURE 2.1: NFPS FISCAL AND PRIMARY BALANCES
(% of GDP)

Source: MEF, IMF and World Bank staff estimates.

shorter periods of fiscal adjustment, particularly before the early 1990s. The main component of the deficit was the Central Government (CG) imbalance, which represented about three fourths of the average NFPS deficit. The first period reflected high deficits resulting from persistent macroeconomic disorders, negative primary surpluses with either short-lived or half-hearted efforts at fiscal adjustment. The lower deficits of the second period came from continuous primary surpluses that became the norm rather than the exception (Figure 2.1).

The impact of a severely deteriorated economy during 1970–90 left a long-lasting memory among Peruvians about the paramount need to preserve stabilization. As GDP growth deteriorated after 1975, the tax ratio ranged from 8 to 16 percent of GDP, with the most striking decline occurring throughout the late 1980s, reflecting the hyperinflation crisis (Figure 2.2). As a result, the average fiscal deficit increased to 6.0 percent of GDP and stayed high until the end of the decade. Such high deficits were financed by resorting to either domestic financing, leading to hyperinflation levels in the late 1980s, or to huge increases in external indebtedness, with the ratio of public external debt to GDP increasing from about 14 percent in the mid-1970s to over 56 percent in the late 1980s (Table 2.1). The governments' heavy reliance on debt led to an explosive rising share of interest payments of total CG expenditure from 5 percent in 1970 to 40 percent in

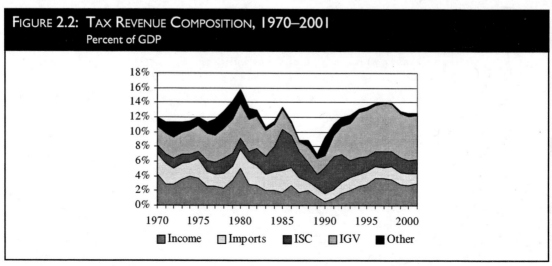

FIGURE 2.2: TAX REVENUE COMPOSITION, 1970–2001
Percent of GDP

Source: MEF, IMF and World Bank staff estimates.

| TABLE 2.1: KEY MACROECONOMIC VARIABLES 1969–89 | | | | |
|---|---|---|---|---|
| Period | Fiscal Balance (% GDP) | Average Inflation Rate (%) | GDP Growth (%) | Public External Debt/GDP (%) |
| 1969–75 | –3.9 | 10.6 | 5.5 | 14.1 |
| 1976–79 | –6.8 | 48.6 | 0.7 | 32.3 |
| 1980–85 | –6.0 | 94.2 | 0.5 | 41.5 |
| 1986–89 | –5.9 | 445.8 | –1.5 | 56.2 |

*Source:* World Bank staff estimates based on MEF and IMF data.

1990. Only after 1990 was the share of interest payments dramatically reduced, following the restoration of normal relations between Peru and the international financial community, prompt payment of arrears to multilateral institutions, and debt restructuring agreements with Paris Club lenders, and other bilateral and private creditors.[2] By 2001, the share of interest payments of total expenditure had been reduced to 12 percent (Table SA.4).

Long-run changes in the tax revenue structure are relevant. The three most important tax categories[3] were the income tax, the general sales tax (VAT), and the excise tax (or selective tax on consumption, ISC) (Figure 2.2). Four subperiods can be identified according to which of these three categories dominates. In the first period (1970–75), the income tax matched the VAT; in the second period (1975–85), it was the VAT that played the leading role; in the third period (1985–93) the ISC prevailed; and in the fourth period (1994–2000), the VAT recovered its major significance. The declining trend of the income tax—which fell from a dominant share of 35 percent in 1970 to 23 percent in 2000—and the exceptional major role that the excise tax played during 1984–92—were the outcome of the excessive number of income tax and VAT deductions and exemptions, and the serious deficiencies in tax administration.

Long-run trends in public expenditure are determined by two structural factors: the role of the public sector in the economy, and output performance. Three subperiods can be distinguished. In the first one (1970–78), total expenditure exhibited an increasing trend, rising from 15 percent to about 20 percent of GDP, as explained by the steady expansion of the role of the State in the economy during the Velasco government and a strong economic expansion.[4] The average ratio of public investment to total investment stood at a high 27.0 percent[5] (Paredes and Sachs 1991). The second subperiod (1979–91) featured the opposite trend—that is, CG expenditure declined as a share of GDP, which reflected the severe deterioration of tax collection and the economy. The third subperiod (1991–2001) reverted to an accelerated expenditure expansion: from the deep trough of 14.5 percent of GDP in 1991, CG expenditure increased to an average of 17.6 percent of GDP during 1999–2001, close to the high levels reached during the era of strong state intervention, pushed by current spending rather than by capital investment (Table SA.5).

---

2. Relations between Peru and the international financial community deteriorated throughout the 1980s. According to Larrain and Sachs (1991), "Peru first partially suspended its debt service in 1983, but the magnitude of the suspension was small. In 1984, renegotiations failed and the country started to accumulate more significant arrears. These increased dramatically after 1985, when President Alan Garcia announced the government's unilateral decision to limit the service of foreign debt to 10 percent of export revenues, a restriction that would apply in principle to all foreign creditors."

3. Taxes on foreign trade transactions were excluded from the comparison.

4. Peru's economy grew an average annual rate of 5.5 percent between 1969 and 1975 (Table 2.1).

5. Compare with the value of the same indicator in a recent period (1999–2001), which was just 18 percent (Table SA.2). The difference was the result, of course, of the privatization in the 1990s of about 80 percent of the large number of State enterprises that the Velasco government bequeathed to its successors.

## TABLE 2.2: ELASTICITY TO GDP, 1970–2000

| Variable | Estimated Coefficient |
|---|---|
| Total tax revenues | 0.998 |
| Income tax | 0.972 |
| Import tax (tariffs) | 0.972 |
| Total VAT | 1.007 |
| Internal VAT | 0.999 |
| Imports VAT | 1.024 |
| Total ISC | 1.010 |
| Gasoline ISC | 1.032 |
| Other ISC | 0.992 |
| Total non-financial expend. | 0.962 |
| Current | 0.965 |
| Wage and salaries | 0.926 |
| Goods and services | 0.995 |
| Transfers | 1.001 |
| Capital | 0.944 |
| Investments | 0.971 |

*Source:* MEF, IMF and World Bank staff estimates.

Fiscal variables were highly procyclical before and during the 1990s. Regression analysis over the entire period shows that all tax and expenditure categories exhibit an almost unitary elasticity with respect to GDP (Table 2.2); that is, they were highly procyclical.[6] Most fiscal variables also have significant correlation coefficients (above 0.5) with the growth rate (Arias and others 2000), and the cyclical components of the primary balance and GDP growth are almost perfectly correlated (Figure 2.3).

Fiscal variables were extremely volatile in both periods. The volatility of fiscal variables is associated to Peru's growth rate volatility (measured by the standard deviation). In the 1990s, it was 33 percent higher than its average for Latin America and the Caribbean (LAC), itself twice as high as in industrial economies (De Ferranti and others 2000). Unstable international export prices and terms of trade, financial shocks, and limited openness in the financial system explain GDP growth volatility. The volatility of fiscal variables, however, appears much higher than the one for GDP growth during 1970–1996: almost six times in the case of tax revenues, five times in the case of public salaries and transfers, more than seven times in the case of capital investments, and 11 times in the case of fiscal deficits (Figure 2.4). In the 1990s, tax revenue volatility is explained by continuous changes to tax policy and administration, the external environment,[7] the legacy of hyperinflation of the late 1980s, and elections in the late 1990s. For its part, public expenditure volatility is explained by erratic policies affecting capital investment, debt payments, the public payroll, and transfers: It reflects the continuous use of capital outlays as the typical procyclical adjustment variable (elasticity

---

6. Regressions are estimated with a simple ordinary least squares (OLS) model: nominal revenue and expenditure from each category was the dependent variable and nominal GDP was the explanatory variable. Variables for 1970–2000 were in logarithms and adjusted by a first-order autocorrelation coefficient to take into account serial autocorrelation. R-square exceeded 0.99 and the t-statistics indicated that the coefficients were different from zero at a significance level of 99 percent.

7. Tax revenue volatility originates in the external sector in a twofold sense: while during 1970–90 the share of export taxes on total revenue was significant, which made tax collection vulnerable to Peruvian commodity-export prices in the world markets, in the 1990s, the Peruvian economy became sensitive to capital inflows surging from the opening of the capital account.

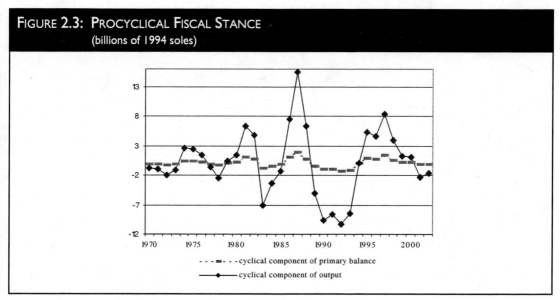

FIGURE 2.3: PROCYCLICAL FISCAL STANCE
(billions of 1994 soles)

Source: World Bank staff estimates.

of almost 2), the high variability of debt interest flows (elasticity of 7.1), and the swinging patterns of wage policy (it had an elasticity of −1.7) (Table 2.3).

The biggest policy mistake (and lesson) of the early 1990s is not to have taken the opportunity to save the transitory additional revenue generated with the economic boom. Since 1993, strong capital inflows dominated Peru's economic performance and brought about a strong economic boom. During 1993–97, GDP grew at an average annual rate of 7.0 percent. Instead of developing a countercyclical fiscal policy, the expansive fiscal stance adopted magnified the boom and increased the risks associated with it. Hence, the overall fiscal deficit increased to 3.0 percent of GDP in 1995, prompting the current account deficit in the balance of payments to widen from 5.7 percent in 1994 to 7.7 percent of GDP in 1995, which made the country's external position more vulnerable. In 1996, the government had no choice but to undertake a severe fiscal adjustment: the fiscal deficit

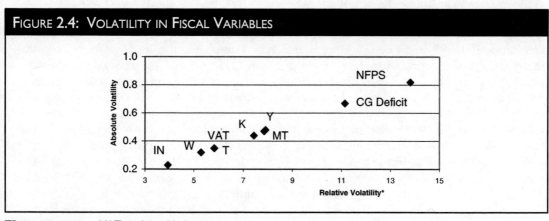

FIGURE 2.4: VOLATILITY IN FISCAL VARIABLES

TR - tax revenue     VAT - value added
YT - income tax     W - wages expenditure
MT - import tax     IN - interest expenditure     KX - capital expenditure
*Relative is ratio of standard deviations wrt GDP
Source: World Bank staff estimates

| TABLE 2.3: ELASTICITIES AND GROWTH VOLATILITIES FOR PERU (1990–2000)[a] | | | | | |
|---|---|---|---|---|---|
| | Absolute Volatility | Relative to Growth Volatility[b] | % of Total Revenue/ Expenditure | Elasticity | t-ratio |
| GDP | 5.0 | 1.0 | 100.0 | | |
| Central Government | | | | | |
| Revenue | 8.3 | 1.7 | 100.0 | 1.6 | 15.3 |
| Expenditure | 15.7 | 3.2 | 100.0 | 1.0 | 5.5 |
| Current Revenue | 7.9 | 1.6 | 98.8 | 1.5 | 14.5 |
| Tax Revenue | 8.0 | 1.6 | 87.8 | 1.4 | 11.6 |
| Non-Financial Expenditure | 16.8 | 3.4 | 80.6 | 1.7 | 14.5 |
| Current Expenditure | 14.8 | 3.0 | 61.9 | 1.7 | 13.0 |
| Capital Expenditure | 32.0 | 6.4 | 18.7 | 1.9 | 3.6 |
| Interest Expenditure | 27.2 | 5.5 | 19.4 | 7.1 | 3.9 |
| Wages | 16.4 | 3.3 | 17.0 | −1.7 | −5.3 |
| Subsidies and Current Transfers | 10.2 | 2.1 | 31.8 | 1.2 | 11.7 |
| Fiscal Balance | 13.6 | 2.7 | | | |
| Primary Balance | 20.3 | 4.1 | | | |

a. Volatilities are computed as standard deviations over a 10-year period in annual percentage rates of growth.
b. Volatility in the rate of growth of the fiscal variable divided by GDP growth volatility.
*Source:* World Bank staff estimates based on MEF and IMF data.

was reduced to 1.1 percent of GDP in 1996, and to an average of 0.3 percent of GDP during 1997–98, a situation of virtual balance.

## The Current Fiscal Disequilibria, 1999–2001

In the late 1990s, fiscal difficulties originated from adverse external developments, but were later accompanied by expansionary domestic policies. Financial contagion hit the Peruvian economy in mid-1998 as foreign banks drastically curtailed the availability of credit lines to the Peruvian banks in the wake of the Russian crisis of August 1998. The turmoil also affected the stock market, resulting in portfolio outflows and a sharp drop in stock prices. The reduction of foreign credit lines to the Peruvian banks was especially deleterious, as the banks had relied heavily on them to finance the 1993–97 credit boom. The ensuing credit crunch was a major blow for an economy that was barely recovering from the effects of another shock: the *El Niño* phenomenon, which struck in the first half of the year. The capital outflows episode thus came to a close, and the well-known vicious circle of credit reduction, decline in output and demand, lower sales, rising difficulties for firms in servicing their debts, deterioration of bank loan portfolios, and further credit reduction, set in. In 1998, the economy entered into a recession, with private investment significantly falling, both in real terms and as a percentage of GDP. Declining economic activity led to lower tax revenue and public expenditure, which also deepened the economic contraction. As a result, the overall fiscal deficit increased to an average of 2.9 percent of GDP during 1999–2001. Three domestic reasons also contributed to this outcome. On the expenditure front, the political business cycle deteriorated the fiscal accounts, as in the run-up to the 2000 presidential elections, the CG expanded current noninterest expenditures from 11.8 percent of GDP in 1998 to 12.7 percent of GDP in 2000. On the revenue side, the strong decline in tax revenue from an average 13.8 percent of GDP during 1995–97 to 12.3 percent during 1999–2001 was mainly associated not with the cycle, because the deviation of the cyclically adjusted balance with respect to the observed primary balance was small, which would suggest that the effect of cyclical factors was

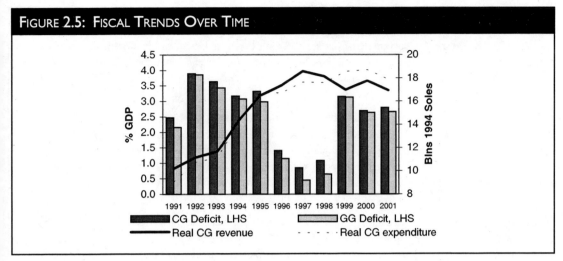

FIGURE 2.5:  FISCAL TRENDS OVER TIME

*Source:* World Bank staff estimates based on MEF and IMF

small, but rather with a structural shift in tax revenue behavior caused by frequent changes to the tax regime.[8]

Real revenue decreased and real expenditure increased. Fiscal vulnerability becomes more apparent when tax revenue and CG expenditure are considered in real terms. In 1999, tax revenue fell to pre-1995 levels (below 12.5 percent), while expenditure rose considerably (about 19 percent of GDP). As a result, the CG (and combined General Government) primary balance has been negative since 1999, and fiscal deficits have surged (Figure 2.5). An increased—mainly short and domestic—public debt (as a percentage of GDP from 42.7 percent in 1998 to about 46.5 percent in 2001) and privatization receipts financed the deficit. Barely 8 percent of public debt is short term, and prospects for improving public debt ratios in the medium term are favorable. However, public debt is exposed to currency risk. Debt service, which already increased from 3 percent of GDP in 1998 to a projected 3.8 percent of GDP in 2002, will contribute to tightening scarce resources in a shrinking budget. Had Peru kept government tax and expenditure constant in real terms during 1998–2001, it would have preserved a fiscal deficit below 1 percent of GDP.

Peru did not fully comply with its Fiscal Prudence and Transparency Law of 1999. The Law established a set of procedural and numerical fiscal rules (Box 2.1), and established five numerical targets for (a) the overall deficit; (b) the difference between the inflation rate and the annual growth rate of consolidated General Government's non-financial expenditures; (c) the total debt increase of the non-financial public sector; (d) the General Government's non-financial expenditures during the first seven months of an election year[9] as a percentage of budgeted non-financial expenditures of the General Government for the entire year; and (e) the overall deficit in the first half of each election year as a percentage of the budgeted deficit for the year. Government compliance with numerical targets was mixed, but the main target referring to the overall deficit was not

---

8. In a simple framework where tax revenues are a function of income, the cyclical effect can be seen as a movement along the revenue curve in response to a lower level of income. The deterioration of the tax system, by contrast, should be seen as a downward shift of the entire tax revenue curve, entailing lower revenues for any given level of income than in the situation prior to the deterioration. Our quantitative estimates indicate that the effect of the business cycle on the primary deficit during 1999–2001 was a worsening of just 0.1 to 0.2 percent of GDP.

9. Due to well-known political events in Peru, both 2000 and 2001 turned out to be election years.

**BOX 2.1: THE FISCAL PRUDENCE AND TRANSPARENCY LAW**

The Fiscal Prudence and Transparency Law was approved in December 1999 (Law No. 27245) and its regulations issued in April 2000 (Supreme Decree No. 039-2000-EF). It was suspended in December 2001 (Law No. 27577). The Fiscal Stabilization Fund was slightly amended through the 2002 Budget Law (Law No. 27573), which has three components:

*Numerical rules* include (a) a zero fiscal deficit in general (over the cycle), but below 2 percent of GDP in 2000, 1.5 percent in 2001, and 1 percent in 2002; (b) an increase of the non-financial general government spending below 2 percent in real terms; (c) electoral expenditure ceilings on the non-financial expenditure below 60 percent in the first seven months, and a public sector deficit below 50 percent in the first semester. These rules have two exceptions allowing for a fiscal deficit below 2 percent of GDP: one for emergency situations and another for recessions.

*Procedural rules* require the introduction of transparency criteria established in the IMF Code of Fiscal transparency from 2002, including (a) a Transparency Decree of Acceso Ciudadano, detailing periodic information to be published in the *Portal de Transparencia Económica;* (b) a multiyear budgeting framework; (c) a mandated pre-election fiscal report; (d) an annual review of contingent fiscal risks and tax expenditure to be published in the annual budget; and (e) a quarterly report on budget expansions and their implication over the macroeconomic framework.

The Fiscal Stabilization Fund was created from 75 percent of privatization proceeds, 50 percent of concessions, and excess revenue (above 0.3 percent its average of the past the years). Its resources should be mainly dedicated to poverty-alleviation programs, and activated when current revenue is at least 0.3 percent of GDP below its average in the last three years.

met, and the Law was suspended in December 2001. Although a case could be made that this was due to revenue-growth slowdown-related factors beyond the control of Peruvian officials, the fact is that President Fujimori's late Administration weakened the fiscal balances with new tax exemptions and electoral spending. In addition, the increase of non-financial expenditures in 2000 and 2001 built on their already high level reached in 1999.[10]

The present level of public debt needs to be reduced to more sustainable levels. Three years in a row of fiscal disequilibrium has led to an increase in public indebtedness and a reduction of long-term public savings. The accumulated deficit during 1999–2001 amounted to 8.8 percent of GDP. Its financing came from domestic credit (4.6 percent), external credit (2.0 percent), and depletion of privatization proceeds (2.2 percent). The stock of total public debt increased from an already high 42.7 percent of GDP in 1998 to 45.8 percent of GDP at the end of 2001. While the net public external debt ratio increased only slightly,[11] the domestic public debt ratio rose from 6.3 percent of GDP to 9.8 percent of GDP. (All domestic debt is in U.S. dollars.) External debt represents around 70 percent of total public debt and has moderate risk, because virtually all of it is long term. However, its service rapidly increased from 3 to 4 percent of GDP between 1998 and 2002, amounting to 23 percent of total expenditure in 2002, which is a considerable burden on tight fiscal balances. Two additional vulnerabilities are the foreign-currency risk exposure of the domestic debt and the rollover risk to changes in foreign investor confidence. Peru reopened its access to international markets with a US$500 million, 10-year bond placement combined with a retirement of Brady Bonds amounting to US$930 million in 2002, which lowered its debt servicing costs, although at the expense of a shorter maturity. Given the low tax revenue situation and expenditure pressures, Peru requires not only a fiscal adjustment, but also a prudent debt management strategy.

---

10. In terms of GDP, combined general government non-financial expenditures in 1999 were the highest for the entire decade of the 1990s (18.9 percent of GDP).
11. From 34.7 percent of GDP in March of 1999 to 35.1 percent in December 2001.

## The Macroeconomic Consistent Expenditure Envelope, 2002–03

The medium-term outlook for the economy is favorable. Since the focus of this chapter is on analyzing expenditure trends, the starting point for such analysis is the determination of an aggregate level of spending that is consistent with medium-term macroeconomic objectives (that is, a sustainable fiscal deficit and public debt ratio) (Table 2.4). A base-case scenario assumes that real growth of about 4 percent a year and low inflation inside the 2 to 3 percent range a year would be achieved on the basis of the recovery of the mining sector, increased productivity, and increased private sector investment and capital inflows attracted by sound macroeconomic policies, political stability, and the privatization program. It also assumes the combination of an increased export capacity, continuous implementation of structural reforms, a managed floating exchange rate regime, and a successful fiscal adjustment, supported by the IMF program. Mining production should benefit from the first full-year operation of the Antamina project. Structural change should lead to completion of the privatization program and improved regulations of private sector activities, developing public sector modernization and decentralization, strengthening financial supervision, and developing pension and social sector reform policies. In sum, under a low inflation and moderate growth scenario, present fiscal imbalances are expected to be gradually corrected provided the Government of Peru (GOP) adopts an urgent tax reform; cuts unnecessary outlays; protects expenditure shifted toward social priority needs; minimizes the cost of potentially significant contingent liabilities, like those from pensions, and maintains a prudent debt management strategy.

This macroeconomic scenario is entirely consistent in the short term with the stand-by arrangement agreed with the IMF. However, significant constraints remain, including limited policy credibility following a long period of political instability and a poor GOP track record in complying with fiscal rules; policy uncertainty due to continuous changes in the tax regime and regulations that affect prospects for attracting foreign investment; fiscal adjustment delays due to Congress inheriting populist-oriented and spending-prone fiscal decentralization measures; weak domestic consensus about further pension reform and the GOP's privatization plans; and a poor rule of law due to an inefficient judicial system and poorly managed local government institutions.

*Recommendations:*
Authorities should:

- Redouble efforts to build credibility before the Law is revamped
- Offset several measures introduced by the transition government that had negative implications for the fiscal balances with revenue resulting from tax reform
- Set rules to prevent decentralization from increasing transfers to regional and local governments that are not offset by similar improvements in revenue collection
- Stabilize the regulatory framework for private sector activities and strengthen the rule of law to diminish uncertainty that erodes the authority of rules and institutions that are essential to promote domestic and attract foreign investment.

Peru's most pressing fiscal challenge is to obtain primary surpluses, because negative primary fiscal balances are unsustainable.

*Recommendations:*
- In the short term, under the base case, the mid-term revised adjustment program aims at a gradual reduction in the combined fiscal deficit to 2.3 percent in 2002 and 1.9 percent of GDP in 2003. Most of the adjustment would be achieved through cuts in public spending, while reorienting and protecting priority social programs; and tax reform, combining tax policy measures, changes to the exemptions regime, and an improved tax administration (Box 2.2; Table 2.5). This scenario also assumes that the privatization of energy enterprises and the granting of a few concessions will materialize during 2002–03, averaging a minimum

## TABLE 2.4: KEY ECONOMIC INDICATORS

| | 1996 | 1997 | 1998 | 1999 | 2000 | 2001p | 2002e | 2003e |
|---|---|---|---|---|---|---|---|---|
| Real GDP Growth | 2.5 | 6.7 | -0.5 | 0.9 | 3.1 | 0.2 | 3.7 | 3.5–4.0 |
| Inflation (% CPI average) | 11.5 | 8.5 | 7.3 | 3.5 | 3.8 | 2.0 | 2.5 | 2–3 |
| **Key Macro Indicators (% of GDP)** | | | | | | | | |
| Gross Domestic Fixed Investment | 22.5 | 23.8 | 23.5 | 21.7 | 20.1 | 18.3 | 18.8 | 19.2 |
| Government investment | 4.3 | 4.4 | 4.5 | 4.8 | 4.0 | 3.2 | 3.1 | 3.0 |
| Private investment | 18.2 | 19.4 | 19.0 | 16.8 | 16.2 | 15.1 | 15.7 | 16.4 |
| Gross National Savings | 16.4 | 18.2 | 17.3 | 18.0 | 17.3 | 16.5 | 16.5 | 16.7 |
| Current Account Balance | -6.1 | -5.2 | -6.4 | -3.7 | -3.0 | -2.1 | -2.3 | -2.5 |
| **Central Government (% of GDP)** | | | | | | | | |
| Current Revenue | 15.7 | 15.6 | 15.7 | 14.5 | 14.7 | 14.1 | 13.9 | 14.1 |
| Tax revenue | 13.9 | 14.1 | 13.8 | 12.5 | 12.0 | 11.9 | 11.9 | 12.4 |
| Nontax revenue | 1.8 | 1.5 | 1.9 | 2.0 | 2.7 | 2.2 | 2.0 | 1.7 |
| Current Expenditure | 13.9 | 13.1 | 13.7 | 14.6 | 14.9 | 14.7 | 14.4 | 14.1 |
| Interest | 2.4 | 1.8 | 1.9 | 2.1 | 2.2 | 2.1 | 2.0 | 2.2 |
| Interest on external debt | 2.3 | 1.7 | 1.8 | 2.0 | 1.9 | 1.9 | 1.7 | 1.9 |
| Interest on domestic debt | 0.1 | 0.1 | 0.1 | 0.1 | 0.3 | 0.2 | 0.3 | 0.3 |
| Current Transfers | 2.9 | 3.1 | 2.0 | 2.8 | 2.3 | 2.3 | 2.4 | 2.4 |
| Consumption | 8.6 | 8.3 | 9.8 | 9.7 | 10.4 | 10.3 | 10.0 | 9.5 |
| Primary Balance | 1.0 | 0.9 | 0.8 | -1.0 | -0.5 | -0.6 | -0.4 | 0.3 |
| Overall Balance | -1.4 | -0.8 | -1.1 | -3.1 | -2.7 | -2.8 | -2.3 | -1.9 |
| **NFPS Balance (% of GDP)** | -1.0 | -0.1 | -0.8 | -3.1 | -3.2 | -2.5 | -2.3 | -1.9 |
| Privatization | 3.9 | 0.9 | 0.5 | 0.8 | 0.8 | 0.6 | 0.6 | 0.5 |
| **NFPS Debt** | | | | | | | | |
| Public sector debt/GDP | 45.2 | 31.9 | 42.7 | 48.0 | 45.9 | 46.5 | 44.9 | 40.9 |
| Public sect. debt service/GDP | 4.1 | 3.3 | 3.4 | 3.9 | 3.8 | 3.9 | 3.8 | 4.5 |
| *Memo:* | | | | | | | | |
| GDP Nominal (millions N$) | 136,929 | 157,274 | 166,514 | 174,719 | 186,756 | 189,532 | 200,083 | 13,205 |

*Note:* This table has minor differences with Table SA.5, based on Central Bank data, and Tables 1–6 in Annex A, based on preliminary data. Tax revenue is net of tax on assets of public enterprises and of CG-IES payments.

*Source:* World Bank staff estimates.

## BOX 2.2: TAX REGIME AND PROPOSED CHANGES

**Income tax on individuals.** This tax is levied on four classes of income: real estate, other capital assets, self-employed labor, and wage labor. The maximum marginal tax rate for net income greater than 54 *Unidades de Ingreso Tributario* (1 UIT = about US$828) is 30 percent. The marginal rate for net income between 7 UITs and 54 UITs is 15 percent. Labor income below 7 UITs is exempted. Dividends are not taxed. The interest income from savings with the national financial system and capital gains from the sale of securities and real estate are exempted. During 1997–2000, revenue from the income tax on individuals was, on average, 1.0 percent of GDP (Kopits and others 2000; Schenone 2001). Over 75 percent of this revenue comes from wage-earners' income and only about 10 percent from the self-employed. This is tantamount to the existence of a high degree of horizontal inequity. The situation is worsened by underreporting of income from independent professionals' services and rents from real estate. The considerable number of exemptions also blunts the intended progressivity of this tax category, which detracts from the system's claim to vertical equity. The exemption on interest income from bank deposits is 0.1 percent of GDP (Kopits and others 2000; and Schenone 2001).

**Recommendations:** *(a) Elimination of exemptions on all forms of capital gains including the sale of securities and real estate, on interest income, and other income from financial assets; (b) introduction of a more gradual structure of marginal tax rates (for example, with three rates, 10, 20, and 30 percent) instead of the current two-rate structure; and (c) introduction of presumptive-income methods for self-employed taxpayers.*

**Income tax on corporate income.** The taxable base for the corporate income tax is the worldwide income of enterprises legally regarded as domiciled in Peru. The rate is 20 percent. Exemptions are numerous and include interest income from savings with the national financial system; interest income from registered instruments issued by corporations; capital gains from the sale of securities; "native" agriculture and/or transformation or processing of products described as "native," and/or alternative crops in the Amazon region; enterprises operating in the Centers for Export, Transformation, Industry, Commercialization, and Services (CETICOS); and income from agricultural enterprises with sales under 50 UIT. Rate reductions and other tax benefits are agriculture (a rate of 15 percent); income of enterprises engaged in agriculture, aquaculture, fisheries, tourism, and manufacturing activities associated with the processing, transformation, and marketing of commodities from the aforementioned activities, the processing of forestry products and forest extraction (a rate of 5 percent if the business is located in the departments of Loreto and Madre de Dios, and in some districts of the Ucayali department, or 10 percent if it is located anywhere else in the Amazon region); accelerated depreciation is allowed in mining, hydrocarbons, tourism, agriculture and agribusiness; and tax discount for reinvestment in mining, education, and manufacturing industry, and for enterprises located in the Amazon region. The effects of this type of tax benefits are well known: the neutrality of the tax system is impaired and the revenue-yielding capacity is damaged. Collection from the tax on corporate income fell from 2.2 percent of GDP in the first quarter of 1999 to 1.4 percent in the fourth quarter of 2001. The fiscal cost of exemptions on deposits of corporations in the banking system is 0.2 percent of GDP. Moreover, in the case of foreign firms, a part of the benefits granted ends up as a transfer to the treasuries of foreign governments where the firms in question have their headquarters. In many cases, these types of tax incentives are not instrumental in attaining the desired investment objectives and lack transparency because it is very difficult to quantify the benefits given to a particular sector or region of a country.

**Recommendations:** *(a) An across-the board elimination of sector- and region-specific exemptions is desirable; (b) alternatively, if the authorities want to subsidize specific productive sectors and/or regions of the country, explicit transfers should be included in the national budget; and (c) exemptions on all forms of capital gains from portfolio investments must be eliminated.*

**Import tariffs.** Tariffs are levied on imports of goods on the basis of their CIF value. There are two basic tariff levels: a 12 percent general tariff (applicable to 5,780 customs items); and a special tariff of 20 percent (applicable to 752 items). In addition, there are two types of surcharges: one on agricultural products (surcharge rate of 5 percent) and one on meat products (surcharge rate of 10 percent). Only one exemption raises serious

(continued)

## Box 2.2: Tax Regime and Proposed Changes (Continued)

concern: the exemption from tariffs for foreign goods introduced into the CETICOS that do not pay import duties and can be reexported. This exemption impairs the horizontal equity of the tax system in that it provides for unequal treatment of enterprises that are otherwise equal just because they are located in different places.

**Recommendation:** *The CETICOS regime must be abolished.*

**The Extraordinary Solidarity Tax.** This is a tax on firms' payroll. The taxable base is the wage compensation to workers classified in tax code categories 4 and 5, excluding national holidays and Christmas bonuses. It has long been recognized as a burden on the competitiveness of enterprises and is being phased out. The current government reduced its rate from 5 percent to 2 percent. The government is seeking congressional approval for its complete elimination.

**Recommendation:** *The government's decision to eliminate the Extraordinary Solidarity Tax is adequate.*

**The General Sales Tax.** The general sales tax (VAT) has a rate of 18 percent and is levied on the domestic sales of movable goods, the provision or use of services in Peru, construction contracts, the first sale of structures by their builders, and imports. The following goods are exempted: fish and seafood, cochinilla, bull semen, whole raw milk, potatoes and other root vegetables, dried vegetables, other vegetables and fruits, cereal seeds, rice, raw coffee, tea, cocoa, unprocessed tobacco, wools and pelts, raw cotton, nonmonetary gold, vehicles for diplomatic use, books for educational institutions, and the first sale of structures valued at less than 35 UITs. The following services are exempted: financial services, public passenger transportation (except for air transport), international cargo transport, live shows declared of cultural value by the National Cultural Institute, sale of beverages and food at snack bars and universities, construction and repair of foreign ships, interest on transferable securities issued by enterprises pursuant to the Securities Market Law, life insurance polices, postal services intended to complete such services originating abroad, and exports of goods and services. Apart from the aforementioned list of exemptions, there are a few special regimes for the VAT. First, the Hydrocarbons Act exempts the import of goods and inputs required in the exploration phase of oil contracts, and the sale of petrol, natural gas, and derivatives, for internal consumption, in the departments of Loreto, Madre de Dios, and Ucayali. The Amazon Investment Promotion Act of 1999 exempts from the VAT the sale of all goods and services for internal consumption and construction contracts in the Amazon region. Furthermore, it allows a fiscal credit of 25 percent or 50 percent on the VAT for sales to the rest of the country. The Agriculture Act exempts from the VAT agricultural producers the annual sales of which are below 50 UIT. The first sale of homes below US$35,000 is also exempted. There is, finally, a special rate for rice (5 percent). In analyzing the fiscal impact of the VAT exemptions we must distinguish between the general exemptions and the special regimes. Defenders of the general exemptions contend that, by selecting items of popular consumption, they introduce a desirable element of progressivity in this tax and hence a positive redistributive effect. It has been demonstrated, however, that, to the extent that they include items that are also consumed by the rich, exemptions to the VAT are, at best, powerless to generate positive redistributive effects and, at worst, deepen the negative redistributive effects that are an inherent feature of this tax. For their part, the special regimes damage the VAT's revenue-yielding capacity. In the case of the Amazon-region exemptions, they not only deprive the national treasury of revenue in the Amazon region itself, but open the door for VAT evasion on the part of taxpayers from regions other than the Amazon region through the simple expedient of doing their shopping in the latter region. Finally, the exemption for agricultural producers the annual sales of which are below 50 UIT breaks its universality and neutrality.

**Recommendations:** (a) VAT exemptions for the Amazon region must be eliminated; (b) VAT exemptions granted by the Hydrocarbons Law must be eliminated; and (c) the 50-UIT threshold for agricultural producers must be eliminated.

| TABLE 2.5: RECOMMENDATIONS FOR TAX REFORM | |
|---|---|
| **Recommended Measure** | **Revenue Impact (% of GDP)** |
| **Income Tax** | |
| Elimination of exemptions on interest income and capital gains | 0.27 |
| Introduction of a three-level structure of rates for individuals | 0.10 |
| Elimination of sector- and region-specific exemptions | 0.60 |
| **Value Added Tax** | |
| Elimination of VAT exemptions for Amazon region | 0.25 |
| Elimination of exemptions granted by Hydrocarbons Act | 0.10 |
| Elimination of the 50-UIT threshold for agriculture | 0.30 |
| **Selective Tax on Consumption** | |
| Elimination of ISC exemptions for the Amazon region[1] | – |
| Elimination of exemption on fuels used by power industry[2] | – |
| Unification of ISC for vehicles at 25-percent rate | 0.10 |
| **Import Tariffs** | |
| Elimination of the CETICOS regime | 0.13 |
| **Special Regime for Mining** | |
| Introduce a system of mining royalties[3] | 0.10 |
| ***Extraordinary Solidarity Tax (EST)*** | |
| Elimination of the EST | –0.20 |
| **TOTAL IMPACT** | **1.65** |

1. The elimination of both the VAT and ISC exemptions for the Amazon region is estimated to have a total revenue impact of 0.10 percent of GDP. This is the reason why no revenue impact figure is entered in this row of the table.
2. The revenue impact of this measure as a percentage of GDP is very small. This is the reason no figure is entered in this row.
3. The revenue impact would depend on the characteristics of the royalties regime (see Chapter VIII).
*Source:* Schenone (2002) and World Bank staff estimates.

of 0.6 percent of GDP a year. Under these assumptions, continuous implementation of a managed floating exchange rate and an open trade regime, the external current account deficit is projected to be about 2.5 in 2003, and the international reserve position is projected to gradually decline to comfortable levels (7.5 months of imports by 2005).

■ In the medium term, our estimates of the potential output and structural fiscal balance under the base-case scenario indicate that, in order to stabilize debt indicators, the present deficit in the non-financial public sector primary balance should rapidly shift to a surplus of 0.9 percent of GDP by 2004. The consolidation of this effort would require NFPS primary surpluses to reach between 1.0 and 1.3 percent of GDP during the second half of the decade (Annex B).

Public debt ratios should decrease to more sustainable levels in the medium term and debt currency risk should be reduced. A public debt ratio of 46.5 percent of GDP is too high, especially for a country the balance sheet of which contains a significant currency risk, which exposes it to external shocks. Such risk originates from the fact that most of Peru's public debt (external and domestic) is in dollars, while the government's earnings are mostly in soles (trade taxes are the only revenue that is dollar-linked). Existing dollar-denominated debt also actually puts authorities in the position of being against their own commitment to let their own currency float freely, thus pressing them to continue intervening to avoid its depreciation.

## Recommendations:

■ Under a baseline scenario, a debt sustainability analysis estimates the target public debt-to-GDP ratio to be reached in 2010 is 36.2 (Annex A, Table A.4). Such ratio would require a fiscal correlation in the structural primary surplus of 1.6 percent of GDP (cyclically adjusted) between 2001 and 2010 (Annex B, Table B.1). Such estimates take into account the debt exchange of the Peruvian Brady bonds with private creditors in 2002 and its slightly shortened maturities. If sustained fiscal efforts are promptly developed, the public-debt-to-GDP ratio is projected to improve substantially from about 46.5 percent in 2001 to 39.3 percent in 2005, and then decrease until its benchmark ratio in 2010. The resulting path toward sustainability in the public external debt service, however, is a longer one. As a percentage to GDP, debt service should increase from about 3.8 to 6.0 percent between 2001 and 2005, and then decrease to 4.6 percent of GDP in 2010.

■ Under the extreme case of a modified baseline scenario with shocks derived from the impact of a sudden financing stop (a real exchange rate depreciation and the materialization of contingent liabilities contained in short-term debt), the target public-debt-to-GDP ratio to be reached in 2010 would increase to 40.8 percent. Such ratio would require a fiscal correction in the structural primary surplus of 2.4 percent of GDP (cyclically adjusted) between 2001 and 2010 (Annex A, Table A.4).

■ **On public domestic debt.** Developing a market for domestic public debt issued in soles would contribute to reducing its currency risk and bringing more credibility to the inflation-targeting policy. Despite being small,[12] an inflation-indexed public debt in local currency, hopefully placed beyond the short term, would also contribute to reducing inflationary surprises.

■ **On public external debt.** The initial focus of the new Peruvian officials has been on reducing rollover costs, widening maturities, and refinancing debt with Paris Club creditors. Increased coordination between the MEF and the Central Bank of Peru (BCRP), and strengthened management of the maturity and currency composition of external debt, would facilitate debt servicing. Approval of a General Debt Law in 2002 is expected to deal with debt management issues.

Peru should start making provisions for contingent liabilities. These could materialize in the near future, thus making more difficult projected recovery of budget discipline. There are at least three main sources of contingent risk that could become a government liability: nonperforming bank loans, pension payments, and municipal debt (not counting those that could originate from *Banco Agrario* or public enterprises loan guarantees).

■ The World Bank's broad estimates of the potential fiscal exposure of a banking crisis is 4 percent of GDP, which is considered in the lower bound of comparable—mostly double-digit—world standards. Moreover, official estimates put nonperforming loans at about 10 percent of the Bank's portfolio in 2001, but such a ratio appears to be stabilizing in 2002.

■ The pension system is a potentially significant fiscal liability. Pension reform has generated two nonbanking debts with the private sector that are actually paid through annual trans-

---

12. Internal debt was very small during most of the 1990s, because the GOP associated it to the decades of large deficits and inflation. Bonds were reissued in 1999 to support a bank merger, the purchase of the bad asset portfolio of a bank taken over by the government, and two bond-for-loan swap programs. In 2000 and 2001, new bond issues were made under the Financial System Consolidation Program. The BCRP has strict limits on purchasing government debt.

fers: one is to cover the pension of public employees retiring under the public pension system, and the other are *bonos de reconocimiento* of those who already migrated to the private pension system. Official transfers to social security represent 0.6 percent of GDP in 2002, and conservative projections indicate they might increase to about 0.6 to 1.0 percent of GDP per year during 2005–07 (IMF data, and Arias and others 2000).

▪ Registered municipal debt is not a threat to macroeconomic stability, but this is not an indication that the problem is not very serious at the local level. Indeed, it is significant and explosive, because some local governments are likely to become nonsolvent and illiquid, like those of Arequipa and La Victoria (Fernandez 2002). These two local governments will have severe difficulties assuming additional responsibilities with decentralization due to financial constraints. Nationwide, total registered debt represents a third of the corresponding national debt (current national liabilities considered as short-term debt). Nonregistered municipal debt adds up to such a burden.

### Recommendations:

▪ Peru should start making budgetary provisions for contingent liabilities, so a first step would be to make a comprehensive assessment of all potential sources and quantify them.

▪ Financial contingent liabilities should be monitored through an adequate prudential supervision. Those eventually arising from a sudden stop of external financing due to contagion, can only be avoided with sound macroeconomic management (Annex A).

▪ Reducing contingent liabilities in pensions will likely require more structural solutions.

▪ Identifying nonsolvent municipalities and their eventually nonregistered short-term debt, and developing a plan for the gradual repayment of their registered debt are essential steps before districts assume further responsibilities under the forthcoming decentralization process.

▪ The revamped Fiscal Prudence and Transparency Law should continue preventing government officials from resorting to the Central Bank for financing of its own expenditure, and should add specific prohibition to incoming subnational governments (or ceilings) on acquiring future debts (Chapter V).

There are also additional external and domestic risks to this scenario that would make Peru's growth potential uncertain, increase credit risk, reduce financing needed for a sustained social policy, or weaken the institutional leadership on social reform and fiscal decentralization. On the *external* front, a prolonged slowdown of the global economy, adverse regional developments, or unexpected shocks in the international capital markets could lead to a significant decline in external demand for Peruvian exports, or in mineral prices, and/or to private capital outflows. This could reduce export dynamism and growth, destabilize the domestic currency, put strong pressure on both the public and corporate sectors, which are heavily indebted in foreign currency, and impose additional stress on the banking sector. On the *domestic* front, the new Administration and Congress could fail to agree on the implementation of the necessary policy measures needed for an effective fiscal adjustment and a financially sound State reform and decentralization process. Lack of consensus could also delay or revert the comprehensive legislative reform of the tax system to be introduced in 2002. Authorities should be supported in their efforts to:

▪ Build a contingent financing plan based on (a) the prompt materialization of external donor financing to the incoming Poverty-Reduction Strategy, (b) increased and enhanced access to international capital markets by further placement of sovereign bonds, and (c) the completion of the privatization process.

▪ Develop consensus-building mechanisms on fiscal issues, aimed at reaching a common, shared, medium-term vision with the private sector and civil society. Such consensus should be adequately reflected in the revamping of the Law.

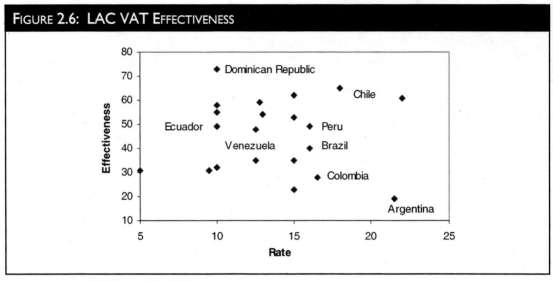

FIGURE 2.6:  LAC VAT EFFECTIVENESS

*Source:* Schenone (2002) and IMF (2000).

## The Fiscal Adjustment Effort

Fiscal adjustment requires a certain combination of expenditure-reduction-cum-revenue-increase. In 2002, Peru's required revenue increase will not likely result from a rapid recovery of the economy, because the cyclical component of the fiscal balance is very small (Figure 2.13). Besides, economic recovery has had limited impact on tax collection due to the prolonged debate that took place in Congress on the *desagio tributario* (a quasi tax amnesty) and the granting of additional income tax exemptions. This points out the need for a combination of expenditure cuts with structural remedies on the revenue side. A long-lasting fiscal adjustment requires measures to (a) strengthen the tax regime and administration; and (b) revert the trend toward increased current outlays, while curbing inefficient expenditure.

### Strengthening the Tax Regime

Continuous changes in the tax regime are weakening the successful tax reform of the 1990s. In 1993, Peru carried out a well-designed reform of its tax system: the reform aimed at simplifying the tax system, broadening the tax base, and increasing revenue yield (IMF 2000). The number of tax categories was reduced from almost 70 to 4 basic categories: the general sales tax (VAT), the income tax on individuals and corporations, the selective tax on consumption (an excise tax), and tariffs on imported goods. The income tax brackets were reduced from 5 to 3, and business income was taxed at a flat rate of 30 percent. Dividend income was excluded from the tax base and the net-wealth tax was eliminated. The minimum income tax, based on gross assets, was maintained. The base for the value added and excise taxes was broadened and most exemptions eliminated. Later, in 1994, the base for the income and value added taxes were broadened further.[13] However, since 1996 a long series of exemptions and other preferential regime measures was introduced, which severely eroded tax collection capacity. Despite having a VAT collection effectiveness ratio that is average in LAC terms—about 50 percent (Figure 2.6)—the main tax breaks represent a minimum of 2 percent of GDP of direct tax losses (Table SA.21). Strengthening the tax regime requires a set of specific actions

---

13. In the institutional domain, the Superintendency for Tax Administration (SUNAT) was created with effective administrative and budgetary autonomy. Personnel policies were reformed to get highly qualified staff and endow them with up-to-date computational equipment. The tax code was modified to enhance SUNAT's ability to audit taxpayers, increase fines and penalties, simplify procedures, and strengthen tax courts.

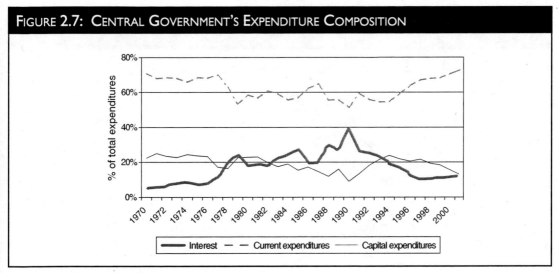

**FIGURE 2.7:  CENTRAL GOVERNMENT'S EXPENDITURE COMPOSITION**

*Source:* MEF, IMF and World Bank estimates.

to improve the equity, neutrality, simplicity, and revenue-yielding capacity (Box 2.2). A specific set of ensuing tax policy recommendations could generate an estimated potential revenue-generating capacity of 1.65 percent of GDP (Table 2.5).[14]

### Reverting Expenditure Trends
Current expenditure is increasing explosively. Since the mid-1990s, Peru's current expenditure has been increasing at an accelerated pace. It rose from about 50 percent of total CG expenditure in 1990 to almost 73 percent in the early 2000s (85 percent for the CG in 2001). These very high levels by Peruvian standards were characteristic of strong State intervention in the 1970s (Figure 2.7). One could argue that the levels of current and capital expenditure are broadly in line with LAC regional averages (Table SA.29); but what is worrisome is its increasing trend and present composition. In 2001, as a share of total expenditure, Peru's 39 percent wage bill was second highest in LAC, and as a share of GDP, Peru's 6.6 percent figure was higher than the 6.3 percent LAC average. These ratios suggest an increasing sense of overstaffing and do not include additional "services" hired as temporary contracts under goods and services categories (Chapter VI). It also suggests a high level of budget rigidity (Chapter III). Such a rising trend would not have been possible unless capital expenditure and interest payments had not decreased their share below 15 percent. Contrary to the early 1990s, interest payments have been below the region's average. For its part, Peru's capital expenditure (3 percent of GDP) is among the lowest in LAC (Figure 2.8) and keeps decreasing (see Table SA.5). Indeed the budget priority in the 1990s was not to increase the capital stock.

### Recommendation:
■ The proposed comprehensive reform of the State should examine proposals to combine a gradual reduction of current expenditure, especially wages and salaries, while developing a more qualified and efficient labor force under a civil service reform (Chapter V).

Public investment remains low and only recently has given priority to the social sectors. In the 1990s, capital expenditure was more volatile and procyclical than all the other expenditures cate-

---

14. Both proposals, the tax regime changes and the set of tax policy recommendations, are based on Schenone (2002).

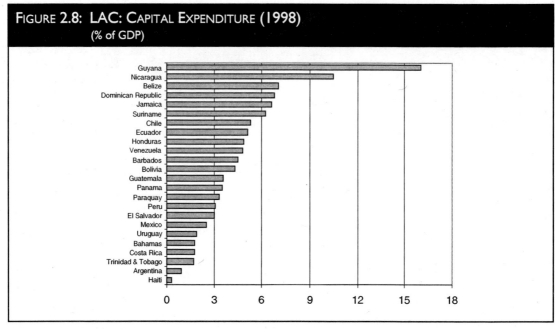

FIGURE 2.8: LAC: CAPITAL EXPENDITURE (1998)
(% of GDP)

*Source:* World Bank staff estimates.

gories (Table 2.3). In addition, the average level of CG capital expenditures as a percentage of GDP was below 2.8 percent in recession years and 4.0 percent in boom years.

These outcomes reflect the fact that, to a great extent, public investment continues to be the residual item in the budget—that is, the one that bears the brunt of fiscal adjustment efforts. The composition of fixed capital formation has suffered important changes. Whereas investment in economic infrastructure played a dominant but declining share as a percentage of total capital investment, falling from 72 percent in 1990 to 54 percent in 2000, the share of investment in social infrastructure increased from 12 percent to 19 percent of total expenditure (Figure 2.9). The disaggregated analysis of the internal decomposition of investment in economic infrastructure shows that, by far, the biggest decline was in the share of public investment devoted to agriculture, which more than halved, from 46 percent to 19 percent of total capital formation, whereas the energy

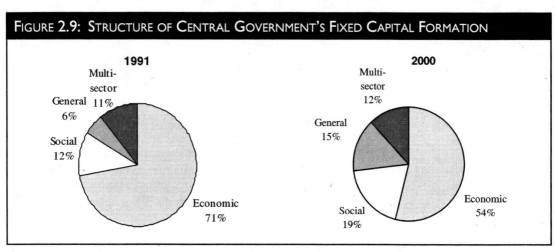

FIGURE 2.9: STRUCTURE OF CENTRAL GOVERNMENT'S FIXED CAPITAL FORMATION

*Source:* MEF.

and mining sector increased its share from almost nil in 1990 to 10 percent in 2000. For its part, the transport and communication sector essentially maintained its share at roughly a quarter of total capital formation (Table SA.7b). The doubling share of investment in social infrastructure is a very positive trend inherited from the 1990s. This effort is also reflected in the pattern of total social expenditure, which seemingly rose from 3.9 percent of GDP in 1990 to 6.9 percent in 2000, and remained steady until 2002 despite the economic slowdown.[15]

*Recommendation:*
- Peru has the capacity to gradually fill its financial gap in the social sectors by raising its historically underfunded education and health expenditure ratios of 2.9 and 3 percent of GDP, respectively, in 2000, to at least the average LAC ratios of 4.1 and 3.2 percent of GDP, respectively, in the next five years.

The observed increase in fixed capital formation of the "general sectors"—mainly including general public services like military expenditures—is a matter of concern. As a percentage of total capital investment, such share almost tripled from 5.6 percent to 14.8 percent, reflecting, to a considerable extent, the leading role assigned to military expenditures within total public expenditures. In a similar vein, during 1998–2000, defense and national security expenditure averaged 2.9 percent of GDP. Such a relatively high level of military expenditure no longer seems to be justified by the needs of a country in the aftermath of the successful peace process with Ecuador, and by a country now far removed from the civil conflict that afflicted it in the mid-1990s. Moreover, such expenditure turned out to be prone to corruption, evidenced by lack of any control.

*Recommendations:*
Authorities should redress this situation by:

- Reducing resources devoted to military outlays to the budgeted 2.1 percent of GDP in 2002, and shifting part of those savings to social expenditure; and
- Completing the application of SIAF subsystems to military expenditure to make it more transparent and accountable.

Developing effective countercyclical *fiscal* and *social* policies remains a priority, especially in good times. Both policies are, in general, complementary. The most significant increases in total (and social) spending took place in the early-to-mid-1990s, when growth was high. Then, in the late 1990s, real social spending remained fairly constant even during the economic downturn of 1998 and, later, in 2001 (Figures 2.10 and 2.11). How expansive total and social expenditures were despite fiscal contractions is an empirical question. The percent changes and point elasticities of total and social expenditures were negative in 1998 (Table 2.6). During 1991–2002, the level of social expenditure was not protected compared to fiscal adjustments. The elasticity of all categories of social expenditure was positive and equal to or higher than unity—which reveals their procyclical behavior (Table 2.6). These findings are all supportive of procyclical policies.

- However, on one hand, Peruvian officials have developed the basic institutional framework required for a countercyclical *fiscal* policy with the creation of the Fiscal Stabilization Fund as part of the Law of Fiscal Prudence and Transparency. Short of resources, however, the Fund has played a rather marginal countercyclical role.
- On the other hand, since 2001, and in the midst of another economic downturn, Peru's government opted for a countercyclical *social* policy, as can be inferred from the nonnegative

---

15. Authorities indicated that such increase could partly be due to a reclassification of line items grouped under social expenditure.

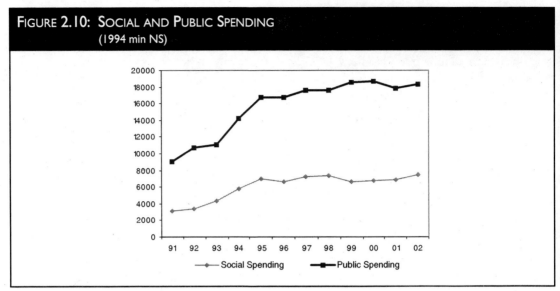

FIGURE 2.10: SOCIAL AND PUBLIC SPENDING (1994 min NS)

Source: MEF.

growth of real social spending, when compared to the actual decrease in real total expenditure (Figure 2.11). In a similar pattern, point elasticities for social, health, nutrition, justice, and social security expenditure in 2001 were also negative, indicating that in a year of fiscal contraction, expenditure in these sectors actually increased.[16] These results for fiscal contraction appear robust to period changes.

## Revamping the Fiscal Rules

Peru needs a fiscal rule to help stabilize its fiscal balances in the medium term, reduce its volatile and procyclical fiscal deficit bias, and consolidate credibility. As mentioned, Peru is under considerable fiscal stress, with only a mild countercyclical social policy in the early 2000s. Procyclical and deficit-biased fiscal policies can be explained by the combination of faulty measures, especially during election years, fiscal conservatism, and weak institutions to attempt (and succeed) in running surpluses during the economic boom of the mid-1990s. If respected, a fiscal rule might strengthen credibility because it reverses political incentives for achieving fiscal stabilization in favor of disciplined compliance, promotes accountability and transparency when supported by sanctions and open access to information, and tends to eliminate the deficit bias if supported by countercyclical, eventually automatic, stabilizers. Peru's Law of Fiscal Prudence and Transparency is one of the most comprehensive in Latin America (Table SA.23b). It contains numerical and procedural rules, and a Fiscal Stabilization Fund (Box 2.3).

Compliance with the Law was mixed. The main numerical target was not met, and compliance with procedural rules was also unsatisfactory, especially with respect to required reporting. However, a multiyear budgeting framework has been established, supported by a *Portal de Transparen-*

---

16. Elasticities were calculated such that $e_i = X_i/X$, where $e_i$ is the elasticity of expenditure in the i sector, $X_i$ is the percentage change in real expenditure in the ith sector, and X equals the percentage change in total real expenditure. The higher the magnitude of the elasticity, the greater the responsiveness of that category of expenditure to variations in total expenditure. Sectors that are favored in periods of fiscal contraction of total government expenditure have elasticities of less than unity, that is, they would be expected to experience reductions of a proportionately smaller magnitude than the total expenditure cutback, or even real increases if the elasticity is found negative. An elasticity of exactly equal to zero means that the sector is completely protected, and those greater than unity suggest that this is a relevant category of expenditure.

**FIGURE 2.11: GROWTH RATES IN SOCIAL AND PUBLIC SPENDING**

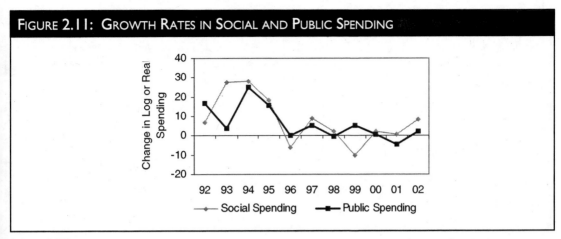

*Source:* MEF.

*cia*, but all mandated reports are missing (Table 3.1): the semiannual progress report of the multi-year framework, the annual report on contingent risk and tax expenditure, and the quarterly report on budget expansions (Valderrama 2002).

Peru faces four broad dilemmas in revamping its Law. First, adding *flexibility versus credibility* for a more rigid rule would imply higher credibility, if the probability of fulfilling it is high; second, looking for more *simplicity versus complexity,* since a simpler rule would allow an easier understanding by the public; third, adding more *procedural versus numerical* rules, since numerical rules seem easier to understand, but harder to comply with; and fourth, opening for *participation versus confidentiality* in the revamping process of the Law, because a consensus-built rule would allow for enhanced credibility, but would delay its approval.

Two LAC best practices seem particularly appealing for revamping Peruvian Fiscal Law: Brazil and Chile.

■ On one hand *Brazil* has a complex, still credible Fiscal Responsibility Law that was built under an extremely participatory process and that combines a mix of procedural-cum-numerical-based rules. It is not clear whether adherence to such rigid targets fully eliminates

**TABLE 2.6: SOCIAL EXPENDITURES ARE PRO- OR COUNTERCYCLICAL?[a]**

|  | Elasticity (1991–2002)[b] | Percent Change in 1998 | Point Elasticity (1998) | Point Elasticity (2001) |
|---|---|---|---|---|
| Total Expenditures | . . . | −0.28 | . . . | . . . |
| Social Expenditures | 1.19 | −1.50 | −8.32 | −0.17 |
| Education | 0.99 | −0.66 | 5.01 | 1.78 |
| Health | 1.15 | −5.58 | −1.87 | −5.83 |
| Nutrition | 2.35 | 0.81 | 13.74 | −1.13 |
| Justice | 1.75 | −0.39 | 58.38 | −3.2 |
| Social Security | 1.47 | −0.75 | −17.01 | −3.34 |
| Other Social Investment | 1.66 | −2.75 | −61.87 | 2.32 |

a. Elasticities are with respect to total real expenditure of the consolidated public sector.
b. Significant at 1 percent.

*Source:* World Bank staff estimates.

## BOX 2.3: PERU: EVALUATION OF THE TRANSPARENCY LAW 2000–01

| | 2000 | | 2001 | |
|---|---|---|---|---|
| | **Law** | **Actual** | **Law** | **Observed** |
| **CPS deficit as % of GDP** | 2.0% | 3.2% | 1.5% | 2.3% |
| Difference between annual growth rate of general government's non-financial expenditures and inflation, less than 2%. | 2.0% | 0.6% | 2.0% | -5.0% |
| **CPS debt increase (adjusted) no greater than NFPS deficit** | <US$ 5,983 | US$ 4,534 | <US$ 4,893 | US$ 5,978 |
| Election year: general government's non-financial expenditures during the first 7 months no greater than 50% of GG annual budget. | <60% | 58% | <60% | 56% |
| Election year: CPS deficit in the first semester no greater than 50% of budgeted deficit. | <50% | 39% | <50% | 20% |

CPS = Consolidated Public Sector = NFPS deficit—net result of local government.
*Source:* Central Bank and Ministry of Economy and Finance.

the deficit bias, because an economic slowdown may force authorities to cut public spending, impeding the operation of automatic stabilizers and deepening the downturn (Perry 2002). However, the Law is accompanied by a Fiscal Crimes Law, establishing an extensive list of sanctions, and a full set of budgetary and financial information, including information about contingent liabilities. Since most intergovernmental transfers in Brazil to subnational governments are automatic, the Fiscal Responsibility Law does not cover them, but discipline in such accounts is enforced through recent government-led individual debt-restructuring deals that have imposed tight indebtedness restrictions and a severely limited ability to borrow in cases of economic slowdowns (Gonzalez, Rosenblatt, and Webb 2002).

■ On the other hand, *Chile* has an extremely simple numerical target of 1 percent of structural annual surplus (after removing the cycle on revenues and variations in copper prices). The fact that the deficit benchmark is set in structural terms forces the government to run surpluses during booms and high copper prices, and to run moderate deficits during downturns and low copper prices, thus playing an effective countercyclical policy, curbing political pressures, and enhancing its credibility in the markets. The Law was also accompanied by a long institutional process devoted to careful technical design and sensitive political validation, broad coverage of the potential risk of contingent liabilities, and consistency checks with the monetary program. The Law does not have, however, any clause with respect to subnational governments.

The Fiscal Stabilization Fund (FSF) is well conceived, but given its limited revenue sources has little potential to sustain a meaningful countercyclical policy. In 2001, the FSF barely contributed with US$59.4 millions to finance 0.1 percent of GDP of the fiscal deficit. Even under a high-case privatization scenario that would generate US$1,400 million in privatization proceeds during

2002–03, the FSF would contribute with resources equivalent to 0.3 to 0.4 percent of GDP of deficit financing. Therefore, other possible resources could be collected from excess revenues, but their expectations of materializing are unrealistic as long as the government refrains from implementing a comprehensive tax reform and recovery does not take a rapid pace. Since there is little evidence that FSF resources have been effectively applied to poverty-alleviation programs, in practice, the FSF has, rather, played the role of a small contingency fund.

Revamping the Fiscal Prudence and Transparency Law requires work on many fronts. The Law is not a substitute, but a complement, to building credibility in the overall economic program. Hence, credibility depends, first, on the capacity of Peruvian officials to comply with their previous commitments under the 2002–03 macroeconomic program agreed; and, second, on an expected positive external environment that would minimize the external risk of another economic downturn. Early noncompliance with a revamped Law would damage the reputation of the macroeconomic program.

### Recommendations:

- ▨ *On previous requirements.* Issuing a new law should be preceded by a building process of (a) institutional strengthening regarding the human and technical inputs required by the design and implementation of the Law; (b) consensus-building participatory mechanisms led by Peruvian officials, with a draft design of the Law being published in advance to receive comments through the web; (c) enhanced SIAF-supported and user-friendly budget transparency (Chapter III), to allow open access by Congress and civil society to monitor implementation of the Law once it is approved; and (d) a comprehensive evaluation of contingent liabilities, so adequate and precautionary budget provisions can be made under the new rule.

- ▨ *On procedural norms.* From recent experience, it is clear that (a) budget reporting needs— human resources and technical tools—have to be significantly strengthened, (b) the multi-year budgeting framework also requires improvement (Chapter III), (c) introduction of a set of sanctions for noncompliance is unavoidable, and (d) upgraded oversight capacity to evaluate and enforce sanctions by the Comptroller's office is needed.

- ▨ *On numerical targets.* Two main measures aimed at simplifying the framework for quantitative benchmarking are proposed. The first measure would consist of targeting an estimated *structural* NFPS *primary surplus* of 1 percent of GDP (Annex B) by 2008–10, which would be roughly equivalent to targeting a *structural* NFPS *deficit* close to 1 percent of GDP. These targets are set in structural terms and do not take into account the cyclical component of the deficit. Progress toward meeting such target should be done through incremental steps. Following Banks' detailed estimates of the potential output and the structural deficit (Figures 2.12 and 2.13) and assuming a prompt recovery under a baseline scenario since 2002, adjusting for the cyclical component would require primary surpluses of about 0.9 as early as 2004, and reaching 1.3 percent of GDP in 2010 (Annex A).[17] Although broad convergence exists between the Banks' and Peruvian officials' estimates, an eventual official benchmark would need to be thoroughly reviewed and published by the officials.[18] The second measure would propose eliminating some of the less-important numerical rules. Not only do a few of them overlap with the main rule, but they are ineffective, as happened to those applied during election years: they did not take into account strong end-year public spending seasonality.

- ▨ *On fiscal rules for subnational governments.* Introducing fiscal rules at the subnational level is a critical priority for the revamped Law, given the pace of the decentralization process

---

17. The estimated cyclical component of the fiscal deficit is small and varies between 0.1 and 03 percent of GDP between 2000 and 2002, but might increase a bit, especially if recovery takes place (Annex B).

18. Notice that Banks' estimates are particularly close to those made by Deutsche Bank (2001) of 0.8 percent of GDP, the Central Bank of Peru (2002) of 1.3 percent of GDP, and Jiménez/MEF (2002) of 1.1 percent of GDP. None, however, includes any provision for the materialization of contingent liabilities.

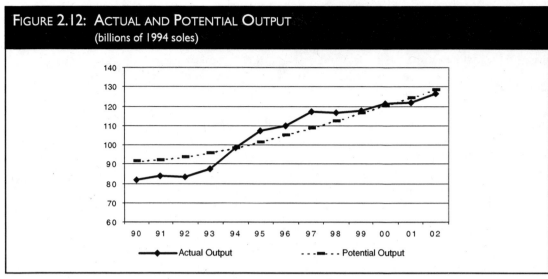

FIGURE 2.12: ACTUAL AND POTENTIAL OUTPUT
(billions of 1994 soles)

*Source:* World Bank staff estimates.

under the present Administration, *and justify its upgrade to a Responsibility Law.* Although there is no consensus on presetting limits or ceilings for specific fiscal indicators at the subnational level, the vulnerability of the overall fiscal situation requires a hard budget constraint, in terms of a modified golden rule—to include capital expenditure—or zero operational deficit. Rules should also be more restrictive during the last year of an administration to avoid electoral cycles, and be more flexible in the presence of exogenous and unexpected shocks. Tight noncontingent municipal debt restrictions are needed. Finally, because there is little knowledge, but partial evidence (Chapter V) about the existence of a

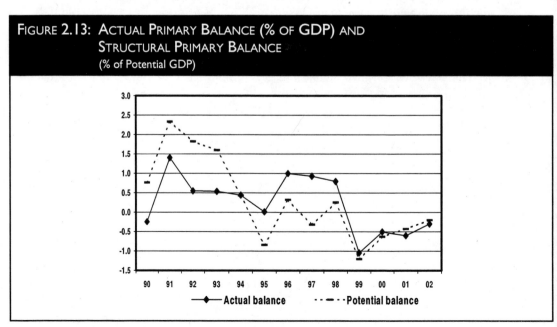

FIGURE 2.13: ACTUAL PRIMARY BALANCE (% OF GDP) AND
STRUCTURAL PRIMARY BALANCE
(% of Potential GDP)

*Source:* World Bank staff estimates.

significant contingent municipal debt, debt restructuring deals (supported by its previous comprehensive evaluation) should precede the adoption of any local government rule.

▓ *On the Fiscal Stabilization Fund.* There is no sense expecting a significant countercyclical policy as long as growth remains low and fiscal revenue is stagnant.

Additional features of the to-be-revamped Law include (a) redesigning an effective special clause for election years, because the three past election episodes provoked a clear fiscal deterioration; (b) making room for changes that will affect the structural balance over time, including those affecting the productive capacity of the economy, external prices of main mining exports, and the taxation structure; and (c) strengthening existing inflation-targeting mechanisms consistent with a revamped fiscal rule, and supported by enhanced coordination mechanisms between the Central Bank and the MEF.

# REORIENTING THE BUDGET TOWARD PRO-POOR EXPENDITURE

*Reorienting the budget toward effective poverty reduction requires an overall reform effort of public expenditure management. Such reform includes a modern financial management system, a pro-poor and performing budgeting system, a clear definition of medium-term social objectives, an effective tracking system of the shift of budget allocations toward these priorities, and transparent information access to an outcome-oriented budget. Since the late-1990s, Peru has made promising inroads in all these areas and, although remaining challenges are still significant, its implementation record provides a solid foundation for further developments. This chapter assesses progress in pro-poor budgeting management.*

Tangible progress in public expenditure management (PEM) in Peru over the past few years is impressive. It includes:

- Creation of an Integrated Financial Management System (SIAF) in 1998;
- Development of an upgraded budget management system since 1999, with improved transparency of budget execution supported by the website *Portal de Transparencia* in 2000, which includes for the first time defense and national security spending and a participatory method for budget formulation scheduled from 2002;
- Passage of the Law of Fiscal Prudence and Transparency and creation of a Fiscal Stabilization Fund (FSF) in 1999;
- Strengthening of accounting institutions and procedures, compatible with world standards, applied to the entire public sector since 1999;
- Introduction of performance management contracts of State-owned enterprises under the National Fund for Financing Government Enterprise Activity (FONAFE) in 1999;
- Adoption of a medium-term expenditure framework in 2000, based on a Multiyear Macroeconomic Framework for 2001–03 and a Multiyear Budget (MAB) Plan for 2001–05; and
- Adoption of budgetary provisions for a set of Protected Social Programs (PSPs) in 2000.

---

**BOX 3.1: MAIN IGR/PEM ISSUES**

The IGR identified several factors affecting financial accountability in PEM (World Bank, 2001b):

- Excess dominance by the Executive through the use of Presidential Decrees: between 1994 and 2001, Congress passed 1,152 laws or legislative resolutions, while the President issued 870 (86 percent Urgency) Decrees;
- Concentration of spending authority in a few central ministries—Economy and Finance, and Presidency—to maximize discretionary control of budgetary resources: in 2001, the share of the consolidated budget (excluding debt service) assigned to these two institutions represented 63 percent;
- Insufficient Congressional oversight of budget execution;
- Local governments still do not have the necessary checks and balances to implement decentralization properly; and
- Severe institutional disorder in a state in which highly modern institutions coexist with antiquated entities, and multiple social agencies overlap their service delivery efforts.

---

In spite of ongoing reforms, persistent weaknesses remain. Some of them were identified in the Peru Institutional and Governance Review (IGR) (Box 3.1) and undermine budgetary transparency and accountability. These include:

- An incomplete SIAF;
- Excessive concentration of budget authority in a few ministries, and budget rigidity reflected in inertial spending;
- A disconnect between multiyear and annual budgeting, the latter being amended by continuous Presidential decrees;
- A fragile and uneven institutional framework for developing an effective medium-term social policy and for decentralization; and
- Inadequate and user-unfriendly external budget monitoring and reporting, which does not facilitate its virtual oversight by authorities themselves, Congress, and civil society.

## Modernizing Financial Management

Peru has developed a well-performing, integrated financial management system. It aims to increase the control, efficiency, accountability, and transparency of public spending, and to support the future decentralization to line ministries and regional and local governments of the primary responsibility for managing resources and improving service delivery in Peru (Box 3.2).

At present, it combines efforts in the areas of Treasury, accounting, and debt management. Its role begins once the annual budget is approved and monthly ceilings are authorized by the Budget Office and Cash Oversight committee. The SIAF is linked with Treasury to register all operations (revenue, expenditure) approved for the budget execution cycle through 580 EUs dependent on the budgetary envelopes (*pliegos*) of various ministries, Transitory Councils of Regional Administration (CTARs), and public institutions.[1] The SIAF contains three operational elements: (a) *single registry* of each EU transaction, and virtual transmission of this information to the Budget Office, the Treasury Office, and the Accountant General; (b) *cash payments management,* but only for those financed by Treasury ordinary resources; and (c) *financial reporting.* In

---

1. The Peruvian public sector is divided into five categories of entities: the CG with 580 EUs, the National Fund for Financing Government Enterprise Activity (FONAFE) with 42 entities, the General Directorate for the Public Budget (DNPP) with 99 entities, 1,826 municipalities, and 101 public beneficiaries. The CG has 26 sectors, divided into 141 envelopes (*pliegos*) comprising 580 EUs, which account for about 60 to 65 percent of the public budget.

---

**BOX 3.2: THE INTEGRATED FINANCIAL MANAGEMENT SYSTEM (SIAF) OF PERU**

SIAF was created by Vice-Ministerial Resolution No. 029-98-EF/II on 22 October 1998 as the mandatory Internet-based system for the recording of all data related to revenue and expenditure execution carried out by the Executing Units (EUs) of the public sector budget at the national level. According to the procedures and norms approved by MEF:

- It covers all Central Government and most decentralized entities: a total of 580 EUs (including Defense and National Security since 2002), all public enterprises, supervisory bodies (SUNAT, Customs, regulators, municipal enterprises), and 23 municipalities (June 2002).
- It contains four modules: Treasury, which receives budget ceilings prepared by the commitment calendar of the Budget Office and preapproved by the Cash Oversight Committee; Accounting; Financial Statement Reporting; and Public Debt, the latter managed as an EU. Public enterprises use only the financial accounting module.
- It has very strict budget execution control mechanisms. Once payments have been previously authorized by Treasury through the system and are daily registered in SIAF, then the *Banco de la Nación* (BN) proceeds to alert and transfer funds to the EU's bank accounts or issue checks.
- The expansion to include financial accounting since 2000 has provided reliable and timely information to the Accountant General, who is now responsible for preparing financial statements. Recording of transactions at the EUs is organized into two parts: administrative (commitment, accrual, payment, and disbursement), and accounting (under standard categories). To record a commitment, it is necessary to use a specific expenditure classification, a financing source, and an objective corresponding to the expenditure. The system then verifies that the operation is in accordance with budget limit criteria and the commitment calendar. An accrual is done only when a commitment exists and the EU receives verification that the goods or services have been provided according to the "best date" (prompt payment—no later than one month) concept. After full payment, the registry is updated with the correct disbursement information provided by the BN.
- All expenditures, revenues, and complementary operations use an SIAF Matrix Operations Table that integrates budget classifications with the government's chart of accounts.

*Note:* This box is based on WB/IADB (2001a).

---

three years, the SIAF has consolidated itself as the instrumental financial management tool of the public sector.

*Overall Efficiency Gains.* After three years of reform efforts, quantifiable savings have emerged from several outcomes: (a) duplication of financial transactions is eliminated as payments are entered once and instantly in a reliable database system; (b) poorly controlled quasi-extra-budgetary funds are significantly reduced; (c) electronic transfers are replacing the use of checks, thus reducing payment lags, transaction costs, and risks of fraud or lost or stolen checks; and (d) unused funds are virtually eliminated, since once a payment is authorized by the Cash Oversight Committee, the banking transfer is executed within 72 hours and remains available for only one month.

*Overall Effectiveness Gains in Budget Management.* Outputs arising from a better mix of public resources consist of (a) the elimination of arrears on floating debt to suppliers, a major budgetary distortion in the past; (b) an enhanced cash management that prevents shortages of counterpart funds to external projects; (c) an improved level of budget execution by the Central Government (CG); (d) control for the first time of the previously sensitive spending "black hole" ministries, Defense and National Security, now fully adopting SIAF systems and procedures; (e) enhanced expenditure control and transparency due to a unique database which offers virtual information through the web; (f) the simplification of the functions of accounting and auditing, which reduces the scope of fraud and corruption; and (g) an enhanced public debt management, since the system also prevents external arrears.

Despite its impressive progress, Peru's SIAF still faces significant challenges. SIAF core sub-systems are incomplete. The lack of a budget module, in particular, is a severe handicap for improving budget efficiency, participation, and transparency. Contrary to similar systems in Latin America, the Peruvian SIAF does not have a budget module, but fundamentally works as a virtual payment system. As a result, Peru's budget formulation and in-year global budget modifications remain little known externally, centralized, and decided at MEF's discretion, and known only ex post, when they are registered monthly in the SIAF. Despite individual ministries providing inputs to overall budget formulation and same in-year modifications, they do it on a bilateral basis with MEF and have little control over ex post decisions regarding charges to their global allocations.

## Recommendations:

- A user-friendly budget module is urgently needed to allow virtual access with no restrictions. It would help assess consistency of budget proposals with macroeconomic conditions in early stages, build a stronger link between budget formulation and multiyear strategic priorities, facilitate monitoring of in-year budget modifications consistency with inter- and intrasector budget priorities in a participatory and transparent way, and allow Congress' legal mandatory oversight of the budget execution.

- The SIAF's budget module requires a multiyear submodule too, that is, one with capacity to track the Government of Peru's (GOPs') compliance with multiyear budgeting benchmarks. On one hand, the SIAF registers only current-year transactions. On the other hand, the Law of Fiscal Prudence and Transparency requires biannual reports on compliance with multiyear benchmarks, but such commitment has not been fulfilled. The separate submodule should allow a historic database, virtual monitoring of compliance with annual executed expenditure, and help produce mandated biannual reports on compliance with MAB targets.

- Among other possible SIAF modules, the one on human resources management is critical. Others that could gradually be developed are national assets, procurement, a national investment system, contingent liabilities risk, and regional and municipal financial management. The human resources module is essential for civil service reform. The one on national assets should have due registry of state assets. The module on procurement, the starting point for e-government, is critical for anticorruption efforts, the most vulnerable area of governance. The module on public investment should help prioritize multiyear investment plans. The module on contingent liabilities risk would help to register them and make proper budgetary provisions, while the one on subnational management would prepare SIAF support for an accelerated scheme of fiscal decentralization, because future regional and municipal governments require a twin-decentralized SIAF and training. Such developments should take place over many years.

- The existing SIAF subsystem to track financial and physical performance indicators, a critical tool for an outcome-oriented budget, supported by benchmarks—final and intermediate— and performance management contracts, requires a thorough conceptual review before completion. The pilot subsystem has too many useless indicators and their inputting and tracking are poor.

- Due to their complexity and the already overcommitted limited technical and human resources capacity of the SIAF team at MEF, all development of new SIAF modules requires detailed prioritization and permanent training. Authorities should support and outsource the creation of a superior university degree in management of SIAF systems.

- Finally, international experience indicates that two important modules, like a fiscal cadastre (essential for a predial municipal tax), or an e-government website (including e-procurement or an e-geo-referenced expenditure map at the district level, for targeting purposes) should be developed outside, but with links to the SIAF.

---

**BOX 3.3:** INTRODUCING THE SIAF AT THE MINISTRIES OF DEFENSE AND NATIONAL SECURITY (INTERIOR)

Until December 2000, the five Executing Units (EUs) of the Ministry of Defense (MINDEF) did not register their transactions in SIAF. An administrative mechanism, known as *libramiento,* allowed MINDEF's UEs to transfer their budget resources to about 870 open bank accounts that worked as authentic "black boxes": Resources in these accounts did not belong to Treasury, were neither monitored by the Cash Oversight Committee nor audited, and end-year nonspent funds were never returned to Treasury. In January 2001, however, all MINDEF EUs were suddenly incorporated into SIAF, and *libramientos* were eliminated. Because this decision was political, and no previous technical preparation was done, all EUs were allowed to operate their new SIAF-registered bank accounts under a transitory mechanism known as *encargo* to operational units (OUs). But, a few control issues appeared:

- About half of MINDEF's EUs operations (Army, Navy, and Air Force) were executed through *encargos* to OUs;
- OUs did not properly register their direct purchase of goods and services, did not use the SIAF or, in the case of some located outside Lima, did register them, but manually.

To address these problems, in January 2002, the SIAF moved to:

- Maintain a limited number of EUs;
- Eliminate OUs operating in the same office of the EU;
- Design and install a tailored-made pilot SIAF2 special module in 100 OUs executing *encargos;*
- Develop an accelerated training program in SIAF2;
- Reduce the number of OUs located outside Lima and improve criteria to define them; and
- Replicate such exercise at the Ministry of Interior.

As a result, (a) 100 percent of defense and national security expenditure will be managed through SIAF by end-2002; (b) the SIAF2 module will be expanded through all active OUs; (c) an administrative reorganization of the Army will be implemented to support it; and, (d) also by end-2002, for the first time all five MINDEF EUs will submit full and transparent financial statement reports.

---

Control of decentralized budget execution by the SIAF is partly diluted beyond EUs through *encargos.*[2] In 2001, a little less than 35 percent of the budget was not devoted to salaries, financial obligations, or pensions. At least 12 percent (NS/1.4 billion) of this share of the budget was executed through *encargos.* The *encargo* is an ad hoc mechanism. It transfers funds from the EUs to a myriad of at least 50,000 Operational Units (*Unidades Operativas,* OUs) dispersed nationwide (including schools and health posts), most of which are outside SIAF control. Operationally, it works like this: Following reception of funds, if the EU decides to commit an *encargo* to an OU, it registers it as a transfer in the SIAF. This transfer is endorsed in a bilateral institutional agreement that has no legal authority. Ensuing budget execution control by the SIAF then faces multiple deficiencies: (a) late registration, because the UEs can receive a complete report of the use of those funds only by end-year; (b) no direct data entry, because most OUs do not use SIAF software; (c) poor auditing, because not all EUs have adequate administrative capacity to internally audit their OUs; and (d) misallocation of resources, because there are no expenditure tracking mechanisms established to verify that resources have effectively been assigned to the original purpose of the transfer. The use of *encargos* is generalized in the health, transport, agriculture, and defense sectors, which use them to speed up execution of their investment program. The abuse of *encargos* has obstructed and delayed the proper application of the SIAF Treasury module at the Ministry of Defense. However, since 2002, it has become the pilot ministry for urgently reengineering *encargos* registry by an SIAF2 special module (Box 3.3). Lessons from this pilot ministry should be replicated.

---

2. Among other SIAF control failures, only one is significant: internal *encargos,* also known as *anticipos,* the 2001 amount (NS/1.3 billion) of which was very close to the one of *encargos,* and are mainly used for travel advances. Other leaks like petit cash used as a revolving cash fund are less significant and are later registered.

*Recommendations:*
- ▨ The SIAF2 special module should be expanded through all active OUs.
- ▨ An administrative reorganization of the EUs should be implemented to support it (see below).
- ▨ Quarterly deadlines should be set for all OUs to submit full and transparent financial statement reports.

The SIAF has reproduced the State's broad institutional disorder in its own internal structure since no homogeneous criteria for defining an EU exist. Below budget envelopes (*pliegos*), there are 580 EUs nationwide. In theory, an EU is the lower level defined by the MEF as the one with full administrative capacity to register the use of funds into the system.[3] In practice, budget size, geographic location, and political affiliation appear to be guiding principles to determine its creation. Becoming an EU is equivalent to having direct control of the checking account, which makes it a much-desired milestone to achieve by OUs, Regional Directorates of Ministries, and ministerial units like the *Unidades de Servicios Educativos* (USEs). All nationwide CTARs are considered as budget envelopes (*pliegos*), and each budget envelope (*pliego*) has the capacity to propose the creation of an EU and assign its budget. However, no standard minimum requirements for the creation of an EU exist, which contributes to their lack of homogeneity, wide dispersion of the budget amounts—an average of between NS/14.1M in Uyacali to NS/122.4M in Lima—per unit (Table SA.45), and perhaps unnecessary bureaucracy. For instance, the Ministry of Education has 72 EUs, and this includes up to eight different management models in a menu of widely heterogeneous institutions with different hierarchical responsibilities, like Regional Directorates of Ministries, Sub-Regional Directorates, and USEs.

*Recommendations:*
- ▨ Taking advantage of the incoming decentralization process, it would be advisable to have a gradual reordering of EUs, both at the regional and district level. In fact, Supreme Decree No. 001-2002-PCM opens the door to their restructuring. This could sound very technical, but it is very important because it shapes incentives faced by those delivering goods and services, and the oversight/accountability arrangements (checkbooks) of those units below EU status. This is a sensitive matter, though, because new regions could assume that the reordering of EUs is taking away their actual budget resources. Hence, this process could be demand-driven by the to-be-decentralized social sector ministries at the regional level, and/or supply-driven by the Executive. In both cases, it would be suitable to examine and enforce a set of standard minimum norms before a unit reaches (or is confirmed as having) EU status.
- ▨ Complementary to the above, multiple types of EUs (and SIAF software) could be considered, depending on their budget size (usually correlated with population), location, and functions. SIAF requirements could be stricter as their budget gets larger, as provincial districts are involved, or as more complex functions are developed. A simplified SIAF-software (it could be called SIAFITO) could be considered in support of small budget or distant EUs. SIAFITOS could be easier to handle by regional and local governments than the standard SIAF.

## Upgrading the Budget Management System
Peru is upgrading its budget management system at an accelerated pace. Recent innovations in budget practices include lengthening the time horizon of budgeting from a single year to multiple

---

3. The authority of the EU is significant: Whereas the *pliegos* are in charge of budget formulation and sector policy norms, the EU has the capacity to make budget commitments, order payments, and execute spending. Whereas budget changes between EUs require a resolution from the head of the *pliego*, authority to approve changes within an EU (for example, from one program to another or within programs) may be delegated from the head of the EU to the OU. The EU is also free to reassign resources among diverse expenditure items, except when required for compensation purposes.

years, setting explicit fiscal targets that limit aggregate expenditure, and developing baseline projections for estimating the impact of proposed policy changes on future budgets. The budget process has four stages: formulation, approval, execution, and evaluation (Box 3.4).

Results following a standard assessment of the Peruvian PEM system, in consultation with country authorities, indicate that it requires some upgrading (Table 3.1 and Annex C). The assessment covers 15 indicators covering critical elements of PEM systems deemed necessary for tracking expenditure. Seven of the indicators relate to budget preparation and four each to execution and reporting. The total number of satisfactory benchmarks met, 8 in the case of Peru, can be viewed as an indicator of the quality of a country's PEM system. According to IMF/WB standards, a country is deemed to require "little or no upgrading" if at least 11 of the benchmarks were met, "some upgrading" is required if between 8 to 10 benchmarks are met, and "substantial upgrading" is required if less than half (7 or fewer) of the benchmarks were met.

Peru scores unsatisfactory in some areas of budget formulation and execution, and satisfactory in most areas of budget reporting, other than external.

## BOX 3.4: PERU: PRINCIPAL STAGES OF THE BUDGET FORMATION

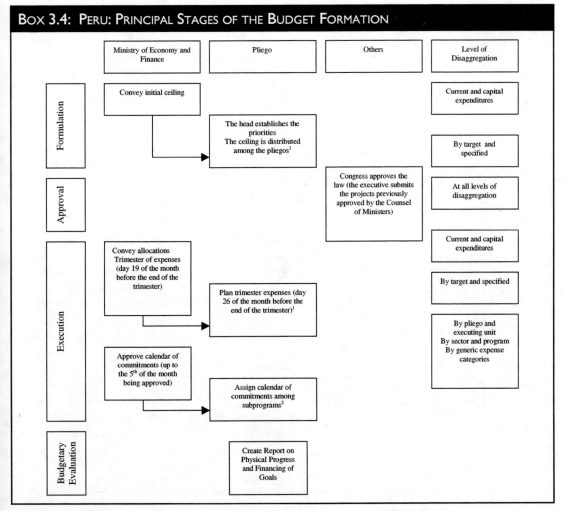

1. Discretion of the Pliego's Budgetary unit to decide how much to assign to each executing unit.
2. Additional discretion when there is no executing unit.

*Source:* Budgetary norms by MEF

## TABLE 3.1: PERU: STATUS OF BUDGET MANAGEMENT BENCHMARKS

| Budget Management | Benchmark | Status of Compliance: S=Satisfactory; P=Partial; U=Unsatisfactory |
|---|---|---|
| **Formulation–Comprehensiveness** | | |
| 1. Composition of the budget entity | Meets IMF–Government Finance Statistics definition of general government | (P) The annual budget covers Central Government expenditure. Coverage of the consolidated general government budget has minor discrepancies and does not include regulatory agencies, local governments, and social funds. |
| 2. Limitations on using off-budget transactions | Extra or off-budget expenditure is not substantial | (S) Quasi-extra-budget expenditure was about 18 percent in 2002, mostly linked to external credit, and rapidly declining. |
| 3. Reliability of budget as guide to actual expenditure | Level and composition of actual expenditure is "quite-close" to budget | (P) The level is close—below 10 percent deviation in 2001—but its composition still shows significant differences. |
| 4. Data on external financing | Both capital and current donor-funded spending included | (S) External credit is duly registered, except for a few donor off-budget accounts. |
| **Formulation–Classification** | | |
| 5. Classification of budget transactions | Functional/program information provided | (S) The budget contains proper functional and program classification. |
| 6. Identification of poverty-reducing expenditure | Identified through use of a classification system (e.g., a virtual poverty fund) | (P) Broad and detailed (beyond the usual social sectors) mapping of budget for poverty-reducing expenditure is possible, but it is neither virtual, nor user-friendly; and requires continuous consistency checks between SIAF and the Budget Directorate. |
| **Formulation–Projection** | | |
| 7. Quality of multiyear projections | Projections are integrated into budget formulation and close fit to actual numbers | (U) Multiyear projections are not integrated into the budget, are subject to significant modifications each year, and their execution has a poor fit to actual numbers. |

## TABLE 3.1: PERU: STATUS OF BUDGET MANAGEMENT BENCHMARKS (CONTINUED)

| Budget Management | Benchmark | Status of Compliance: S=Satisfactory; P=Partial; U=Unsatisfactory |
|---|---|---|
| **Execution–Internal Control** | | |
| 8. Level of payment arrears | Low level of arrears accumulated | (S) SIAF requires payment arrears to be cleared within one month. |
| 9. Quality of internal/external audit | Effective internal/external audit | (P) Good quality of internal audit, but infrequent and poor quality (e.g., no program costs are reported) of external audits (WB/IDB 2001). |
| 10. Use of tracking[1] surveys | Surveys used on a regular basis | (U) Nonexistent until recently[2] |
| **Execution–Reconciliation** | | |
| 11. Quality of fiscal/banking data reconciliation | Reconciliation of fiscal and monetary data carried out on routine basis | (S) Satisfied permanently |
| **Reporting** | | |
| 12. Timeliness of budget reports | Monthly expenditure reports provided within 4 weeks of end-of month | (P) Regular *internal* reports are provided within 4 weeks of end of the month; but *external* reports are annual, 6 months after year-end. MEF has announced quarterly budget reports in the web since mid-2002. |
| 13. Classification used for budget tracking. | Detailed functional reporting derived from classification system | (S) Existing functional reporting derives from the classification system. Its program and project decomposition could be improved. |
| **Reporting–Final Audited Accounts** | | |
| 14. Timeliness of accounts closure | Accounts closed 2-months before year-end | (S) Accounts close one month after year-end. |
| 15. Timeliness of final audited accounts | Audited accounts presented to Legislature within one year | (S) Audited accounts submitted on June 30th. |

1. Tracking is defined here as the identification and reporting of budgeted and executed outlays. Tracking surveys are usually needed when the financial management system does not have the capacity to regularly identify, monitor, and report expenditure at the lowest levels of the government, such as districts (IMF/WB 2002).
2. Public Expenditure Tracking Surveys (PETS) are rare in LAC: only Honduras (for service quality) and now Peru (for quantitative leaks and service quality) have developed them (see Chapter IV).

*Source:* Interviews conducted by project team.

## TABLE 3.2: COMPOSITION OF CG BUDGET SOURCES

| | Percent | | |
| --- | --- | --- | --- |
| | 2001[b] | 2001[P] | 2002[b] |
| Ordinary | 80.7 | 70.7 | 75.1 |
| Canon/Sobrecanon* | 0.5 | 0.6 | 0.6 |
| Customs | 0.4 | 0.4 | 0.0 |
| Self-Raised Funds | 6.8 | 6.5 | 6.9 |
| External Credit* | 7.7 | 16.9 | 13.2 |
| Grants | 0.4 | 0.7 | 0.2 |
| Contrib. to Funds | 3.5 | 4.2 | 3.9 |
| Total | 100 | 100 | 100 |

*Quasi-EBFs. b = budget. p = preliminary.
*Source:* MEF.

### Recommendations:

▨ Budget classification should be made fully consistent with the Government Financial Statistics (GFS) definition of General Government.

▨ The quality of budget projections (especially in function and sector composition) needs to be upgraded if social priorities are to be sustained in the medium term.

▨ Multiyear projections also require significant improvement and adequate integration with the annual budget process.

▨ The creation of a budget module and refinement of the existing set of financial and physical indicators in the SIAF should facilitate a user-friendly tracking of pro-poor expenditure and an effective results-based control system in budget execution.

▨ Sector tracking surveys should be developed randomly on a regular basis.

▨ External reporting of budget execution, multiyear budgeting, and audits should be frequent, timely, and comprehensive.

▨ Full adoption of the IMF Code of Fiscal Transparency requires a thoroughly defined and supported technical assistance program.

This assessment should, however, be used with caution, since not all indicators are of equal importance. Its bias in favor of process measures (such as audit reports) to the detriment of impact outcomes (such as questioned audit reports) is usually not optimal in a country context, and may miss critical issues of PEM, like the ones outlined below.

Although the share of quasi-extra-budgetary funds (EBFs) in Peru is rapidly declining, its importance is significant for a single category: external credit (Table 3.2).[4] Following the elimination of the *Fondo Nacional de Vivienda* (FONAVI), the housing EBF, which accounted for about 6 percent of the budget in 1999, the CG budget coverage of all resources increased from 65 percent in 1999 to 82 percent in 2002. Self-raised revenue by local governments, customs proceedings, and grant funds are now controlled through the single Treasury account managed by the *Banco de la Nación*. However, three main sources of quasi-EBFs remain: (a) external credit accounts (in local

---

4. In OECD terms, EBFs comprise all government transactions that operate outside the normal budgetary process. Peruvian "quasi" EBFs are considered as such since they are capped monthly and are reported in the SIAF as part of the overall budget envelope, which is unusual for such types of resources, but conform to other EBFs features: their effective allocation takes place only if they become available; funds are managed through commercial bank accounts separate from the Central Government budget account; and, despite standardization efforts, they still might have separate accounting systems and classification.

currency), which manage salary payments to top-ranked public servants serving external projects and whose eventual late registration might affect reporting on executed expenditure; (b) contribution to funds (especially ESSALUD); and (c) the *canon/sobrecanon* revenues from mining, oil, gas, and other natural resources activities.

## Recommendations:

- Total reduction in the number of EBFs would not only improve control over the level and quality of public expenditure, but would also reduce the cost of *sobregiro* fees that Treasury pays when seasonal shortages of tax revenue collection by SUNAT lead to insufficient cash availability to cover all public payments.
- Other less visible EBFs, like tax expenditures, should continue to be registered from 2003 onward.
- Accounting of external credit should be fully made in the SIAF and have timely and transparent reporting.

There is a budget paradox that needs to be addressed: budget formulation remains centralized in the MEF, while budget execution is decentralized. While budget formulation is centralized and a high proportion of budget expenditure remains under the authority of government agencies located in Lima, roughly 56 percent of the CG nonprevisional, nonfinancial budget is executed through the regions in a decentralized fashion (Table SA.39). Hence, although larger and decentralized entities appear to be tightly controlled politically and may operate as means for distributing political spoils (World Bank 2001a), they preserve enough spending authority to modify the budget at their discretion.

Inertial expenditure is a major constraint for budget formulation. Peru is ranked among countries with the most inflexible budget not only in LAC, but also worldwide. In addition to Brazil, India, and a few HIPC countries, which have above 90 percent of their total revenue fixed, Peru has 91 percent and 86 percent of ordinary and total budget resources, respectively, in 2002, assigned to inertial commitments (Table 3.3). Budget rigidities originate from different sources, including (a) wage and benefits considered as *derechos adquiridos* by the Constitution; (b) permanent contracts hidden as nonpersonal services (NPS)—no less than 40 percent of the total budget allocated to NPS, according to estimates of Peruvian officials; (c) inertial payroll under prolonged investment projects; (d) earmarked transfers to municipalities and the private sector, as the *Vaso de Leche* and *Comedores Populares;* and (e) misuse of the budget contingency reserve, which finances the March school bonus, and the July and December salary supplements (*aguinaldos*). The high share of inertial current expenditure explains not only its rapid expansion, but also the complexity that attempting to reverse such pattern will require.

## Recommendations:

- An immediate general hiring freeze under the NPS category is critical, accompanied by a case-by-case short-term renewal of existing temporary contracts, upon their prior revision.
- Authorities had no option but to review their present policies regarding pension and wage benefits in a comprehensive civil service reform (Chapter VI).
- Funds assigned to *Vaso de Leche* and *Comedores Populares* need to be streamlined (Chapter IV.
- The use of the contingency reserve requires review to fulfill its true role: filling unpredicted in-year budget needs.[5]

End-year excessive seasonal spending is another critical shortcoming of budget execution. Notwithstanding the purpose of the creation of the SIAF—which is to enhance and improve budget

---

5. Authorities reported that such review was achieved in the formulation of the 2003 budget.

## TABLE 3.3: REVISED PROJECTION OF THE 2002 BUDGET
(Millions of NS and % of Total Expenditure)

| Structure of Expenditures | All Sources | | Ordinary Resources | |
|---|---|---|---|---|
| **Expenditures by Category** | **21,790** | **59.9%** | **17,290** | **3.3%** |
| **Fixed Component** | **16,820** | **46.2%** | **14,844** | **4.3%** |
| Goods and Services | 3,200 | 8.8% | 2,170 | 7.9% |
| Investment | 1,330 | 3.7% | 868 | 3.2% |
| Financial Investments | 171 | 0.5% | 139 | 0.5% |
| Other Current Expenditures | 1,967 | 5.4% | 1,770 | 6.5% |
| Other Capital Expenditures | 25 | 0.1% | 25 | 0.1% |
| Personal and Social Obligations | 9,272 | 25.5% | 9,016 | 33.0% |
| Contingency Reserves | 856 | 2.4% | 856 | 3.1% |
| **Flexible Component** | **4,970** | **13.7%** | **2,446** | **8.9%** |
| Goods and Services | 1,714 | 4.7% | 1,124 | 4.1% |
| Investment | 2,933 | 8.1% | 1,258 | 4.6% |
| Other Current Expenditures | 36 | 0.1% | 31 | 0.1% |
| Other Capital Expenditures | 288 | 0.8% | 33 | 0.1% |
| **Structural Obligations** | **13,982** | **40.1%** | **9,438** | **6.7%** |
| **Financial Expenditure** | **7,787** | **23.1%** | **4,495** | **8.7%** |
| **Previsional Expenditure** | **6,195** | **17.0%** | **4,943** | **8.1%** |
| **TOTAL** | **35,772** | **100.0%** | **26,728** | **100.0%** |

Source: MEF.

control—the persistent pattern of excessive deficits in the last quarter of the last six years, coupled with small budget surpluses in the first quarter, remains a constant and fiscally damaging seasonal concern—whether they occur in an election year or not (Figure 3.1). Such budget behavior is not specific only to Peru. Most public budgets in LAC have such fiscal expansions to cover not only end-year cumulative and additional payments, but for building fiscal provisions for the slowly opening expenses of the next year's first quarter. A similar pattern is also typical of the LAC political business cycle, and Peru is no exception (López-Cálix 2002). However, deficits appear for both the CG and the NFPS, and following SIAF creation, their size is difficult to justify for reasons other than fiscal indiscipline. In 2000, the quarterly deficit developed since the third quarter, lasting until end-year, while in 2001, it grew with respect to 2000 (in particular the deficit of the CG).

### Recommendations:

- Given its persistence throughout so many years, the first step for the GOP (and its Cash Management Committee) is to assess the deep implications that this seasonal episode is having on fiscal imbalances and monetary policy (possibly affecting short-term interest rates).
- A thorough review of cash management and budget planning for the closing fiscal year is needed to examine structural—revenue and expenditure—factors that might explain end-year cumulative deficits and determine effective measures aimed at smoothing them.
- Under the present situation, setting and meeting realistic revenue projections and tight quarterly expenditure ceilings looks critical to make room for end-year impulses.
- Until this seasonal pattern is significantly corrected, meeting midyear tighter expenditure ceilings, especially in an election year, is particularly meaningful for fiscal discipline.

As Peruvian PEM modernizes, it will need to adopt further contemporary innovations in budget practices, in terms of both rules and procedures that will be required eventually under the new MEF Code of Budget Transparency.

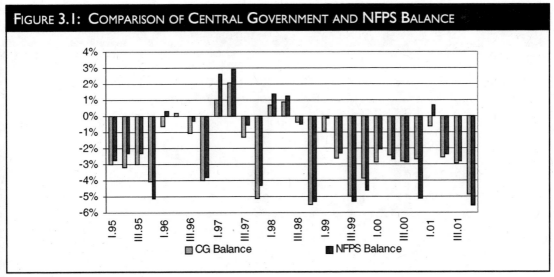

FIGURE 3.1: COMPARISON OF CENTRAL GOVERNMENT AND NFPS BALANCE

*Source:* MEF and IMF.

*Recommendations:*
- Define procedures for identifying the government's exposure to contingent liabilities, particularly those associated to the financial system, pensions and public enterprises guaranteed debt, and other fiscal risks; and
- Attempt (cautiously) accrual accounting for certain commitments, at least on the expenditure side.[6]

## Building a Medium-Term Expenditure Framework

In the past two years there has been an important shift in the budget toward pro-poor expenditure. In spite of the recession and resulting fiscal retrenchment, the share of social expenditure to GDP remained constant between 1999 and 2002 (Figure 3.2). Likewise, significant inter- and intrasectoral pro-poor spending reallocation began to take place between 2000 and 2002. The budget decreased for defense and national security from 2.9 to 2.1 percent of GDP; increased for education, health, and social assistance from 5.3 to 5.6 percent of GDP; and decreased for ESSALUD (nontargeted public health insurance administration) from 1.5 to 1.3 percent of GDP (Figure 3.3). On the other hand, the share of poverty-reduction programs in social expenditure (consisting of programs with universal coverage—education and health—and targeted spending) increased from 57 percent in 2000 to 60 percent in 2002 (Table 3.4).

Peru has taken promising steps toward a medium-term expenditure framework (MTBF). Since 2000, as part of the Law of Fiscal Prudence and Transparency, the GOP has published Multiyear Budgets (MABs), themselves based on Multiyear Strategic Sector Plans (PESEMs). MABs have introduced the initial framework for a shared strategic vision in the ongoing overhaul of the budgetary process, emphasizing a poverty focus, output-driven program budgeting, transparency in the use of

---

6. The IMF Code of Fiscal Transparency does not require accrual accounting. Countries are allowed to adopt it at their own speed. Its implementation continues to have mixed results, with Australia experiencing particular difficulties and New Zealand and Brazil claiming to have had a relatively smooth conversion. Among opposing "big bang" and "incremental" approaches, the latter appears closer to the Peruvian way to PEM reform, since the country has, de facto, modified accrual, since it already captures some commitments upstream in the expenditure chain. Accrual accounting may confuse the definition of fiscal deficit among civil society and other stakeholders and must be developed with caution.

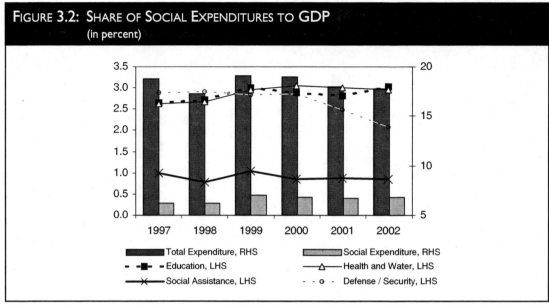

FIGURE 3.2: SHARE OF SOCIAL EXPENDITURES TO GDP
(in percent)

*Source:* MEF.

budget information, and political prioritization in the medium term. MABs provide the bridge between sound technical preparation of annual budgets and political priorities of multiyear budgets. Rolling five-year sector budgets are published by Executive Decrees and are made consistent with rolling three-year monetary programs. These allocations provide an indicative analysis of ex ante expenditure ceilings reflecting inter- and intrasector policy priorities at the formulation stage, and set referential medium-term broad performance indicators based on several monitoring benchmarks. Revised and approved before the annual budget proposal to Congress is sent by the Executive, MABs are intended to be living processes, adjusted consistent with macro aggregates certified by the Central Bank, and supported by interministerial teams, under the leadership of the MEF and the Central Bank.

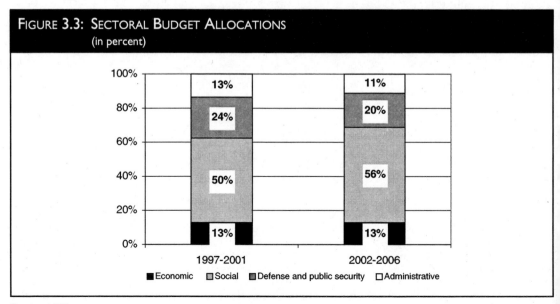

FIGURE 3.3: SECTORAL BUDGET ALLOCATIONS
(in percent)

*Source:* MEF.

| TABLE 3.4: COMPOSITION OF SOCIAL EXPENDITURE 1999–02* (millions of nuevos soles) | | | | |
|---|---|---|---|---|
| Categories | 1999 | 2000 | 2001ᴾ | 2002ᵉ |
| Universal Coverage—Education & Health—Programs | 8,378 | 8,804 | 9,113 | 10,170 |
| Targeted Programs (Extreme Poverty) | 3,257 | 3,043 | 2,979 | 3,531 |
| Nontargeted Social Programs | 7,909 | 8,928 | 8,960 | 9,175 |
|   ESSALUD | 2,489 | 2,801 | 2,666 | 2,695 |
|   Pensions | 5,330 | 6,127 | 6,294 | 6,480 |
|   FONAVI | 90 | 0 | 0 | 0 |
| Total Social Expenditure and Pensions | 19,544 | 20,775 | 21,051 | 22,877 |
| *Memo:* | | | | |
| Poverty Reduction Programs (I+II)/Total (%) | 59.5 | 57.0 | 57.4 | 59.9 |
| Extreme Poverty Reduction Programs (II)/Total (%) | 16.7 | 14.6 | 14.1 | 15.4 |
| Nontargeted Programs/Total (%) | 40.5 | 43.0 | 42.6 | 40.1 |

*Includes ESSALUD, FONAVI, and pensions.
ᴾPreliminary.
ᵉEstimated.
*Source:* MEF.

Revisions of the 2002–06 budget by the new Peruvian officials also reflect a shift toward pro-poor and decentralized expenditure, and a search for a more efficient safety net system. The first 2001–05 MAB was modified to accommodate the difficult transition period during the electoral cycle and reflect the priorities of the Toledo Administration. Major changes in multiyear budget allocations 2001–05 and 2002–06 were (a) a reduction of about 10 percent in the overall expenditure amount; (b) a significant reduction of defense and security outlays; (c) a slight increase in health expenditure; (d) a significant increase in the safety net programs grouped under the Presidency, supporting the new countercyclical *A Trabajar* program and the decentralization process; and (e) an election campaign-promised salary bonus of 50 soles to public servants, and a conversion from temporary to permanent teacher hiring status. In sum, when compared to 1997–2001, the 2002–06 MAB projects a higher share allocated to social spending (adding up to about 56 percent of the budget), offset by lower shares allocated to defense and security (falling to about one fifth of the total budget) and to public administration (falling to 11 percent) (Figure 3.3). Such priorities are being revised under the national dialogue, but the intended shift toward pro-poor and decentralized expenditure looks irreversible.

Significant inter- and intrasectoral pro-poor spending reallocation also took place between 2000 and 2002. The budget for defense and national security decreased from 2.9 to 2.1 percent of GDP. The budget for education, health, and social assistance increased from 5.3 to 5.6 percent of GDP. Complementary to these major shifts, ESSALUD expenditure (nontargeted public health insurance administration) decreased from 1.5 to 1.3 percent of GDP. In a similar vein, the share of poverty-reduction programs (consisting of programs with universal coverage—education and health—spending and targeted spending) to social expenditure increased from 57 percent in 2000 to 60 percent in 2002 (Table 3.5).

MABs' framework, however, has four weaknesses when compared to international standards:

■ *Low technical content.* The quality of MABs' projections have two important limitations: (a) they barely project budget sector institutional allocations, but exclude more familiar ones like economic or functional classifications; and (b) their forecasting horizon—five years—is too long to be credible, and its consistency with monetary aggregates (and ceilings) published by the Central bank is too broad.

## TABLE 3.5: COMPARING MULTIYEAR BUDGETS BY SECTOR
(Billion NS and %)

| Sector | 2001–05 | | 2002–06 | | Absolute Variation |
|---|---|---|---|---|---|
| Agriculture | 1,085 | 3.23 | 1,010 | 3.37 | –74 |
| Transport, Communication, & Housing | 2,154 | 6.41 | 2,062 | 6.88 | –92 |
| Mining and Energy | 506 | 1.50 | 435 | 1.45 | –71 |
| Education | 8,906* | 26.49 | 4,662 | 15.56 | –4,244* |
| Health | 2,863 | 8.51 | 3,024 | 10.09 | 161 |
| Presidency (Social Assistance) | 4,701 | 13.98 | 6,745 | 22.51 | 1,994** |
| Justice | 586 | 1.70 | 553 | 1.84 | –33 |
| Judicial Court | 804 | 2.40 | 711 | 2.37 | –92 |
| Defense | 4,476 | 13.31 | 3,210 | 10.71 | –1,266 |
| Security | 4,375 | 13.01 | 2,812 | 9.38 | –1,564 |
| Others | 3,169 | 9.42 | 4,744 | 15.80 | 1,624 |
| TOTAL | 33,625 | 100.00 | 29,968 | 100.00 | –3,657 |

*Reflects an overestimation of the education payroll originally budgeted in the multiyear budget, but not approved, to hire teachers outside Lima by the Ministry of Education.
**Includes projected support to *A Trabajar* and to regional and local governments.
*Source:* MEF.

- *Weak link to the annual budget.* MABs are produced three to four months before the draft new fiscal year budget appears, which should allow time for fine-tuning, yet they are not the main basis for formulating or determining actual modifications to annual budget allocations. Moreover, broad institutional allocations assigned ex ante to strategic priorities per sector are modified ex post throughout the year, with little consideration of the original priorities; there is no link with the planning function of the Investment Office; and, in fact, their actual benchmarks are so numerous and inadequate that compliance by public institutions is not regularly evaluated.
- *Fragile institutionalization.* MAB's institutional framework, which was born as part of a Fiscal Law that was not totally complied with, is weak and should be strengthened. Because it is an internal MEF exercise, it bears fundamental review of such questions as, Why are MABs produced? Who are the users of this information? How is this information relevant to policy design and implementation?
- *Public's misperception about MAB's transparency.* As an MEF-led exercise and despite the *Portal's* existence, MAB's transparency is also constrained by public misperceptions about the budget. The fact that a module on multiyear budgeting is not yet part of the SIAF, and that mandated biannual evaluations of the MABs are neither regularly prepared nor published, contribute to such misperceptions.

In the medium term, MABs should consolidate their role in determining the strategic priorities of annual budget allocations. To achieve this, authorities expect to carry out certain improvements in the MABs' framework from 2002 onward.

### Recommendations:
- The annual budget investment formulation is following an innovative participatory process and, from 2003 onward, MABs will be broadened to take into consideration regional priorities.

- MAB's five-year horizon should be reduced to three to make it consistent with the three-year horizon macroeconomic program.
- Revenue estimates should be opened to external and hopefully independent review to gain credibility.
- MABs' link to annual budget priorities should be strengthened, and mandated reports should be prepared twice a year to correct for deviations.
- The SIAF should design and implement MAB's performance-monitoring indicators, and the Ministries' budget execution should regularly be monitored against their benchmarks.
- MABs's reporting should be regularly published on the web to enable Congress and civil society to monitor and oversee expenditures—both programmed and executed—thereby ensuring both accountability and compliance with the annual budget. This is especially critical in light of national dialogue.
- As the SIAF improves its monitoring indicator system, a very basic costing-per-unit-arrangement system could be developed for selected poverty benchmarks.
- Finally, projected performance-based contracts in the public sector by end-2002—starting with pilot social ministries, programs, or projects—will require SIAF-monitored benchmarks in accordance with agreements under the MABs.

## Protecting the Budget as a Medium-Term Social Policy

Poverty-reduction efforts in the 1990s also included an innovative but hardly known emphasis on protecting priority social expenditure. In the 1990s, social expenditure in Peru was mostly pro-cyclical, such that their spending rose during periods of economic growth, but fell during economic downturns when such interventions were most needed. In this context, the fact that the last two GOPs have actively protected social spending in a fiscally retrenched economy, with total expenditure decreasing from 19 percent of GDP to 17.8 percent of GDP during 1999–2002 (about one seventh in dollar terms), is exceptional. Indeed, the share of social expenditure to GDP, which evolved from 3.9 percent of GDP in 1990 to 7.0 percent in 1999 and then remained steadfast until 2002, is a positive outcome.

Social programs were highly procyclical until 2000, but anticyclical afterward when, as part of actions leading to an effective social protection strategy, authorities guaranteed floor budget financing for a series of Protected Social Programs (PSPs), initially conceived during periods of recession.[7] This approach consisted of assigning a global budget allocation to nonsalary current and capital spending for 11 broadly selected programs, distributed among 8 sectors (functions): education (pre-primary, primary, and secondary); health (collective and individual); social and community assistance; transport; justice and peace; water and sanitation; agriculture; and energy. In 2001, the minimum aggregate budget allocation was about US$1.0 billion, equivalent to 12.7 percent of the ordinary budget and 1.9 percent of GDP. Preliminary projections for end-2001 budget execution show that the GOP complied with such commitment by transferring an aggregate amount of US$1.1 billion, equivalent to 13.1 percent of ordinary budget or 1.9 percent of GDP, and slightly above its target despite recessionary trends in 2001. Such anticyclical behavior in social expenditures was atypical in Peru, particularly in light of the significant economic slowdown all year due to unfavorable external and internal events. Moreover, in 2002, the GOP proposed an aggregate allocation of 2.0 percent of GDP to the PSPs (Table 3.6).

Meeting PSPs' expenditure floors was accomplished in 2001, but not without difficulties. Protected expenditure was maintained despite a fiscal retrenchment of about 0.8 percent of GDP. However, a few individual programs exhibited significant variations between target and actual

---

7. Other actions include introduction of a countercyclical workfare program; improved targeting and consolidation of food and nutrition programs; and reduction of the public pension system deficit, while exploring options for expanding social insurance options for the poor who are currently employed in the informal sector.

## TABLE 3.6: BUDGET FOR PROTECTED SOCIAL PROGRAMS
### (Nonsalary Current and Capital Budget, million soles)

| Program Code | Sector | PSRL I Target* 2001 | PSRL I Executed* 2001ᴾ | PSRL II Target** 2002ᶠ | PSRL II Approved* 2002 |
|---|---|---|---|---|---|
| 026 | Pre-Primary Education | 132 | 66 | 230 | 160 |
| 027 | Primary Education | 467 | 152 | 229 | 255 |
| 028 | Secondary Education | 467 | 107 | 212 | 175 |
| 063 | Collective Health | 196 | 420 | 432 | 479 |
| 064 | Individual Health | 471 | 660 | 835 | 847 |
| 014 | Social & Community Assistance*** | 315 | 414 | 383 | 609 |
| 052 | Transport | 686 | 503 | NA | 385 |
| 002/022 | Justice & Peace | 559 | 583 | NA | 655 |
| 052 | Water and Sanitation | 89 | 67 | NA | 79 |
| 009 | Agriculture | 85 | 606 | NA | 310 |
| 035 | Energy | 74 | 73 | NA | 54 |
| | **TOTAL** | 3,541 | 3,650 | 2,321 | 4,008 |
| | **% of Ordinary Budget** | 12.7 | 13.1 | 8.7 | 15.0 |
| | **% of National Budget** | 9.9 | 10.2 | 6.5 | 11.2 |
| | **% of GDP** | 1.9 | 1.9 | 1.2 | 2.0 |
| | *Memo:* | | | | |
| | GDP | 189,800 | 189,800 | 201,002 | 201,002 |
| | Ordinary Budget | 27,812 | 27,812 | 26,728 | 26,728 |
| | National Budget | 35,712 | 35,712 | 35,772 | 35,772 |

*PSRL = Programmatic social reform loan.*
*NA = Not applicable.*
ᴾ *Preliminary.*
ᶠ *Forecast.*
*Includes ordinary resources.
**Includes ordinary and external resources under restructured PSPs.
****Vaso de Leche* resources are excluded; under restructured PSPs in 2002, those corresponding to *Comedores Populares* and *A Trabajar* are excluded, as well.
*Source:* Bank staff estimates supported by MEF data.

expenditures, for example, underexecution in education and overexecution in health, social, and community assistance, and agriculture. Overexecution was mainly due to a moderate expansion of rural health programs and school breakfast programs, and unexpected expenses associated with natural disasters like the Arequipa earthquake, or prevention work required to deal with potentially adverse effects of *El Niño* on agriculture production. Underexecution in education programs was needed to make room for converting teachers from *contratados* to *regularizados* by the Paniagua transition government. Because the definition of the set of protected programs was broad, it prevented the assessment of the efficiency of individual programs in accomplishing their ultimate outcomes.

The government has agreed to go beyond the initial countercyclical role of the PSPs—that is, providing budget protection when a downturn occurs—to sustain their spending floors in the medium term while improving their focus, efficiency, monitoring mechanisms, and transparency. The ongoing restructuring of PSPs will be accompanied by expenditure shifts in broad sector functions, since both will have a central role in a poverty-reduction strategy.

*Recommendations:*

To *institutionalize* this key social policy, the GOP has announced several intentions:

- At the sector function level, assigning a broad aggregate amount of earmarked resources to education, health and sanitation, and social assistance. This amount is considered not only a budget-protection tool when a downturn occurs, but the sustained floor required to make progress toward Peru's medium-term development goals.[8] The aggregate 2002 budget allocation for the three priority social-sector functions—education, health and sanitation, and social assistance—is at least similar to its 2001 level in real terms, and shows an increase from 5.3 percent of GDP in 2001 to 5.6 percent of GDP for these sectors. In addition, in 2003, at least a similar aggregate expenditure floor should be agreed, in real terms, in the approved Budget Law.
- At the program level, reduce the number of virtually selected PSPs to six (Table 3.6), and group under three sectors: education (pre-primary, primary, and secondary), health (collective and individual), and social assistance. The aggregate earmarked expenditure to this revised set of PSPs is set at 1.2 percent of GDP in 2002, down from the previous 1.9 percent of GDP in 2001.[9] This reduction of 0.7 percent of GDP makes room for increased budget flexibility. In addition, in 2003, a similar aggregate expenditure floor should be agreed, in real terms, in the approved Budget Law.
- At the project level, establish monitoring indicators for specific projects grouped under the selected PSPs and, in a few cases, add performance management contracts to improve their efficiency (for example, the Integral and Mother and Child Health Insurances, SIS-SMI).
- Introduce budget flexibility on executed PSPs expenditure by including escape clauses at the sector function level to make provisions for budget underexecution or a major budgetary shortfall; and at the program and project levels, by allowing internal reallocations from underperforming to overperforming programs or projects, but maintaining global spending floors.[10]
- Design and develop a tailor-made and user-friendly SIAF-supported monitoring and evaluation tool.
- Consider the possibility of converting the de facto "virtually" protected budget into an Enhanced Virtual Poverty Fund. This enhanced mechanism would consist of tagging certain budget lines that meet or approximate the definition of poverty-reducing spending (the so-called "virtual" fund) and draw principally on the experience of Uganda's Poverty Action Fund (Box 3.5). It is rapidly expanding through highly indebted poor countries (HIPCs).[11] In some countries, its creation has also involved making changes to the existing budget and accounting systems (Zambia), introducing new reporting templates to track spending lines (Mauritania, Mozambique, and Tanzania), or producing additional

---

8. Peru has defined a set of about 20 medium-term development goals.

9. The revised set of programs, however, increases its global allocation as a percentage of GDP from 1.0 percent in 2001 to 1.2 percent in 2002. The reduced level of protection in the revised set is the direct result of the narrow number of PSPs considered.

10. These ceilings for budget reassignments are required, on one hand, to maximize the effective use of protected funds that could be left unused by underperforming projects in priority programs and, on the other hand, to guarantee a minimum level of budget execution in priority programs.

11. In 1996, the IMF and the World Bank launched the HIPC initiative to reduce the debt stock of debt-stressed countries. In 1998, they launched the Enhanced HIPC initiative to provide faster, deeper, and broader debt relief, and strengthen the links between debt relief and poverty reduction through a poverty-reduction strategy produced by the country. Uganda is committed to channel cash-flow savings on interest payments resulting from the reduction of the stock of debt under HIPC toward PAF programs.

---

**BOX 3.5: PERU: INSTITUTIONALIZING A VIRTUAL POVERTY FUND: A LOOK AT BEST-PRACTICE UGANDA**

The virtual Poverty Action Fund (PAF) is focused on implementing the government of Uganda's highest priorities within the Poverty Eradication Action Plan (PEAP). The PAF is funded by a combination of HIPC debt relief, donor—general or sector-earmarked—support, and the government's own resources. The *operational framework* of the virtual PAF has the following components: (a) budget priorities are defined by a rolling three-year medium-term expenditure framework (MTEF); (b) it is not a separate fund, but a subset of the overall budget; (c) the government commits not to cut its funds; (d) all expenditures fall under full Congress and Auditor General oversight; (e) it is managed by sector- and ministerial-level working groups; and (f) PAF programs have a structured and participatory institutional framework that ensures that they are properly planned, budgeted, and implemented. This includes:

*Eligibility Criteria:* A program qualifies if it meets four criteria: (a) it is part of the PEAP; (b) it directly reduces poverty (with involvement by the poor); (c) it delivers a service to the poorest 20th of the population; and (d) it has a well-developed implementation plan (with costs, outcome, and output targets clearly identified). Programs are reviewed once a year.

*Administration:* Five percent of PAF resources are set aside for improving program effectiveness and transparency.

*Size:* At least a constant proportion of the original budget.

*Reporting:* An overall quarterly report by central or local governments should be produced by the Ministry of Finance and distributed countrywide. Biannual sector performance evaluations are also required. Audits should cover all Central Government-led programs and at least 60 percent of district-led programs. Sector expenditure tracking studies are required when there is inadequate audit information. Civil society independently monitors reviews.

*Safeguards:* (a) In case of budgetary shortfalls, underallocation to PAF should be lower than cuts in non-PAF programs; (b) in case of underperformance, funds can be reallocated to other PEAP programs or to PAF programs in the following fiscal year.

---

information on all poverty-reducing spending (Honduras) (IMF 2002). Often, virtual funds are believed not to be needed in countries that already have a system of program classification or are well on the way to setting up such systems. However, in the case of Peru, not only does such a Virtual Fund exist, with the support of the SIAF and the decision of the GOP's authorities to tag protected spending, but the Fund's recent successful experience proves that virtual tagging is not the only sufficient condition for sustaining pro-poor expenditure in the medium term. An Enhanced Virtual Poverty Fund, tailor-made to Peruvian needs, would essentially require adding two new features: (a) the development of its institutional framework providing open access and reporting; and (b) the definition of monitoring indicators and evaluation mechanisms in a participatory way. Such a proposal would definitely strengthen a medium-term social policy with one of the finest tools for a solid poverty-reduction strategy, supported by the SIAF's full development and expansion throughout the public sector.

## Budget Transparency

There is no question that Peruvian officials have made tremendous progress toward making the budget process more transparent and accountable to civil society (Table 3.7). In 2000, a few social programs were first in posting on the web their district-by-district expenditures. Then, two popular

## TABLE 3.7: BUDGET TRANSPARENCY RATINGS
### (November 2001)

| Area/Score | Peru<br>A | LAC Mean*<br>B | A–B |
|---|---|---|---|
| General Knowledge (Overall Score) | 3.4 | 3.6 | −0.2 |
| Formulation | | | |
| Legislative powers | 3.8 | 3.4 | 0.4 |
| Civil society participation | 1.6 | 1.8 | −0.2 |
| Budget is inertial | 2.1 | 2.5 | −0.4 |
| Budget follows M–T priorities | 1.6 | 2.4 | −0.8 |
| In-Year Modification | | | |
| Legislative participation | 3.0 | 2.9 | 0.1 |
| Awareness of the civil society | 1.7 | 2.2 | −0.5 |
| Execution | | | |
| End-year impact evaluation | 1.5 | 2 | −0.5 |
| Monitoring on physical targets | 1.8 | 2.2 | −0.4 |
| Budget Transparency Indexes (General) | 2.7 | 3.0 | −0.3 |
| Formulation | 2.5 | 2.7 | −0.2 |
| Approval | 2.4 | 2.6 | −0.2 |
| Execution | 2.4 | 2.6 | −0.2 |
| Fiscalization | 1.9 | 2.3 | −0.4 |
| Data Quality | | | |
| Trustworthiness of INE data | 2.4 | 3.2 | −0.8 |
| Independence from executive | 2.1 | 2.7 | −0.6 |
| Supervision | | | |
| Openness to bidding prices | 2.4 | 2.8 | −0.4 |
| Knowledge of public salaries | 2.4 | 2.6 | −0.2 |
| Trustworthiness of internal audits | 1.7 | 2.6 | −0.9 |
| Comptroller's office fights corruption | 1.9 | 2.6 | −0.7 |
| Sanctions for misuse applied | 2.7 | 3.1 | −0.4 |
| Reporting Timeliness | | | |
| Formulation | 1.9 | 2.0 | −0.1 |
| Approval | 2.2 | 2.8 | −0.6 |
| Execution | 1.8 | 2.3 | −0.5 |
| Fiscalization | 1.5 | 2.0 | −0.5 |

*Also includes Argentina, Chile, Mexico, and Peru.

Source: Morón (2001).

infrastructure programs—*Caminos Rurales* and Rural Electrification—also posted on the web the areas covered by their work. In February, the MEF launched the Economic Transparency website (*Portal de Transparencia Economica*), including detailed information on budget execution. This provided citizens and civil society organizations with the necessary tools to begin exercising control over social and decentralized programs—to verify that expenditure outlays are actually spent as indicated, whether targeting is appropriate, and whether there appears to be any politically motivated wrongdoing in the use of public resources. Finally, the rapid expansion of the SIAF throughout the government will allow, in an unprecedented move for LAC countries, full disclosure of the budget of the ministries of Defense and National Security by end-2002. The SIAF is also getting ready to support decentralization to subnational governments.

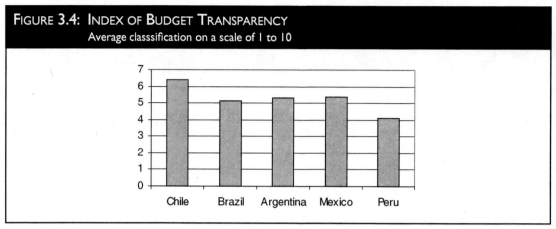

FIGURE 3.4: INDEX OF BUDGET TRANSPARENCY
Average classsification on a scale of 1 to 10

Source: Morón (2001).

Despite such efforts, Peru still ranks lowest in LAC in terms of overall budget transparency. Comprehensive national surveys developed in five LAC countries found that Peru ranks fifth below Chile, Argentina, Mexico, and Brazil (Figure 3.4). The survey was developed by the *Universidad del Pacifico* (Morón 2001). It approached Congressmen from all political parties, journalists, think tanks, and NGOs. Why, despite multiple recent efforts, did Peru obtain such a low ranking? A look at the multinational survey shows detailed features about Peru's legal framework and, more important, prevailing perceptions on budget transparency existing in the civil society.

Peru ranks favorably in terms of the legal framework surrounding budget transparency. The survey underscores existing regulations that favor public knowledge of the budget and mechanisms like the *Portal,* which promotes a transparent management of public expenditure, or the SIAF, which improves budget execution. Budget formulation, though, faces one obstacle: inertial spending, which prevents an adequate fit between budget allocations and priorities. For its part, budget auditing is affected by the diminished role of the Comptroller's Office in controlling public expenditure. Furthermore, this office has no legal authority to issue sanctions against public servants found guilty of wrongdoing. Finally, the survey also finds that no minimum reporting format requirements exist in the SIAF, thus preventing a user-friendly reading of the budget database.

In spite of a positive legal framework, the major obstacle to budget transparency is that the public remains skeptical in Peru. The budget transparency ratings allow a detailed reading of the issues found by the survey (Table 3.7), classified per stage: formulation, in-year modifications, and execution; or per area: overall transparency indexes, data quality, supervision, and reporting timeliness. Our analysis of selected perceptions is associated either to a higher differential (gap) between Peru and the rest of LAC, or to a low score obtained in the survey:[12]

■ *Budget formulation.* Perceptions suggest that the Peruvian Congress has above-average leverage to be able to influence budget formulation, and others affirm that the budget does not follow medium-term priorities. The first finding is surprising since about 69 percent of surveyed responses also think that congressmen do not have the capacity to assess the budget.

■ *In-year modifications.* The public's perception is that the Peruvian Congress has a higher participation in budget in-year modifications than is assumed in the rest of LAC, but that civil society's awareness of such adjustments is significantly lower than in other countries.

12. Scores are the average total response in a 1 to 5 rating.

■ *Budget execution.* Monitoring and evaluation of public expenditure in Peru appears to significantly lag compared to other LAC countries.
■ *Overall transparency indexes.* The public's perception is quite homogeneous with respect to the gaps perceived in the different stages of the budget process, with the lowest score assigned to budget fiscalization.
■ *Data quality.* The public clearly mistrusts INEI data and its independence from the Executive. INEI ranks low in regional terms.
■ *Supervision.* The public's perception assigns the lowest supervision ratings to internal audits and the Comptroller's Office. The degree of openness to bidding processes and sanctions for misuse of public funds are perceived as requiring improvements.
■ *Reporting timeliness.* Budget formulation shows a rating that is close to other LAC countries. The public's perception points to significant gaps in fiscalization, approval, and execution.

In the interim, the GOP is making extraordinary efforts to improve transparency. An internal survey developed by the MEF on reporting, and the degree of compliance with directives referring to budget transparency in all public sector entities, shows impressive progress in compliance (Table SA.25 and Figure 3.5). In 2002, the only remaining reports to be published on the web are (a) MEF—the consolidated balance of the public sector, the balance of the Fiscal Stabilization Fund, and the evaluation of the financial and physical indicators; (b) FONAFE—audits of financial statements and results of the evaluation of management indicators; and (c) *Oficina de Normalización Provisional* (ONP, Pensions)—consolidated financial statements of both the provisional reserve and the National Savings Fund (FONAHPU). Regarding the degree of compliance with directives, the only common area where generalized weaknesses are found is in the hiring of public employees and procurement contracts. For their part, CTARs and most public entities do not reveal their strategic plans, whereas public enterprises still do not reveal economic information related to their investment projects.

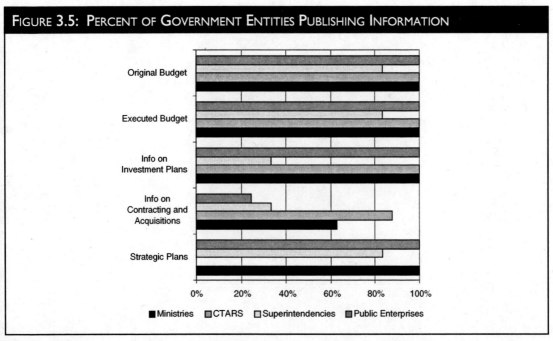

FIGURE 3.5: PERCENT OF GOVERNMENT ENTITIES PUBLISHING INFORMATION

*Recommendations:*
A set of additional actions is proposed to enhance transparency.

- Strengthen training and advice with improved learning tools for budget oversight by Peruvian Congress and civil society. The recent creation of a joint MEF–Congress Commission of Economy is a positive step in the right direction.
- The budget for internal auditing and for the Comptroller's office should be increased. Lack of due fiscalization and corruption-prone practices are recurrent themes in this report.
- SIAF reports should be made user-friendly,[13] and nationwide capacity building for its use should be considered a permanent priority.
- A special effort should be made to develop procedures for outputs to reach populations outside Lima, especially in regard to transfers to subnational governments, because they will be critical in supporting the decentralization process.
- Complete ongoing official plans to make public sector publications fully available.

---

13. SIAF officials reported to have completed a *Portal Amigable* (special module) last August.

# IV

# IMPROVING THE EFFICIENCY OF PUBLIC EXPENDITURE

*Does higher public expenditure buy better results in social outcomes? In Peru, there has been little empirical effort to evaluate the evidence supporting such a common belief and assess the efficiency in the use of increased resources. However, it is commonly recognized that reducing unproductive outlays, increasing social expenditure, and improving its efficiency and quality are critical elements of countries that have achieved macroeconomic stability and have decided to actively pursue poverty reduction. Leakages and poor targeting are two critical shortcomings that affect the efficiency of pro-poor expenditure. On one hand, a highly decentralized budget execution brings the possibility of significant leakages in the flow of resources to the final beneficiaries of social programs. Leaks may undermine social policy by their ability to prevent a critical input—public expenditure—from producing desired social outcomes. The introduction of an innovative tool—a Public Expenditure Tracking Survey (PETS)—reveals major leakages in revenue transfer mechanisms to local governments and downward, in particular for the* Vaso de Leche *program, the most important food supplementary program in Peru. The same national survey indicates that the most significant leaks are not at the origins of the chain, between the Central and local governments, which is a very positive achievement for the financial management system, but at the mid- to lowest levels of the chain, as resources get closer to beneficiaries. Transfers to local governments are also compounded by insufficient audit control and poor transparency. On the other hand, poor targeting deviates pro-poor outlays to the non-poor. Targeting rates in social programs vary tremendously in Peru, and their degree of regressivity/ progressivity provides a mixed picture. Household-survey-based findings show that targeting is adequate for* Desayunos Escolares, *but inadequate for others, such as* ESSALUD *and* Comedores Populares. *This chapter briefly addresses the empirical evidence supporting the rationale for increasing expenditure in the education and health sectors, describes the main findings of Peru's PETS, and assesses the quality of targeting of pro-poor expenditure in Peru.*

## Does Higher Government Expenditure Buy Better Results in Education and Health Care?

Increased public expenditure in health and education improves both access to and attainment in schools, and reduces mortality rates for infants and children.[1] There is increased recognition that expenditure allocations in favor of education and health can boost economic growth while promoting equity and reducing poverty. The rationale for higher public spending in education is often based on its impact on individuals' lifetime incomes (that is, the social rate of return, highest in primary education, then in secondary). Similarly, the rationale for increased spending in health is justified on the grounds that it reduces the impact of diseases on the productive life years of the population. Empirical evidence, however, has not been conclusive, especially if public resources are used inefficiently and inequitably, and public expenditure crowds out private spending on the social sectors. Using a model and a cross-sample database developed by Gupta, Verhoeven, and Tiongson (1999), data from Peru are added to a sample of about 50 countries, and ensuing estimation followed an ordinary least squares (OLS) and two-stage least squares (2SLS) linear regression technique (Tables 4.1a and 4.1b).[2] Highly robust results for education and health indicators show that:

- ▨ Total education spending has mixed coefficients—a statistically significant one as a determinant of enrollment rates in secondary education, but insignificant ones as a determinant of enrollment rates in combined gross primary and secondary education. In the 2SLS gross secondary education regression, the coefficient of combined primary and secondary education spending is also statistically significant.[3] Overall, the F-statistics are significant at the 1 percent level. Other variables the coefficients of which also appear statistically significant are population, child mortality rate, per capita income, and urbanization.
- ▨ Total health spending has a statistically significant effect on both outcomes, infant and child mortality. Its coefficient appears weakly significant in the 2SLS infant and child mortality regressions. Other variables the coefficient of which appears statistically significant are the adult illiteracy rate and income per capita.

The policy implications of such findings are obvious.

### Recommendations:

- ▨ The Government of Peru (GOP) has made the right decision in deciding to increase the share of public resources allocated to education and health. However, caution is required in using these figures to estimate budgetary resources needed to achieve specific targets in social areas, because the verified lack of significance for some critical coefficients (that is, for combined primary and secondary education spending on gross primary and secondary enrollment rates) confirms that there are also other important determinants to take into account.

---

1. This section draws on Gupta, Verhoeven, and Tiongson (1999), who kindly shared the IMF database and allowed us to include Peru in their consistent dataset in order to facilitate the estimates leading to the findings submitted here.

2. OLS are corrected for heteroskedasticity and 2SLS is used to address the problem of reverse causality (that is, higher spending on primary education may have a positive effect on enrollment, but a higher demand for primary education, reflected in higher enrollment rates, may also provide a push for higher spending). We also applied a third method of estimation, the seemingly unrelated regression (SUR) procedure, and our findings remained robust to changes in specification, instruments, and weights defined. In evaluating the regression results, it should be borne in mind that some degree of multicollinearity among variables affects the standard errors of coefficients. Fortunately, the variables for overall sectoral spending are generally not correlated with other independent variables, except health spending with adult illiteracy. White's technique is used to correct for heteroskedasticity and Sargan's test is used to assess 2SLS specification.

3. Regressions do not permit drawing conclusions about changes in the level of spending on primary and secondary education as opposed to the share of such spending in total expenditure.

**TABLE 4.1A: REGRESSION RESULTS FOR EDUCATION INDICATORS: LINEAR REGRESSIONS[a]**

| | Enrollment Rates | | | |
| | Gross Primary and Secondary | | Gross Secondary | |
| | OLS (weighted)[b] | 2SLS (weighted)[c] | OLS (weighted)[b] | 2SLS (weighted)[c] |
|---|---|---|---|---|
| Constant | 53.81 | 36.28 | 23.04 | ***31.10 |
| | (42.65) | (27.38) | (18.92) | (11.25) |
| Primary and secondary education spending | −.19 | −.20 | .12 | *.22 |
| (% of total educ. spending) | (.30) | (.31) | (.11) | (.11) |
| Education spending (percent of GDP) | 1.18 | .80 | ***2.43 | *1.86 |
| | (1.47) | (1.52) | (.95) | (1.08) |
| Population aged 0–14 (percent of population) | .17 | .85 | **−.76 | ***−.77 |
| | (.98) | (.77) | (.37) | (.26) |
| Child mortality rate (per thousand of | **−.12 | ***−.21 | ***−.01 | *−.07 |
| children 0–5 years) | (−.06) | (.07) | (.03) | (.03) |
| Income per capita in PPP terms[d] | 1.82 | −.086 | ***3.07 | **1.65 |
| | (2.20) | (1.32) | (1.16) | (.81) |
| Urbanization (percent of population) | .53 | **.71 | ***.45 | ***.45 |
| | (.37) | (.32) | (.15) | (.13) |
| Adjusted R-squared | 53.78% | 48.46% | 78.15% | 81.05% |
| Number of observations | 43 | 42 | 44 | 43 |
| F-statistic | ***17.45 | ***12.29 | ***60.40 | ***81.64 |
| P-value | 0.00 | 0.00 | 0.00 | 0.00 |

a. Robust standard errors are in parenthesis: *** indicates significance at the 1 percent level, ** significance at the 5 percent level, and * significance at the 10 percent level.
b. By adult illiteracy.
c. Instruments used: aid in percent of government expenditures, military spending in percent of government expenditures, share of unallocated education spending, and total government spending.
d. Multiplied by 1,000. PPP = Purchasing Power Parity.
*Source:* World Bank staff estimates.

■ There are mutually reinforced positive implications between social outcomes: that is, a higher illiteracy rate has a positive impact on health outcomes; ditto for a lower mortality rate on higher education enrollment.

■ As the study reported on below shows, increasing resources is not enough. Improving efficiency through the reduction of leaks and improvements in targeting in order to assure funds actually reach their intended beneficiaries is critical for achieving desired outcomes.

Further analysis shows that the efficiency of Peru's public expenditure is below Latin America's average for health, but above average for education. Similar results hold true in relation to world averages, but these indexes should be taken with a grain of salt.

■ Peru's level of efficiency in reaching health outcomes is below both Latin American and world averages. Two indexes—technical and relative—measure the efficiency of public expenditure on health among Latin American countries during 1990–98 (Table 4.2). These indexes combine five outcomes: life expectancy, infant mortality, under-five mortality, height-for-age malnutrition, and weight-for-age malnutrition. The Technical Efficiency Index varies from 76 to 94 percent, well below LAC and world averages in most health

### TABLE 4.1B: REGRESSION RESULTS FOR HEALTH INDICATORS: LOG-LOG REGRESSIONS[a]

| | Infant Mortality | | Child Mortality | |
|---|---|---|---|---|
| | OLS | 2SLS (weighted)[b] | OLS | 2SLS (weighted)[b] |
| Constant | ***5.64 | ***5.49 | ***6.44 | ***6.31 |
| | (.89) | (.87) | (1.13) | (1.15) |
| Health spending (percent of GDP) | −.11 | *−.14 | .11 | *−.14 |
| | (.09) | (.08) | (.076) | (.07) |
| Adult illiteracy rate (percent of population | ***.35 | ***.39 | ***.36 | ***.39 |
| 15 or older) | (.07) | (.07) | (.08) | (.08) |
| Income per capita in PPP terms | **−.30 | **−.34 | **−.37 | **−.39 |
| | (.12) | (.13) | (.15) | (.15) |
| Urbanization (percent of population) | −.19 | −.12 | −.24 | −.19 |
| | (.18) | (.22) | (.19) | (.20) |
| Access to sanitation (percent of population) | .06 | .08 | .10 | .11 |
| | (.10) | (.11) | (.12) | (.13) |
| Adjusted R-squared | 75.75% | 79.89% | 77.97% | 78.85% |
| Number of observations | 31 | 29 | 31 | 29 |
| F-statistic | 27.49 | 50.99 | 46.10 | 65.00 |
| P-value | 0.00 | 0.00 | 0.00 | 0.00 |

PPP = Purchasing Power Parity
a. Robust standard errors are in parenthesis: *** indicates significance at the 1 percent level, ** significance at the 5 percent level, and * significance at the 10 percent level.
b. Instruments used: aid in percent of government expenditures, military spending in percent of government expenditures, and total government spending.
*Source:* World Bank staff estimates.

indicators, particularly in malnutrition-height, under-five mortality, and life expectancy. The relative efficiency index is below 100 in most cases (except malnutrition-weight), which reflects that, compared to LAC benchmarks and given its inputs—health spending and a time-trend (a proxy for technological progress)—Peru could do better in improving its health outcomes (Jayasuriya and Wodon 2001).[4]

■ Outcome indicators for Peru's educational inputs look acceptable compared to LAC and world averages, but severe quality and equity shortcomings remain. Net enrollment rates in primary and secondary education are the outcome indicators for the education sector; and education spending, adult literacy (which is not an outcome but an input, since we are looking at performance in primary and secondary education), and a time-trend are inputs. Peru's Technical Efficiency Index for net primary enrollment is 77 percent, on a par with other Latin American countries, whereas for net secondary enrollment it is 72 percent, much above the LAC average of 51 percent. In spite of this progress, severe educational shortcomings are still relevant in terms of the very low quality of education services and

4. The Technical Efficiency Index values depict country-level efficiency of spending, with a value of 100 indicating that a country has reached the maximum possible outcome given its inputs. The Relative Efficiency Index measures each country's spending efficiency relative to a Latin American regional benchmark efficiency, with the benchmark being the straight average for the countries in the sample. The inputs taken into account for the analysis are the level of health spending, adult education levels (as measured by the share of the adult population which is literate), and time. Sensitivity tests have been performed with additional input variables, such as GDP per capita, but the relative ranking of various countries does not change much.

TABLE 4.2: PERU: EFFICIENCY OF PUBLIC EXPENDITURE IN REACHING SOCIAL OUTCOMES 1990–98

| | Technical Efficiency | Relative to | | Technical Efficiency | Relative to | | Technical Efficiency | Relative to | |
|---|---|---|---|---|---|---|---|---|---|
| | | LAC | World | | LAC | World | | LAC | World |
| **HEALTH** | *Life Expectancy* | | | *Infant Mortality* | | | *Under-Five Mortality* | | |
| Peru | 81.6 | 97.7 | 100.9 | 94.5 | 98.6 | 98.8 | 89.9 | 98.1 | 98.3 |
| Latin America | 83.4 | | 103.2 | 95.9 | | 100.3 | 91.6 | | 100.2 |
| World | 80.9 | 96.9 | | 95.6 | 99.7 | | 91.4 | 99.8 | |
| | *Malnutrition-Height* | | | *Malnutrition-Weight* | | | *Combined Health* | | |
| Peru | 76.2 | 89.2 | 91.5 | 94.3 | 101.3 | 107.7 | 87.3 | 97.1 | 99.5 |
| Latin America | 85.4 | | 102.5 | 93.1 | | 106.3 | 89.9 | | 102.4 |
| World | 83.3 | 97.6 | | 87.6 | 94.1 | | 87.8 | 97.6 | |
| **EDUCATION** | *Net Primary Enrollment* | | | *Net Secondary Enrollment* | | | *Combined Education* | | |
| Peru | 77.1 | 100.9 | 104.1 | 71.8 | 141.0 | 132.8 | 74.4 | 116.9 | 116.2 |
| Latin America | 76.4 | | 103.1 | 50.9 | | 94.2 | 63.7 | | 99.4 |
| World | 74.1 | 97.0 | | 54.0 | 106.2 | | 64.1 | 100.6 | |

*Note:* The value 100 reflects the average for the LAC region.

*Source:* Jayasuriya and Wodon (2001.)

teacher qualifications, especially in the rural areas, and in terms of the high inequality of resources devoted to private and public education (Apoyo Institute 2002b; Wodon 2002).

## Tracing Leakages of Public Funds in Peru—A Public Expenditure Tracking Survey

This section focuses on the leakages of public funds through municipalities (districts) in Peru.[5] "Leakage" is defined as the portion of public funds that does not reach its ultimate targeted beneficiary, but instead is diverted for other purposes, including private gain or other potentially legitimate, but clearly unintended, purposes. This particular study of leakages is different from the study of corruption per se. Studies of corruption examine the bald diversion of public funds and the taking of bribes by public officials that are both clearly illegal and fraudulent in intent (Rose-Ackerman 1999; Seligson 2002; Treisman 2000). Research on leakages, instead, begins by asking the question: Why do public expenditures often not produce concomitant increases in social outcome indicators?[6] While there are many factors that go into the answer to that question, only recently has it been appreciated that part of the explanation lies in the fact that institutional factors, as well as local organization constraints, or private gain prevent some public funds from ever reaching their intended targets. This "leaking away" of public funds in Peru is the subject of the present investigation.

Work on leakages of public expenditure is in the pioneer stage worldwide. It builds on the seminal work developed by the World Bank in Africa, more particularly in Uganda. Reinikka and Svensson (2002) found that only 13 percent of the nonwage expenditures made by the CG were received by the local schools in Uganda. The study of Peru deepens the approach followed in the Uganda study, mainly because it is able to trace leakages at *each* level in the chain, from the first emission of public funds at the central level, down to the consumer at the household level. The Uganda study looked only at the national/individual leakage, and thus was unable to attribute leakages to each stage in the chain. As a result of this more comprehensive and disaggregated focus, surprising findings presented here emerge, especially because it is possible to identify the specific steps where main leakages occur and to quantify them. Moreover, the Peru PETS, because it pinpoints the locus and key causal factors responsible for the leakages, gives policymakers clear direction for dealing with the problem.[7] In doing so, it looks at how resources are procured and distributed, and examines both provider and household behavior, which allows both identification of how much the government spent on the wrong goods or wrong people, and inferences about those instances in the chain where a reasonable presumption of corruption could be pinpointed as "worst offenders." Finally, the Peru PETS is preceded by a thorough discussion of the system of CG transfers to the municipalities, and its shortcomings.

The approach taken to measure leakages is to employ survey instruments at each level in the process of transference of government funds from the central authority down to the household. The study employed data on 120 of the 1,828 municipalities in Peru. Data were obtained from the CG on four transfers to municipalities managed by the GOP: FONCOMUN, *Canon Minero, Canon/Sobrecanon Petrolero,* and the *Vaso de Leche* ("Glass of Milk", VDL) program. Since all but the last of these programs do not extend below the municipality level, the deepening of the research on leakages is on the VDL program. It is in tracing the flow of funds in this program that the

---

5. This section draws on the findings of a national survey jointly developed with Apoyo Institute (2002a).

6. A recent parametric model (Simulations for Social Indicators and Poverty, SIMSIP) developed by the World Bank (Wodon and Hicks 2001) to estimate the projected impact of fiscal inputs on selected social outcomes, especially the Millennium Goals, does not take into account country differences in leakages of public spending in its estimates, and assumes them constant in its projections. If developed regularly and in several countries, PETS could not only modify SIMSIP results, but set baselines for countries with similar levels of leakages.

7. The study gets as detailed as identifying the entities presumed as "worst offenders" in producing leakages (and their estimated amount).

research attempts to make its most innovative, but not unique, contribution. Using survey data at the municipality, local milk distribution committee, and beneficiary household levels, it is possible to trace the flow and leakage of central funds from the top of the chain to the last link at the bottom. The methodology is very complex, not only because it involves multilevel comparisons, but because the input itself is transformed from cash to commodities as the funds move from the top to the bottom, and as "the commodity itself" actually becomes commodities, since the program is not limited to milk or milk products alone, despite its name. The product is then transformed at the household level, as the food products are mixed with other foods before being served. Yet, despite this complexity, it has been possible to determine the relative magnitude of leakages at each level.

The survey findings send an important warning signal: leakages in Peru are significant and far more pervasive and extensive at the bottom of the chain than at the top. Of the entire amount of public funds intended for the VDL program, barely 29 percent get to their intended beneficiaries. This does not mean that 71 cents of each dollar are fully lost in corruption costs. Rather, the diverted resources get leaked away through a combination of off-budget administrative costs, expenditure on noneligible products, in-kind deliveries to nonbeneficiaries, fees for overpriced items, and sheer corruption. Results also challenge the predominant view of the last decade that organizations that are closer to the people necessarily perform better in service delivery. This is not necessarily the case if the program does not have a proper design or if the local organizations are not transparent and do not practice accountability, which seems to be the case of the VDL Committees in Peru.

These are hybrid organizations where both the government and the beneficiaries are represented. They are made up of three government representatives and three representatives of the beneficiaries of the program, democratically elected by the rank and file. The government representatives are the mayor of the municipality, another municipal official, and a representative of the Ministry of Health. Additionally, a representative of the Association of Agricultural Producers of the region is entitled to participate in the committee.

The relationship between these committees and the direct beneficiaries is characterized by at least two features. First, there is asymmetric information: final beneficiaries have limited access to the information about the decisions made by the committees. The beneficiaries also have limited information about how much resource they are entitled to receive from the program and which procedures they should employ to secure them. Second, there is a lack of transparency and accountability of the committees vis-à-vis both the beneficiaries and the upper echelons of government. In addition to these two features there likely is, in many committees, a somewhat low level of management capacity. The fact of the matter, anyway, is that committees so dominate the running of the program at the local level that they may divert resources from their original purpose, without being held accountable or sanctioned for doing so, since both the higher official authorities (the Ministry of Economy and Finance, [MEF], for example) and the intended beneficiaries do not know about it. The committees then dispose of the resources at their own discretion and sometimes end up vitiating, even unwittingly, the program's expected effects.

This arrangement is, of course, a far cry from the desirable participatory setting where the citizens of a community could directly observe, talk to, and even argue with, those providing them key services and where they would be able to hold those individuals and institutions accountable for their actions. On the contrary, in the VDL program we have the case of hybrid committees (made up of both government and elected representatives) placed in direct control of a development program, which, due to lack of accountability and transparency, can distort its goals and/or become rent-seekers benefiting not the collectivity, but their own narrow interests. This, of course, points to the fact the program has severe design problems. These committees are beyond the reach of common citizens and are frequently dominated by self-serving, rent-seeking, self-styled "representatives" of the program beneficiaries. The evidence amassed in this study enables us not only to directly compare diversions (referred to here as "leakages") of public resources for private gain or for a distorted purpose at each level of the public assistance "food chain," but also to conclude that, in this case, the *lower* we go "down the chain," the *greater* the diversion. Thus the conventional belief that every local body is necessarily more accountable than the national and public authorities is turned on its head.

There are some caveats to the anticipated main findings presented above. The survey was con-ducted in a country that in the past three years has undergone a restructuring of the way public expenditures are managed and controlled by the Integrated Financial Management System (SIAF) (Chapter III). For that reason, it may be the case that our central finding is one that is not easily replicated elsewhere. The SIAF facilitates nearly all CG expenditures getting to the municipalities for which they were intended, and our findings confirm that most arrive without extensive delays, although their volatility and supervision remain somewhat of a problem in some instances. Where the leakages are extensive, however, is below the level of the municipality. Thus, in Peru, the leak-ages increase exponentially as central funds move away from the capital and move down to the committees and families. Future studies in other countries in which central funds are less well con-trolled may well find that leakages remain extensive at the local level, but perhaps would be far greater at the upper levels than they are in Peru. In both cases, leakages are extensive and have serious negative implications for development. In addition, a tracking survey is needed because a municipal SIAF is not yet installed in all municipalities. So, even though transfers from the CG to municipalities are well recorded, there is no further virtual control of what happens inside the municipality once it receives its transfer and moves it downward. PETS methodology does not allow direct measurement of other types of leaks, such as inflated prices of milk products. However, it does it indirectly through comparison of price variation for the same milk or milk-derived prod-uct, and through the measure of their overprice with respect to supermarket retail prices.

## The Significance of Intergovernmental Transfers

The Government of Peru (GOP) has committed itself to improving the efficiency of its social spend-ing and the quality of the provision of social services at the local level, including its nutritional pro-grams. It has recognized that increased social spending needs to be decentralized and that this implies delegating more budgetary responsibilities to Regional Units of Ministries (particularly Education and Health), and efficient mechanisms to transfer resources to local governments. While these improvements are important, they may not necessarily translate into actual increases in public funds reaching their intended destinations. That is because the GOP lacks a solid baseline to evaluate the quality, efficiency, and efficacy of public expenditure below the national level. In fact, very little is known about how resources are channeled (particularly outside of Lima), and even less is known about how much of these resources initially allocated actually gets spent on their original purpose, what percentage really reaches their intended beneficiaries, or what are the magnitudes of transfer delays. Supervision is also very poor. For instance, we found that in 78 percent of the municipalities visited, the CG had not carried out any supervision regarding the use of resources in the VDL pro-gram. Moreover, in rural areas, only 14 percent of the municipalities had any supervision.

This study applies Public Expenditure Tracking Surveys (PETS) to (a) detect, analyze, and quan-tify the leakages and delays in the transfer of public expenditure, and (b) assess their effects on munic-ipal service delivery deficiencies. In this section, we deal with the latter topic. In the next section, a quantitative PETS is developed collecting information currently nonexistent and otherwise very diffi-cult, if not impossible, to obtain systematically. The information is surveyed at the different levels involved: CG, decentralized government unit (if any), final service units, and any intermediate units.

In Peru, public resources are distributed by two mechanisms: those that are centrally allocated and administered through branch offices of the CG, and those that are transferred to local govern-ments (municipalities). The education budget is an example of the former, while the VDL program is an example of the latter. In both cases, there is a long chain of intermediaries between the origi-nal CG budgeting office and the intended recipient. Findings presented here focus on the latter mechanism, in contrast to the work in Uganda.

It is difficult to overstate the importance of transfers to municipal governments. For the dis-tricts outside of Lima, transfers, on average, represent 72 percent of their total income and, among the districts of the poorest stratum, they can represent in excess of 90 percent of total income. The CG's four main transfers include the *Fondo de Compensación Municipal* (FONCOMUN) and VDL for all municipalities, and *Canon Minero* and *Canon/Sobrecanón Petrolero* for provinces and districts in regions where mining and petroleum products are extracted or the mining and petroleum company headquarters are located.

In 2001, these four major CG transfers totaled NS/1.9 billion (roughly $560 million).[8] Total transfers to municipalities in 2001 can be broken down in three major ways: (a) by separating Lima from the rest of the country, (b) by dividing the sample into urban versus rural and population size, and (c) by level of poverty (Annex D).

- The largest of the four transfers is the FONCOMUN, which accounts for NS/1.4 ($413 million) of the NS/1.9 billion in 2001 (in some districts it represented over 90 percent of total income).
- The second-largest CG transfer is the VDL transfer, which totaled NS/330 million ($97 million) in 2001. By law, approximately 7 percent of public social spending in Peru is dedicated to nutrition programs. Much of this effort involves the VDL program. This transfer, unlike the others, is earmarked specifically for use in the purchase of VDL products. This program is very important: excluding Lima, the municipalities in our survey reported a total of 645,346 direct beneficiaries; expanding this to the national population equals 3,693,406 (2,207,209 being children aged 0 to 6), which would suggest, roughly, coverage of 92 percent for children aged 0 to 6, and pregnant and nursing mothers.
- The third largest of the four major transfers is the *Canon/Sobrecanon Petrolero,* which totaled NS/128 million (roughly $37 million) in 2001. The importance of the total figure is misleading, however, at the local level. For municipalities that are eligible to receive this transfer, it can represent as much and, in some cases, more resources than, the FONCOMUN.
- Of the four transfers, only the *canon minero* is not variable month to month. It is the fourth-largest transfer, with about US$24 million distributed in 2001.

How meaningful are these transfers to the individual Peruvian? On a per capita basis, FONCOMUN transfers—the largest of the programs—average $8.57 in Lima per year and $18.61 per year in the rest of the country. In a country in which the GNP per capita (Atlas method) is in the neighborhood of $2,080, the largest of the transfers (FONCOMUN) amounts to no more than nine tenths of a percent of GNP per capita. A similar comment applies to the *canons.* Yet, these calculations are somewhat misleading since the funds are designated for the poor—not the entire population; and, since the poor receive the highest portion of the transfers, transfers are higher on a poor per capita basis. In addition, such comparisons are misleading in the case of VDL. The cash value of those funds is not the only factor to consider because the transfer provides, at least in theory, key nutritional supplements for children, whose nutritional status during childhood could impact their future health and productivity.

Expenditure on intergovernmental transfers shows a significant degree of progressivity. Using Lorenz curves, the highest degree of progressivity happens with the distribution of the *canon minero,* followed by FONCOMUN and VDL, which exhibit a distribution almost similar to a social program with universal coverage (Figure 4.1).[9] These results are consistent with the laws that govern them, and with the findings of our survey. According to the legislation, all but *canon petrolero* transfers are to be distributed according to per capita population, adjusted for poverty levels.[10] This is especially so for the FONCOMUN allocation formula, which counts each rural resident (who are usually the poorest in the country) twice as much as each urban resident. This should mean that the transfers would be higher in the rest of Peru than in Lima, and would also be higher in the

---

8. A comprehensive and detailed description of the transfer mechanisms is in Annex D.

9. Since these are progressive distributions, curves are above the 45-degree line. Otherwise, standard regressive Lorenz curves are depicted below it.

10. The *canon/sobrecanon petrolero* is distributed by other criteria, but introducing the urban/rural factor indirectly takes into account poverty as part of the criteria.

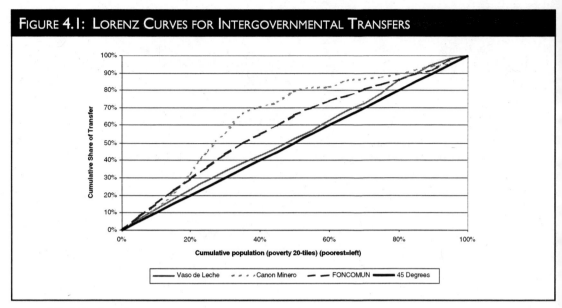

FIGURE 4.1: LORENZ CURVES FOR INTERGOVERNMENTAL TRANSFERS

*Source:* World Bank staff estimates.

more-impoverished areas than in the less-poor areas. In practice, the FONCOMUN per capita contributions are clearly far higher in the rest of the country than in Lima. The same pro-poor poverty bias appears in the *canon minero* and, to a much lesser extent, in the VDL program (Table 4.3).

*Recommendations:*
- The formula (and criteria) used for determining the *canon minero* and FONCOMUN transfers do not need any change and should be kept.
- Since transparency about the amount and timeliness of transfers is the main issue, it is in the interest of Peruvian officials to have them fully available to the public and the direct beneficiaries through the SIAF and the *Portal de Transparencia.*

Volatility of most transfers is significant. One of the most serious long-term problems faced by local governments in Latin America is the consistent lack of reliability of CG transfers. In many countries, such transfers often result in arrears. Volatility is calculated as the standard deviation of the annual percentage changes in the transfer amounts. While volatility is not directly a leakage issue, it does make planning difficult and does cause suffering when milk and other foodstuffs are not delivered on time. In Peru, using the new financial management system that is now in place, volatility has been reduced, but not eliminated, as the results of our survey show. In the worst case, volatility for the VDL transfer, outside of Lima, often exceeds 10 percent, with the poorest districts averaging over 15 percent (Annex D).

*Recommendation:*
- SIAF expansion among municipalities should continue, but alternatives to diminish the remaining volatility of transfers should be explored. Structural volatility in the *canon minero* transfers (related to international mineral prices) may require a Stabilization Fund (Chapter VIII).

Understanding of the amount of the transfers at the local level is insufficient and knowledge about the arrival day of the transfers is poor. Overall, most of the officials interviewed in the munic-

## TABLE 4.3: PER CAPITA TRANSFERS TO MUNICIPALITIES IN 2001
(in U.S. dollars)

| | FONCOMUN | Canon Minero | Canon/Sobrecanon Petrolero | Vaso de Leche |
|---|---|---|---|---|
| **PERU** | **15.35** | **1.20** | **12.51** | **3.73** |
| Lima | 8.57 | 0.09 | NA | 3.99 |
| Urban | 8.33 | 0.09 | NA | 4.00 |
| Rural | 25.24 | 0.19 | NA | 3.33 |
| *No. of observations* | 177 | 171 | NA | 177 |
| Rest of Peru | 18.61 | 1.89 | 12.51 | 3.60 |
| Less poor | 14.38 | 1.55 | 10.97 | 2.96 |
| Poor | 18.94 | 2.07 | 11.16 | 3.54 |
| More poor | 22.54 | 1.99 | 19.47 | 4.35 |
| Urban | 15.46 | 1.54 | 10.22 | 3.14 |
| Rural | 22.73 | 2.25 | 17.37 | 4.21 |
| Small | 31.97 | 1.84 | 48.15 | 4.37 |
| Medium | 20.05 | 1.77 | 19.40 | 4.13 |
| Large | 16.28 | 1.92 | 10.62 | 3.39 |
| More accessible | 17.33 | 1.81 | 9.81 | 3.39 |
| Less accessible | 23.72 | 2.15 | 20.90 | 4.47 |
| Nonprovincial capital | 16.98 | 1.48 | 11.95 | 3.73 |
| Provincial capital | 21.60 | 2.69 | 13.09 | 3.41 |
| *No. of observations* | 1,641 | 1,296 | 142 | 1,641 |

*Source:* MEF and World Bank ttaff estimates.

ipalities surveyed claim to have a reasonable understanding of the various transfer programs. However, the same is not true at the neighborhood level. For example, the survey found that 90 percent of the municipalities in the Lima area and 79 percent in the rest of the country claimed to know the *allocation criteria* used for the FONCOMUN program. Yet, the survey also found that when questioned, only 11 percent of the municipal officials in Lima—who earlier claimed to have knowledge of the criteria—actually did. Surprisingly, in the rest of Peru the knowledge was higher among those who claimed to know, since 67 percent actually did. As for the *amount of transfers* expected from FONCOMUN, the knowledge base is more reasonable since only 5 percent in Lima and 15 percent in the rest of Peru claimed not to know. In poor and rural areas outside Lima, however, this percentage of uncertainty increased to nearly one third. In the case of *Canon/Sobrecanon Petrolero* transfers, there is considerable uncertainty as to the expected amounts, with the majority in the rest of Peru districts not knowing. Knowledge of the date of arrival of the transfers was far weaker in Lima, with 40 percent of the municipalities not knowing. In the rest of Peru, 33 percent did not know. Similar percentages are found for FONCOMUN and *canon minero* (Table 4.4).

### Recommendation:
■ The GOP's decision to include monthly transfers to each municipality in a user-friendly format in the SIAF from 2002, also including the methodology used for their estimates, should be complemented with adequate permanent training of and information to major and local authorities (for example, VDL Committees).

Supervision of transfers to municipalities is extremely poor. On average, only 6 out of 10 of the municipalities are audited with regard to FONCOMUN and *canon minero,* and barely a third of those eligible for the *canon/sobrecanon petrolero* are supervised by some CG entity. Furthermore, the

**TABLE 4.4: MUNICIPALITIES THAT DO NOT KNOW THE ARRIVAL DAY OF THE TRANSFER**
(in percent)

|  | FONCOMUN | Canon Minero | Canon/Sobrecanon Petrolero |
|---|---|---|---|
| **Lima** | 40 | | |
| Urban | 42 | NA | NA |
| Rural | 38 | NA | NA |
| *No. Observations* | *20* | *NA.* | *NA* |
| **Rest of Peru** | **33** | **35** | **40** |
| Not Poor | 27 | 29 | 2 |
| Poor | 49 | 63 | 94 |
| Extreme Poor | 38 | 30 | 40 |
| Urban | 61 | 87 | 35 |
| Rural | 28 | 28 | 47 |
| Small | 30 | 30 | 38 |
| Medium | 39 | 36 | 31 |
| Large | 45 | 62 | 44 |
| More accessible | 18 | 21 | 15 |
| Less Accessible | 66 | 66 | 64 |
| Nonprovincial capital | 34 | 33 | 41 |
| Provincial capital | 28 | 50 | 29 |
| *No. Observations* | *99* | *74* | *32* |

Source: Instituto Apoyo (2002).

CG audits are reaching only the more accessible districts, while leaving the poorer, midsize, urban, and more remote districts wholly unsupervised (Table 4.5). CG supervision is not only rare, but also irregular, since the bulk of audits in about 80 percent of FONCOMUN and *canon minero* cases (43 percent for the *canon petrolero*) are done on a yearly basis (Apoyo Institute 2002a).

*Recommendation:*
- Auditing procedures to districts should be overhauled, including training, management reform, and more periodic internal and external audits by the Comptroller's Office. This reform is particularly urgent in the case of the *canon petrolero*.

Leakages in the transfer of FONCOMUN and the *canon minero* appear to be very small. This leak is defined as the percentage of transfer reported by the MEF that is unaccounted for by the municipality. Leakages amount to 1.5 percent in Lima and 0.5 percent in the rest of Peru for FONCOMUN, which is the largest program, but rise to 7.1 percent in the *Canon Minero* program in Lima (essentially driven by two outliers), but only 0.7 percent in the rest of Peru for this program[11] (Table 4.6). These so-called small leakages are tolerable and can be safely assumed to be mainly due to reporting errors (round-off) or simply bad recollection due to poor or nonexistent records at the municipality level.

*Recommendations:*
- SIAF-proposed expansion at the municipal level should be able to trace these leaks on a regular and virtual basis.
- Registry of the *canon/sobrecanon petrolero* transfers must be overhauled.

---

11. *Canon/sobrecanon petrolero* figures provided by the MEF were not trustworthy and complete, so were not included, but point out an area of priority reform.

## TABLE 4.5: MUNICIPALITIES THAT ARE SUBJECT TO CG SUPERVISION
(in percent)

| | FONCOMUN | Canon Minero | Canon/Sobrecanon Petrolero |
|---|---|---|---|
| **Rest of Peru** | **61** | **61** | **34** |
| Not Poor | 75 | 75 | 34 |
| Poor | 27 | 29 | 16 |
| Extreme Poor | 52 | 42 | 58 |
| Urban | 32 | 31 | 21 |
| Rural | 67 | 65 | 55 |
| Small | 67 | 67 | 0 |
| Medium | 30 | 28 | 31 |
| Large | 58 | 50 | 51 |
| More accessible | 78 | 79 | 23 |
| Less accessible | 26 | 19 | 46 |
| Nonprovincial capital | 62 | 61 | 30 |
| Provincial capital | 58 | 56 | 65 |
| *No. Observations* | *100* | *73* | *33* |

*Source:* Instituto Apoyo (2002).

## TABLE 4.6: LEAKAGES IN FONCOMUN AND CANON MINERO
(in percent)

| | FONCOMUN | Canon Minero |
|---|---|---|
| LIMA | 1.52 | 7.12 |
| Urban | 0.15 | 5.88 |
| Rural | 3.66 | 8.90 |
| *No. of Observations* | *18.0* | *17.0* |
| REST OF PERU | 0.45 | 0.70 |
| Less Poor | 0.00 | 0.00 |
| Poor | 1.11 | 0.03 |
| More Poor | 1.02 | 2.47 |
| Urban | 0.00 | 0.00 |
| Rural | 0.89 | 1.13 |
| Small | 1.56 | 2.76 |
| Medium | 0.35 | 0.06 |
| Large | 0.00 | 0.00 |
| More Accessible | 0.39 | 0.40 |
| Less Accessible | 0.65 | 1.38 |
| Nonprovincial capital | 0.83 | 1.10 |
| Provincial capital | 0.00 | 0.00 |
| *No. of Observations* | *96* | *64* |

*Source:* Instituto Apoyo (2002).

Important shortcomings surround the lack of evidence available to determine how much of the transfers of FONCOMUN, *Canon Minero,* and *Canon Petrolero* actually go toward current expenditures. In 2001, FONCOMUN law required a ceiling of 30 percent devoted to current expenditure (100 percent devoted to capital expenditure and milk products in the cases of *canon minero* and VDL transfers). In 2002, FONCOMUN restriction was eliminated, and the GOP allowed each municipality to decide how best to combine its resources. Survey findings show that the percentage assigned to current expenditure from FONCOMUN resources varies between 27 and 41 percent, but such evidence is inconclusive because a significant number of respondents (more than half in the case of the *canons*) did not know how the transfers were used. Other respondents accounted for more than 100 percent of the transfer, and yet about another one third of respondents could account for only less than 70 percent of *canon minero/petrolero* funds (in implicit violation of the law) (Table 4.7). However, these findings show an important shortcoming in transfer mechanisms—that is, the readiness of municipalities for having any idea about the exact use of funds and complying with required current expenditure/capital ratios.

*Recommendation:*
  ▨  If current expenditure/capital ratios are to be respected, present procedures for their auditing and accountability should be upgraded; otherwise, due to the lack of the GOP's enforcement capacity, the present ratios should be eliminated and it should be left to municipalities to decide how best to allocate their own resources.

*Leakages in the Vaso de Leche Program*
The *Vaso de Leche* program is the only one of the four main transfers to municipalities that can be traced from the top of the chain to the bottom. It targets as direct beneficiaries children aged 6 or younger, and pregnant and nursing mothers. However, the law under which the program operates also allows for *leftover resources* to be used for children aged 7 to 13, the elderly, and those suffering from tuberculosis. The transfer criteria from the CG to the municipality are based on per capita poverty formulas. At the municipal level, the local government is required, via special committees set up for the purpose, to use 100 percent of the funds for milk products, which must be overwhelmingly produced nationally. These committees are nearly ubiquitous, with 98 percent of the urban municipalities and 95 percent of the rural municipalities having them, according to the survey. The products should be purchased through competitive bidding, which is supposed to help ensure employment of the lowest-price criterion. However, the study found that while bidding was predominant, 19 percent of the products purchased were done through other mechanisms, and some excessively high prices were also found.

Despite its name, the *Vaso de Leche* program in fact includes milk, milk products, or milk substitutes, and other products such as oatmeal, quinua, and other grains. This flexibility in the program produces the unfortunate effect of reducing both the protein and calcium intake of the

| TABLE 4.7: FRACTION OF TRANSFERS USED FOR CURRENT EXPENDITURE | | | | |
|---|---|---|---|---|
| | **Unrestrictive Definition[a]** | | **Restrictive Definition[b]** | |
| | **Percent** | **No. of Observations** | **Percent** | **No. of Observations** |
| FONCOMUN | 41 | 61 | 27 | 61 |
| Canon/Sobre Canon Petrolero | 35 | 16 | 29 | 16 |
| Canon minero | 8 | 45 | 0 | 45 |

a. Employee payrolls (white and blue collar), pensions, road maintenance, sanitation, other current expenditures.
b. Employee payrolls (white and blue collar), pensions, other current expenditures
*Source:* Instituto Apoyo (2002).

beneficiaries, since milk and milk products contain the highest levels of these nutrients compared to grains. The fieldwork determined that only 15 percent of all municipalities distribute milk alone, with the vast majority "diluting" the milk with the distribution of cereal, a combination of milk and cereal, or distributing cereal only. Once these products are purchased, they are transferred to the next level down the chain; that is, to the local committees or clubs comprised of mothers, which are neighborhood or village-based volunteer groups. These local groups then distribute the "milk" on some sort of regular cycle (daily, weekly, monthly, bimonthly) depending on local circumstances, presumably based on the legal criteria mentioned above, and on locally determined criteria for need. Within the recipient household, presumably the "milk" is then fed to the children and mothers for whom it was designated. As we shall see, much of the above is more theoretical than real, as the fieldwork for this research determined.

Leakages in the VDL program occur at many levels, but measurement of these leakages is an extremely complex task. Perhaps the major complexity emerges from the law itself. According to the law, the foods can be distributed to beneficiaries in prepared form. This could mean, for example, mixing of powered milk into a cereal or other cooked product. It would be virtually impossible for any study to then measure with exactitude how a given amount of milk input arrives in the stomach of the beneficiary. But, more important, from a practical point of view, distribution committees often cannot reasonably prepare the food, since the beneficiaries are preschool children whose parents cannot transport them on a daily basis to a central distribution point. Consider the mother who is nursing two preschoolers, and whose partner works outside the home. She cannot reasonably be expected to visit a central kitchen each day to feed her children.

In addition, and more important according to our findings, the overhead costs of preparing the food, including distance, time, materials, and spoilage for unconsumed food, deter many committees from attempting to follow the law. As a result, 60 percent of the committees in the sample do not prepare the food, and distribute it unprepared. For the purposes of the study, this is a plus, since it allows us to more precisely measure the distribution, since we can more easily count cans of milk, pounds of cereal, and so forth. However, it brings an additional challenge in that many of these products are marketed in units that are not easily divisible. For example, if a household is entitled to 1.5 cans of milk based on the number of children, the committee could not reasonably be expected to open a can and divide it and pour the remainder into a glass for another beneficiary family. The result is that individual families will receive more or less than their exact ration of milk and other products, a factor which makes calculation of leakages at the household level even more complex.

The problem of food distribution and preparation is exacerbated by the widespread absence of knowledge of the municipalities about the program, (and committees), and no effective training of the mothers. The survey found, for example, that only 20 percent of the municipalities in the rest of the country (and 43 percent in Lima) were familiar with the CG criteria for allocation of the "milk." At the level of the committee, barely 2 percent in the rest of the country outside of Lima have knowledge of the allocation criteria used by municipalities (and 5 percent in Lima). And, at the level of the mothers, only 27 percent reported having received training in the preparation of the "milk," and 26 percent reported receiving training on its proper allocation within the household. Most disturbing was that the level of training *declined* as poverty levels increased (Table 4.8), so that training was lowest where it was needed the most.

### "Milk" Leakage Stage 1: Central Government to Municipality

A first and very small leakage occurs during the transfer of the CG to the municipalities.[12] It represents on average 0.06 percent in Lima and 0.02 percent in the rest of Peru, which could be determined by rounding and recording errors. Thus, at the top level, where one often assumes the greatest level of corruption (and therefore the greatest leakage), the leakage is virtually nonexistent. This is a

---

12. See Annex D for the exact formulas applied to estimate each leakage.

### TABLE 4.8: BENEFICIARY HOUSEHOLDS THAT RECEIVED TRAINING/INFORMATION (in percent)

| Urban/Rural | Yes | No |
|---|---|---|
| Urban | 34 | 66 |
| Rural | 20 | 80 |
| **Stratum** | | |
| Least poor | 36 | 64 |
| Poor | 20 | 80 |
| Most poor | 19 | 81 |
| **Accessible** | | |
| Less accessible | 15 | 85 |
| More accessible | 32 | 68 |

*Source:* Instituto Apoyo (2002).

major accomplishment for the SIAF system. However, considerable volatility remains in VDL transfers outside Lima. Volatility in 2001, calculated as the standard deviation of monthly percent changes of VDL transfers, was virtually zero in Lima, but in the rest of Peru it averaged 11.6 percent, with a high of 15.4 percent in the poorest areas. Hence, the less accessible the area, the more volatility there was at that level. Despite this volatility, none of the municipalities in Lima and only 1.7 percent in the rest of the country were unsure of the amount of VDL funds they would be receiving. However, in the municipalities of Lima, 40 percent have no knowledge of the date on which they will receive their VDL transfer, while 31 percent of the districts outside of Lima claim the same problem, a surprising result given the relative simplicity of the transfer mechanism at the CG level. In Lima, 21 percent of the municipalities suffered delays of seven or more days, while in the rest of Peru this level reached 25 percent. Furthermore, given that these delays imply that children and other beneficiaries are kept expecting food, a major basic need, the large percentage of municipalities the arrival time variation of which is more than seven days is quite serious (Table 4.9).

### "Milk" Leakage Stage 2: Unaccounted for Conversion of Transfer to Products

Once the transfer reaches the municipality, a second leakage occurs when the funds are converted to products to be given to the local committees. From the municipal level onward, the transfer of resources for the VDL program becomes in-kind transfers such that no subsequent stages of execution receive money, but rather receive the transfer in-kind. Our fieldwork team was instructed to get prices and quantities of VDL product purchases made by the municipality in December 2001 and to verify this information through signed contracts, purchase orders, or receipts. The quantities were in most cases obtained from the municipality's distribution roster (*padrón municipal*), which includes the amounts allocated and distributed to each mother's committee within the municipality's jurisdiction. This leak is defined as the percentage of the amount transferred to the municipality from the CG for the month of December 2001 that is unaccounted for by the total expenses of the municipality for that month (in terms of products purchased for the VDL program).

Leakages found at this stage were also quite small. In Lima, they appear to have amounted to 3.03 percent of the totals transfer, whereas in the rest of Peru they amounted to 0.63 percent. We say "appear" because of the larger urban districts surveyed in the province of Lima—which all have populations exceeding 200,000—most refused to provide our team with any price information or price-related documentation. This refusal supports the qualitative information collected by our team at later stages of the execution path that suggest there is considerable misuse of funds at the municipal level within these districts. We were, however, able to document a number of worst-case offenders. We found one municipality in Lima in which this leak was 18 percent of the transfers, and another where it was 15 percent, again keeping in mind that most larger municipalities refused

| TABLE 4.9: VASO DE LECHE TRANSFER SCHEDULE | | | | |
|---|---|---|---|---|
| | **Municipalities with No Knowledge of Next Arrival Date (%)** | **Arrival Time Variations** | | |
| **Days** | | **1–2 Days** | **2–7 Days** | **7+** |
| **Lima** | **40** | **26** | **53** | **21** |
| Urban | 42 | 27 | 55 | 18 |
| Rural | 37 | 25 | 50 | 25 |
| *No. Observations* | 20 | 20 | 20 | 20 |
| **Rest of Peru** | **31** | **43** | **32** | **25** |
| Not poor | 25 | 0 | 29 | 71 |
| Poor | 45 | 49 | 51 | 0 |
| Extreme poor | 35 | 45 | 23 | 33 |
| Urban | 57 | 0 | 43 | 57 |
| Rural | 26 | 47 | 31 | 21 |
| Small | 29 | 58 | 0 | 42 |
| Medium | 30 | 47 | 43 | 10 |
| Large | 42 | 17 | 64 | 18 |
| More accessible | 67 | 45 | 33 | 22 |
| Less accessible | 13 | 41 | 32 | 27 |
| Nonprovincial Capital | 31 | 42 | 32 | 26 |
| Provincial capital | 32 | 48 | 33 | 19 |
| *No. Observations* | *100* | NA | NA | NA |

to cooperate with us on obtaining this data. In the rest of Peru, we found 4 municipalities out of 76 surveyed in which the leakage at this stage was over 10 percent, with one reaching 15.5 percent. Thus, although the national averages are low, these isolated cases in which the leakage at this point exceeds 10 percent of the total transfer amount are serious.

Without taking into consideration any of the leakages at subsequent transfer stages, the beneficiaries—mainly children aged 0 to 6—already are receiving less than 90 cents on the dollar. About one tenth of all municipalities surveyed were found to have leaks higher than 5 percent. In addition, one would have to consider the possibility of overpricing reflected in two facts: the high price variability found among districts for purchasing similar products, and the premium paid when comparing those prices to leading retail supermarket prices, even when adjusting them for quality and transportation costs. For instance, (a) the price of generic *Enriquecido Lácteo*, a milk substitute, distributed in 32 out of 100 districts visited, varies from NS/.1 to NA/15 per kilogram; and (b) in some cases, the registered price of cans of milk outside Lima was twice as high as in a Lima supermarket!

Private gains are not the only possible reason for these leaks. One explanation for the leakages at this stage could be a diversion of VDL funds to cover the program's operating expenses (personnel, bookkeeping materials, transportation costs, and warehousing costs). Although prohibited by law, this kind of leak is not a result of a corrupt act. Indeed, the leakages at this stage are found more significant in small, rural, and less-accessible districts. In many cases, it was found that in small rural districts, there are severe budget and personnel limitations that make the operating costs of the program prohibitive. Moreover, given the large and organized network of VDL mothers representing a unified and powerful faction of the constituency that exerts considerable pressure on the mayor, it is no surprise that there may exist many cases in which the municipality supplements the CG transfer with municipal resources. Indeed, we find that often, leak 2 turns out to be negative, that is, the municipality spent more in December 2001 than the amount allocated to it by the MEF.

| TABLE 4.10: LEAKAGE STAGE 3: MUNICIPALITY TO LOCAL COMMITTEES (in percent) | |
|---|---|
| | **Leak 3** |
| **Lima** | 10.06 |
| Urban | 6.83 |
| Rural | 18.77 |
| *No. of Observations* | 37.0 |
| **Rest of Peru** | 2.59 |
| Less poor | 0.54 |
| Poor | 5.67 |
| More poor | 5.22 |
| Urban | 1.26 |
| Rural | 4.52 |
| Small | 2.83 |
| Medium | 4.23 |
| Large | 2.25 |
| More accessible | 2.31 |
| Less accessible | 3.70 |
| Nonprovincial capital | 3.10 |
| Provincial capital | 1.97 |
| *No. of Observations* | *320* |

Source: Instituto Apoyo (2002).

## "Milk" Leakage Stage 3: Transfer from the Municipality to the Local Committees

Leakages found from the municipality to local committees were more significant. In Lima, they averaged over 10 percent, but were far lower—only 2.6 percent—in the rest of Peru (Table 4.10). However, it is obvious from the results that the poorer, more remote areas have far higher leakages at this level. Every municipality has an allocation formula based almost entirely on the size of the target population that each VDL committee services. Thus, criteria of *relative* poverty do *not* play a role here; only the number of poor counts. The roster of beneficiaries is centralized at the municipal level and provides detailed information on the quantities distributed to each committee within the district. This roster was used to randomly select four VDL committees in order to verify the veracity of the municipal distribution roster. This information was compared to the quantities that the committees visited declared to have received from the municipality in the same period for every product distributed. This allowed us to calculate leakages associated with the transfer from the municipality to each of four randomly selected committees. This leak was defined as the percentage of the amount registered as delivered by the municipality, not accounted for by the VDL committee, but estimated using municipal and committee data computed at the committee level.

A clearer picture of the magnitude of the leakage problem that occurs in the transfer from local government to civil society is obtained by examining the worst offenders. The national averages do indeed hide very important information (Table 4.11). There are 27 districts/VDL committee pairs (about a tenth of the total surveyed) with leakages in excess of 20 percent, and 10 pairs that exceed 40 percent. In the case of such top-ranked worst offenders, the beneficiaries receive 36 cents of every dollar without taking into consideration all the leakages in prior segments of the chain of distribution![13] A possible explanation of these very high leakages is that in some cases municipalities

---

13. It is important to note that this leakage was computed at the committee level with 320 observations. A lot of committees had zero leakage, which was much lower than that of the worst offenders. A complete list of worst offenders is found in Instituto Apoyo (2002).

| TABLE 4.11: WORST OFFENDERS, LEAKAGE STAGE 3 (in percent) | |
| --- | --- |
| Rank | Leak 3 |
| **Lima** | |
| 1 | 84.5 |
| 2 | 57.4 |
| 3 | 48.2 |
| 4 | 44.8 |
| 5 | 43.8 |
| 6 | 24.4 |
| **Rest of Peru** | |
| 1 | 63.7 |
| 2 | 55.1 |
| 3 | 53.2 |
| 4 | 49.6 |
| 5 | 47.4 |
| 6 | 47.2 |
| 7 | 41.7 |
| 8 | 40.1 |
| 9 | 40.0 |
| 10 | 40.0 |
| 11 | 38.9 |
| 12 | 34.8 |
| 13 | 34.0 |
| 14 | 34.0 |
| 15 | 31.8 |
| 16 | 29.4 |
| 17 | 28.6 |
| 18 | 27.8 |
| 19 | 27.2 |
| 20 | 26.7 |
| 21 | 25.4 |
| 22 | 24.3 |
| 23 | 23.5 |
| 24 | 23.0 |
| 25 | 22.6 |
| 26 | 22.3 |
| 27 | 20.7 |

Source: Instituto Apoyo (2002).

may make changes to the allocations to every committee, keeping one product already assigned for later distribution. Such an informal arrangement significantly diminishes the transparency of the program and should be prohibited.

## "Milk" Leakage Stage 4: Committee to Beneficiary/Household

A fourth leakage occurs between committees and beneficiaries. Estimation at this step became very difficult because when evaluating the situation inside the committee, we found that it is very difficult to quantify what happens to the products distributed to beneficiaries. This is because the committee representatives do not follow the criteria established by program regulations. Instead, they make decisions at their discretion as to how to proceed regarding the distribution of the product. In most cases, the committee representatives have been democratically elected and mostly rely on the approval of the population of their communities. So, our methodology originally contemplated the comparison of per-beneficiary rations at the household level with the total per-beneficiary rations at the committee level. This was complicated, however, due to the fact that multiple products get distributed to beneficiaries and the only way to aggregate them was to use a common measurable indicator. To further complicate matters, in the cases of distribution of "prepared" products, there was no way to gauge whether the servings-per-container directive was followed, and therefore there was no way to measure the amount of raw product a household was actually receiving. Therefore, we eliminated from the sample the cases in which the product was not distributed in raw form.

Estimation of this leakage was done by calculating the monetary values of each product (using municipal price figures) and adding them up. This allowed a comparison of the monetary value of the amount of all the products received by the VDL committee per beneficiary with the monetary value of the amount received by the individual households per beneficiary (excluding the committees that distribute prepared products). The first variable would be obtained from the quantities declared by the mothers' committee representative in the VDL committee survey (in the four committees surveyed in each municipality). The second variable would be obtained from the quantities declared by the beneficiaries' household representative in the beneficiary household survey (in the four households surveyed for each VDL committee). Although implementation of the proposed formula faced several operational problems, it provided very important insights into the distribution process to individual households. Some of the problems that made it impossible to quantify the rations received by the beneficiaries are due to the very large variation of types, units, and frequencies of the distribution and products—which makes the program less transparent and thus more difficult to evaluate and supervise—and to products distributed already prepared (approximately 40 percent of the committee cases). Although the municipality reported (in most cases) the number of rations that could be obtained by each package of product, the VDL committee did not necessarily follow the recommended recipe. Many committee representatives indicated that their objective is to try to service the largest possible number of recipients. Furthermore, the households receive a ration in a large variety of ways—as a cup, a glass, a handful, or just a ration. So, we standardized frequencies, units, and products, and eliminated all cases in which the products were distributed in prepared form by the committee or in committees with unclear target beneficiaries.

Leakage at this level is quite high. On average, over a quarter of the product is lost at this stage outside of the Lima area (for which we have no data, as shown in Table 4.12). Leaks are markedly more serious in urban districts (34 percent), in provincial capitals (40 percent), and in large districts (29 percent). To further understand the subtleties of the program, which made this leakage difficult to quantify, one must look at the law itself, which provides for an unnecessarily broad definition of its target beneficiaries. According to the law, indirect beneficiaries need not be exclusively young children, but may include children aged 7 to 13, the elderly, and others in need—but *only if there are enough resources left.* The result is that this open-ended definition allows such a broad interpretation of eligibility that leakages seem bound to occur, which causes confusion in the committees and in the population in general as to who are the intended beneficiaries. This problem is further complicated by the indivisibility of the formula chosen and the ad hoc decisions made at the discretion of committee representatives as to the criteria of distribution. These include number of household members, number of children, equal quantity for each household, or other criteria that the study was unable to identify, many of which alter the originally estimated quantities per beneficiary in each household of the same committee and municipality.

### "Milk" Leakage Stage 5: Within the Household (dilution of the ration)
A fifth leakage happens at the household level. This leakage was estimated using household-level data. As a final stage, the fieldwork team visited four households per committee in order to quantify

**Table 4.12: Leakage Stage 4: Vaso de Leche Program**
(at household level, in percent)

| | Leak 4 |
|---|---|
| **LIMA** | NA |
| Urban | NA |
| Rural | NA |
| *No. of Observations* | *NA* |
| **REST OF PERU** | 26.70 |
| Less poor | 26.67 |
| Poor | 19.21 |
| More poor | 32.91 |
| Urban | 34.53 |
| Rural | 25.01 |
| Small | 24.41 |
| Medium | 22.83 |
| Large | 29.63 |
| More accessible | 25.71 |
| Less accessible | 28.32 |
| Nonprovincial capital | 22.72 |
| Provincial capital | 40.31 |
| *No. of Observations* | *488* |

*Source:* Instituto Apoyo (2002).

the amounts of the in-kind VDL transfers that actually reach the intended beneficiaries. Because of the complications concerning the "target population" mentioned in the previous section, the analysis is restricted to direct beneficiaries only: children aged 0 to 6, pregnant women, and breastfeeding mothers. The leak attributed to "beneficiary dilution" is defined at the household level as one minus the percentage of household members who consume VDL products who are official direct beneficiaries (Table 4.13).

Results make clear that, upon reaching the households, there is considerable dilution. On average, target beneficiaries receive only 41 percent of the ration that arrives at the household (not taking into account all the losses associated with earlier leakages). This dilution effect is possible because in most cases the beneficiaries do not receive their rations directly from the committee, but the children receive the rations filtered through their mothers (and in some cases the fathers), who pick up the total rations allocated to her or his household for later distribution. Consistent with evidence in studies of other nutritional assistance programs worldwide, the official distribution criteria are very difficult if not impossible to enforce at this level. In most cases, it is impossible to exclude non-targeted members of the household. Furthermore, in about 60 percent of the committees visited, the products are distributed in nonprepared forms. As noted above, this is understandable, since the transaction costs of receiving daily prepared rations could be too high, but nonprepared forms frequently result in mixing the nutrition ration with the families' overall food intake. In these cases, considerable variation appears in their final use.

In sum, the PETS survey reveals that targeted beneficiaries get on average 29 cents of each dollar initially transferred by the Central Government. The survey indicates, surprisingly, that the leak is much higher at the bottom (VDL committees and households leaks 4 and 5) levels than at the top (CG and municipalities, leaks 1–3) levels of the ladder. This not only demonstrates significant improvements in the official financial management of resources by the SIAF/MEF, but also challenges the predominant view that local private organizations are more accountable in manag-

## TABLE 4.13: LEAKAGE STAGE 5
### (at beneficiary household level)

| | Leak 5 |
|---|---|
| **LIMA** | NA |
| Urban | NA |
| Rural | NA |
| *No. Observations* | NA |
| **REST OF PERU** | **58.89%** |
| Not poor | 59.93% |
| Poor | 57.89% |
| Extreme poor | 59.15% |
| Urban | 59.26% |
| Rural | 58.70% |
| Small | 59.01% |
| Medium | 61.46% |
| Large | 57.90% |
| More accessible | 60.75% |
| Less accessible | 56.11% |
| Nonprovincial capital | 58.69% |
| Provincial capital | 59.32% |
| *No. Observations* | *985* |

*Source:* Instituto Apoyo (2002).

ing resources than official organizations (Figure 4.2). Transfers appear also compounded by the generalized lack of audit controls, poor transparency, and volatility. Finally, leaks clearly affect the poorest, urban, and provincial municipalities more than others, but their level appears similar among districts of different sizes and distances to the province (Table 4.14).

Recommendations based on the PETS findings can be grouped into two areas: those referring to accountability of transfers and municipal management issues, and those referring to the VDL.

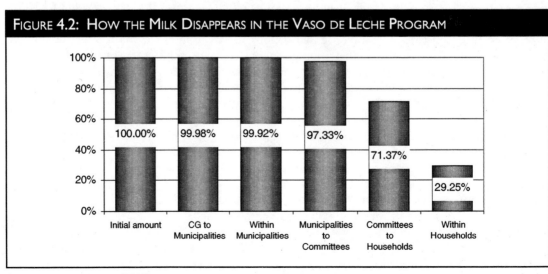

## FIGURE 4.2: HOW THE MILK DISAPPEARS IN THE VASO DE LECHE PROGRAM

*Source:* Instituto Apoyo (2002).

**TABLE 4.14: VASO DE LECHE LEAKAGES**
(in percent)

| | Leak 1 | Leak 2 | Leak 3 | Leak 4 | Leak 5 | Combined |
|---|---|---|---|---|---|---|
| **Lima** | **0.06** | **3.03** | **10.06** | NA | NA | NA |
| Urban | 0.03 | 2.73 | 6.83 | NA | NA | NA |
| Rural | 0.11 | 3.58 | 18.77 | NA | NA | NA |
| *No. Observations* | *20* | *14* | *37* | *NA* | *NA* | *NA* |
| **Rest of Peru** | **0.02** | **0.63** | **2.59** | **26.70** | **58.89** | **70.84** |
| Not poor | 0.00 | 0.13 | 0.54 | 26.67 | 59.93 | 70.81 |
| Poor | 0.00 | 1.36 | 5.67 | 19.21 | 57.89 | 68.34 |
| Extreme poor | 0.12 | 1.30 | 5.22 | 32.91 | 59.15 | 74.39 |
| Urban | 0.00 | 0.42 | 1.26 | 34.53 | 59.26 | 73.77 |
| Rural | 0.05 | 0.85 | 4.52 | 25.01 | 58.70 | 70.70 |
| Small | 0.11 | 0.05 | 2.83 | 24.41 | 59.01 | 69.94 |
| Medium | 0.00 | 0.59 | 4.23 | 22.83 | 61.46 | 71.68 |
| Large | 0.00 | 0.84 | 2.25 | 29.63 | 57.90 | 71.29 |
| Accessible | 0.00 | 0.54 | 2.31 | 25.71 | 60.75 | 71.67 |
| Remote | 0.09 | 0.82 | 3.70 | 28.32 | 56.11 | 69.98 |
| Municipal | 0.04 | 0.87 | 3.10 | 22.72 | 58.69 | 69.35 |
| Provincial capital | 0.00 | 0.21 | 1.97 | 40.31 | 59.32 | 76.25 |
| *No. Observations* | *95* | *76* | *320* | *488* | *985* | *N/A* |

*Source:* Instituto Apoyo (2002).

**Recommendations:**

■ *On financial management accountability.* There is a need to (a) increase the transparency of transfers to municipalities through a monthly report by the SIAF, accompanied by thorough dissemination of their redistribution criteria; (b) build local capacity to manage them; (c) reduce their volatility, particularly among poorest recipient municipalities; (d) as a priority, upgrade auditing procedures of municipal governments not only by the Comptroller's Office, but also by means of internal audits of the municipal administrations themselves; and (e) overhaul the registration of the *canon/sobrecanon petrolero.*

■ *On the Vaso de Leche program.* A major lesson of the VDL experience is that a poorly designed social program, with a presumed high degree of participation of community leaders grouped in a committee, can be inefficient—voluntarily or involuntarily—and unaccountable to both its agents (constituent beneficiaries) and its principal (municipal authorities), thereby missing the original purpose or intention of the program. Further, although there is a need to recognize that the dilution effect allows households to reach indirect beneficiaries, and thus overcome rigidities in CG guidelines, the nutritional impact on direct beneficiaries is, however, diminished.

Suggested priority actions are:

*In the short term,* focus on amending regulations to enforce accountability of the municipalities and committees: (a) review VDL regulations, particularly regarding products to be distributed and the form of distribution, to make the list of selected milk derivatives shorter and more homogeneous, and thus raise chances of improving the nutritional impact of the program; (b) establish a proper registry of VDL beneficiaries, if possible supported by the SIAF; (c) undertake information campaigns and training sessions for VDL committees and individual beneficiaries to raise their awareness of new information available and the rules; (d) undertake surprise audits of worst offenders (municipalities and committees) in the near term, to eliminate major deviations; and (e) establish a policy of no budget increase in real terms of the VDL annual budget. Implementation of these actions requires a significant overhaul of the system, and should be accompanied by the design of a new comprehensive framework for food supplementary programs in Peru (discussed below).

In the *medium term*, given its failures and defective design, the question is, should the VDL program be transformed into a cash-transfer program? The answer could be yes. Mexico's *Programa de Educación, Salud y Alimentación* (PROGRESA), which successfully moved its food supplement program to an integrated and better-targeted model of social assistance, is a good example. However, since this proposal goes beyond the sole issue of leakages and also addresses targeting, we will return to this subject at the end of the chapter (Box 4.1).

## Enhancing Targeting of Social Programs

The GOP's policy of programs targeted to the poor has been fundamental in the poverty-reduction achievements of recent years.[14] As a percent of GDP, total social spending increased from 3.6 percent in 1993 to 6.9 percent in 2002. Commitment by Peruvian officials to a set of comprehensive safety net programs has been reflected in a multiplicity of safety net programs specializing in development and relief components. The *development component* provides permanent access to improving human capital accumulation of the poor in the form of health, education, and basic infrastructure services. The *relief component* provides a consumption floor for the poor through two types of mechanisms: temporary employment or cash programs, like *A Trabajar*—Urban and Rural—and direct transfer programs usually in the form of food or basic services.

As a point of departure, the new authorities are not increasing resources to existing safety net programs, but rather are attempting to improve the efficiency in their administration and targeting. The budget share assigned to *extreme*-poverty-reduction programs as a percentage of GDP increased from 1.1 percent in 1994 to about 1.7 percent in 1998, and has remained constant until 2002. This level is considered adequate for existing needs (World Bank 2000). Striking the right balance between the two types of safety nets, however, requires further assessment of their performance. Indeed, until the creation of *A Trabajar* in 2002, direct transfers dominated the landscape of relief and safety net programs in Peru. At present, however, such a temporary employment program competes for scarce resources. Furthermore, ongoing unification of rural infrastructure projects under one administration—*Proyecto Nacional de Mantenimiento de Cuencas Hidrográficas y Conservación de Suelos* (National Project for the Water Management of Sheds, PRONAMACHCS), *Instituto Nacional de Dessarollo* (National Institute for Development, INADE)—is an initial step to reduce administrative costs and overlaps and gaps in coverage.[15] This leaves targeting as a major issue requiring efficiency improvements. Fortunately, Peru already has a well-developed poverty map.[16]

Broad geographic regional targeting remains regressive in Peru. While adequate targeting of social programs is a critical component to optimize scarce resources and deal with prevailing heterogeneity in program resources *to reach the poor,* it is also needed to offset broad mistargeting in regional public expenditure. Simple correlation coefficients between per capita spending by department (and by CTAR) and poverty and extreme-poverty rates produce negative results, whereas they should have been positive, had they been allocated to the department with the highest poverty rates.

---

14. This section partly draws from the work done by Diaz (2001).

15. Gaps in other infrastructure projects, like the National Office for Popular Cooperation (COOPOP), *Caminos Rurales,* and others from the Ministry of the Presidency, remain.

16. Peru has an excellent FGT2-based poverty measure, which takes into account both the number of people below the poverty line, and the severity of their poverty (the gap between their incomes and the poverty line). The MEF map combined information from the 1993 census with a household survey conducted by the National Institute for Statistics and Information (INEI) in 2000 to "impute" the consumption of households in the census. This, in turn, was aggregated up to the district level, and combined with information on the poverty line to estimate the number of households in each district below the poverty line (the headcount index), the poverty gap, and the FGT2 (square poverty gap).

## TABLE 4.15: CORRELATION EXPENDITURE AND POVERTY BY DEPARTMENT

|  | Correlation | Expected Direction if Poverty Targeted |
| --- | --- | --- |
| Dept. Expenditure Per Capita to Poverty, by Definition |  |  |
| Poverty rate | −0.522 | Positive |
| Extreme poverty rate | −0.463 | Positive |
| MEF poverty ranking | 0.265 | Negative |
| INEI poverty ranking | 0.458 | Negative |
| INEI extreme poverty ranking | 0.507 | Negative |
| CTAR Expenditure Per Capita to Poverty, by Definition |  |  |
| Poverty rate | −0.207 | Positive |
| Extreme poverty rate | −0.130 | Positive |
| MEF poverty ranking | 0.397 | Negative |
| INEI poverty ranking | 0.202 | Negative |
| INEI extreme poverty ranking | 0.135 | Negative |

Source: World Bank staff estimates.

Furthermore, correlation coefficients are positive between per capita spending by department and poverty rankings, ordered from poorest to richest, whereas they should be negative (Table 4.15). Such severe misallocation is explained by the rigid components of the budget, particularly in current expenditure.

### Recommendation:

■ Broad geographic targeting of public expenditure should carefully be reviewed, particularly in light of the incoming process or regional decentralization, giving greatest weight to departments with the poorest populations.

Access by the poor to social programs is in general progressive, but important differences remain among individual programs. Poor household access to social programs is high. A total of 82 percent of poor households have access to social programs (84 percent for those in extreme poverty), and 69 percent have access to at least two social programs (73 percent for extreme poverty) (Table 4.16). Poor rural households have proportionally been more adequately reached by social programs than urban households. Among major social programs, FONCODES (excluding *A Trabajar PESP-Urbano*), joined by *Caminos Rurales,* has the best record in progressive spending, adequately reaching poor beneficiaries (Figure 4.3). The *Programa Nacional de Asistencia Alimentaria* (National Food Assistance Program, PRONAA), however, has lost ground and joined the VDL program in the mild progressivity of its programs. No doubt, their targeting has worsened. Finally, the program *Trabajar Urbano* has started on the wrong foot. Its overall progressivity, particularly at the first four poorest levels of the population (which goes beyond the population in extreme poverty), reveals that self-targeting of the most needy beneficiaries is failing. The reason for this is to be found in the seemingly too-high wage rate being paid to attract workers from only the poorest deciles.[17]

---

17. The current wage rate appears even more generous in the *A Trabajar Rural* program, but this is less alarming because of the sharing income mechanism often employed de facto by the rural communities, with members being assigned to a project but actually sharing the working time, or the monthly wage, or both. Therefore, the wage rate does not work as a tool for individual self-targeting the way it does in urban areas. Notice that the success of the program is not measured only by the share of beneficiaries found in the poorest income quintiles, but also by the income gains received as a result of participating in the program and the coverage of the program with a proportion of unemployed poor having access to the program, and the efficiency with which it operates (ratio of wages to administrative costs and material inputs) (Schady 2002).

## TABLE 4.16: HOUSEHOLD ACCESS TO SOCIAL PROGRAMS BY POVERTY LEVEL, 2000

| Geographic Area | Total | Extreme Poverty | Nonextreme Poverty | Total Poverty | Non-Poor |
|---|---|---|---|---|---|
| TOTAL | 5,632,815 | 1,161,588 | 845,355 | 2,006,943 | 3,625,872 |
| Beneficiaries | 59.1% | 83.9% | 79.7% | 82.1% | 46.4% |
| One program | 13.4% | 10.5% | 17.2% | 13.3% | 13.5% |
| More than one | 45.7% | 73.4% | 62.5% | 68.8% | 32.9% |
| Nonbeneficiaries | 40.9% | 16.1% | 20.3% | 17.9% | 53.6% |
| URBAN | 3,607,764 | 266,243 | 607,221 | 873,464 | 2,734,300 |
| Beneficiaries | 50.8% | 81.9% | 78.8% | 79.7% | 41.6% |
| One program | 14.9% | 19.1% | 19.1% | 19.1% | 13.5% |
| More than one | 36.0% | 62.7% | 59.7% | 60.6% | 28.1% |
| Nonbeneficiaries | 49.2% | 18.1% | 21.2% | 20.3% | 58.4% |
| RURAL | 2,025,051 | 895,345 | 238,134 | 1,133,478 | 891,573 |
| Beneficiaries | 73.9% | 84.5% | 81.9% | 84.0% | 61.1% |
| One program | 10.8% | 7.9% | 12.3% | 8.9% | 13.3% |
| More than one | 63.1% | 76.6% | 69.6% | 75.1% | 47.8% |
| Nonbeneficiaries | 26.1% | 15.5% | 18.1% | 16.0% | 38.9% |

*Source:* Diaz (2001).

### Recommendation:

■ *A Trabajar* should offer a wage rate that makes it attractive only to poor households. To do this, the GOP should undertake an evaluation study, including assessment of household targeting outcomes, and lower the wage should the study indicate poor urban targeting outcomes. A similar study should be done regarding *A Trabajar Rural*. The study should be widely disseminated to support the GOP's decisions.

The main social sector programs also reflect a mixed picture in terms of the progressivity/regressivity of their resources allocated nationwide. On one hand, health expenditure appears with

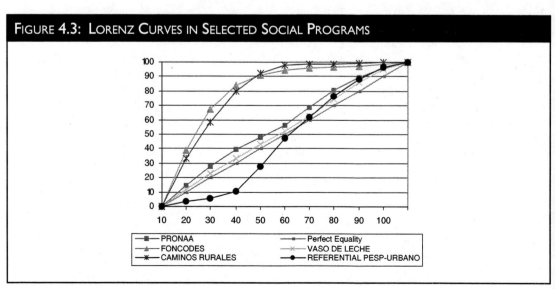

## FIGURE 4.3: LORENZ CURVES IN SELECTED SOCIAL PROGRAMS

*Source:* Diaz (2001).

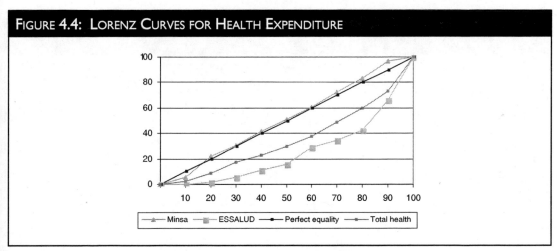

FIGURE 4.4: LORENZ CURVES FOR HEALTH EXPENDITURE

*Source:* Diaz (2001).

significant *regressivity,* much exceeded by ESSALUD, the services of which clearly focus on the population located in the non-poor deciles, but offset by Ministry of Health (MINSA) programs, which show mild progressivity thanks to a few local service delivery programs that clearly target most needy beneficiaries (Figure 4.4). On the other hand, education expenditure shows some degree of progressivity, certainly reflecting a similar feature in primary education, barely offset by the mild regressivity of expenditure in secondary education (Figure 4.5).

In general, safety net programs reach less than 40 percent of their intended extreme poverty beneficiaries. This is the case of the VDL and *Comedores Populares* programs (Table 4.17). *Desayuno Escolar* and School Text and Materials, however, are the exceptions, with an acceptable 51 percent and 44 percent of their beneficiaries, respectively, belonging to the three poorest deciles. *Seguro Escolar* (School Health Insurance) ranks relatively better among health programs, whereas *Planificación Familiar* (Family Planning) is found among the worst-targeted programs. This ranking also broadly corresponds to the level of access—measured by the ratio of beneficiaries to the total population—that these programs have, with *Comedores Populares* and *Planificación Familiar* having the lowest targeting scores (Figure 4.6).

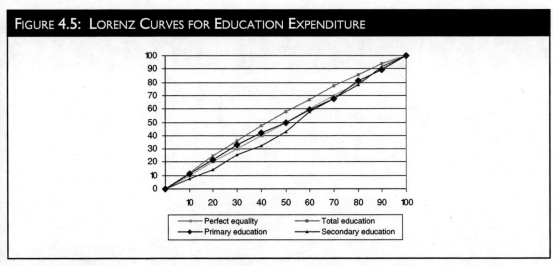

FIGURE 4.5: LORENZ CURVES FOR EDUCATION EXPENDITURE

*Source:* Diaz (2001).

## TABLE 4.17: TARGETING BY FOOD ASSISTANCE, HEALTH, AND EDUCATION PROGRAMS, 2000

| Social Program | No. of Beneficiaries | Total (%) | Extreme Poverty (%) | Nonextreme Poverty (%) | Total Poverty (%) | Non-Poor (%) |
|---|---|---|---|---|---|---|
| **Food Assistance** | | | | | | |
| Desayuno Escolar | 2,972,859 | 100 | 51.1 | 18.7 | 69.8 | 30.2 |
| Vaso de Leche | 2,283,919 | 100 | 40.1 | 24.1 | 64.2 | 35.8 |
| Comedor Popular | 746,134 | 100 | 40.2 | 14.5 | 54.7 | 45.3 |
| **Health** | | | | | | |
| Regulating child growth | 1,729,899 | 100 | 33.7 | 18.4 | 52.1 | 47.9 |
| School health insurance | 1,157,912 | 100 | 36.8 | 20.6 | 57.4 | 42.6 |
| Family planning | 870,942 | 100 | 22.1 | 24.8 | 46.8 | 53.2 |
| **Education** | | | | | | |
| School text and materials | 2,970,567 | 100 | 44.4 | 19.7 | 64.1 | 35.9 |

*Source:* Diaz (2001).

### Recommendations:

▨ In the *short term,* application of a common poverty-targeting methodology and criteria—based on the Foster, Greer, and Thorbecke 2 (FGT2) poverty map updated every three years—in all social programs should be made more explicit, transparent, and focused on populations that are extremely poor, and should be accompanied by complementary training, information campaigns, community mobilization, or nutrition education.

▨ Programs with substantial mistargeting should be redesigned, merged, or closed. To regularly evaluate this, benchmarks in terms of the share of expenditure reaching extreme-poor beneficiaries (the lowest 4 quintiles) should be established explicitly for at least the 10 main social programs, and progress toward meeting such benchmarks should also be monitored on an annual basis, with SIAF and INEI support. If their evaluation indicates that programs overlap or do not meet their objectives, their immediate restructuring will be necessary.

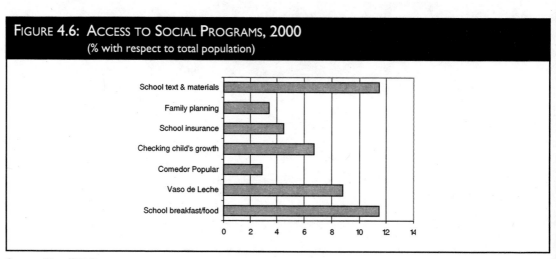

## FIGURE 4.6: ACCESS TO SOCIAL PROGRAMS, 2000
### (% with respect to total population)

*Source:* Diaz (2001).

---

**BOX 4.1: MEXICO: INTEGRATING SOCIAL PROGRAMS FOR IMPROVED EFFICIENCY— THE CASE OF PROGRESA**

In 1996, the Mexican government designed and successfully implemented the *Programa de Educación, Salud y Alimentación* (PROGRESA), a single and integrated social assistance intervention replacing a series of disparate food subsidies, and education, health, and other social programs. PROGRESA's unified approach provides immediate financial transfers to the rural poor, while at the same time promoting investment in children's human capital (future earnings) through increased schooling and improved health and nutrition status. The program provides cash transfers to selected poor rural families, selected with household surveys updated every three years, conditional on keeping children in school and providing them with basic preventive health care and nutrition. A key feature of the program is the provision of the cash transfer to registered mothers, a mechanism designed to ensure that the money is well invested in children and as an incentive to empower women in rural communities. In 2001, the program covered 3.2 million rural families (well over half of the rural poor), at a cost of 2.3 percent of the government's social expenditures, or 0.2 percent of GDP. The program is highly efficient, with administrative costs of about 4 percent; therefore, over 95 percent of its expenditure is transferred as cash directly to poor households.

Six years later, an independent evaluation confirmed PROGRESA's impressive results: (a) an increase of about 1 percent in the primary enrollment rates for girls, and an increase of 8 percent for girls and 5 percent for boys in the secondary enrollment rates; (b) an increase of about 10 percent in children's educational achievement, which would represent an increase of 8 percent in their future earnings; (c) an increase of 8 percent in prenatal care in the first trimester of pregnancy; and (d) a decrease of 12 percent in the incidence of disease among children under 5, and a decrease in the probability of malnutrition among children aged 12 months to 36 months.

---

Some of them, like VDL, already showing significant leakages and not meeting nutritional objectives, require immediate major restructuring.

- In the *medium term*, a comprehensive restructuring of the main social programs dealing with extreme poverty is necessary, perhaps following the example of PROGRESA (Box 4.1) in Mexico. Given very limited fiscal resources, budget rigidities, and low levels of efficiency for a substantial amount of resources already devoted to extreme poverty programs, this seems a rather urgent task. The restructuring of social programs in Peru should aim at several goals: (a) improving the quality of service delivery; (b) expanding the coverage of social programs, particularly among the most vulnerable rural groups; and (c) generating fiscal savings that could be used to increase coverage of the most effective programs at the local level.[18]
- Restructuring Peru's feeding programs into a unified intervention along the lines of PROGRESA (or, more ambitiously, folding other programs into this unified structure) is a very viable option that Peru might consider. This offers a broad coverage of the poor under a single program structure, with proper targeting and very powerful positive impacts on poor families. Rough calculations based on PROGRESA's costs per beneficiary ($80 per year) indicate that to cover the *entire* rural poor population of Peru (4.5 million people) with a similar unified intervention (primary education, basic preventive health, and food supplement) would entail a *maximum* cost of $360 million—or NS/1,200 million (0.6 percent of GDP). Interestingly, this amount represents about a third of total budget expenditure devoted to extreme-poverty programs, just over three times the current cost of the VDL program, or the combined sum of the VDL, *Comedores Populares, Desayunos Escolares*, and *Seguro Materno-Infantil* programs. Obviously, if the selected target population were the extreme poor, the cost would be considerably lower.

---

18. A recent study found that the educational impact of *Desayunos Escolares* in terms of rate of attendance, rate of repetition, and drop-out rates is small, but not negligible: about 10 percent in attendance, between a 1 and 3 percent drop in repetition, and a 0.3 to 1.6 percent reduction in drop-out rate.

# V

# ADDRESSING THE PROMISES AND RISKS OF DECENTRALIZATION

*In the past decade, Peru made considerable progress toward redefining the role of the State, but the reform process remains unfinished. In the early-to-mid-1990s, the size and scope of the public sector was reduced to more manageable proportions; the nature of government shifted from ownership of productive firms and excessive intervention to market regulation and provision of social services; and many State enterprises were privatized or closed. However, in the mid-to-late-1990s, the State reform process lost steam and some key tasks of State reform were not even initiated. Instead, authoritarian tendencies and open hostility to any democratization or deepening of State modernization gained the upper hand. Not surprisingly, public service delivery, governance, and corruption indicators deteriorated toward the end of the decade. Prominent among the reforms that were set aside by the authoritarian leadership were decentralization of the State and public administration, restructuring of the civil service, implementation of progovernance and anticorruption policies, and the design of sound mining fiscal and environment policy agendas. These pending reforms are the subjects of the next four chapters.*

*This chapter is devoted to the issue of decentralization. Its point of departure is the fact that, in Peru, there is a consensus among both the political leadership and civil society about the need to decentralize political power and the management of public resources. It points out both the promising potentialities and the serious risks entailed in the decision to decentralize, drawing on the lessons learned from other Latin American experiences with decentralization. It concludes with an examination of the issues raised by the decentralization of education and health as key social services. The main message of the chapter is that the Peruvian resolve to decentralize has both promises and risks. If appropriately executed decentralization can increase both the efficiency of the delivery of government services and the responsiveness of government to the needs of citizens. However, decentralization also poses formidable risks to fiscal discipline, and thereby to macroeconomic stability, in the form of recurring central government deficits, an overexpanded public sector, and the inability to use fiscal policy to adjust to economic shocks.*

## The Decision to Decentralize: Promises and Risks

Following almost a decade-long centralized authoritarianism, Peru is a relative latecomer to decentralization in Latin America. The decision to decentralize initially was motivated more by the rejection of the political and social consequences of centralization than in an explicit message as to the purposes, content, and goals of decentralization. A number of recent decisions by the new Administration are evidence that there is a growing consciousness about the scope of, and the potential advantages and serious risks entailed in, the decision to decentralize. In the meantime, the decision to decentralize has been taking shape in a number of initiatives, such as:

- The passage of a framework Law for State Modernization and the introduction of a framework Law for Decentralization in January 2002;
- The decision to hold regional elections next November;
- The recent creation of the Public Management Secretariat at the Presidency of the Council of Ministers, charged with formulating a strategy for both CG modernization and State decentralization;
- The Ministry of Economy and Finance's (MEF's) decision to implement regional and participatory budgeting;
- The Executive decision to create Regional Coordination Councils, integrating Transitory Councils of Regional Administration with social sector ministries representatives;
- The legal acknowledgment by the Legislature of the departmental *Mesas de Concertación* (Dialogue Roundtables) as consultative bodies of the regional governments; and
- The passage in late June 2002, of the Law to Lay the Bases of Decentralization.

The dominant force behind decentralization is political. The current government's decision to decentralize is part of a broader, positive trend toward democracy in the LAC region (Burki, Perry, and Dillinger 1999). However, there is no single regional paradigm for decentralization, and experiences vary greatly (Box 5.1). In the particular case of Peru, the decentralization process is seen by the political leadership as an integral component of State reform, and there is a basic convergence of views between Congress and the Administration. In the view of one of its leading congressional proponents, the process aims at devolving power to the regions and the local citizenry, promoting autonomous and sustainable regional development, fostering citizen participation in public affairs and citizen control of elected officials, and improving efficiency and efficacy of the local public administration. For its part, the Executive branch's view emphasizes seven principles: efficiency in service provision, macroeconomic stability, gradualism, heterogeneity, equity, participation of civil society, and political independence.

The decision to decentralize contains big promises and risks. If appropriately carried out, decentralization can, indeed, increase both the efficiency of the delivery of government services and the responsiveness of government to citizen needs. This is because devolving resource-allocation decisions to locally elected leaders can improve the match between the mix of services produced by the public sector and the preferences of the local population. Local officials have better knowledge of local conditions and are more accessible to their constituents. This gives them both the means and the incentive to be responsive. Decentralization may also improve public-resource management since, through sheer proximity, local officials can be held more accountable for their performance. Where the population is mobile and citizens can "vote with their feet," decentralization may also result in local governments competing with each other better to satisfy the wishes of citizens. Decentralization may, however, pose serious risks in the political sphere, in the area of service provision, and for macroeconomic stability. The risks in the political sphere have to do with the possibility that the local administration can be captured by local power elites and be put to the service of special interests. The risks in the area of public service provision have to do with the possibility that, because of the small size of some communities and hence insufficient scale in service

## BOX 5.1: LESSONS FROM DECENTRALIZATION EXPERIENCES IN LATIN AMERICA

**There is no single paradigm for decentralization in LAC.** Decentralization experiences in LAC are highly varied in their political, functional, and fiscal dimension, be it for multitier countries (Argentina, Brazil, Colombia, Mexico, and Venezuela) or single-tier countries (Bolivia, Chile, and Guatemala) (Table SA.46). At the *political* level, some countries introduced elected authorities at the regional or municipal level; others did not. At the *functional* level, some countries were explicit in reallocating functions at the level of regional governments; others did it at the level of municipal authorities, and others did not do it explicitly, but in an incremental way. At the *fiscal* level, increased revenue sharing or earmarked transfers accompanied new functions of states or municipalities (Table SA.47).

**Why decentralize? In theory, three main reasons have been argued in LAC: (a) to promote territorial deconcentration of productive activities and generate employment; (b) to increase efficiency in the delivery of public service; and (c) to raise local participation in the generation of fiscal revenue.** For the most part, however, outcomes in LAC have been disappointing (CEPAL 2001).

- The reduction of territorial concentration of productive activities does not appear positively correlated with decentralization processes. Two highly decentralized countries, Argentina and Brazil, showed higher territorial disparities after decentralization than before. In Colombia, territorial disparities increased as decentralization advanced. Chile, a country with a low level of decentralization, is the exception, with regional disparities decreasing only temporarily as a result of decentralization.
- On the expected increased efficiency in service delivery, the experience is mixed. Decentralization appears to decrease efficiency in education and primary health services in seven LAC countries: Argentina, Bolivia, Brazil, Chile, Colombia, Mexico, and Nicaragua (CEPAL 1998). Exceptions in education are Colombia at improving the allocation of resources, and Chile and Nicaragua, due to the increased participation of parents in school financing and management. In Bolivia and Colombia, however, the cost per student increased and quality decreased following decentralization. Exceptions in health are Argentina and Colombia, and this is explained by the existence of enhanced demand–subsidy mechanisms that have also slightly reduced the acceleration in sector spending levels that usually accompanies the decentralization of health services.
- On the expected increased participation of local government in generating additional fiscal revenue, LAC empirical evidence has been disappointing. It shows, rather, a persistent trend in local expenditure to increase faster than local revenue as decentralization proceeds. Being mostly based on increased transfers from the center, decentralization tends to increase the size of the total government sector (Burki, Perry, and Dillinger 1999). Such widening subnational deficits not only had increased national expenditure, but threatened macroeconomic stability in the short term, and aggravated the sustainability of subnational debt in the medium term, thus adding new pressures to already fragile fiscal stances. This was the case in Argentina, Bolivia, Brazil, Chile, and Mexico.[1]

**Where does the greatest risk lie?** The Latin American experience clearly shows that it lies in the potential that decentralization harbors for fiscal instability. Brazil's 1988 Constitution, for example, required a major increase in federal tax sharing by the subnational governments, without providing for any devolution of federal spending responsibilities. This threatened to provoke recurrent deficits at the federal level. Colombia decentralized both revenues and expenditures, but ended up maintaining and even increasing CG spending on education and health several years after those functions were transferred to the subnational governments. Mexico substantially increased transfers to municipalities without a reciprocal reduction of spending at the federal level. As a result, Colombia and Mexico have been forced to maintain preexisting levels of spending while funding and expanding volume of intergovernmental transfers. This has contributed to significant CG deficits. Attempts to eliminate such deficits by raising taxes may lead to overexpansion of the public sector. Brazil's mismatch between revenues and expenditures, for example, was ultimately resolved not by reducing CG expenditures, but by increasing federal taxes. Finally, decentralization can reduce a country's ability to respond to adverse economic shocks. Governments in Brazil and Colombia, for instance, which must share nearly half of their tax revenues with subnational governments, find it difficult to raise taxes sufficiently to compensate for revenue shortfalls.

---

1. An important caveat is that following cross-section analysis for several decentralized countries, the steady state level of subnational borrowing does not appear associated with higher CG spending or deficits. However, when subnational borrowing increases, the CG seems to have to spend and borrow more in the subsequent periods, which points to an intertemporal macroeconomic management problem that not many countries, certainly none in LAC, have adequately prevented (Burki, Perry, and Dillinger 1999).

provision, or due to institutional weakness of the local governments, the services rendered may turn out to be of lesser quality or more inefficiently provided.

The macroeconomic risks are especially troublesome. They may take the form of recurring CG deficits, an overexpanded public sector, or the inability to use fiscal policy to adjust to economic shocks. First, CG deficits can worsen if subnational governments are unable to reduce expenditures or increase revenues to finance the cost of assuming new responsibilities. Second, governments may find themselves decentralizing both revenues and expenditures, but being unable to reduce existing levels of CG spending in those functions that have been decentralized. Third, decentralization can hamper a government's ability to respond to economic shocks if it reduces central control over aggregate public sector revenues and expenditures. This is generally the case in countries with high budget rigidity, like Peru. In addition, subnational government prodebt policies and indebtedness behavior can also undermine overall fiscal discipline. Subnational governments may end up borrowing excessively in the expectation that the CG will bail them out.

In the case of Peru, the decentralization challenge is compounded by several factors: a vulnerable fiscal stance, at both the aggregate and local level; multiple governance issues afflicting local governments; and the incredible institutional fragmentation in the social sectors in the delivery of services. A variety of vertical programs resulting from years of gradual "add-ons" respond to particular needs with little internal coordination, multiple and overlapping levels, and partial coverage through a variety of institutions. In the health and education sectors, the absence of a unified regulatory structure or regular evaluation and monitoring systems based on results compounds the problem of both quality control and the assurance of productivity.

## The Deconcentration of Central Government Spending and Transfers to the Municipalities: Intergovernmental Fiscal Relations

The current system of expenditure allocation to the regional and local levels rests on two pillars: deconcentrated spending by the CG and budget transfers to the municipalities. Peru has 25 states (called *departamentos,* or departments). Unlike most countries in Latin America, however, in Peru there are no intermediate-level governments, because the *departamentos* are not administrative entities but merely geographical divisions of the national territory toward which the population has historical and cultural attachments. In contrast, the local level of government is fully established. There are two types of municipalities: the provincial municipalities and the districts. Sizewise, the relationship between the two types of municipalities is hierarchical in that each provincial municipality consists of a (variable) number of districts. Provincial municipalities are hence bigger than the districts nested by them. In the absence of an intermediate level of government, the CG executes its department-level spending through the deconcentrated organs known as Transitory Councils of Regional Administration (CTARs) and through the regional directorates of the CG ministries. The other pillar in the current system of expenditure allocation is based on the transfer of resources from the CG to the provincial and district governments.

Region-level expenditures by the CG are a significant share of the national budget. More than half of the CG budget is executed through the deconcentrated organs at the department level. This amounts to a substantial 6.0 percent of GDP (Table 5.1). The role of CTARs is quite important because they execute over 42 percent of the total expenditure outside Lima (Table 5.2). The relative significance of region-level spending (outside Lima) is much higher if we exclude debt service and pensions from the budget: in 2002, regional allocations accounted for about half of CG current expenditure and 81 percent of CG capital investments (Table SA.39), which means that approximately 4 out of every 5 dollars of public investment in Peru is executed outside Lima. The downside of this is that regional and CTAR expenditures are particularly punished when, as a result of an economic downturn, there are cuts in public investment outlays. For instance, in 2000, while total expenditure outside Lima was reduced to 88.4 percent of its budgeted amount, the executed budget for capital investment was much less reduced—to 67.5 percent of its respective approved

| TABLE 5.1:  BUDGETED EXPENDITURE FOR THE PUBLIC SECTOR FOR FY02 | |
|---|---|
| **Sector** | **Percent of GDP** |
| National government | 11.4 |
| Regional level | 6.0 |
| Local government | 1.8 |
| Public entities | 1.2 |
| Firms (Fonate) | 6.7 |
| TOTAL | 27.5 |
| US$ millions | 15,686 |

*Source:* MEF.

amount (Table 5.3). Hence, if budget autonomy is conceded to future regional governments, the CG would have much less capacity to invest nationwide, and much less freedom (due to budget rigidity) to reduce expenditure when needed.

Region-level expenditure in health and education represents a very high share of total regional budgets. In 2002, education and health expenditures represented 50 percent and 27 percent, respectively, of total budgeted regional expenditure by the CG (Tables SA.39 and SA.40). These ratios show that a future decentralization of both sectors could be tantamount to a de facto transfer to the future regional governments of up to about three fourths of current region-level budget resources. In fact, if we deduct current expenditure from total regional expenditure, education and health budgeted capital outlays jointly represent a very high 95 percent of the total regional budget devoted to investment (Tables SA.39 and SA.40). This share underscores the fact that the burden of budget cuts over regional investment is borne by these two sectors.

Transfers to local governments are small when compared to region-level expenditures, but constitute the bulk of municipal government revenues. The transfers to local governments amount to 15.8 percent of the CG budget (1.8 percent of GDP). However, in the case of municipalities other than Lima, they are the most important source of revenue. As a percentage of total municipal revenue, CG transfers represented 48 percent in 2001, and a high 73 percent when Lima is excluded (Figure 5.1). CG transfers are concentrated in the four most important ones: *Fondo de Compensación Municipal* (FONCOMUN), *Vaso de Leche* (VDL), petroleum canon, and mining canon, with 67, 17, 7, and 4 percent, respectively, of total budgeted transfers in 2002 (Figure 5.2). When it comes to the locally based sources of revenue, the main revenue items are fees (*tasas*)—which in 2002 represented 45 percent; taxes—which barely represented a low 25 percent; fines, with 11 percent; public service fees, with 6 percent; and real estate income—which barely represented a low 5 percent (Table SA.40). No doubt, these sources of revenue will have to be strengthened through a municipal tax reform if municipal autonomy is to be strengthened.

Local government finance is additionally constrained by severe liability problems. The municipal debt is not a serious threat for macroeconomic stability, but that is not an indication that the problem is not serious or generally significant, and even explosive, for some municipalities that face severe liquidity and solvency problems. Municipal debt explains a third of the corresponding national registered debt—short-term current liabilities—but this varies widely by municipality. Solvency at the local level can be a serious concern. A World Bank survey of nine municipalities[2] shows that four of them had a current liability/revenue ratio above 1, meaning that they require more than a one-year income to cover their present debts (in some cases, the ratio is above 3). Debts have been growing at a rapid annual rate (13 percent on average during 1997–2000) and

---

2. The sample consisted of three provincial municipalities (Arequipa, Lima, and Trujillo) and six district municipalities (Characato, Jacobo Hunter, La Esperanza, La Victoria, Poroto, and San Juan del Lurigancho).

TABLE 5.2: EXPENDITURE COEFFICIENTS BY CTAR, 2001

| Departments | No. of EUs | Population | Expenditure (Mlns of NS) | Budgeted Expenditure by CTAR (i) | Actual Expenditure by CTAR (ii) | Difference (i)–(ii) | Coefficient of Actual CTAR Expd. by Pop. | CTAR Expd./Dept Expenditure (%) |
|---|---|---|---|---|---|---|---|---|
| Amazonas | 12 | 420,606 | 215.3 | 89.6 | 100.4 | (10.8) | 23.9 | 46.6 |
| Ancash | 27 | 1,092,662 | 591.4 | 277.5 | 284.1 | (6.6) | 26.0 | 48.0 |
| Apurimac | 14 | 455,637 | 299.0 | 125.5 | 129.2 | (3.7) | 28.3 | 43.2 |
| Arequipa | 19 | 1,067,469 | 913.8 | 261.7 | 275.0 | (13.3) | 25.8 | 30.1 |
| Ayacucho | 20 | 541,427 | 465.1 | 163.5 | 187.3 | (23.8) | 34.6 | 40.3 |
| Cajamarca | 20 | 1,480,690 | 547.0 | 250.9 | 264.9 | (13.9) | 17.9 | 48.4 |
| Callao | 13 | 774,604 | 547.0 | 133.4 | 71.0 | 62.5 | 9.2 | 13.0 |
| Cusco | 17 | 1,194,275 | 716.6 | 264.0 | 275.2 | (11.3) | 23.0 | 38.4 |
| Huancavelica | 11 | 435,596 | 215.6 | 105.3 | 108.0 | (2.7) | 24.8 | 50.1 |
| Huánuco | 12 | 800,543 | 322.0 | 148.1 | 151.2 | (3.1) | 18.9 | 47.0 |
| Ica | 14 | 676,249 | 464.6 | 181.6 | 184.6 | (3.0) | 27.3 | 39.7 |
| Junín | 20 | 1,232,343 | 660.2 | 278.9 | 286.0 | (7.1) | 23.2 | 43.3 |
| La Libertad | 32 | 1,483,681 | 741.1 | 277.6 | 287.3 | (9.7) | 19.4 | 38.8 |
| Lambayeque | 14 | 1,110,129 | 553.5 | 173.6 | 185.2 | (11.6) | 16.7 | 33.5 |
| Lima | 194 | 7,617,193 | 23,747.2 | 9.3 | 9.5 | (0.2) | 0.1 | 0.0 |
| Loreto | 18 | 894,307 | 511.7 | 314.8 | 331.4 | (16.6) | 37.1 | 64.8 |
| Madre de Dios | 8 | 96,703 | 80.0 | 42.5 | 42.7 | (0.2) | 44.2 | 53.4 |
| Moquegua | 6 | 153,383 | 147.7 | 61.5 | 66.9 | (5.4) | 43.6 | 45.3 |
| Pasco | 8 | 259,137 | 172.7 | 72.1 | 75.4 | (3.4) | 29.1 | 43.7 |
| Piura | 16 | 1,611,573 | 788.1 | 350.8 | 376.6 | (25.8) | 23.4 | 47.8 |
| Puno | 33 | 1,247,494 | 651.2 | 304.9 | 323.7 | (18.7) | 25.9 | 49.7 |
| San Martín | 23 | 746,202 | 445.1 | 177.3 | 176.1 | 1.2 | 23.6 | 39.6 |
| Tacna | 9 | 286,539 | 222.2 | 93.0 | 99.8 | (6.8) | 34.8 | 44.9 |
| Tumbes | 8 | 197,605 | 179.1 | 81.1 | 90.3 | (9.2) | 45.7 | 50.4 |
| Ucayali | 16 | 450,693 | 225.6 | 149.0 | 158.5 | (9.5) | 35.2 | 70.2 |
| Total | 584 | 26,326,740 | 34,422.69 | 4,387.54 | 4,540.29 | (152.75) | 17.2 | 13.2 |
| w/o Lima | 390 | 18,709,547 | 10,675.50 | 4,378.25 | 4,530.79 | (152.54) | 24.2 | 42.4 |

Source: MEF.

TABLE 5.3: EXPENDITURE BY DEPARTMENT, 2000 (MLN NS)

| Departments | Total Expenditures | | | Capital Investments | | | Goods and Services | | |
|---|---|---|---|---|---|---|---|---|---|
| | Budgeted | Executed | Executed/Budgeted | Budgeted | Executed | Executed/Budgeted | Budgeted | Executed | Executed/Budgeted |
| Amazonas | 338.5 | 206.2 | 60.9 | 154.9 | 77.9 | 50.3 | 70.8 | 26.8 | 37.9 |
| Ancash | 641.2 | 598.2 | 93.3 | 203.5 | 158.6 | 77.9 | 70.4 | 57.5 | 81.8 |
| Apurimac | 367.2 | 292.7 | 79.7 | 182.4 | 124.1 | 68.0 | 48.1 | 35.8 | 74.3 |
| Arequipa | 917.0 | 881.2 | 96.1 | 300.9 | 231.8 | 77.0 | 104.4 | 93.7 | 89.8 |
| Ayacucho | 553.0 | 481.3 | 87.0 | 259.9 | 208.8 | 80.3 | 70.0 | 56.5 | 80.7 |
| Cajamarca | 640.7 | 494.3 | 77.2 | 263.1 | 116.3 | 44.2 | 61.9 | 52.7 | 85.2 |
| Callao | 448.1 | 407.7 | 91.0 | 148.5 | 106.5 | 71.7 | 108.8 | 122.8 | 112.8 |
| Cusco | 819.1 | 698.0 | 85.2 | 342.3 | 237.8 | 69.5 | 116.6 | 103.7 | 88.9 |
| Huancavelica | 278.1 | 240.5 | 86.5 | 109.9 | 87.3 | 79.4 | 41.0 | 34.8 | 84.9 |
| Huanuco | 346.2 | 313.2 | 90.4 | 117.6 | 79.3 | 67.4 | 42.9 | 38.9 | 90.7 |
| Ica | 471.7 | 453.0 | 96.0 | 68.2 | 57.0 | 83.6 | 55.2 | 47.4 | 86.0 |
| Junín | 695.8 | 613.3 | 88.2 | 162.9 | 83.0 | 51.0 | 86.6 | 72.8 | 84.0 |
| La Libertad | 782.2 | 766.6 | 98.0 | 193.8 | 138.2 | 71.3 | 79.7 | 69.4 | 87.0 |
| Lambayeque | 583.5 | 574.3 | 98.4 | 136.1 | 96.5 | 70.9 | 65.9 | 59.7 | 90.6 |
| Lima | 24,297.4 | 17,889.1 | 73.6 | 2,427.6 | 1,718.0 | 70.8 | 4,341.8 | 2,759.7 | 63.6 |
| Loreto | 538.4 | 505.9 | 94.0 | 175.0 | 125.8 | 71.9 | 80.2 | 69.9 | 87.2 |
| Madre de Dios | 106.2 | 79.4 | 74.8 | 59.6 | 33.2 | 55.6 | 14.4 | 12.0 | 83.2 |
| Moquegua | 138.9 | 124.2 | 89.4 | 48.3 | 31.1 | 64.3 | 16.5 | 13.7 | 83.1 |
| Pasco | 206.8 | 165.7 | 80.1 | 42.7 | 20.0 | 46.7 | 27.3 | 24.5 | 89.6 |
| Piura | 919.3 | 781.8 | 85.0 | 379.7 | 221.5 | 58.3 | 92.0 | 97.2 | 105.7 |
| Puno | 815.8 | 731.6 | 89.7 | 323.0 | 244.3 | 75.6 | 89.6 | 79.0 | 88.2 |
| San Martín | 469.6 | 408.2 | 86.9 | 206.8 | 141.5 | 68.4 | 52.1 | 45.3 | 87.0 |
| Tacna | 253.4 | 231.6 | 91.4 | 74.9 | 63.7 | 85.0 | 33.4 | 33.7 | 101.1 |
| Tumbes | 195.9 | 152.4 | 77.8 | 69.1 | 38.2 | 55.2 | 19.3 | 15.9 | 82.3 |
| Ucayali | 260.4 | 219.0 | 84.1 | 81.2 | 46.8 | 57.7 | 47.2 | 39.2 | 83.2 |
| **Total** | **36,084.4** | **28,309.1** | **78.5** | **6,532.0** | **4,487.0** | **68.7** | **5,836.0** | **4,062.7** | **69.6** |
| w/o Lima | 11,787.0 | 10,420.0 | 88.4 | 4,104.5 | 2,768.9 | 67.5 | 1,494.2 | 1,303.0 | 87.2 |

Source: MEF.

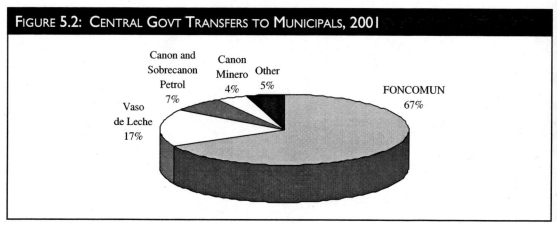

FIGURE 5.1: MUNICIPAL REVENUES, 2001
(excluding Lima)

Transfers
from central
government
73%

Own revenues
27%

*Source:* MEF.

FIGURE 5.2: CENTRAL GOVT TRANSFERS TO MUNICIPALS, 2001

Canon and
Sobrecanon
Petrol
7%

Canon
Minero
4%

Other
5%

FONCOMUN
67%

Vaso
de Leche
17%

*Source:* MEF.

the debt situation appears to be deteriorating faster in large provincial municipalities (Arequipa) and urban districts (La Victoria in Lima). Debt dynamics are explained essentially by two factors: arrears (*cuentas por pagar*) with suppliers and public utility companies (about 55 percent), and nonregistered pensions with former municipal employees (21 percent). The municipalities are also becoming increasingly illiquid as all but two had a current-revenue/current-expenditure ratio below 1, reflecting that their present current revenues are hardly enough to cover their present current expenses. The problem is becoming explosive, since contingent liabilities are threatening to materialize, mainly because of resolution of labor disputes, the amount of which is projected to grow 25 percent in the next few years (Fernandez 2002). Municipalities like Arequipa and La Victoria, in particular, are not going to be able to assume additional responsibilities under decentralization if they do not solve their debt problems. The Government of Peru (GOP) seems to have neither an adequate regulatory framework nor an appropriate institutional arrangement for assessing and controlling growth of municipal debt.

## The Emerging Legal Framework for Decentralization in Peru

Both the government of President Toledo and the Congressional leadership are committed to laying the political and legal bases for the decentralization process. As a result, in late January, the legislature approved the *Framework Law for the Modernization of State Management* (Law 27658). The Law is an effort to provide the legal base and principles for initiating the process of implementing modernization reforms. It promotes six objectives: (a) a service-provider state, (b) effective access for participation, (c) decentralization and deconcentration, (d) transparency, (e) a new civil service—well qualified and remunerated, and (f) fiscal balance. The Law focuses strongly on the need to redimension the State both in its role and in its size. The State is then perceived less as an actor than as a regulator of actions, while retaining basic human-need-attention functions in health and education. To accomplish this paradigm shift, the Law offers three principal tools: (a) fusion of State entities to reduce duplication; (b) introduction of Management Contracts (*Convenios de Gestion*) in conjunction with Multiyear Strategic Sector Plans (PESEM) in the context of the Multiyear Macroeconomic Framework (MMM) objectives and goals; and (c) pilot programs for modernization through the gradual introduction of *convenios*. The initial pilot programs will be carried out at the Ministry of Transportation and the Presidency of the Council of Ministers.

The Law also defines three lines of action for the CG in terms of the need to (a) clarify functions and structures, (b) introduce a system of management contracts based on results, and (c) modernize administrative systems. As a framework document, the new Law was a step in the right direction. It provided objectives to aim at while remaining flexible. It also opened the door for sector ministries to pursue different avenues of action. By virtue of this Law, the newly created Public Management Secretariat at the *Presidencia del Consejo de Ministros* (Premier's Office, PCM) was rightly given a leading role.

In late June 2002, the Peruvian Congress overwhelmingly approved the *Ley de Bases de Decentralization*. The Law defines the purpose, principles and objectives, regulations, and transition measures guiding the decentralization process. It distinguishes two sets of principles on which it is based: general principles and specific principles for fiscal decentralization.

- The general principles include (a) decentralization is a permanent State policy, of a mandatory character for all the constitutional branches of the State, the autonomous constitutional entities, and the government as a whole; (b) the process of decentralization is defined as dynamic and requires a constant monitoring and evaluation of its ends and objectives; (c) it is irreversible; (d) it is democratic in that it promotes equality of opportunity; (e) it is integral in that it encompasses the whole State in the national territory and calls for carrying out the process in a gradual manner, so that a sequence of steps must be followed; and (f) the process is premised on the principle of subsidiarity, implying that functions and competencies must be assigned to the level of government closest to the citizens that can efficiently perform a given public service.
- The specific principles are next: (a) a clear definition of competencies, (b) transparency and predictability, (c) fiscal neutrality to avoid any transfers of resources that are not accompanied by a transfer of responsibilities, (d) public sector indebtedness is an exclusive competency of the national government, and regional and local governments can contract debt only with CG guarantee, (e) fiscal responsibility is to be materialized in fiscal rules for the subnational governments, which must include rules on indebtedness and limits on annual expenditures of the subnational governments so that the decentralization process can be sustainable. Prominent among the objectives defined by the Law are (a) institutionalization of the regional and local governments; (b) economic development and competitiveness of the different circumscriptions, according to their productive potential; (c) modernization and simplification of administrative systems and processes; and (d) citizen participation in all forms of organization and social control. The Law creates intermediate-level governments—the regional governments—and mandates that regional government officials be directly elected.
- The normative foundations are also considered. On this account, the Law defines (a) three types of competencies: exclusive competencies, shared competencies, and delegatory competencies; (b) a Constitutional Tribunal is called for resolving conflicts of jurisdiction; (c) the creation of a Regional Compensation Fund (FONCOR), which will finance regional investment projects to be executed by the regional governments; and (d) new sources of revenue in the national budget and as a percentage of privatization proceeds.

■ The Law also creates the National Council for Decentralization to lead the decentralization process. The Council will be composed of representatives from the CG, the regional governments, the provincial municipalities, and the district-level municipalities. The Council's main responsibility is to oversee the process of transfer of competencies from the CG to the subnational governments, and manage an Intergovernmental Decentralization Fund (FIDE) to promote cofinancing of projects by subnational governments. The transfer process will be carried out gradually over several years, in successive stages that initially affect sectors like transport and housing, and at a later stage education and health. The Council will also discharge functions of coordination, technical support, and training for the subnational governments.

■ Finally, the Law includes transition measures of utmost importance, including the elimination of the Ministry of the Presidency and the CTARs by 31 December 2002.

This emerging legal framework will be completed with forthcoming laws. These include the Organic Law for the Executive Power, the Law on Regional Governments, the Law of Municipalities, the Law on Fiscal Decentralization, the Law to Create the Regional Compensation Fund, and the Law of Economic and Productive Decentralization.

## Entering a Decentralization Path

Peru's recent efforts toward modernization and decentralization offer the general principles that will guide the transition process, while complementary laws will apply them to specific components of such a process. Because decentralization is the result of political will and consensus—not simply of technical expertise—a broad and participatory dialogue (and patient persuasion), supported by the National Dialogue and the Concertation Roundtables, has taken place in the past eight months. Since decentralization should be demand-driven, the binding thread for the process must be the idea that its ultimate purpose is to increase the coverage and improve the quality of public services so that the citizenry assumes ownership of both the process and its results.

The latent risk that fiscal discipline may turn out to be a casualty of the decentralization process will continue to be high until a clear framework for intergovernmental public finances is finally enacted and enforced. The guiding criterion for such a framework must be the establishment of hard budget constraints for the expenditure and indebtedness decisions of subnational governments. The road ahead must then be carefully trodden if the appropriate framework for fiscal discipline of the subnational governments is to be attained. Some critical actions that will help secure that outcome seem to be in order.

The issues of substance relate to the rules of the game in the process of decentralization. Five issues deserve special consideration: (a) the degree of autonomy to be given to the subnational governments in their future provision of social services, (b) the kind and extent of expenditure responsibilities to be transferred to the subnational governments, (c) the rules and institutional mechanisms for transferring resources from the CG to the subnational governments, (d) the allocation of taxing powers to the subnational governments, and (e) the rules subnational governments must follow in contracting debt.

A higher degree of autonomy is desirable. The higher the autonomy subnational governments can enjoy, the higher the likelihood that the potential benefits of decentralization will be realized. Both the ability of the local governments to respond to the demands of the local population and the participation of the citizenry in local political life will be enhanced if a high degree of autonomy is allowed. However, for the decentralization not to be a travesty of local democracy, higher degrees of autonomy must be accompanied buy higher accountability on the part of subnational governments vis-à-vis the local population. But autonomy has its risks as well. Autonomous subnational governments may end up spending irresponsibly and accumulating unsustainable debts if they are not subject to stringent budget and indebtedness rules.

There are no hard and fast rules on the kind and extent of expenditure responsibilities to be assigned to subnational governments. The extent to which expenditure and service-provision responsibilities are to be transferred depends mainly on the institutional strength and administrative capability of regional and local governments. In this respect, two broad facts in the Peruvian situation are of compelling importance. First, regional governments are yet to be constituted after the November 2002 elections. There is no reason to expect that the soon-to-be-born regional governments will quickly become capable and efficient administrative apparatuses. Quite to the contrary, there is every reason to predict that the constitution of truly capable regional governments will take some time. Second, with the exception of a few provincial municipalities and even fewer district municipalities, local governments are weak. In light of these two facts, it stands to reason that the transfer of responsibilities must be gradual.

In designing the transfer of responsibilities, due account must be taken of the markedly different degrees of development of administrative capability in the subnational governments. In addition, in the Peruvian case, the difficulties of any transfer process are compounded by the sheer existence of the two levels of municipalities, the provincial municipalities, and the district municipalities. This implies that, unlike most countries, after the implementation of the regional government, Peru will have four levels of government rather than three. Most district municipalities are very small to assume responsibility for the more demanding public services, and can discharge only the relatively less complex tasks and, in any case, only those where economies of scale are not crucial. Assignment of responsibilities to the two levels of municipalities must be carefully designed, keeping in mind size and human-resource and administrative-capacity constraints at the two levels. Finally, the one mistake that should be avoided at all costs is the lack of clarity and precision in the distribution of functions between the CG, the regional governments, the provincial municipalities, and the district municipalities. Legal and institutional confusion about the distribution of functions is likely to lead either to situations of duplication and overlapping of effort, or to some public services being left unattended and underinvested.

The GOP intends to change the way decisions are made about the amount of resources transferred from the CG to the subnational governments. In the past, these transfers have been (a) tied to variable sources; (b) to a certain extent, subject to discretional decisions at the central level, sometimes under the guise of formulas that have not been very transparent; and (c) procyclical. It is expected that, in the new legal framework, both procedures that are more transparent and decision-making criteria, will be established. From the standpoint of transfer policy, the two key institutional pieces in the new framework are going to be the Compensation Funds and the FIDE.[3] Defining their long-term financing mechanisms and criteria for accessing their resources is a short-term priority. Both types of funds will follow explicit formulas in the calculation of the transfers to a given regional or local government. As is customary, these formulas will take into account the size of the population and income and poverty indicators. There is, however, an important difference between the two types of funds. Whereas transfers from the Compensation Funds will be applied in an unconditional manner, that is, regardless of the particular local government's fiscal and service-delivery performance, FIDE's transfers will be conditional on each subnational government's meeting predefined targets of performance in public service provision and on its adhering to explicit standards of fiscally disciplined performance.

There must be a close connection between the transfer of responsibilities and the transfer of resources. The double golden rule to be followed is that (a) the transfer of resources must be accompanied by the transfer of responsibilities, and (b) responsibilities must not be transferred unless an adequate level of resources to discharge them is available at the subnational level in most cases as a result of a combination of resource transfers from the CG and the subnational government's own tax revenue.

---

3. We showed the degree of progressivity of FONCOMUN and saw little reason to modify its redistribution criteria.

Subnational governments must be given powers of taxation within appropriate boundaries. It would be a monumental mistake were Peru to decide that the subnational governments are to rely only on the resource transfers from the CG. The experience of other countries teaches that an institutional scheme where local governments do not have the power to collect taxes weakens accountability at the local level; reduces incentives to pay any kind of taxes, including taxes to the national government; and weakens the CG's willingness and commitment to refrain from bailing out the subnational governments when and if they incur insurmountable financial difficulties stemming from lack of fiscal discipline. It is therefore fundamentally healthy that subnational governments have their own sources of tax revenue and make an effort of their own to optimize their tax revenue, taking into account both issues of incentives to entrepreneurial efforts and issues of redistributive justice, and the need for local public goods.

In this respect, the Law already defines a procedure by assigning to the Executive the sole responsibility for submitting regional tax proposals—the management of which will be undertaken by regional governments—to Congress. The menu of taxes that can be imposed on the populations of the subnational entities by their governments must be unambiguously defined by law, and any tax that is outside that menu will be illegal. The types of taxes that are appropriate at the subnational levels are a matter of considerable consensus in both the literature and practical experience. Real estate taxes and taxes on industry and commerce are the most common at the municipal level. Excise taxes on specific consumption goods such as tobacco products, liquor, and beer are the most frequent at the intermediate, regional level. Within the confines of the tax menu defined by national legislation, subnational governments must be given a fair degree of autonomy to define the bases and rates for their tax systems.

Subnational government indebtedness must be subject to stringent rules and procedures. There are good reasons to allow subnational governments to use debt as a source of finance. As a way of spending anticipating future income, the resort of subnational governments to debt makes as much sense as it does for any other economic agent. The issue then is not whether debt should be allowed. Rather, the issue is to which constraints must subnational government indebtedness be subject, to prevent these constraints from becoming a source of national instability and local ruin. A related issue is how to avoid the moral hazard that becomes rampant when and if subnational governments are given (implicit or explicit) assurance that they will be bailed out. Since neither the market nor the spontaneous workings of the political system enforces debt discipline, it is necessary to impose limits on subnational indebtedness. A positive initial step is that the Law already specifies that external debt is an exclusive competence of the national government and its amount must be consistent with the overall public sector debt ceilings. It also states that subnational governments can contract only new debt supported by a State guarantee. However, domestic and contingent—registered and unregistered—debts are not mentioned directly, and should be addressed in the upcoming reform of the Law of Fiscal Prudence and Transparency.

### Recommendations:

- ▣ There is an immediate agenda of urgent issues that must be addressed. The agenda includes issues of paramount importance such as designing alternatives for intergovernmental fiscal relations, hard budget and indebtedness constraints on subnational governments, the specific functions and competencies to be decentralized by sector (see Annex F), the characteristics and funding sources of the future Regional Compensation Fund, and any possible changes in the transfers scheme for municipalities. As the Law of Fiscal Prudence and Transparency gets revamped, adding a section on subnational fiscal responsibility would be a positive development (Chapter II).
- ▣ A critical goal of decentralization is to develop an increased local revenue-generating capacity, based on local governments' own tax systems. Measures to be taken may include (a) increasing the real estate tax in the short term and upgrading it with a new system (a territorial-based tax on property extension) in the medium term with the support of a

fiscal cadastre, initially piloted in a few municipalities; (b) transferring the proceeds of gasoline taxes to subnational governments; (c) abolishing obsolete taxes; and (d) promoting horizontal technical assistance on the basis of best-practice municipalities.

▨ The issue of local governments' already existing—domestic and external, registered and nonregistered—debt must be urgently tackled. A curative approach would include a full diagnosis of all municipalities and design of a transparent program for the restructuring of the existing debt. Its implementation would be another essential precondition for assuming new functions and administrative responsibilities. A preventive approach would establish prior conditions for contracting further debt and limits to its size.[4] Ditto for future regional governments.

▨ The building of institutional capacity both in the current local governments and in the future regional governments is critical for the success of decentralization, especially regarding the development of integrated financial management systems at the regional and local levels in advance of, and as a prior condition for, decisions about transfers of expenditure responsibilities. The resulting local and regional systems must be linked to the national SIAF to have consolidated accounts for all levels of government.

▨ The use of performance contracts has proved useful and should be promoted. Peru's experience with the National Fund for Financing Government Enterprise Activity (FONAFE) in developing management contracts with public enterprises is a success story for the LAC region (Annex E). The experience can be applied, under a pilot approach, to deconcentrated ministerial units and subnational governments. Special incentives can be given to such units and governments to entice them to enter into management contracts. FONAFE's success would provide important lessons and examples because, in the end, decentralization and reform place a premium on accountability. This is not simply probity, transparency, and internal efficiency in the use of resources. It is also an emphasis on results, performance, and social accountability. Success breeds success, and the demonstrative effect of carefully monitored successful pilot experiences can prove fruitful and critical in the public's support for the process.

## Decentralization in the Education Sector

Specialists have noted that public education in Perú remains among the most centralized in Latin America[5] (Box 5.2). During the decade of the 1990s, the effort to decentralize public education was limited to a series of "on-again, off-again" initiatives driven more by political interests than technical reasons (Ortiz de Zevallos and others 1999). These initiatives were also short-lived. Opposition of municipalities and labor unions, and the fear of the loss of free public education, doomed these efforts from the outset. As a result, few efforts had any major impact on either a deconcentration or decentralization of the educational system. Further, even as recent (2001) policy directives with strategic objectives have been formulated, there is little consensus as to the mechanisms or organizational units that should be the agents of the process.[6] What is not clear is whether the agent of decentralization should be the future regional governments, the existing Educational Service Units (*Unidades de Servicios Educativos*, USEs), the municipalities, or the schools, and what is the appropriate role of the community in the process. Worst of all, the

---

4. Two interesting examples of good subnational risk monitoring are Brazil and Colombia. In the former, complementary limits are established in the Brazilian Fiscal Responsibility Law. In the latter, rules are embedded in the Colombian "traffic light system" that links each subnational government's debt to its payment capacity and uses indicators as traffic lights to alert the CG about potentially excessive subnational debt (Ma 2002).

5. The next two sections partly draw from the mimeograph prepared by Richard Moore (2002).

6. These directives provide an ambitious set of measures and goals. Three objectives are noted: (a) quality basic education for all; (b) strengthening at the school level with increased autonomy, participation, and quality learning; and (c) dramatic improvements in the condition and qualifications of teachers (MED 2001).

---

**BOX 5.2: THE DECENTRALIZATION DRIVE IN EDUCATION IN LAC: SOME CASES**

In the case of **the state of Paraná in Brazil,** the decentralization effort has aimed at the municipalization of basic education. Recent efforts in **Ecuador** have focused on the extension of networks, both for pedagogical and administrative reasons and on a model of voluntary municipalization of education. That municipalization process is incipient and not subject to any evaluative criteria (Moore and Rosales 2001). In **rural Mexico,** parents have been authorized to certify teacher attendance under national jurisdiction, while transfers to state education boards have been extended since 1998. Municipalization combined with direct decisional control has been a successful model in **Nicaragua.** School autonomy in Nicaragua is based on three elements: fiscal transfers to schools based on both technical and equity criteria (formula based), parental control of fiscal resources through Parent Councils, and complete local authority over hiring and firing decisions. While the effort has been successful in the transfer of decisional control and in the encouragement of community and parent involvement in the educational process, educational quality has not been noticeably affected (Arcia and Belli 1999). In the **Dominican Republic,** recent reforms and training efforts aim at increasing the role of parent associations in monitoring teacher attendance, receiving the transfer of some funds for local operating costs, and exercising a more participatory role in local schools. In **Venezuela,** a current decentralization effort focuses on the transfer of management authority to the school level ("the school as the center of basic education") and introducing and certifying (vocational) educational training at the level of the workplace (*cada empresa una escuela*). In **Chile,** a variety of efforts have been attempted, including where parents have been given the option to select among publicly financed schools (Winkler and Moore 1996). In **El Salvador,** rural parents associations have been reinforced and have been empowered to enter into contracts to successfully manage schools. *Educación Comunitaria* (EDUCO) schools lie outside the purview of the Ministry of Education's regular school system. They are located in remote rural areas principally, and were/are intended as a means of extending coverage. The management of financial resources is the responsibility of community educational associations (ACEs) based on annual plans. The transfer of funds to the ACEs is based on these annual plans and these are received monthly as earmarked funds (salaries, operations). Personnel decisions are the responsibility of the ACE, but pay scales are Ministry responsibilities. The ACE has clear governance responsibilities, although the Ministry names the director. Pedagogical concerns and standards remain ministerial responsibilities. The evidence to date suggests that, as a means for increasing community participation and parental involvement, the model has been successful, but as a means for improving educational quality, there is no clear evidence that EDUCO has accomplished much. Finally, in **Guatemala,** four different models of decentralization have been pursued simultaneously: local management autonomy and control (PRONADE), limited decisional authority at the school level (*Juntas Escolares*), the decentralization of a competitive system of teacher recruitment and selection, and the deconcentration of finance and supervision to departmental governments.

---

institutional framework for the delivery and administration of educational services has become a sort of labyrinth of fragmented units.

The first element of this fragmentation stems from the creation of CTARs. They are directly responsible to the Ministry of the Presidency and charged with responsibilities over the bulk of the regional recurrent budget in both health and education. Under the current scheme, the Ministry of Education has little control over the allocation of resources within its own sector at the regional level. In addition, even at the central level, the confusion of authority between the Ministry of the Presidency and sector ministries remains.

The second element of this fragmentation is the myriad of institutions exercising administrative and/or decisional responsibility at the regional level. The result is a high degree of overlap and duplication of responsibilities and authority. The responsibility for providing educational services resides in Regional Directorates of Education (DREs), yet these entities depend fully on transfers from the CG. The DREs exercise their functions (normative, financial, regulatory, and supervisory) in a very partial manner and contingent upon the relationship of any individual Director with the Ministry of Education (MED). At the regional and subregional level, institutional fragmentation is even more pronounced due to the existence of a variety of institutions exercising some functions, yet the roles of which in the process of deconcentration or decentralization are unclear. No fewer than five organizational units play a role at this level: DREs, CTARs, AEs, USEs, and ADEs. Under the DREs, there exist no less than three units or levels of action. Areas of Execution (AEs) and Educational Service Units (USEs) are administrative units charged with purely administrative functions. The USEs are line units with responsibilities for exercising budget functions, yet they receive large portions of that budget from the CTAR. They are responsible for the management of 58,000 schools and 18,000 nonformal educational programs. In some cases, there are regions with sub-DREs with essentially the same administrative functions as USEs. In addition, under the DREs, there exist educational supervisory bodies, the Areas of Educational Development (ADEs). The sector fragmentation is further evidenced in the extreme degree of confusing, poorly coordinated, and overlapping jurisdictions, particularly in the case of the 82 USEs and 189 AEs.

Historically, relations between Regional Directorates and both the central level of the Ministry of Education (MED) and the local level have been conflictive, mainly due to MED-limited budgetary control, and poor regulatory and managerial capacity. While, theoretically, MED exercises regulatory authority over DREs, in fact appropriate control is not exercised. This regulatory weakness on the part of the MED over its own bureaucratic apparatus is in part a function of the sheer size of the sector, and in part a function of limited budgetary control. There are more than 300,000 teachers in the public sector, and budgetary control over the labor force rests with the CTAR. The weak managerial capacity, in turn, is a function of several factors, including the low quality of functionaries of MED, high rotation among ministers and regional directors, and limited communication between those charged with educational planning and execution.

Finally, the triplication of authority between the Ministry of the Presidency, the MED, and the CTARs affects capacity and coordination. The first—through transfers to the CTARs—transfers funds to executing units and exercises control over payroll. The MED has, in theory, educational quality as its principal concern, but also exercises control over hiring of teachers. CTARs have a discretional focus on nonpersonnel budget austerity and control. Perhaps the most fundamental manifestation of the lack of coordination resides in the area of payroll and personnel policy, also reflected by the absence of a generalized information system, or even an inventory of personnel (Chapter VI).[7] This historical multiplicity of functions also affects the quality and supervision of education. At the same time, inadequate regional supervisory capacity and quality results in a supervisory function that is virtually bereft of a concern for pedagogical quality in the face of administrative and bureaucratic demands.

The legal framework for the sector is not particularly propitious for decentralization. Both the Teachers' Law (*Ley Magisterial*) and the General Education Law are rigid in terms of preventing the conditions for flexible response at either the school level or in terms of local functions that might be exercised.

However, a promising beginning toward a redefinition of the legal framework for decentralization is evident in the Executive Decree promulgated in February 2001. This decree (a) expanded and fortified the role and functions of the school director; (b) created *Consejos Escolares Consultivos* (CEC) at the local level; (c) strengthened the role of Parents Associations, intensifying relations among MED, teachers, and the community; and (d) mandated the introduction of planning and participation at the local level for the formulation of Institutional Development Projects (PDI) at the school level and to do this through the (optional) creation of the CEC.

A 2001 pilot exercise in the creation of the CEC in some 467 schools has been positive, but is still far from expectations. In November 2001, the incoming director of the program made a very

---

7. Currently, there is an effort to create this information system. However, to date only Lima-Callao is included in the system and there are pressures not to implement it at the regional level for fear of loss of regional discretionary authority. In the effort to link the information system to a system of payroll, a problem that needs to be addressed in the near term is the inconsistency in the definitions of benefits (*bonificaciones*).

cursory evaluation of the experience as follows: (a) the experience has been positive and should be expanded; (b) there is a need to create a baseline for monitoring and evaluating the program; (c) the principal limitation of the effort to date is its voluntary character and the fact that the functions of the CEC are limited to advise and consult; (d) the CEC has no resources and its leveraging capabilities are weak; (e) support from USEs, DREs, or the MED in the formation, training, and capacity to evaluate on the part of the CEC has been extremely limited; and (f) little promotion of the program has occurred. As a result, there is little incentive to participate in or even create the CEC at the school level.

### Recommendations:

- Both the Teachers' Law and the General Education Law need to be revised in this context. They are too rigid for most forms of decentralization.
- Decentralization should follow a sequential process. CG reorganization prior to decentralization, but with an eye to decentralization, needs to be first. The suggested model for defining functions and structure in Annex F should be carried out within the central ministry and with the participation of key personnel from the various structural units.
- The current institutional morass of jurisdictional levels needs to be integrated. The decision to transfer funds and functions from CTARs to DREs is only a partial move. The proposed Law of Decentralization offers broad guidelines for jurisdictional levels (regions, municipalities), but the nonexclusive nature of which level promotes, develops, and regulates activities of education (and health) leaves gaps for defining these functional differences.[8] What is clear is that the creation of multiple levels of intermediation may not be an appropriate strategy, and may well inhibit deeper forms of decentralization to the provider level. Therefore, as the process of redefinition of roles and functions progresses, there must be a simplification of administrative units and a clarification of responsibilities at the intermediary level.
- The introduction of management or performance contracts should wait for a more advanced stage of the decentralization of the education sector. Once the institutional morass is simplified and monitoring indicators are agreed, they could serve as an agent for culture change, for the transformation from an organizational culture based on norms, bureaucracy, procedures, and inputs to an organizational culture founded on transparency, individual and institutional responsibility and authority, and results. Performance agreements must be accompanied by individual performance agreements evaluating teachers regularly.
- The new legislation should clarify the role of service providers and local councils. Much of the current move to decentralize in education focuses on direct transfers authority, finance, and accountability mechanisms to educational providers: schools and their communities.
- The CEC model should be expanded, but with strengthened functions. Examples from LAC countries would encourage greater school autonomy and the use of tools of social/legal accountability, such as institutional development plans and management agreements.
- Authorities need to create political "space" for the introduction of modalities of decentralization with a reasonable level of consensus. Such consensus does not exist in the educational sector today. The National Consultation on Education is a good beginning.

## Decentralization in the Health Sector

The public provision of health services is characterized by the ministerial absorption of multiple vertical programs, fragmentation, inefficiency, and limited programmatic integrity, driven by the supply of programs for health care rather than the demand for health services (Box 5.3). In addi-

---

8. During the Public Expenditure Review (PER) main mission, a brief seminar was held with the technical leadership of the MED. It practiced a methodology for initiating the dialogue on functions and structures, based on technical workshops led by key technical personnel at the central level (central restructuring) and participation from regional directors and their technical staff.

---

**BOX 5.3: DECENTRALIZATION OF THE HEALTH SECTOR IN LAC**

A review of decentralization efforts in the health sector in six countries of Latin America shows that the results have been very uneven (Burki, Perry, and Dillinger 1999). Efforts to reform the health sector invariably aim at the separation of financing from service delivery, a split between purchaser and provider, and often the introduction of management or performance contracts. Decentralization involves the transfer of parts of the public sector health institutions from the central to subnational governments. Central governments retain policymaking, overall financing, and highly specialized operations, and subnational governments have been given primary (often municipal), secondary, and tertiary hospital care (states and provinces). More often than not, efforts to decentralize have generally failed at either improving coverage or efficiency, and when successful have often included some form of contractual agreement, such as management contracts.

In **Nicaragua,** for instance, there is an ongoing effort to decentralize a number of basic institutional characteristics (provision and acquisitions, finance, personnel management) to both hospitals and to regional/local units (SILAIS) through the introduction of management contracts. The experience of two years with management contracts in hospitals has not been successful, although the learning curve has improved the quality of these contracts, particularly in terms of moving from input-based criteria to output- and outcome-based criteria for contractual agreement.

---

tion, there is limited focus on preventive health care and the promotion of health care, because the supply of curative health services dominates the terrain. Today, there exist no fewer than 23 vertically controlled programs administered from the center, each with its own disconnected set of norms, procedures, supervision system, evaluation, databases, training, and mechanisms for accessing local-level participation. The result is an incredible fragmentation of policy and administration in the national system.[9] Further, at the regional level many of these vertical programs maintain their own coordinators for administration, monitoring, data collection, and training, virtually independent of the regional directorate. Here, too, the result is fragmentation in the financing of health services and little coordinated control over policy direction or planning. The Regional Directorates for Health (DISA) suffer from a minimum of authority, the inability to program in a coordinated fashion, and a high degree of fragmentation. As is true in the case of education, the financing functions that reside in the CTAR further erode any authority that the DISA might have. DISAs have very little programming authority and receive mostly preprogrammed funds, including earmarked *entrusted funds* (Altobelli 2001). Finally, barely 20 percent of the health expenditure budget is devoted to preventive health care, which reflects its lower priority compared to curative health.

Ironically, while the health care system has become increasingly centralized, the central line ministry has minimal control over any attempt to integrate the health care system. Rather, there are three areas or initiatives that favor decentralization in the health care system, and these should be promoted: (a) the Performance-Contracts Administration Program (*Programa de Administración de Acuerdos de Gestión,* PAAG); (b) the Regional Directorates of Health (DISA); and (c) the recently created *Unidades de Seguro Integral de Salud* (USIS).

The *Programa de Administración de Acuerdos de Gestión*/Local Committees of Health Administration (PAAG-CLAS) Program is a very useful model for health decentralization that should be strengthened. PAAG already executes some 17 percent of the Ministry of Health (MINSA) budget under financial management rules of its own. There are approximately 550 CLAS and some 1,200 health establishments (approximately 20 percent of total health

---

9. Recent documents provide excellent diagrammatic representations of the institutional disorder in the health sector. They offer dismaying evidence of the chaos in the sector. See World Bank (2001a) and Cortez (2001).

establishments) under the system. It was created in 1994 as a means of improving the quality of health care expenditures, to bring transparency to the system, to improve the cost-effectiveness of service delivery, and to promote (private) community participation in health care management. The CLAS model builds on the existing local and community organization, and essentially was designed to increase coverage in rural and periurban communities, in areas where existing health services were weak or absent. Similar to *Convenios de Gestión Institucional,* the CLAS model provides for a management contract. However, one fundamentally different characteristic of the contract is that the model applies private law to the use of public resources, and by doing so proffers greater flexibility in the management and use of public resources. CLAS not only combines community and public health services in the planning process, but also gives CLAS direct control over hiring and firing of contracted health personnel and assures a unique degree of social accountability.

In its initial stages, the formation of CLAS was very localized: each CLAS managed a single establishment or health center. It became apparent that this approach was less than ideal in terms of the potential coverage of the system, and gradually the CLAS became a management contract over a group of establishments in a network. While this change in scope and structure seems to be more effective in terms of economies of scale, there is a danger that increasing scale reduces "local" social control at the community level, in favor of control at the site of the center of the network. CLAS has shown to be an effective model of comanagement in the financing and provision of services. It has increased the "capture" of local resources (because fee-for-services remains at the local level) and the sense of local accountability. However, CLAS should not be seen as a means for reducing government expenditures on local health care. Further, CLAS has not proven to be as effective in the supervision of the quality of services. By its very nature, members of CLAS are not competent to supervise quality.

### Recommendations:

- Expand the number of CLAS, possibly to attain about 25 percent of health establishments, but this should be done without increasing their size of the CLAS to maintain the sense of local social accountability. Also, the ratio of CLAS to establishments should not be increased.
- Strengthen other entities within the health care system to make them more capable of quality assurance and supervision.

For CLAS to function well requires the reinforcement of Regional Directorates of Health (DISA). The DISA suffers from fragmented authority, which further fragments the coordination of financing in the sector and in the supervision of the quality of health provision. In addition, execution by the DISA is driven as much or more by the supply of services rather than demand for services, and introduces a certain rigidity in the use of funds. However, despite norms and regulations, DISAs have played an important role in the health sector, since they are able to manage financial accounts to their own benefit and to the advantage of the CLAS model if they enjoy a larger role in planning, technical assistance, administrative control supervision, and evaluation of management agreements with various service providers (Altobelli 2001). A positive relationship between DISA and CLAS would allow DISA to ensure that the appropriate transfers of funds to CLAS takes place. The proposed Law of Decentralization correctly provides a legislative framework to strengthen DISA.

### Recommendations:

- The relationship between CTARs and DISAs should change by removing CTARs from sector-driven purposes. This implies a need for the immediate strengthening of the institutional and human resources capacity within DISA.
- DISA's ability and authority to supervise and control the quality of service delivery should improve. The current nature of the finance mechanism and the lack of control over financing at the DISA level have affected it.

- The renewed efforts to consolidate and integrate vertical and virtually autonomous programs implies the need to rethink the planning, administration, supervision, and financing roles for DISA, and to restructure these units in an integrative fashion. Further, DISAs should be increasingly demand driven, relying on local diagnostics of needs.

Another initiative that needs strengthening is the radical transformation of health insurance with the creation of the Integral Health Insurance Unit (USIS) in 2001. The USIS lies outside MINSA and is an ambitious effort to integrate Maternal Infant Insurance (SMI) and the General School Insurance (SEG) programs under one roof. While currently the two program funds remain separate, there is a drive to consolidate them and universalize coverage, separate financing from service provision, and strengthen the decentralization process. The model incorporates a variety of service providers, ranging from public health centers to management contracts with CLAS or private local service providers. There are several concerns. First is the legal status of USIS. Because of the absence of legal autonomous status, USIS cannot act as an executing unit to provide direct financing for services. Rather, most financing by USIS is channeled through the DISA, creating yet another administrative level in financing. Further, the use of DISA as direct administrator of USIS funds generates delays in transfers to providers (and CLAS) and has fragmented the capacity to supervise the cost-effectiveness of service provision.[10] The control and evaluation functions over what is financed and who is providing it rests within the DISA and not in USIS. A second concern is the potential for increased fragmentation in financing local services. Various financing entities provide resources to a local health establishment, and the potential for duplication of payments for the same service is real. A third concern is the limited institutional capacity of the USIS. Currently, USIS is incapable of providing the necessary technical capacity to supervise or evaluate. In addition, quality control over providers (accreditation) is weak or nonexistent.

## Recommendations:

- The solution to the dilemma of indirect financier can be resolved through the granting of legal status to USIS as a Public Decentralized Organism (OPD). It would remove one level of unnecessary administration in financing services, provide strong impetus to the strengthening and extension of the CLAS model, and allow for the separation of finance (USIS) from provision (CLAS, public health centers, private providers) and finance from supervision (DISA).
- Fragmentation should be reduced through the consolidation of existing vertical programs within MINSA.
- The strengthening of the supervisory role of DISA, and of USIS itself, would improve the monitoring, evaluation, and supervision of both the quality of service and of financial accountability.

In recent months, there has been a strong focus on attempting to bring some order to the public health system. This focus can be summarized as an effort to consolidate some of the vertical and somewhat isolated programs within the *Dirección General de Salud Pública* (DGSP), simplification of the CG structure through the reduction of Executive Directorates to three, and renewed interest in decentralization.

## Recommendations:

- It is equally imperative that while pursuing decentralization policies and initiatives, reform of the core of the Ministry of Health also takes place. Until now, the principal focus of efforts

---

10. Not only have there been complaints from CLAS over delays in transfers, but also that, in some cases, the DISA simply has not made the transfers to CLAS (Moore 2002).

has been on restructuring of the central level, and less on decentralization, but both avenues should be pursued simultaneously. There would be a notable improvement in internal communication, whereas previously each vertical program was much an island unto itself.

■ Central ministerial restructuring has been initiated, but must continue, with a greater eye to decentralization. Again, the functional matrix model offered in Annex F is an example of how such an identification of structures and functions can be a useful tool.

■ The work of the Commission on a Decentralized Health Care System (*Sistema Coordinado y Descentralizado de Salud*) is of paramount importance. Its main responsibility is to (a) clarify the roles of the various entities involved in the health care system—MINSA at the central level, DISA, the *Programa de Apoyo a la Reforma del Sector Salud* (Health Sector Reform Program, PARSALUD), municipalities, CLAS, and local health centers; and (b) integrate programs and projects, ending the multiplication of vertical programs and the creation of parallel bureaucracies virtually removed from the core of the MINSA.

■ Prior review, strengthening the regulatory functions of the central and intermediate levels, is increasingly imperative. CLAS is the answer for decentralization of service delivery to locally accountable providers in Peru, and provides the key for longer-term models of decentralization. A program of expansion over the next several years without altering the ratio of CLAS to individual health establishments should be pursued, perhaps at a rate of some 5 to 10 percent per year.

# VI

# UPGRADING THE CIVIL SERVICE

*Civil service reform is the missing link of an outcome- and poverty-reducing-oriented modernization of the State in Peru. The past decade witnessed a severe deterioration of Peru's civil service, with deep implications for the fiscal accounts and the costs of the pensions regime. Hyperinflation of the late 1980s and the beginning of the 1990s sharply reduced the real earnings of civil servants. A poorly conceived downsizing of the Central Government work force in the early 1990s, which, by the end of the decade was reversed, led, however, to the departure of the most capable civil servants. The fiscal burden of the surviving public labor force is very high and unsustainable. There is an entrenched disregard for the provisions of the existing Civil Service Law and its associated regulations. Civil servants are employed under a variety of legal regimes with a wide disparity in salaries for similar tasks. The existing formal salary structure has not been revised in over a decade, so base salaries are increased through resort to a variety of supplements and benefits in cash and in kind.*

*With the proclamation of a ban on hiring into permanent positions 10 years ago, institutions have resorted to hiring on a contractual basis, a process that is not subject to any required procedures for recruitment and selection and that has severe fiscal implications. All these factors have contributed to the existing legacy of a work force that is poorly prepared, poorly trained, poorly supervised, and therefore of very low productivity. Consequently, there is an urgent need for a thorough reform to reestablish some semblance of control over the wage bill and to promote the creation of a more efficient government. Any initiative designed to improve the performance of government must include a major overhaul of the institutional framework that governs public sector employment and of the management of its human resources. The current Civil Service Law has major weaknesses that argue for its replacement by a new legal framework designed to promote a higher level of efficiency in the delivery of government services. A sequencing path of reforms is suggested, starting with a modest, but valuable, pilot effort to rationalize human resources management on a ministry-by-ministry basis and supported by an SIAF-controlled payroll, to the ultimate creation of an autonomous institution or Directorate with the responsibility of administering the civil service system, with normative and enforcement functions.[1]*

---

1. This mostly draws from the mimeograph prepared by Gregory (2002).

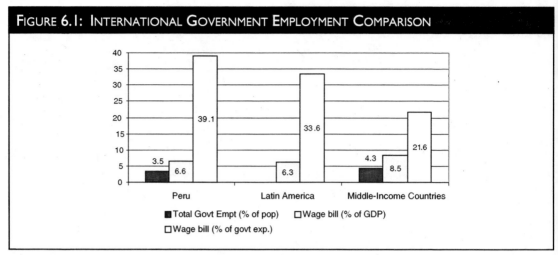

FIGURE 6.1: INTERNATIONAL GOVERNMENT EMPLOYMENT COMPARISON

*Source:* Gregory (2002).

## The Size and Employment Conditions of the Public Sector

There is no sure estimate of the size of public sector employment in Peru. The range varies between 616,200 and 890,728, the latter number including members of the armed forces and police, which represents 7.9 percent of the employed labor force.[2] If we accept the most conservative estimate of 616,200, it represents approximately 2.4 percent of the estimated population for 2000. This ratio closely resembles the average proportion for middle-income countries, 2.5 percent. If total government employment, including police and the armed services, is considered, the ratio to population for Peru is 3.5 percent, which compares favorably to the group of middle-income countries the ratio of which is 4.3 percent (Figure 6.1).[3] Similarly, as a percentage of GDP, the wage bill[4] is lower than the average in LAC or middle-income countries, 6.2 percent. While Peru would compare favorably with other countries, it should be kept in mind that these are poor indicators of whether government employment or remunerations are excessive or inadequate. Such a judgment is made only after taking into account the range of obligations assumed by different governments and the efficiency with which they are carried out.

The fiscal costs of the public servants and the associated pension regimes are very high, bringing rigidity to the budget and absorbing a significant share of it. On one hand, Peru's wage bill, equivalent to 39 percent of total expenditure and 6.6 percent of GDP, is the second highest in LAC, and this ratio does not include public servants hired under other categories. This suggests overstaffing (Figure 6.1). On the other hand—and this is very relevant for a country undergoing fiscal retrenchment—the budgetary cost of the public pension system amounted to a minimum of about 0.6 percent of GDP in 2002, and is projected to peak at at least 1 percent of GDP by 2010. (The public pension system has three components: (a) recognition bonds issued to workers that switched to the private system, (b) unfunded liabilities under the *Oficina de Normalización Previsional* of both current and future workers, and (c) special regimes.)

Furthermore, a negative public perception prevails on the overall performance of the public work force. A World Bank Institute survey on governance and corruption in Peru (Chapter VII) reveals that public servants in Peru rank unfavorably when compared to Honduras and Colombia,

---

2. *Encuesta Nacional de Hogares, op. cit.,* p.11

3. The information for international comparisons is drawn from the World Bank database on Public Sector Employment and Wages.

4. Such a wage bill is significantly underestimated, as explained below.

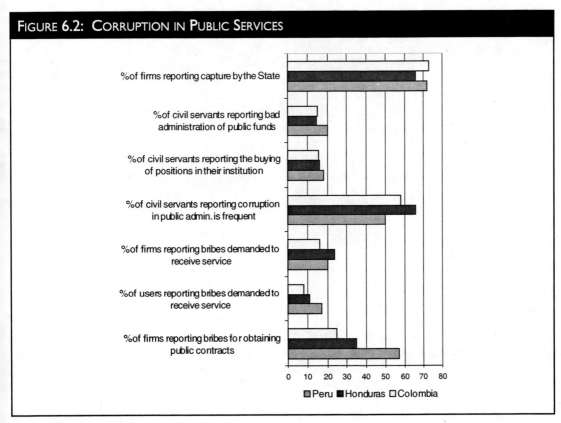

FIGURE 6.2: CORRUPTION IN PUBLIC SERVICES

*Source:* World Bank (2001c).

in terms of bribes paid for obtaining public contracts and services, bad administration of public funds, and the practice of buying positions in public entities (which favor capture of the State by determined groups). Peru ranked better, however, in frequent reporting of corruption in the public administration (Figure 6.2).

Public employment conditions in Peru's public sector are governed by a legal framework that has rarely been fully applied. The 1979 Constitution mandated that a law be enacted that ought to establish merit as the governing principle in defining conditions of employment, and set up a single structure of remunerations and fringe benefits for all covered employments. Hence, the Civil Service Law and the *Ley de Bases de la Carrera Administrativa y de Remuneraciones del Sector Público* were enacted in 1984.[5] Both Laws are basically a statement of principles underlying the employment relationship. The specific norms and procedures regulating that relationship were left to be defined in the Laws' implementing regulations (or *Reglamento*). The initial *Reglamento* was published in 1985 and was superseded by a far more detailed *Reglamento* in 1990. However, for all practical purposes, both Laws have been a dead letter for the better part of their life. Concomitant with a partial reduction in employment between 1991 and 1993, a ban on hiring for permanent positions was decreed. Presumably, all hiring since then has been on a contractual basis and has not been subject to any statutory procedures. Other provisions of the Law, such as the creation of a tribunal to hear appeals by public servants from disciplinary actions, have never been fulfilled.

---

5. Note that the Constitution of 1993 omits any reference to a civil service law or to the principle of merit in public employment.

The present legal framework is weak and the status of civil service is chaotic. The Laws did not create a centralized agency with normative and enforcement functions. Nor did they provide for the creation and maintenance of an employee database. Therefore, there exists no source within the Government of Peru (GOP) that can provide exact and systematic information about the number of government employees, their employment status or histories, and their remuneration. The existing formal salary structure has not been revised in years and is hopelessly inadequate. In short, there is no reliable way to trace the evolution of government employment and remuneration over the past decade. Because of this vacuum, a Multisectoral Commission to Study the Situation of the Central Public Administration Personnel (henceforth the Commission) was created in 2001 and was charged with examining the issues related to public sector employment. The Commission's Final Report provides preliminary information that is available on the state of the government's employment as of the first half of 2001.

## Public Sector Employment and Earnings

There are four classes of public servants:

- Those who entered under the legal provisions of the existing Civil Service Law (Regime 276).
- Those hired under contracts; since the hiring ban was instituted a decade ago, supposedly no appointments to permanent positions have been made. Instead, ministries have resorted to hiring employees under contracts that are also governed by provisions of Regime 276.
- Those subject to no regime and financed from diverse sources, but largely from the budgetary category of goods and nonpersonal services (NPS).
- Those covered under the labor code that applies to the private sector; because of the restrictive provisions of Regime 276, some decentralized agencies have opted for coverage under the labor code that applies to the private sector (Regime 728).

The Commission's preliminary major findings concerning employment and salaries in the public sector are:

- If the two first classes of public employees are aggregated into a single category referred to as Regime 276 public employees, the monthly average salaries under the three regimes are NS/1,439, NS/1,796, and NS/1,775, respectively, for an overall average of NS/1,500. Earnings of employees under Regime 728 would exceed, on average, those of statutory employees by 25 percent, while those under NPS would enjoy a 23 percent premium.
- The high concentration of employees in Regime 276 (82.2 percent of the public work force) is heavily influenced by the inclusion of public servants that do not form part of the administrative ranks of the government (Table 6.1). In fact, if we were to deduct from the total employment appearing in the table, teachers, health professionals, judges, and attor-

### TABLE 6.1: NUMBER OF EMPLOYEES AND THE AVERAGE MONTHLY WAGE BILL

| Regimen | Number of Employees | | Monthly Wage Bill | |
|---|---|---|---|---|
| | Thousands | Percent | Millions of Soles | Percent |
| Regimen 276 | 506.8 | 82.2 | 729.4 | 78.9 |
| Regimen 728 | 49.5 | 8.0 | 88.9 | 9.6 |
| NPS | 59.9 | 9.7 | 106.3 | 11.5 |
| Total | 616.2 | 100.0 | 924.6 | 100.0 |

Source: Comisión Multisectorial Encargada de Estudiar la Situación del Personal de la Administración Pública Central (2002).

neys in the Attorney General's office, the remaining employees would, for the most part, represent the staff of line ministries. When these deductions are carried out, it turns out that only 45.3 percent of the work force *within the line ministries* is employed under Regimen 276, while almost as many, 40.2 percent, represent contract employees under NPS. So, NPS introduces major distortions to the wage bill and overall budgetary flexibility.

Contrary to common belief, the current employment level is higher than in the early 1990s. The number of public servants accounted for by the Commission, 616,200, is slightly higher than that in 1990. The number of employees ascribed to the national government was 591,498 in 1990 (World Bank 1994). An alternative measure of urban employment in public administration, obtained from third-quarter household surveys and data available for 1997–2001, reports a total public employment of 707,000 (Table 6.2).[6]

Household surveys confirm that the ban on new hiring of public employment proved ineffective because a very significant increase in government employment took place during 1997–2001. All but one category increased their number of public servants. In total, public employment is believed to have significantly increased by over 25 percent; but if we correct this number by the likely overestimation of the number of teachers in 2001 (reducing them to approximately the level of 2000), growth in total public employment would still be significant at about 20 percent.

There is also a considerable divergence between the Commission's estimate of earnings and those reported by the household survey for 2001. The former are significantly higher, ranging from 33 to 66 percent greater than the average public sector earnings reported by the household survey for 2001. This is an uncomfortably large difference that cannot easily be explained, except by the frequent tendency of survey respondents to understate their real revenues. However, another difference appears in reported average earnings for all employees, which advanced by almost 40 percent during 1997–2001. Those in central administration reported an increase of almost 52 percent, while educators reported a more modest increase of almost 27 percent. Since the consumer price index rose by only 15.5 percent between the two endpoints of the series, public employees realized real percentage increases in double digits on average earnings during this period.

## Comparison of Public and Private Sector Earnings

The earnings of civil servants in the central administration gained significantly in relation to those of private sector employees[7] during 1997–2001. According to household surveys, in 1997, average earnings in *the central administration* were 87 percent of those in the private formal sector. Earnings reached virtual parity in 2000 and surpassed central administration earnings by about 7 percent in 2001. Average earnings for permanent teachers also surpassed average earnings for the private sector in 2001. Average earnings in the *total government* also increased, but remained below average earnings for formal private employment and above average earnings for informal employment during the same period (Figure 6.3). These findings differ from the Commission's estimates; public sector average earnings, including those of educators, appear to range between 30 and 66 percent above those

---

6. It should be kept in mind that the survey's measure of public employment is not limited to only the CG, but includes municipalities. However, it would seem that the large difference between the two measures of employment is to be attributed to the inflated number of educators reported by the household survey. Whereas government sources estimate the number of teachers to be on the order of 280,000, the survey reports some 377,000 in 2001. No other source comes close to reporting numbers as large as these. Another reference point is provided by a census of schools undertaken in 1999. It reported the existence of 309,000 teachers, of whom 235,000 were public school employees. This compares with the survey's measure of almost 340,000 public school teachers in that same year. Furthermore, the variations in this number during 1997–2001 are larger than one would expect, and the increase of about 45,000 reported for 2001 over 2000 certainly is unlikely to reflect reality (Saavedra, Melzi, and Miranda 2001).

7. The data for the private sector employees is for firms with 10 or more employees.

## TABLE 6.2: URBAN PUBLIC AND PRIVATE SECTOR EMPLOYMENT AND AVERAGE MONTHLY EARNINGS, 1997–2001
(Nuevos Soles)

|  | 1997 | | 1998 | | 1999 | | 2000 | | 2001 | | % Change 1997–2001 | |
|---|---|---|---|---|---|---|---|---|---|---|---|---|
|  | No. '000s | Average Earning | No. '000s | Average Earning | No. '000s | Average Earning | No. '000s | Average Earning | No. '000s | Average Earning | No. '000s | Average Earning |
| Public Total | 561.6 | 771 | 619.7 | 820 | 662.5 | 941 | 648.6 | 1030 | 707.0 | 1078 | 25.9 | 39.8 |
| Permanent | 339.8 | 903 | 397.1 | 851 | 399.4 | 1042 | 389.1 | 1120 | 433.9 | 1175 | 27.7 | 30.1 |
| Fixed-Term Contract | 131.8 | 667 | 127.4 | 881 | 156.8 | 888 | 156.6 | 950 | 145.0 | 1134 | 10.0 | 70 |
| Other | 90.0 | 422 | 95.2 | 609 | 106.3 | 638 | 102.9 | 812 | 128.1 | 685 | 42.3 | 62.3 |
| Private Informal | 1001.9 | 482 | 1149.6 | 521 | 1147.9 | 521 | 1089.0 | 523 | 1223.6 | 443 | 22.1 | -8.1 |
| Private Formal | 1217.1 | 1042 | 1373.6 | 1288 | 1279.9 | 1369 | 1305.8 | 1246 | 1255.3 | 1285 | 3.1 | 23.3 |

Source: Gregory (2002).

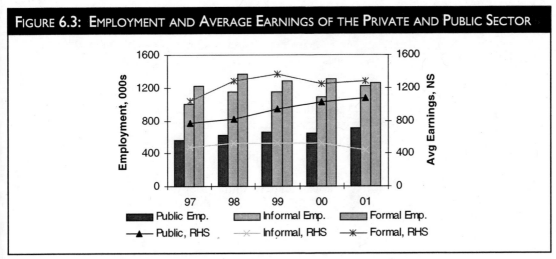

FIGURE 6.3: EMPLOYMENT AND AVERAGE EARNINGS OF THE PRIVATE AND PUBLIC SECTOR

*Source:* Gregory (2002).

in the private sector. The Commission's number, however, has a larger margin than one would find in most other countries of similar or higher incomes.[8]

A third more accurate but conflicting measure of private sector earnings is derived from establishment surveys that extract data from payrolls. In June 2001 average monthly earnings were reported to be NS/1,854, compared to the NS/1,285 reported for private formal sector employees by the household surveys.[9] Relative to this value, the average monthly earnings of public employees reported in Table 6.2 are only six tenths.

In view of the conflicting data, it is very risky to make definitive pronouncements regarding the actual earnings of civil servants and their relationship to those from the private sector. The safest statement that can be made is that public sector earnings appear to have gained relative to those in the private sector during 1997–2001. Since the establishment surveys are a more accurate source of information regarding private sector earnings, it can be concluded that while the gap between the two sectors has narrowed, public sector earnings are probably still somewhat below their private sector counterparts.[10]

## Earnings by Occupational Category of Public Employees

The salary payroll is highly inconsistent and fragmented; the official payroll barely covers less than half the real one. The formal payroll of the central administration for employees covered by Regimen 276

---

8. A note of caution is needed in evaluating these findings. Household surveys of income and expenditures typically fail to capture all income actually received. Aggregate incomes reported generally fall short of those recorded in the aggregate national income accounts by 15 to 20 percent, and in the case of Peru may be understated by as much as 30 percent. It is reasonable to believe that private sector incomes are more likely to be understated than those of salaried public servants. If so, the reported margin by which public earnings exceed private earnings may be exaggerated.

9. *Ministerio de Trabajo y Promoción Social, Encuesta Nacional de Sueldos y Salarios* as reported in *Informe Estadístico Mensual, Agosto 2001*, p. 39.

10. The importance of the level of public sector remunerations relative to the private sector should not be underestimated. According to the World Bank's 1997 *World Development Report* (p. 8), there is a clear and strong inverse relationship between public sector wages relative to those in manufacturing and the incidence of corruption. The higher public sector salaries are relative to those in manufacturing, the lower the incidence of corruption. Regardless of whether one refers to the *Encuesta Nacional de Hogares*'s (National Household Survey, ENAHO) average monthly earnings in the central administration in 2001, NS/1,379, or the Commission's average, NS/1,500, both fall far short of the average monthly wage in urban manufacturing in June 2001 of NS/2,337.

is called the Unified Payroll (*Planilla Unica de Pagos*, PUP). The Commission's study reports that only 41 percent of all salary payments are charged to the PUP. The rest of the payments are made by resorting to over 40 different salary supplements in cash and in kind, such as incentive payments, vacation bonuses, birthday bonuses, consumption subsidies, family food baskets, monthly bonuses, transportation, schooling subsidies, and uniforms. The result of these ad hoc arrangements is a total loss of transparency and coherence in the formal salary structure. Employees in the same salary grade or performing the same tasks receive widely disparate salaries, and the salary relationships existing among the different levels of the salary structure obey no consistent or transparent relationship to the skills required to perform the assigned tasks, as reflected by the minimum and maximum salaries in each salary grade that are financed out of the PUP (Table 6.3).

- The ratios of the highest to the lowest salary within grades vary greatly. For example, the maximum salary in grade F1 is 5.55 times greater than the minimum, while in F7 the ratio is 1.36.
- There is no perceptible order in which this ratio moves along salary grades from the minimum to the maximum, and the overlap of salaries is extreme. For example, the maximum

**TABLE 6.3: DISPERSION OF SALARIES CHARGED TO THE PUP BY OCCUPATIONAL GROUP AND SALARY GRADE**
(Nuevos Soles)

| Occupational Group | Salary Grade | Maximum Value | Minimum Value | Ratio of Max/Min |
|---|---|---|---|---|
| | F8 | 2,594 | 1,326 | 1.96 |
| UPPER MANAGEMENT | F7 | 1,574 | 1,154 | 1.36 |
| | F6 | 1,651 | 1,059 | 1.56 |
| | F5 | 1,928 | 1,005 | 1.92 |
| | F4 | 1,458 | 964 | 1.51 |
| MIDDLE MANAGEMENT | F3 | 2,695 | 906 | 2.97 |
| | F2 | 2,934 | 669 | 4.39 |
| | F1 | 3,805 | 686 | 5.55 |
| | SP A | 2,670 | 651 | 4.10 |
| | SP B | 1,608 | 620 | 2.59 |
| | SP C | 1,798 | 600 | 3.00 |
| PROFESSIONALS | SP D | 2,469 | 576 | 4.29 |
| | SP E | 1,382 | 551 | 2.51 |
| | SP F | 1,158 | 598 | 1.94 |
| | ST A | 1,960 | 526 | 3.73 |
| | ST B | 1,725 | 518 | 3.30 |
| TECHNICAL | ST C | 816 | 520 | 1.57 |
| | ST D | 788 | 508 | 1.55 |
| | ST E | 778 | 507 | 1.53 |
| | SA A | 1,765 | 502 | 3.52 |
| | SA B | 1,555 | 500 | 3.11 |
| AUXILIARY | SA C | 1,748 | 491 | 3.56 |
| | SA D | 1,052 | 498 | 2.11 |
| | SA E | 1,803 | 480 | 3.76 |

*Note:* Grade F8 does not include the President of the Council of Ministers.
Some Secretaries General (F6) have a rank of Vice-Minister (F7).
*Source:* Comisión Multisectoral, *op. cit.,* p. 2.

TABLE 6.4: MAXIMUM, AVERAGE, AND MINIMUM EARNINGS BY OCCUPATIONAL
GROUP AND REGIMEN
(Nuevos Soles)

|  | Permanent | | | Contract | | |
|---|---|---|---|---|---|---|
|  | Min | Avg | Max | Min | Avg | Max |
| Upper Mgmt | 13,634 | 23,360 | 43,083 |  |  |  |
| Middle Mgmt | 700 | 3,377 | 12,438 | 932 | 4,047 | 5,016 |
| Professionals | 684 | 1,943 | 5,554 | 764 | 2,246 | 6,770 |
| Technical | 679 | 1,373 | 3,816 | 579 | 1,499 | 3,488 |
| Auxiliary | 498 | 1,209 | 3,779 | 578 | 1,106 | 2,416 |

Source: Gregory (2002).

salary in the bottom grade (SA-E) is greater than the maximum salary in 10 of the next 11 higher grades.[11] Indeed, it is greater than the maximum recorded for vice-ministers and secretary general.

On average, contracted personnel earn more than permanent personnel, except for auxiliary personnel, but salary dispersion is high (Table 6.4 and Figure 6.4). Peru's civil service regime appears to offer higher-than-market rates of pay for employees at the bottom of the occupational hierarchy, while paying less-than-market salaries to highly skilled employees. Managerial personnel with permanent status under Regime 276 appear to earn less, on average, than do those contracted under the same regime, but the Commission's report says that more disaggregated data by salary grade reveal that the permanent managers actually earn more.

A wholesale reform of employment and remuneration practices in the public sector is in order. Public employment is growing rapidly and uncontrollably. Salary levels are being assigned without reference to any benchmarks. There is no mechanism for assuring that individuals performing similar tasks at similar levels of productivity receive similar pay.

## Reforming the Legal and Institutional Framework

Neither the Laws, nor the *Reglamento* establish procedures and offer benefits to employees that are more likely to discourage rather than encourage efficiency:

- A glaring omission of the Laws is the absence of any entity responsible for enforcement. The 1985 *Reglamento* leaves enforcement to the human resources offices at the ministry level.[12] This is a weak reed on which to place such a responsibility. Typically, the human resources offices are poorly staffed and exercise little authority. To the extent that their directors serve at the pleasure of the higher authorities, there would be little disposition to oppose the authorities should they wish to bypass procedures outlined in the law or regulations.
- Upon appointment to a post, a civil servant immediately acquires tenure, since the 1990 *Reglamento* expressly rejects the use of probationary periods.
- The *Reglamento* seems to reflect a determination to move employees upward through the occupational and salary structure as quickly as possible. It calls for setting annual quotas for promotions based on either existing vacancies or by the reclassification of a civil servant's

---

11. However, the Commission report notes that this particular anomaly is not normally observed within institutions.

12. *Reglamento Inicial del Decreto Legislativo No. 276, Decreto Supremo No. 018-85 PCM, Disposiciones Generales*, 2.

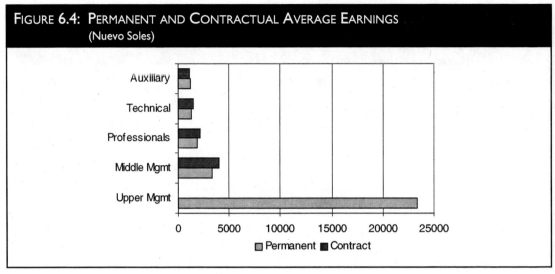

FIGURE 6.4: PERMANENT AND CONTRACTUAL AVERAGE EARNINGS
(Nuevo Soles)

*Source:* Gregory (2002).

existing post. Rather than restricting access to promotion to maintain a strong incentive for excellent performance, it creates a mechanism that risks converting the promotion into a pro forma event. Since the *Reglamento* seeks to fill all vacancies above the entry level from an occupational group from within the existing personnel pool, this limits the flexibility required to ensure that the best possible candidate is selected.

The procedures outlined for the recruitment and selection of new employees conform to standard practice in theory, but prove ineffective. Vacancies at the entry level must be advertised, and selection follows a competitive process in which applicants' backgrounds are evaluated and examinations may be required. But there are loopholes. For example, individuals hired on a contractual basis are not required to undergo a competitive selection process, and after one year may be granted permanent status if a vacancy exists. Then, after three years on contract an individual acquires a right to become permanent if the institution decides it needs to retain the position (Art. 40). Clearly, these provisions are inconsistent with procedures to ensure that the best candidates are hired into tenured positions.

Monetary rewards are merely a function of tenure. Article 51 grants a 5-percent increase in the basic salary after each five years of service. Article 52 provides for bonuses that are a function of family size. Both provisions violate the principle of equal pay for equal work and certainly have no link to performance. Article 53a provides for a bonus to be paid to those occupying positions of responsibility or supervision. No definition of "responsibility" appears either in the Laws or in the *Reglamento*, so it obviously lies within an area of discretion of the institution's authorities.[13] Moreover, Articles 140–46 of the *Reglamento* oblige all government institutions to provide a variety of welfare benefits extending to the employee and his or her family. Among the benefits to be provided are meals; transportation; in-house medical services; housing; nurseries and educational subsidies; cultural, social, and recreational activities; and subsidized credit.

---

13. Why a salary supplement should be necessary is not clear. After all, the job evaluation process is supposed to take account of the duties and responsibilities that characterize each post and assign it to the appropriate salary category. No further supplement should be required. But even less understandable is the granting of a permanent bonus in recognition of past supervisory services after one moves to a nonsupervisory position. The *Reglamento* provides for this salary supplement for those serving in a managerial position for at least three years, though it does not specify what proportion of the bonus becomes permanent (Art. 124).

## The Need for a Civil Service Directorate

Peru intends to enact a new Civil Service Law and *Reglamento* designed not only to protect the legitimate rights of employees, but also to create the incentives for a higher level of efficiency and improved quality of services to the public.

## Recommendations:

It is advisable for a new Civil Service Law to establish a central entity—a Directorate—with authority for normative and enforcement functions. Ideally, the Directorate must be autonomous from the executive power. The person who heads the Directorate should be viewed as apolitical and have had professional experience in the area of human resources management. The qualifications for the position should be clearly set forth in the law.[14] The Directorate could be assigned a variety of functions designed to ensure a measure of consistency in the administration of human resources across the various institutions of government. Among these could be to:

- Prepare the *Reglamento* of the new Civil Service Law.
- Prepare a model *Reglamento,* (subject to the approval of the Council of Ministers), which would serve as a basis for institution-level *Reglamentos.*
- Create and maintain a database containing personnel information of all government employees.
- Design of a single system of job description and evaluation that could be applied across all government agencies.
- Design and implement the training program of the personnel assigned to the human resources offices in the public entities.
- Provide technical assistance to the institutional human resources offices.
- Assist ministries in assessing training needs and training programs, maintaining a listing of qualified sources of training.
- Design an appropriate wage structure that permits government to recruit and retain employees of the desired quality.
- Perform periodic surveys of the labor market to identify salary trends on the basis of which it could offer policy recommendations to the executive designed to maintain public salaries in the desired relation to the market.
- Perform technical analyses of public sector employment.

## Personnel Management

The procedures outlined in the existing *Reglamento* are, for the most part, adequate, but could be improved. They prevent opening all vacancies to competitive qualification by both internal and external candidates. Some greater degree of regulation of the process of contracting would appear to be desirable, since it is an area that could give rise to abuse. Currently, an institution can contract anyone it wishes without resort to a competitive process of qualification.

## Recommendations:

- For contracts with a duration of less than one year, the current practice can be followed, but contracts should be nonrenewable to prevent avoidance of the competitive process.

---

14. The appointment process to be followed is of the utmost importance. One possible appointment mechanism is the constitution by law of a nominating panel with representation from Congress, civil society organizations, and the business sector, which would forward a short list of approved candidates to the President from which he or she would make the appointment. The Director (*Rector*) should enjoy a rank equivalent to that of a minister and hold such position for a term longer than that of the President. Removal from the position would require a demonstration of incompetence. In the absence of such a demonstration, renewal of the director's term would be expected.

- Contracts of longer duration should be filled through a competitive process. Holders of longer-term contracts should also be entitled to all other benefits, such as paid vacations and participation in a pension plan.
- Consideration must be given to employing occupants of all professional and managerial positions on a contractual basis rather than on a permanent basis. To compensate for the increased risk of separation, a premium could be offered over the position's salary grade, say 10 percent, to those choosing the contract option. The increase in flexibility afforded by the contractual arrangement could well be worth such a premium.

*Remunerations and Other Incentives to Perform.* The Directorate should be made responsible for developing a single market-oriented salary structure designed to accommodate the full range of services employed in government, from the unskilled service worker to the minister.

### Recommendations:

- Budgetary provisions should be made for payment of bonuses to employees as rewards for superior performance.
- The budget should allocate to each institution some proportion of its wage bill for the distribution of such bonuses. Each institution would be responsible for administration of the bonuses.
- Permanent payments that are unrelated to performance, such as length-of-service supplements, should be avoided. If it is desired to grant some recognition for length of service, it would be preferable to grant a lump-sum award when recognition is due rather than to make a permanent addition to the basic salary, as the current law provides.
- The new Civil Service Law should provide that salary increases mandated for all employees be made in proportional form, that is, an equal percentage increase for all. The common practice of awarding the same absolute increase to all employees has the unfortunate consequence of reducing relative differentials among salary grades, leading to a compression of the salary structure and to future difficulties in the recruitment of highly skilled employees. It also reduces the incentives to perform in order to better qualify for promotion.
- All new employees should be subject to a probationary period during which they may be discharged without payment of an indemnity.

*Implementation of a New Civil Service Regime.* The new Law and salary structure should not be extended to the whole Central Government (CG) immediately upon its enactment, except for the general provisions governing recruitment and selection. Rather, it should start with modest human resources management reform pilot exercises, developed on a ministry-by-ministry basis. The government ought to use accession to the Law and the new salary structure as an incentive for each institution to undergo a careful review of its mission and structures and their adequacy for meeting future institutional needs.

### Recommendations:

- A basic human resources restructuring process would include (a) the discontinuation of activities that do not fit within the newly defined mission of the institution; (b) the elimination of duplications and consolidation of units; (c) the re-engineering of processes and procedures to simplify the delivery of services, and completion of new job titles, descriptions, and evaluations; and (d) a commitment to the professionalization of management.
- Pilot institutions should be required to prepare a detailed plan of action and a calendar for its completion to qualify for coverage under the Law.
- An appeals procedure is needed for any disciplinary system. The *Ley de la Carrera Administrativa* provided for the creation of a body to hear appeals (*Tribunal del Servicio Civil*). However, it was never established, so it is a priority. Such an entity should lie outside the institution.

*The Scope of a Civil Service Law and Decentralization.* A final note concerns the desirable scope of a new Civil Service Law. The CG is committed to the process of deconcentration of administrative functions of ministries to regional or local political entities. At the same time there is a potential devolution of functions and resources to regional or municipal governments.

*Recommendation:*
- It is imperative that the staffing of subnational units of government be subject to the same rigorous standards and procedures advocated for the CG, if decentralization is to result in better economic and social services to the public.

## Additional Measures for Improving Human Resources Administration
There are additional features that an overhauled human resources administration would require:

- A virtual database integrated into the SIAF system would support the main urgent task of developing a unified payroll system to establish the exact number of public workers and eliminate ghost workers. Any high-performing system of personnel administration requires it also contain a full profile of each employee, including a public sector employment history that records date of entry, positions held, disciplinary actions, classification, salary, supplements, and so forth.
- Gradual simplification of the remunerations package to cash payments; every effort should be made to avoid in-kind supplements. Resorting to a wide assortment of supplements to the basic wage gives rise to difficulties in accounting for the full cost of the remunerations package. Typically, individual welfare or satisfaction is maximized when an individual receives all of his or her income in cash and can allocate it according to his or her consumption preferences.
- The current variety of payment practices should gradually be replaced by a wage structure that provides for a single basic salary for grade and assures that pay differences among employees performing the same tasks are minimized.
- Pension regimes require an ad hoc solution. If a new salary structure were to result in increases in salaries, the government would be faced with an immediate increase in its liabilities to the pensioned population and to its employed work force. Currently, there are some 225,000 beneficiaries of the pension system established by DL-20530 whose pensions are automatically adjusted by the current salary of the positions they occupied prior to retirement, the *cedula viva* arrangement.
- A true system of performance evaluation has yet to be established. The current *Ley de la Carrera Administrativa* adopts merit as a criterion for promotion and for granting performance bonuses, but it has been ignored. Depending on the nature of the tasks, a performance bonus is desirable.
- A prior condition to the introduction of performance contracts is the professionalization of management. Indeed, the introduction of trained managers can lead to improvements in productivity even in the absence of performance bonuses. Able managers can raise productivity by improving the organization of their units, modifying and simplifying work procedures, and motivating employees to perform. It is desirable to make a clear distinction between the policymaking and the executive functions of the ministerial hierarchy. The General Director and all lower-level directors and supervisors would constitute the backbone of the permanent professional management structure.

## The Education Sector
The education sector is a major destination of government resources, and public school teachers constitute, by far, the largest group of public employees. The education sector accounts for about 15 percent of total expenditures and deserves special attention because teachers are not covered by the Civil Service Law that applies to administrative employees, but are governed by their own legal

regimen. The institutional framework is defined by two basic documents, the *Ley del Profesorado*, enacted in 1984, and the *Reglamento de la Ley del Profesorado*, enacted in 1990.

There are various categories of teachers defined by the nature and amount of education and/or training that they possess. Those who hold diplomas in pedagogy from one of the teacher training institutes (*institutos superior pedagógicos*, ISPs) occupy the highest category. In addition, there are five categories of teachers who do not hold a teaching title.[15] In 1997, 62 percent of the approximately 248,000 primary and secondary-school teachers held pedagogic degrees (World Bank 2001b:47). The distribution among schools of teachers with different qualifications is hardly random. The more rural and distant from urban areas a school is, the greater the likelihood that it will employ a larger proportion of untitled and poorly prepared teachers.

Teachers' salaries have shown huge variations in real terms over the past few decades. Salaries attained their peak during the 1970s, declined precipitously during the 1980s, and recovered during the 1990s. By the end of the 1990s, teachers' earnings, in real terms, had recovered to a significant level. Their salary structure had also been severely compressed.

The present assignment mechanisms for teachers engender misallocations because the assignment of a teacher to a post vests an ownership right to the post. As enrollments shift from one school district to another as a result of population changes, schools in districts losing students find themselves with a surplus of teachers, but the surplus cannot be reassigned and the teacher may retain his or her post as long as he or she wishes.

Promotion procedures are inoperative, since they were suspended a decade ago. The result is that most teachers are found in the bottom two levels of the career structure.[16]

The current salary structure does not provide adequate incentives to elicit more efficient teacher performance. Consider, for instance, one of the categories that is likely to encompass a substantial number of teachers—the category that includes those under Pension Regimen 19990 and who are appointed for 30 hours of classroom time. The difference between the salary in Level I and the salary in Level V is only NS/67.75, or barely 10 percent of the starting salary in Level I.[17] The differentials for the other categories are of a similar magnitude.[18]

The adequacy of teachers' salaries is a controversial issue. Comparing the remunerations received by teachers and professionals in the private sector using several different measures of pay for 1997 (Table 6.5) shows that if no allowance is made for hours worked at home by teachers, the hourly earnings of teachers fall short of those of private sector professionals but exceeds those of nonprofessional workers with a university education. The disadvantaged position of teachers relative to the labor market is mainly due to the higher earnings reported in Lima. In the rest of urban areas, teacher's earnings exceed those of other workers with advanced education. If it is assumed that teachers spend an extra 40 percent of classroom hours in school-related work at home, the dis-

---

15. These are (a) individuals who have completed their pedagogic studies but have not completed the degree requirements, (b) those who hold degrees in nonpedagogic fields from institutions of higher learning other than the ISPs, (c) those who have not completed pedagogic studies at a higher level of education, (d) those with incomplete university training, and (e) those with only secondary school education.

16. In theory, teachers with pedagogy degrees have a defined career path consisting of five levels, each of which has a salary associated with it. A teacher must spend at least five years in a level prior to becoming eligible for promotion to the next level. The passage from Level I to Level II is automatic at the end of five years. From then on, promotion depends on the evaluation of the teacher. The evaluation is based on three categories of factors: (a) education and degrees obtained, the number of training courses attended, papers presented at professional meetings, length of service, and posts held; (b) an evaluation of services that is based on attendance and punctuality and participation in joint faculty activities; and (c) meritorious recognition as evidenced by opinions from the State, parent organizations, or intellectual production.

17. The discussion of salary differentials is based on the salary structure in effect in 1999 and does not reflect the 16-percent increases instituted since then (World Bank 2001b).

18. Last year, a 50-soles increase was extended to all teachers, the first of similar increases promised over three years. This practice of granting equal absolute increases across the board to all teachers leads to an even greater compression of the salary structure.

| Area and Occupation | Weekly Hours Worked | Hourly Earnings | Earnings Adjusted for Weeks Worked | Teachers' Earnings (Assuming 20 Hours Worked at Home) | Teachers' Earnings (Assuming 40 Hours Worked at Home) |
|---|---|---|---|---|---|
| **TABLE 6.5: HOURLY EARNINGS BY OCCUPATIONAL GROUPS AND AREAS, THIRD QUARTER, 1997** (Nuevos Soles) | | | | | |
| **Urban Peru** | | | | | |
| Teachers | 26.7 | 5.7 | 7.2 | 6.0 | 5.2 |
| Professionals | 42.2 | 8.1 | 8.2 | 8.2 | 8.2 |
| Univ. Educated | 42.3 | 6.8 | 7.0 | 7.0 | 7.0 |
| **Lima** | | | | | |
| Teachers | 25.4 | 5.8 | 7.3 | 6.1 | 5.2 |
| Professionals | 42.1 | 10.0 | 10.2 | 10.2 | 10.2 |
| Univ. Educated | 42.3 | 8.3 | 8.5 | 8.5 | 8.5 |
| **Other Urban** | | | | | |
| Teachers | 27.2 | 5.6 | 7.2 | 6.0 | 5.1 |
| Professionals | 42.4 | 5.8 | 5.9 | 5.9 | 5.9 |
| Univ. Educated | 42.3 | 5.1 | 5.2 | 5.2 | 5.2 |

*Source:* Saavedra, Melzi, and Miranda (2001).

advantaged position of teachers is accentuated in Lima, though in other urban areas the differences are small.[19]

Whether teachers are earning salaries that approximate or exceed their opportunity cost is an inadequate guide to the salary policy to be pursued in the educational sector. If the goal is to improve the quality of education, one would think that the first objective should be to improve the quality of the teachers entering the profession. To the extent that a higher-quality teacher has a higher opportunity cost than the current cadres, it will be necessary to offer higher salaries in order to attract him or her. However, it makes little sense to raise all existing teacher salaries to the levels required to attract a more promising teacher. What this suggests is that the remunerations policy of the Ministry should be tailored to more closely fit the opportunity costs of those entering the teaching profession.

### A New Institutional Framework for Human Resources in the Education Sector
Taking a closer look at other provisions of the *Ley del Profesorado* and the *Reglamento* provides the opportunity to offer suggestions that might be incorporated in a new legal framework.

### Recommendations:
■ The Ministry of Economy and Finance needs to establish a central employment registry integrated into the SIAF, similar to the one advocated for the civil service sector. This would establish a general single payroll management system, supported by bank transfers.

---

19. The *Reglamento* provides for a monthly bonus equal to 30 percent of total remuneration for class preparation, and it is assumed that the earnings figures reported include this bonus.

■ The remunerations package should be simplified because it would be more transparent and equitable for the sums expended on fringe benefits to be distributed in the form of salary, and should allow employees to purchase the benefits or services they want. The current *Ley* and *Reglamento* are replete with a wide variety of fringe benefits and bonuses. There are 10 provisions for leave with pay; discounts available on public transport and for state-sponsored cultural events; 20 percent of all publicly financed housing is reserved for teachers; there is preferential access to mortgage credit; an automatic annual 2-percent increase in basic pay; family allowances; bonuses for length of service; payments upon the death of a teacher or his or her spouse, parent, or offspring; funeral benefits; upon retirement, a bonus in recognition of years of service; a 30 percent monthly bonus for class preparation; a 5 percent bonus for directors and university professors for performing their tasks; funds for the construction of facilities for the delivery of social services; and for cultural and entertainment purposes, among others. However, the value of these benefits to employees is positive only to the extent that they receive them. Not all employees receive them in equal amounts and, therefore, the compensation package has a different value for different individuals.

## BOX 6.1: THE SEQUENCING OF CIVIL SERVICE REFORM MEASURES

| Stage | Institutional Actions | Civil Service Actions |
|---|---|---|
| I. | Creation of a Reform Commission. | |
| II. | Issuance of invitations to pilot individual institutions to prepare and submit plans for human resources management reform. | Preparation of new Civil Service Law. |
| III. | Preparation of institutional reform plans. | Submission of law to Congress. |
| IV. | Review and approval of reform plans. | Enactment of Civil Service Law. |
| V. | Creation of management structures in to-be-reformed institutions. | Creation and staffing of Civil Service Directorate. |
| VI. | Management training. Start integrating payroll into SIAF by pilot institutions. | Preparation of internal *Reglamento*. |
| VII. | Begin the institutional restructuring process. | Prepare model *Reglamento* for adaptation to institutions. |
| VIII. | Identify the positions and job content required to meet programmatic objective. | Upgrading directors and staff of institutional human resources offices. Training. |
| IX. | Prepare internal *Reglamento*. | Select methodology for job description to be applied throughout the government and train institutional human resources department personnel in application of methodology. |
| X. | Perform job descriptions and evaluations; specify qualifications for filling each post; formalize in manuals. | Prepare model salary structure that reflects market rates of pay. |
| XI. | Staff decisions followed by retraining or recruitment of new personnel. Separation of redundant personnel with severance payments. | Apply Civil Service Law provisions to reformed institutions. |
| XII. | Personnel training. | Design a personnel information system with standard personnel forms and the networking of institutional information systems with a Directorate's centralized database. |
| XIII. | Full integration of payroll into the SIAF. | |

- A new law should also place a heavy emphasis on merit as a condition for entry into the profession and as a determinant of compensation. If committees are viewed as desirable to review the salary recommendations of principals or supervisors, these should be composed of persons of similar rank, perhaps with the participation of parent associations. Union officers tend not to be appropriate members of such committees.

- A more intensive use of contracting of teacher services is bound to provide greater flexibility in the allocation of posts. Contracting would permit the reallocation of positions from schools with declining enrollments to those districts with expanding student bodies. It would also facilitate the process of relieving ineffective teachers of their duties. If, however, contracting of teachers were not to become the standard form of employment, then the procedures for hiring teachers and granting tenure ought to be reformed. Because the removal of ineffective teachers is more difficult under a system that grants tenure, it becomes imperative to place greater emphasis on the way teachers are selected and evaluated. The present practice of holding qualifying exams for entry into the field should be made a legal requirement. Given the large number of potential applicants, the Ministry of Education can afford to establish high standards for entry into the field. We believe it is important that tenure not be granted upon entry to the profession, but rather every new teacher should be subject to a probationary period during which performance can be evaluated.

- A new law should redefine the rationale of a new salary structure for the profession and avoid bonuses or other payments that are unrelated to performance. For example, the current provision of automatic yearly increases rewards good and the poor teachers equally and, therefore, provides no incentive to improve performance. Attendance should also be taken into account to prevent teacher absenteeism.

A suggested sequencing of reform is depicted in Box 6.1.

# VII

# IMPROVING GOVERNANCE AND
# REDUCING CORRUPTION

*The collapse of the Fujimori Administration in the middle of corruption scandals raised awareness in the country about the need for a long-term progovernance and anticorruption strategy. President Fujimori's third term was short-lived: mounting evidence of corruption by close associates forced him to resign, and a Constitutional transition took place. Mr. Valentin Paniagua was converted from President of Congress to Interim President until July 2001, when Mr. Alejandro Toledo was inaugurated as the elected President. In April 2001, the Government of Peru (GOP) established the* Iniciativa Nacional Anti-Corrupcion *(INA), a committee with the task of promoting a national workshop with representatives of major agencies in charge of the fight against corruption and developing an anticorruption strategy. With the support of the World Bank and other international donors, the GOP requested a diagnostic study of corruption in Peru, the results of which follow.*[1]

P eru's most recent scores on governance are mixed. There is strong evidence of a causal relationship between good governance and better development outcomes, including higher per capita incomes, lower income mortality, and higher literacy. World Bank researchers recently compiled a massive cross-country database of some 300 governance indicators, yielding six clusters of composite measures: voice and accountability, political instability, government efficiency, regulatory

---

1. This section summarizes the World Bank Institute's study on governance, rule of law, and corruption for Peru (World Bank 2001c). The study was carried out during February and March 2001 and, although current Peruvian officials have indeed taken actions to address some of the issues identified below, their persistence allows change to take place only slowly. The main objective of the study is to support the anticorruption effort and the GOP's commitment in Peru. The rich survey data collected facilitate the unbundling of the many faces of corruption across governmental agencies and regions, from *administrative corruption* associated to laws, rules, and regulations, to *state capture* by vested interests affecting their actual design and implementation. Overall, Peruvian citizens (1,696 public service users), 401 enterprises, and 1,123 public officials responded. The refusal rates for each of the three surveys were low and, particularly among public officials, very low: barely 11.3 percent of interviewees did not complete the survey.

burden, rule of law, and corruption for two years, 1998 and 2001. Peru's scores in government effectiveness and regulatory quality have dropped significantly as the country has moved from an authoritarian-like regime to one with a more vocal and active opposition (Figure 7.1). Its overall score in corruption remains approaching the LAC average, but some scores are at the upper end, appearing particularly high—close to 60 percent—in procurement contracts of public works. To off-set such a gloomy picture, Peru's scores in voice and accountability, political stability, and rule of law have improved, thus reflecting the political opening that is taking place. Yet, significant challenges remain in these areas, too.

Survey evidence indicates that Peru faces serious corruption challenges (Figures 7.2 and 7.3). More than 85 percent of managers of enterprises interviewed rated corruption as the most serious problem they face. The uncertainty surrounding the decisions regarding the judicial system, the low quality and inefficiency of public administration, unstable economic policies, and the continuous changes in tax regulations are also perceived as very serious problems by more than half the enterprises. Comparing various dimensions of governance and quality of service delivery across four regions (Lima, Resto de Costa, Selva, and Sierra), governance appears uneven across Peru, with the Selva region ranking systematically higher than the other three regions. How costly bribery is for the competitive enterprise sector is suggested by the fact that most enterprises are prepared to materially contribute to controlling corruption. Enterprises report that they are willing to offer on average 6.8 percent of their gross revenues in order to eradicate corruption. This figure is higher only to improve the administration of the fiscal system. This large potential tax contribution is an indicator not only of how costly corruption is financially for many competitive businesses, but is also indicative of the fiscal losses to the Treasury if a more transparent system were to exist. Performance by regulatory agencies is generally well perceived (Box 7.1).

While Congress and the administration of justice are particularly afflicted, other government institutions appear to exhibit good governance and are highly regarded. In all three types of surveys and respondents, it is reported that Congress and rule-of-law institutions rate among the most corrupt state agencies as well as core public security institutions, such as the Police, the Army, and

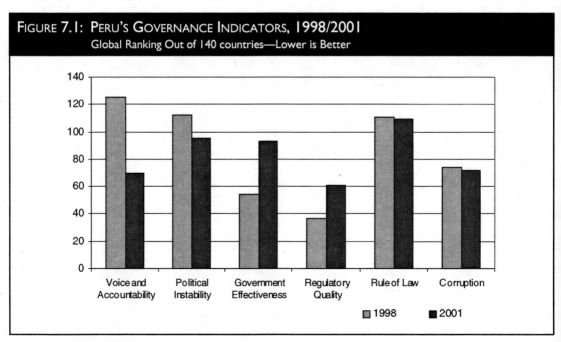

FIGURE 7.1: PERU'S GOVERNANCE INDICATORS, 1998/2001
Global Ranking Out of 140 countries—Lower is Better

Source: World Bank (2001c).

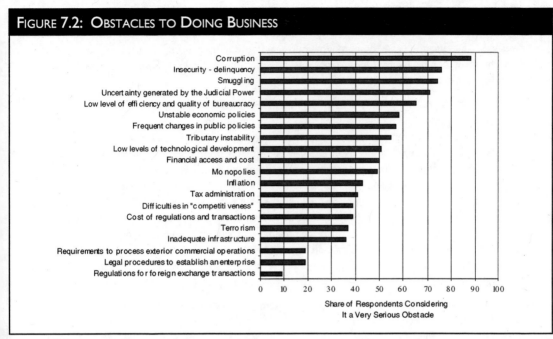

FIGURE 7.2: OBSTACLES TO DOING BUSINESS

*Source:* World Bank (2001c).

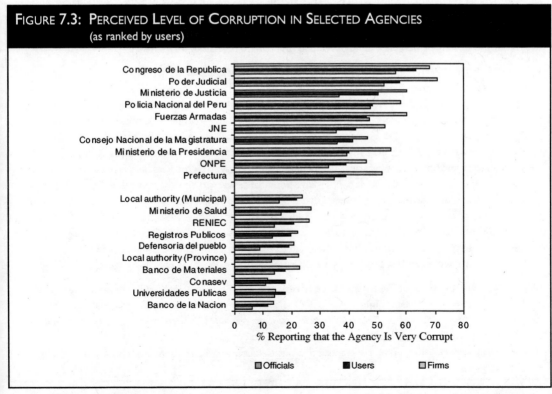

FIGURE 7.3: PERCEIVED LEVEL OF CORRUPTION IN SELECTED AGENCIES
(as ranked by users)

*Source:* World Bank (2001c).

## BOX 7.1: REGULATION OF INFRASTRUCTURE IN PERU

Any evaluation of the effectiveness of a regulatory framework would need to be based more on input than output measures. An evaluation based on output measures, although more appropriate, has nontrivial measurement and interpretation problems. On the input side, however, the evaluation is based on the legal, institutional, organizational, and procedural elements.

In Peru, the *legal and institutional* elements of the regulatory framework are good and above average in the Region. Regulation is grounded on sector-specific laws and complemented by concession contracts. The *institutional* component is good, with separate sector agencies; a single regulator but an advisory board, staffed by mostly professionals and not politicians; a budget financed by sector firms' contributions/fees; pay scales comparable to the private sector; and all the modes of transport regulated by a single agency, a most desirable structure and a rarity in the Region. A problem, however, is security of employment for the regulator, which could be stronger, and the appeal process that relies on the judiciary—but that is also the case practically everywhere else. The agencies also score well on the *organizational* element. They are well structured by functions and sectors, and staffed by competent professionals. Perhaps their major weakness is on the *procedural* side, in the sense that the framework does not give enough guidance on the process to inspire confidence and transparency. For example, there is little to compel the agency to explain or justify its timing and process to reach decisions, and checks and balances are scarce.

The sector is evolving to improve those components. A number of deficient structural elements have been corrected, such as eliminating operators from the regulatory board at *Organismo Superior de Inversión Privada en Telecomunicaciones* (OSIPTEL) and merging the institutional and the tariff agencies in the energy sector. Clarifying the roles of the antitrust agency and the regulatory agency, at least on energy issues, is needed. One weakness identified has been the managerial instability of the transport regulatory agency, *Organismo Superior de la Inversión en Infraestructura de Transporte de Uso Publico* (OSITRAN), which has had five presidents in four years. The agencies score rather well on implementation or outcome measures. They used level of conflicts, delays, price levels, quality of service, compliance with contract, and so forth, as evaluators. The agencies have increased their administrative capacity, trained their personnel, and developed appropriate regulatory instruments.

Regarding their financial and operative autonomy, Peru's regulatory agencies still have to be improved. The institutional base of their autonomy is fragile. This is, fundamentally, because of the absence of effective checks on possible decisions coming from the Executive branch, which undermine their effective independence. In previous governments, when presidential objectives shifted away from efficient, fair, and predictable regulation and toward other priorities, the funding of these agencies declined and their scope narrowed. This has to do with two flaws in their institutional design. First, they enjoy only limited budget independence. Second, these agencies' chief executive officers and board members are vulnerable to being removed by the President or by members of the ministerial cabinet for virtually any reason. They have potential powers to be very effective, if the regulator wishes it to be, and they have shown in general that they do. An indication of their autonomy has been the continuous claims and complaints by the Peruvian Executive and Congress, since 1996, that regulatory agencies have too much power, too many resources, and are accountable to no one. The limited autonomy these agencies have is fragile. The current government was initially inclined to reduce it. Yet it is to be commended for having adopted an open and competitive process for the selection of the heads of the regulatory agencies.

All in all, the perception about the performance of regulations in Peru remains above average in the region. The rankings for the World Economic Forum's 2002 *Global Competitiveness Report* placed Peru among the top four countries in the LAC Region. This framework, however, remains fragile to eventual institutional and legal changes, and can be improved, but future changes need to be done with transparency and predictability, honoring procedures established in the contracts, so as not to increase investor concerns about changing the rules of the game.

the Judiciary (Figure 7.3). About 90 percent of enterprises and users of public services neither believe that the Judiciary is independent from the government or political groups, nor that justice is administered in a fair, just, and transparent manner. In addition, enterprise managers report that bribes are used predominantly to facilitate judicial proceedings. In contrast, the Ombudsman, National Bank, *Comisión Nacional Supervisora de Empresas y Valores* (CONASEV), and provincial authorities are *not* regarded as misgoverned in general—with the notable exception of municipal fiscal/tax collection services, which were not viewed positively.

Bribes are used by firms predominantly to obtain public contracts, deal with the Judiciary, and obtain licenses and permits. Enterprises pay bribes at least twice as often to facilitate judicial procedures and obtain licenses as for import/export documents and other procedures (Figure 7.4). About half of all enterprises *always* pay bribes to win public contracts (Figure 7.5). This number rises to around 67 percent among foreign enterprises. Not only does this estimate of public contracts tainted by bribery reflect widespread and large-scale corruption, but the reported percentage bribe "fee" expected to secure such contracts is also rather large: enterprises report that on average, regardless of their ownership structure, 17 percent of the value of the contract is paid as a bribe. Further, in terms of time spent dealing with the public administration, foreign enterprises appear to spend more time than domestic firms. The poor performance of the Judiciary leads to the use of alternative mechanisms for conflict resolution. In addition, both managers and public officials report that bribes are paid to judicial authorities significantly more frequently than to guarantee contracts or obtain public services.

*State Capture.* Some key "institutions" outside of the public sector appear to also fuel misgovernance by exercising undue influence over the State (hint at modicum of "State capture").

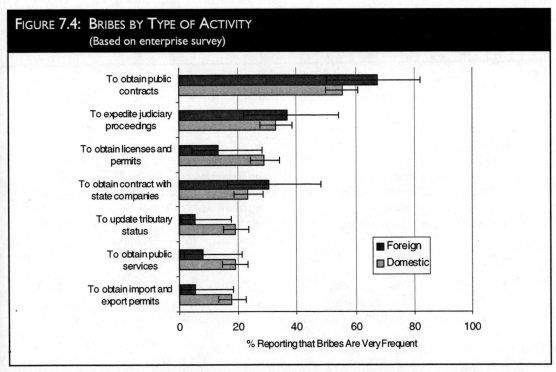

FIGURE 7.4: BRIBES BY TYPE OF ACTIVITY
(Based on enterprise survey)

Note: The thin lines represent margins of errors (or the 95 percent confidence intervals) for each value. They show the range where the true (population) proportion would lie with probability 0.95 if we had drawn a random sample from this population.

*Source:* World Bank (2001c).

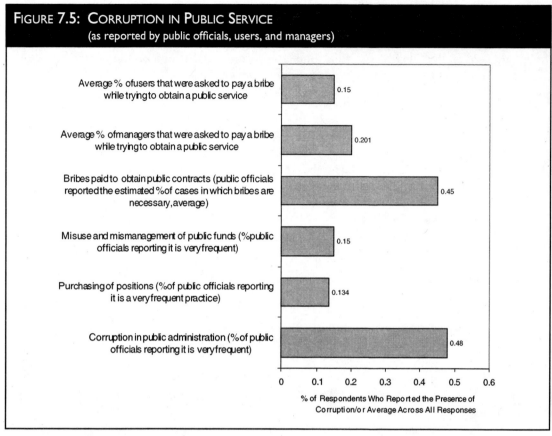

**FIGURE 7.5: CORRUPTION IN PUBLIC SERVICE**
(as reported by public officials, users, and managers)

*Source:* World Bank (2001c).

■ Both drug cartels and large financial and economic groups are perceived as wielding enormous influence in shaping laws, policies, and regulations, in contrast with associations of professionals, trade unions, and so forth, which are not seen as wielding excessive or undue influence.

■ Bribes are used to shape key government functions (high-level judiciary, legislative, and executive) much more often than to obtain public contracts or services.

■ Bribes are also linked to political funding. Nearly 30 percent of enterprises surveyed report that very often firms in Peru make political contributions to affect the political process. Though the majority of managers deny providing campaign contributions during the last elections, one third of firms report that bribe revenues are very often used to finance political campaigns, suggesting the existence of a tight, nontransparent link between government officials and the private sector.

■ Illicit payments are made to secure public administration positions. Thirteen percent of public officials report that this practice exists for some higher-level positions as a "private investment," while this number (and amount) declines significantly for lower-level positions.

## The Costs of Weak Governance and Corruption

Corruption increases inequality. Bribery is a significant and regressive "tax" on public service users. Users report major bribe expenditures extorted from institutions in charge of drivers' licenses and passports, construction permits, taxes, school enrollment, and so forth. Furthermore, the poorer groups are disproportionately affected by corruption, with lower-income users spending three times the percentage of their income on bribe payments that wealthier households spend (Figure 7.6).

## FIGURE 7.6: AVERAGE PERCENT OF INCOME PAID IN BRIBES

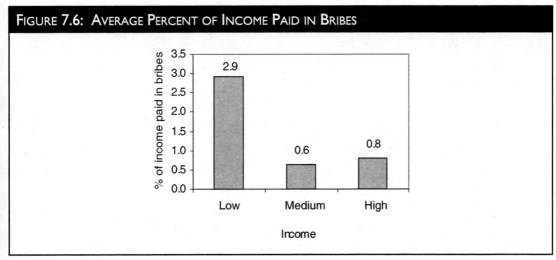

*Note:* Average percentage of income paid in bribes was computed for all respondents that used any public service and reported that they were or were not asked to pay a bribe.

*Source:* World Bank (2001c).

Businesses are also affected negatively by corruption. Enterprises spend more on bribes than on security, and this bribery "tax" is regressive. On average, 5.2 percent of monthly gross revenue of enterprises goes to bribes. For smaller enterprises, the bribery tax is particularly onerous: it accounts for 8.9 percent of their revenue, compared to the 2.5 percent large enterprises pay. And there is evidence that much of the onerous bribery tax on enterprise is indeed extorted, in the sense that on balance the firms do not benefit from it.

Bribes contribute to the lack of effective access to public services by the poor. Users, especially the poorest, are often discouraged by bureaucratic inefficiencies and choose not to seek a public service. Users cite government agencies like *Seguro Social de Salud* (ESSALUD, health services), *Empresa de Agua y Desagüe,* and the Superintendency for Tax Administration (SUNAT) as the ones where they are more likely not to attempt to obtain a service or complete a procedure because they do not provide effective service.

## Impact on Public Service Delivery

Regression analysis shows that, on average, paying more bribes does not result in higher-quality service delivery for the users and firms, and that the opposite might be true, with poor quality and bribery going hand in hand (Figure 7.7). Users report the highest levels of service quality in the offices devoted to issuing identity cards and passports, the real estate registry, and public schools. Users report the lowest levels of service quality in the offices handling national taxation (SUNAT), construction permits, real estate duties, and public health and social security (Figure 7.8). Enterprises report highest levels of service quality by utility companies and the lowest levels by municipal authorities.

*Health and Education Services.* Except in Lima, the quality of education by public schools is fair (more than 50 percent of users rate such service high), somewhat more homogeneous across the country than that of other social services, and bribes are not very frequent (7 percent) (Figure 7.9). However, user survey data also suggest that the most pressing issues of the education system are the quality of the personnel, especially since teacher promotion is very significantly influenced by political power, the high access costs to school, and the poor quality of school equipment. Conversely, the delivery and quality of health services are quite poor and very uneven across regions. While respondents report that they do not pay bribes for health care quite as often as for other services, they are very often discouraged from seeking health care due to its internal inefficiencies.

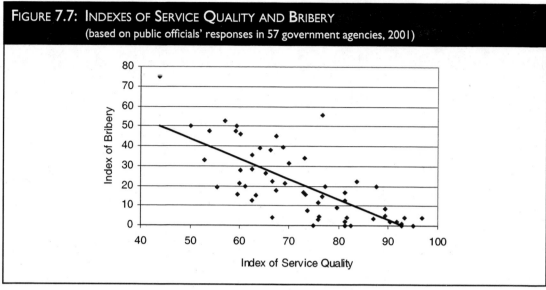

FIGURE 7.7: INDEXES OF SERVICE QUALITY AND BRIBERY
(based on public officials' responses in 57 government agencies, 2001)

*Source:* World Bank (2001c).

There is wide geographical heterogeneity in the quality of public service delivery. The quality of public services appears, on average, to be higher in the Selva region and Lima than in the rest of the country, and significantly greater in the case of offices handling drivers' licenses, judicial documents, basic health services, and schools.

There is also extremely varied service delivery performance across public institutions in Peru. Such variance permits a rigorous analysis to distill the key governance elements that influence ser-

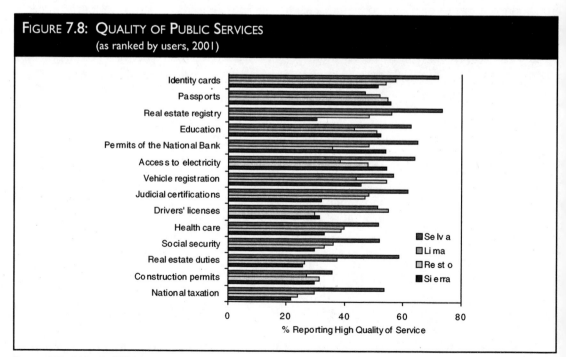

FIGURE 7.8: QUALITY OF PUBLIC SERVICES
(as ranked by users, 2001)

*Source:* World Bank (2001c).

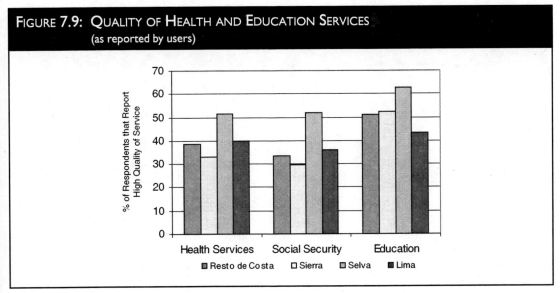

FIGURE 7.9: QUALITY OF HEALTH AND EDUCATION SERVICES
(as reported by users)

*Source:* World Bank (2001c).

vice delivery. This analysis between governance structures (as rated by users, enterprises, and public officials) suggests that the following factors may be important for improving governance:

- *Voice.* Simple and partial correlation analyses suggest that corruption-reporting mechanisms are associated with lower levels of corruption. Complaint mechanisms deter corruption.
- *Transparency.* The relationship between levels of corruption and transparency is statistically significant: agencies with more transparent procedures are less likely to display corruption.
- *Quality of Rules.* When rules and regulations over personnel are clearly specified, there are fewer incentives for corruption.
- *Social Inclusion and Collective Action.* Agencies with employees supporting civil society participation reforms in the public sector display lower levels of corruption.
- *Meritocracy.* Agencies in which personnel decisions are based on merit and performance are not associated with lower frequency of corruption.

Local governments perform much worse than national agencies in service delivery. The survey findings support the extent and seriousness of corruption and governance problems within municipal governments, when compared to national agencies. Overall, the degree of satisfaction in the provision of public services by local governments appears much below other government agencies in terms of quality, low cost, degree of satisfaction with the service expected, and accessibility to the poorest (Figure 7.10). Corruption levels in local governments also appear much higher than those in national agencies (except with respect to bribes paid to obtain a public service (Figure 7.11).

## A Policy Agenda for Improving Governance

Reducing corruption and improving governance is more than just a matter of law enforcement—it requires a societywide set of institutional reforms. A multipronged strategy that addresses the various forms of corruption—from *state* capture to *administrative corruption*—must address political accountability and transparency, promote a competitive private sector, strengthen institutional restraints, improve public sector management, and embrace civil society participation. It is important to emphasize that while the comprehensive approach described in Box 7.2 applies generally, the detailed components described within each box can lead to the determination of reform priorities in Peru.

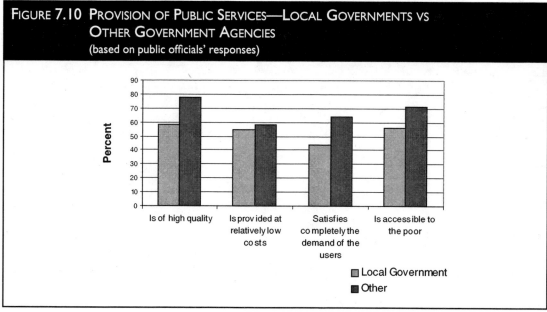

FIGURE 7.10   PROVISION OF PUBLIC SERVICES—LOCAL GOVERNMENTS VS
OTHER GOVERNMENT AGENCIES
(based on public officials' responses)

*Source:* World Bank (2001c).

The strategy needs to center on fundamental public sector reforms, while at the same time
strengthening civil society participation and constructively engaging the competitive segments of the
private business sector—within a coalition-building approach of shared responsibility. The evidence
suggests that public institutions characterized by effective voice and accountability mechanisms,
efficient corruption-reporting mechanisms, clear and well-defined rules, and a reform-minded staff,
perform better and are able to control corruption more effectively. The evidence also identified the

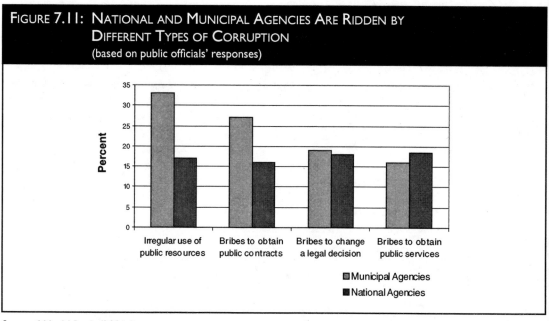

FIGURE 7.11:   NATIONAL AND MUNICIPAL AGENCIES ARE RIDDEN BY
DIFFERENT TYPES OF CORRUPTION
(based on public officials' responses)

*Source:* World Bank (2001c).

---

**BOX 7.2:  A MULTIPRONGED STRATEGY FOR ADDRESSING CORRUPTION AND IMPROVING GOVERNANCE**

**Institutional Restraints:**
- Independent and effective judiciary
- Legislative oversight
- Independent prosecution, enforcement

**Political Accountability:**
- Political competition, credible political parties
- Transparency in party financing
- Disclosure of parliamentary votes
- Asset declaration, conflict-of-interest rules

Anticorruption

**Civil Society Participation:**
- Freedom of information
- Public hearings on draft laws
- Role for media/NGOs

**Competitive Private Sector:**
- Economic policy reform
- Competitive restructuring of monopolies
- Regulatory simplification for entry
- Transparency in corporate governance
- Collective business associations

**Public Sector Management:**
- Meritocratic civil service with monetized, adequate pay
- Budget management (coverage, treasury, procurement, audit)
- Tax and customs
- Sectoral service delivery (health, education, energy)
- Decentralization with accountability

*Source: Anticorruption in Transition—A Contribution to the Policy Debate,* World Bank (2000).

---

support of public officials for civil society oversight and meritocracy reform as anticorruption mechanisms. The survey evidence underscores the importance of implementing reforms to enhance transparency and public oversight.

Design of an anticorruption strategy is facilitated when there is a good understanding of the levels of resistance that are likely to be encountered. Public officials were asked about their levels of support for various reforms. Public officials favor strengthening public administration, in terms of both merit-based promotions and simpler administrative procedures. They are also in favor of the introduction of a system of checks and balances and the oversight of public sector activities by civil society (Figure 7.12).

*The government needs to build credibility.* There is a significant discrepancy between users and public officials on the official commitment to fight corruption. More than half of users, compared to only 20 percent of public officials, reported that the government is not committed at all in the fight against corruption. This lack of trust toward government's commitment to eradicating corruption is especially felt among low-income users of public services. Conversely, the fact that a high proportion of public officials report preparedness of the public sector to fight corruption is an encouraging sign that not only the challenge is recognized within the public sector, but that there would be support among civil servants for an anticorruption and governance improvement program.

*Recommendations:*

- The government needs to make the fight against corruption a top priority. The majority of citizens (users, public officials, and firms) would support it.

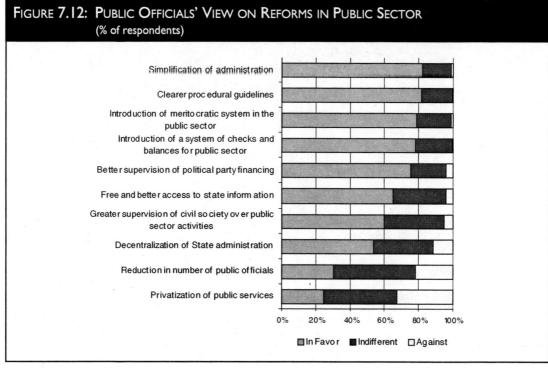

FIGURE 7.12: PUBLIC OFFICIALS' VIEW ON REFORMS IN PUBLIC SECTOR
(% of respondents)

*Source:* World Bank (2001c).

▓ The church and the media should be integrated as potential contributors in the fight against corruption: all respondents indicate they are key players in developing an anticorruption strategy. Low-income users exhibit high confidence in the media.

*The government needs to continue enhancing transparency.* Transparency in government is synonymous with openness. Introducing transparency requires that officials provide the public—civil society organizations, the media, or anyone else who is interested—sufficient information about the budget and its activities in order for the public to serve as an effective check on abuses (Chapter III).

## Recommendations:

▓ The government should consider issuing a freedom of information law that requires governments, national and subnational, to provide information to the public unless there is a valid reason (such as threat to national security) for the information to remain secret.
▓ Sufficient investment in training civil servants producing and handling potential public information is essential to prevent misunderstandings.
▓ A proactive approach that invites open oversight by Congress, civil society, and the media, for example, with respect to large privatizations or important tenders, is usually effective.

*The government needs to be accountable.* Separation of political and economic interests is a challenge facing governments everywhere. Building accountability into political life helps reduce the potential gains for "captor" firms and politicians alike.

## Recommendations:

▓ The GOP should improve its civil service recruiting system and migrate toward a merit-oriented promotion system, while guaranteeing insulation of the civil service from political changes (Chapter VI).

- The GOP should issue an Ethics Code Law for public service, with clear prohibitions of conflicts of interest, and an effective enforcement for both political and civil service positions. This is an essential corruption-deterrence tool. Since income and assets of high-ranking politicians in Peru are already publicly disclosed, the media and the general public may act as allies in uncovering conflicts of interest and questioning politicians who cannot explain their wealth. Such measure should also reach members of Congress, incoming regional presidents, and municipal authorities.
- The GOP should demand transparency of the financing of political parties. Campaigns should make clear the links, both explicit and implicit, between politicians and the interests they support. The GOP should mandate and publicize detailed reports on the finances of all political organizations, identifying contributors and beneficiaries, and providing civil society, the media, and the general public with tools they can use to identify the sources of State capture.
- Other possible measures by the GOP include banning the use of State resources for political campaigns, limiting the amount that can be spent on political campaigns, providing public funding, and prohibiting certain types of entities from contributing to political campaigns.

*The government needs to promote a sound business environment.* Since every bureaucratic and regulatory intervention creates an opportunity for corruption, reducing the regulatory burden on firms is a key element of the strategy.

## Recommendation:

- The GOP should examine and consider reducing the number of regulations and inspections. Clear rules defining when regulation is appropriate, sound analysis of a regulation's impact on firms, and a constant, mandated dialogue with the business community would increasingly be required to make regulatory reform sustainable.

*In sum, the government needs a comprehensive and inclusive approach to deal with governance.* Peru is at a crossroad in governance matters and it is crucial to implement a series of institutional reforms in key areas to improve transparency and accountability of government agencies. By addressing the systematic institutional weaknesses within key public sectors and agencies in Peru, that progress would be possible. Survey results show that reducing corruption is not just a matter of strong enforcement, but also hinges directly on the incentives facing public officials, enterprises, and households. Many reforms that are important in their own right—State and regulatory reform, judicial system reform, civil service development, and openness in government, to name a few—should now be viewed as part of a progovernance agenda. Although there is no single recipe for success, several countries have followed a three-pronged approach focusing on *enforcement* of anticorruption statutes, *education* of the population about their rights when dealing with the public sector and the harm corruption causes, and *prevention* of corruption by improving public sector governance. A sustainable strategy also endorses an inclusive approach with governmental and nongovernmental leaders.

## Recommendation:

- Creating a high-level steering committee, supported by a professional secretariat, can help bring together representatives of governmental bodies, both central and local, to develop a specific action plan to implement the governance strategy. By explicitly including representatives from outside government, the steering committees can further build credibility while mobilizing an important ally for reducing corruption.

# VIII

# FINE-TUNING FISCAL AND ENVIRONMENTAL MINING POLICIES

*While the Peruvian mining sector reform in the early 1990s resulted in the attraction of substantial exploration and development investment and the subsequent increase in mineral production and exports, since the late 1990s, key fiscal and environmental issues have negatively affected the competitiveness and level of acceptance of mining activities by foreign investors and local society, particularly with the local communities. The mining reform brought about the effective opening of the sector to direct foreign investment and the shift of the role of the State from owner-operator to lessor-regulator. This was accomplished by reforming the legal and institutional framework, privatizing the mining State-owned operations, and initiating an environmental management program. While the three reforms have been widely considered successful, three issues remain controversial and in need of adjustment.*

*First, the taxation system might be producing a certain loss of competitiveness. To the extent that it affects rates of return on investment, the effective tax rate in a given country is a major factor influencing the decision of foreign investors about where to invest their capital. Nations the mining fiscal systems of which impose high levels of overall taxation should expect to see lower levels of foreign investment in their mining sectors than countries with lower tax levels. Thus, as the world moves forward in the new century, there is a clear trend for mining taxation systems to become increasingly similar. Second, poor transparency is eroding the business climate. The highly centralized and nontransparent nature of the Peruvian governments of the 1990s created an issue of credibility with the local populations around the mining transfers from the Central Government to municipalities. Although the Mining Law establishes that 40 percent of the income tax generated by the mining operations—the* canon minero—*should go back to the municipalities (20 percent) and the regions (20 percent), and Bank findings show that its overall redistribution has been progressive, management of the* canon *has not been transparent, and there is a widespread perception that the local communities are not benefiting from it. Third, the perception of inadequate environmental control and of widespread conflict between mining companies and local populations is endangering the contribution and stability of a key sector of the Peruvian economy. Furthermore, the environmental information that the Ministry of Energy and Mines (MEM) has received from the mining companies has not been adequately released to the public, resulting in a feeling of mistrust toward mining activities.*

*This chapter offers empirical evidence that supports the view that the current Peruvian mining tax regime is among the most globally competitive systems in the world, and provides an appropriate balance between investor needs and government needs. However, room for improvement is constrained by the need for additional fiscal resources. Finally, it reviews other structural issues and offers detailed recommendations.*

## Background

The mining sector is essential for growth and development in Peru.[1] The sector generates more than 45 percent of the country's export earnings and contributes 5 to 7 percent of GDP.[2] The mining industry has long been Peru's most prosperous sector, with growth rates between 6.6 percent and 15.2 percent, during 1994–99, attracting a total of US$6.3 billion in investments during 1992–2001, and peaking in 2001 at US$1.3 billion. Potential tax revenues from the sector would be highly relevant to achieving its macroeconomic–financial projections. Tax expenditure associated to mining benefits is estimated at 0.4 percent of GDP (IMF 2000). The *canon minero* accounts for about 4 percent of total transfers to municipalities. Over one-quarter million people depend on formal mining for their livelihood, and it is estimated that this could double given the sector's potential. Mining is particularly relevant in some of the mountainous areas of the country, which are among the poorest regions. Attracting and sustaining mining investment in these areas would contribute to reducing the widening inequalities between the coastal areas and the lagging interior. However, investor interest in the sector has recently dropped dramatically, resulting in moderate investment projections of about $500 million per year between 2003 and 2005. The key question for Peru is whether it can institute reforms that will return the sector to its role as an engine of growth like, for example, in Chile.

Past reforms were left incomplete. The Peruvian General Mining Law provided a sound basis for the modernization of the sector. Results of mining reforms in the early 1990s were impressive: While global exploration investment went up 90 percent and grew fourfold in Latin America, between 1990 and 1997 in Peru it grew twentyfold. Since 1997, as a consequence of drastically lower metal commodity prices, the share of exploration investment of most developing countries was reduced substantially, as most international mining companies retreated to their traditional exploration areas. Yet Peru was able to keep its share of the total. This increased investment during the 1990s doubled the mineral production and mineral exports value of Peru. However, structural—taxation and environment—issues and low transparency of revenue transfers have negatively affected the competitiveness and credibility of the mining regime, expanded the perception of inadequate environmental control, and failed to prevent conflict between the government and the local populations, thus endangering the contribution and required stability of this critical source of growth.

## The Peruvian Taxation Regime

The existing Peruvian mining tax system is complex (Box 8.1). The term "tax" is defined as any levy imposed by the government on a productive agent, regardless of whether it takes the form of an explicit tax, a fee, or any other payment that is paid to the government or to another party because the taxpayer is required to do so by the government.

## Comparison of Peru's Tax System to Minerals Tax Systems in Selected Countries

Many of the major tax types of the mineral sector are already applied by Peru. Comparison of mining tax systems among different countries endowed with mineral resources is relevant from the standpoint of determining how attractive a particular country is to foreign investors in a world

---

1. The sections on taxation mainly draw on Otto (2002).
2. Peru's main mineral exports are iron, silver, zinc, copper, lead, platinum, and gold.

## BOX 8.1:  PERU: DESCRIPTION OF THE EXISTING MINING FISCAL SYSTEM

**Income tax:**

- *Distribution:* Fifty percent of income tax paid by a mine to the Central Government is to be remitted back to the canon where the mine is located.
- *Rate:* Twenty-seven percent under the general tax regime. If the taxpayer has elected to enter into a Stability Agreement or Mining Contract, the rate is 29 percent. An additional 4.1 percent tax is applied to net profits remitted (see withholding tax description below).

**Deductions for computing taxable income:**

- *Feasibility studies:* There are two possible interpretations: (a) treated as a development cost; may either be expensed in the year costs were incurred, or costs may be amortized over a period of three years from the year the minimum production is achieved; or (b) treated as a preoperative cost; may either be expensed in the year the cost is incurred, or costs may be amortized over a period of 10 years from the year in which minimum production is achieved.
- *Preproduction exploration costs:* Costs may either be expensed in the year they were incurred or amortized from the year the minimum production is achieved, over a period determined based on the life of the mine.
- *Development expenses:* Costs may either be expensed in the year they were incurred, or may be amortized over a period of three years from the year the minimum production is achieved.
- *Capital costs:* Taxpayer can select the rate of straight-line depreciation up to the allowed maximum; most mining, processing, and power equipment has a maximum of 20 percent per year; roads and buildings have a maximum of 3 percent unless a stability agreement (15 years) is in effect, in which case a 5-percent maximum applies; costs incurred for government-approved infrastructure such as a school, hospital, or recreational facility can be expensed as incurred.
- Costs qualifying for depreciation or amortization may be adjusted for inflation using the whole price index; however, adjustment is not allowed if (a) there is a stability agreement, and (b) the taxpayer has elected to keep its books in U.S. dollars.

The following types of costs may be deducted for computing net taxable income: preproduction exploration expenses, mine site development costs, feasibility study costs, operating costs, capital costs, qualifying loan interest, withholding tax on interest, property tax, fee based on land area, payroll taxes, workers' profit share, value added tax (when the VAT is not used as a credit).

**Excess profits type tax: None.**

**Royalties:** There are no royalties or similar taxes.

**Withholding tax on loan interest paid to foreign lenders:** 4.99 percent is applied to loans from abroad provided monies are sent into Peru, and the maximum interest is less than prime + 6 points or LIBOR + 7 points. Thirty percent is applied for the excess of interest exceeding the maximum limit, in cases where loans are entered into between related partners, and if the lender is a resident of a tax haven.

**Withholding tax on dividends remitted abroad:** None by that name. However, an additional rate of 4.1 percent on income tax is applicable when dividends are distributed.

**Withholding tax on salaries and fees paid to foreign consultants:** Thirty percent tax rate is applied on 80 percent of gross income (thus, in practice, the effective rate is 24 percent) if technical services are rendered in Peru. If technical services are rendered partly abroad and partly in Peru, a 30 percent tax rate is applied on 40 percent gross income (thus, in practice, the effective rate is 12 percent). Services totally rendered abroad are not subject to withholding tax.

**Import duty on foreign equipment:** Rates are generally 12 to 20 percent. The average rate for mining equipment is 12 percent. Import duties are not immediately deductible; rather, they are added to the asset acquisition cost and depreciated at the asset's depreciation rate.

*(continued)*

## BOX 8.1:  PERU: DESCRIPTION OF THE EXISTING MINING FISCAL SYSTEM (*CONTINUED*)

**Export duties on minerals:** None.

**Sales tax on equipment:** None

**Value added tax on purchased goods or services:** Eighteen percent VAT is levied on sales of goods and services, imports of goods, construction contracts, sales of real property by construction concerns, and services rendered abroad, but used in Peru; VAT may be reimbursed by means of assignable credit notes based on export sales; can offset VAT against income tax, or obtain a refund check. If minerals are sold locally, VAT applies to sales except for gold. The amount of VAT that may be credited is restricted to 18 percent of export sales, and any amount exceeding this may be carried forward as a credit against future export sales. VAT paid during exploration is refundable.

**Time to claim back value added tax:** Three to 6 months.

**Education tax:** None.

**Property tax:** Applies only to operations located in urban areas.

**Local development requirement:** None. If a taxpayer voluntarily contributes to local development and that local development project is approved by the proper government ministry, the costs may be expensed as incurred. In practice, approval is difficult or time consuming.

**Land use fees:** A validity tax, also called a good standing fee, is calculated based on the area in mining concession from the moment the claim is filed. The fee is US$3 per hectare per year and is deductible. Seventy-five percent is distributed by the Central Government to the canon where the mine is located.

**Stamp tax:** None.

**Payroll taxes paid by employer:** Extraordinary solidarity tax: 2 percent of salaries paid; health service (ESSALUD): 9 percent of salaries paid; national technical industrial training service, if more than 20 workers: 0.75 percent of salaries paid.

**National Service for Construction Industry Training:** 0.2 percent of total incomes comprised of materials, workmanship, general expenditures, technical direction, profits, or any other item that might be invoiced to the company's clients.

**Workers' profit sharing:** It is obligatory to pay a workers' participation of 8 percent on the net profits; of this amount up to 18 times monthly salary goes to the worker, with the remainder going to a special educational, social, and recreational fund. Disbursements are decided by a Board comprised of representatives of mining companies, government, and workers. The amount paid is allowed as a tax deduction. Not all foreign governments recognize this as a creditable tax, and double taxation can occur.

**Tax incentives:**
- **Loss carry-forward:** Four years.
- **Loss carry-back:** None.
- **Tax credits:** Income tax paid abroad in respect to income of foreign source taxable in Peru, may be deducted against Peruvian income tax within certain limits; qualifying VAT may be credited (see above).
- **Tax stability:** Titleholders of mining activities may enter into several types of tax stability agreements. Two types are defined under the Foreign Investment Law and two others under the General Mining Law. They are not mutually exclusive and a company can have both (one under the Foreign Investment Law and another under the General Mining Law). If an agreement is in place under the Mining Law, the income tax is increased by 2 percent.
     *Under the Foreign Investment Law,* a Stability Agreement (as an investee—the company which received the investment) granted by the National Commission for Foreign Investment and Technology guarantees for

(continued)

**BOX 8.1: PERU: DESCRIPTION OF THE EXISTING MINING FISCAL SYSTEM (*CONTINUED*)**

10 years stability concerning income tax regime, currency exchange regime, free availability of foreign currency, and nondiscrimination). To qualify, the investor must invest a minimum of US$10,000,000 within two years of the Stability Agreement.

*Under the General Mining Law,* an investor can enter into a Mining Contract. The agreements can be for a period of 10 or 15 years: 10-year—the investment must equal US$2 million and be destined to either start up an operation with a production capacity of 350 metric tons per day (Mt/day) to 5,000Mt/day; and 15-year—this agreement targets production of at least 5,000Mt/day and requires an investment of US$20 million for a start-up operation, or US$50 million to capitalize an existing operation. A Mining Contract guarantees the following: free marketing of mineral products for export or domestic sale; free disposal within the country and abroad of foreign currency generated by exports; free convertibility into foreign exchange of local currency generated by mineral sales; nondiscrimination in exchange matters; depreciation rates of 20 percent for mining and processing equipment and 5 percent for buildings (15-year agreements); the electable option to keep books in U.S. dollars (15-year agreements); general tax stability including income tax, regime, compensation and/or tax refunds, customs duties, municipal taxes, and validity fee; nondiscrimination in exchange matters; and freedom to remit profits, dividends, financial resources.

*Tax reduction in Selva regions:* Special tax rules and rates apply to VAT, income tax, and excise tax.

**Requirement to use local goods and services:** None.

**Local equity requirement:** None.

**Government equity requirement:** None.

**No ring fencing principles apply** (may consolidate books).

**Foreign external accounts:** Allowed for receipt of revenues.

**Exchange controls:** No significant restrictions.

*Source:* Otto (2002).

where investment in mining depends on, among other things, decision criteria such as after-tax profitability, the investor's ability to predetermine the applicable tax liabilities, the stability of the tax regime, and the level and method of tax levies (Box 8.1).

Comparisons of mine taxation in different taxing jurisdictions are a complex matter (Table 8.1). An isolated comparison of any one type of taxing mechanism may lead to certain insights, but taken alone may not provide a useful indication of how mine taxation in one jurisdiction compares to that in another. To gain a broader understanding of how overall tax systems compare, it is necessary to analyze them in a holistic manner. Both to facilitate and formalize such an analysis, it is a common practice to define a hypothetical pre-feasibility-type model mine and then apply different taxation systems to that mine and compare the results. In the background work for this chapter, model mines were specified and various measures of taxation and profitability calculated to allow comparison between Peru and other countries.[3]

The current tax system in Peru is globally competitive for mining. When countries are ranked from the standpoint of the foreign investors' internal rates of return (IRR), Peru ranked 11th out of 23 (base metal) and 7th out of 23 (gold), and in the second-lowest quartile (Tables 8.2 and 8.3).

---

3. Yet, this is not the only possible approach. Another familiar one is to analyze competitiveness by level of investments in new deposits and expansion in already existing ones. The model mines used in the background work for this chapter were based on the standard base metal (copper) mine model and gold mine model developed at the Institute for Global Resources Policy and Management at the Colorado School of Mines. Description of the model, its methodology, attributes, and limitations can be found in Otto (2002). The model's estimates are particularly sensitive to price assumptions.

## TABLE 8.1: Mineral Taxes in Peru and Other Countries

| Tax type | Does Peru Impose this Levy? Yes | No | Comments |
|---|:---:|:---:|---|
| Income tax | X | | |
| Excess profits tax | | X | |
| Royalties | | X | |
| Withholding tax on remitted dividends | | X | An additional rate of 4.1 percent (income type tax) is applicable when dividends are distributed (similar to a dividend withholding tax, but it is not technically termed a withholding tax). |
| Withholding tax on remitted loan interest | X | | |
| Import duties on equipment | X | | Equipment imported for temporary use, such as for exploration work, may be imported without payment of import duties if such equipment is reexported within a year. |
| Export duties on minerals | | X | |
| Sales tax on purchased equipment | | X | |
| Sales tax on minerals paid by mine | | X | |
| VAT on services | X | | Fully refundable during exploration (as of the date of this report, refund is not applied because the procedural rules are pending). |
| VAT on equipment | X | | Fully refundable during exploration (as of the date of this report, refund is not applied because the procedural rules are pending). |
| VAT on mineral sales | X | | VAT does not apply if the mineral is sold for export. |
| Property tax/fee | | X | A property tax applies only to mines located within urban areas. |
| Education tax/fee | | X | An education tax is not applied; however, an 8 percent profit-based, profit-sharing requirement is applied, and a portion may go to a special educational, social, and recreational fund. |
| Local development tax/fee | | X | |
| Fees based on land area | X | | Called a "validity tax" or "good standing fee." |
| Stamp tax | | X | |
| Payroll taxes | X | | |
| Excise tax on fuel | X | | Exempted during exploration (the exemption is not applied because the procedural rules are pending). |

Source: Otto (*2002).

### Sensitivity of the Peruvian Tax System to Prices and Costs

Using a standard copper mine model, Peru's mining tax system is quite neutral to changes in prices, operating costs, and capital costs, except when prices become low (Table 8.4). The impact of a tax system on a mine can vary according to its profitability. If the overall effective tax rate (ETR) goes up as profitability goes up, the system is said to be progressive. If the ETR decreases as

| TABLE 8.2: COMPARATIVE MEASURES OF PROFITABILITY AND EFFECTIVE TAX RATE FOR A MODEL BASE METAL MINE IN SELECTED JURISDICTIONS | | |
|---|---|---|
| **Country** | **Foreign Investor's IRR (%)** | **Total Effective Tax Rate (%)** |
| **Lowest Taxing Quartile** | | |
| Sweden | 15.7 | 28.6 |
| W. Australia | 12.7 | 36.4 |
| Chile | 15.0 | 36.6 |
| Zimbabwe | 13.5 | 39.8 |
| Argentina | 13.9 | 40.0 |
| China | 12.7 | 41.7 |
| **Second-Lowest Taxing Quartile** | | |
| Bolivia | 11.4 | 43.1 |
| South Africa | 13.5 | 45.0 |
| Philippines | 13.5 | 45.3 |
| Kazakstan | 12.9 | 46.1 |
| **Peru** | 11.7 | 46.5 |
| Tanzania | 12.4 | 47.8 |
| **Second-Highest Taxing Quartile** | | |
| Indonesia | 12.2 | 48.6 |
| Poland | 11.0 | 49.6 |
| U.S. (Arizona) | 12.6 | 49.9 |
| Mexico | 11.3 | 49.9 |
| Greenland | 13.0 | 50.2 |
| Ghana | 11.9 | 54.4 |
| **Highest Taxing Quartile** | | |
| Papua New Guinea | 10.8 | 57.8 |
| Uzbekistan | 9.3 | 62.9 |
| Ivory Coast | 8.9 | 62.4 |
| Ontario Canada | 10.1 | 63.8 |
| Burkina Faso | 3.3 | 83.9 |

*Source:* Otto (2002).

profitability goes up, it is said to be regressive. Progressive tax systems tax more profitable mines at a higher effective rate than mines with lower profits. Most economists agree that neutral or slightly progressive tax systems are better than regressive systems.

## Comparing Tax Stability Across Countries

In a global survey of mining companies, over 50 percent of the respondents listed tax stability as a "very important" factor in investment decisionmaking. Out of a list of 60 investor criteria, tax system stability ranked 10th in importance. In the mining business the investment horizon is long, and companies are usually reassured by tax systems that reduce tax payment uncertainty and vulnerability, particularly during the loan and project payback periods. However, many governments are hesitant to resort to tax stability agreements. This is because there is a basic tenet that one generation of lawmakers should not be able to tie the hands of future lawmakers. Another relevant consideration is that tax stability is desired by all productive sectors because it reduces uncertainty. Then, if stability is offered to one sector, other sectors will also seek it.

The government faces a tradeoff. On one hand, stability agreements enhance the potential for mineral sector investment, but, on the other hand, they complicate the tax system and raise

## TABLE 8.3: COMPARATIVE ECONOMIC MEASURES FOR A MODEL I GOLD METAL MINE IN SELECTED JURISDICTIONS

| Country | Foreign Investor's Internal Rate of Return (%) | Total Effective Tax Rate (%) |
|---|---|---|
| **Lowest-Taxing Quartile** | | |
| Sweden | 19.2 | 29.1 |
| South Africa | 18.8 | 32.6 |
| Chile | 18.3 | 36.8 |
| Philippines | 18.4 | 38.2 |
| Argentina | 16.6 | 42.5 |
| W. Australia | 15.2 | 43.1 |
| **Second-Lowest Taxing Quartile** | | |
| Peru | 14.7 | 43.3 |
| Zimbabwe | 15.7 | 45.9 |
| U.S. (Nevada) | 15.1 | 49.3 |
| Bolivia | 12.2 | 52.4 |
| Kazakstan | 13.5 | 54.4 |
| Greenland | 14.7 | 54.9 |
| **Second-Highest Taxing Quartile** | | |
| Ghana | 13.6 | 56.7 |
| Tanzania | 12.7 | 57.9 |
| Indonesia | 11.4 | 60.4 |
| Uzbekistán | 11.2 | 62.0 |
| Mexico | 10.4 | 62.9 |
| Ontario Canada | 10.7 | 68.3 |
| **Highest Taxing Quartile** | | |
| Ivory Coast | 9.1 | 69.1 |
| Papua New Guinea | 8.7 | 72.3 |
| China | 7.1 | 73.9 |
| Poland | 3.0 | 90.2 |
| Burkina Faso | −1.6 | 106.0 |

Source: Otto (2002).

## TABLE 8.4: COPPER MODEL: PERU'S TAX SYSTEM SENSITIVITY TO PRICE AND COST CHANGES

| | Effective Tax Rate (%) | System Effect |
|---|---|---|
| **Price Sensitivity:** | | |
| US$0.80/lb | 126 | Regressive |
| US$1.10/lb (base case) | 47 | |
| US$1.50/lb | 39 | |
| **Operating Cost Sensitivity:** | | |
| US$0.40/lb | 45 | Fairly Neutral |
| US$0.45/lb (base case) | 47 | |
| US$0.50/lb | 49 | |
| **Capital Cost Sensitivity:** | | |
| US$550,000,000 | 43 | Fairly Neutral |
| US$610,000,000 (base case) | 47 | |
| US$650,000,000 | 48 | |

Note: A rate higher than 100 percent indicates that the mine is paying taxes in excess of its net income.

Source: Otto (2002)

administrative costs. In addition, if taxes are stabilized for various mines, then an administrative challenge can arise over time. As the underlying tax laws change, each stabilized mine will have a tax regime dating to the time the stability agreement was entered into. This means that, over time, there will be multiple tax regimes and the government agency charged with tax administration will increasingly face a more complicated situation monitoring and enforcing each. This entails costs. (See Table 8.5 for the availability of tax stability in selected jurisdictions.)

Currently, in Peru, there are hundreds of mining concessions with stability agreements. However, because these agreements stabilize taxes for only around 10 to 15 years, over time the affected mines will revert to the general tax system in the future. Stability also carries a price for companies—an additional 2 percent rate is applied to the 27 percent income tax. Stability is, indeed, important to investors—witness the number of mining concession holders who have agreed to pay the premium. One option open to the Peruvian government is to raise the amount of this premium. The effect of raising the stability premium is shown in Table 8.6. As can be seen in the table, for the two model mines a premium of 5 percent on the regular income tax rate of 27 percent reduces the

## TABLE 8.5: AVAILABILITY OF TAX STABILITY IN SELECTED JURISDICTIONS

| Country | Some Form of Tax Stability Available? | Description |
|---|---|---|
| Argentina | Yes | 30 years, provincial & municipal taxes, import duties, exchange rules. |
| Bolivia | No | – |
| Burkina Faso | Yes | During the term of the contract; except mining taxes and fees. |
| Canada (Ontario) | No | – |
| Chile | Yes | 10 years, if mine elects a higher income tax rate (42%). |
| China | No | – |
| Ghana | No | – |
| Greenland | No | – |
| Indonesia | Yes | Tax stabilized for life of mining agreement or a shorter period (Contract of Work). |
| Ivory Coast | No | – |
| Kazakhstan | Yes | Taxes stabilized for life of mining agreement. |
| Mexico | No | – |
| **Peru** | Yes | Two systems of tax stability: mining contracts (10 to 15 years tax stability), and 10-year Legal Stability Agreements that fix the income tax regime and certain other fiscal imposts; 2% additional rate. |
| Philippines | No | – |
| Poland | No | – |
| South Africa | No | – |
| Sweden | No | – |
| Tanzania | No | – |
| U.S. (Arizona) | No | – |
| Uzbekistan | Yes | Most major taxes may be frozen for 10 years from date of establishment; tax experts warn that there may be difficulties with the practical implementation. |
| W. Australia | No | – |
| Zimbabwe | No | – |

Source: Otto (2002).

## TABLE 8.6: TAX SYSTEM SENSITIVITY TO INCOME TAX RATE

| Income Tax Rate | Effective Tax Rate (%) | Investor IRR (%) | Govt Revenue: All Taxes & Fees (US$ millions) |
|---|---|---|---|
| **Copper Model** | | | |
| 25% | 45 | 11.9 | 451 |
| 27% (current) | 47 | 11.7 | 471 |
| 27 + 2 = 29% (stabilized) rate | 48 | 11.5 | 491 |
| 27 + 3 = 30% | 49 | 11.4 | 501 |
| 27 + 5 = 32% | 51 | 11.1 | 521 |
| **Gold Model:** | | | |
| 25% | 42 | 15.0 | 73 |
| 27% (current) | 43 | 14.7 | 76 |
| 27 + 2 = 29% (stabilized) rate | 45 | 14.4 | 79 |
| 27 + 3 = 30% | 46 | 14.3 | 80 |
| 27 + 5 = 32% | 48 | 13.9 | 83 |

Source: Otto (2002).

investor's rate of return by about 1 percent, and the effective tax rate remains at about 50 percent or lower.

*Recommendation:*
■ Companies find tax stability very attractive, and Peru's stability agreements are an incentive to investors. Therefore, it is recommended that tax stability agreements be retained but that the premium for all future such agreements be raised to 5 percent. The disadvantages of such agreements (sector discrimination and administrative burden) are more than offset by the increased tax base that may be created in the future by higher levels of investment, and the higher levels of tax paid based on the 2-percent premium. Investors would probably be willing to pay a higher premium for tax stability.

The income tax rate of 27 percent in Peru is somewhat lower than in some nations (Table 8.7). In addition, a 4.1 percent additional income tax is applied to remitted dividends. The net effect for many foreign companies is a rate of around 30 percent. If a taxpayer desires a stability agreement, and many miners probably would, the base rate is 29 percent.

*Recommendation:*
■ The current income tax rate should be retained.

Peru uses a form of accelerated depreciation for most mine equipment (20 percent straight-line method). The most common form of tax-base incentive for mining is accelerated depreciation. Most nations provide the mining industry with some sort of accelerated depreciation (Table 8.8). Until recently, Peru also provided a form of accelerated depreciation on mine buildings at a rate of 20 percent (straight-line). After tax reform, this was extended to a 3 percent depreciation rate, which is in line with depreciation periods allowed by many other nations.

Unlike most industries, when a mine closes, its buildings usually have no future function—that is, no market value. Thus, mines the duration of which is less than the depreciable life of their buildings will never be able to fully depreciate these buildings. For this reason, some nations allow a shorter depreciation period, or an alternative depreciation method (such as life of the mine).

## TABLE 8.7: INCOME TAX RATES APPLIED TO MINING PROJECTS IN SELECTED JURISDICTIONS

| Country | Corporate Income Tax Rate |
|---|---|
| Argentina | 35% |
| Bolivia | 25% (a surtax may also apply in some cases) |
| Burkina Faso | 35% (0.5% of previous year turnover is the minimum tax) |
| Canada (Newfoundland) | Federal: effectively 29.12%, including 4% surtax); provincial: 14% |
| Chile | 15% (two elective regimes are available) |
| China | 33% (30% to Central Gov't, 3% to provincial gov't) |
| Ghana | 35% |
| Greenland | 35% |
| Indonesia | 30% (previous rates range from 221/2–48%) |
| Ivory Coast | 35% |
| Kazakhstan | 30% (excess profits tax may apply) |
| Mexico | 35% |
| Papua New Guinea | 35% for large (SML) mines, 25% for most other mines |
| **Peru** | 27% (29% for taxpayer with stability agreement) |
| Poland | 2000, 30%; 2000–01, 28%; 2003, 24%; 2004+, 22 |
| South Africa | 30% for other than gold; formula > 30% for gold mines |
| Sweden | 28% |
| Tanzania | 30% |
| U.S. (Arizona) | Progressive based on income (profit level) |
| Uzbekistan | 33% |
| W. Australia | 2000–01, 34; 2001+, 30% |
| Zimbabwe | 35% |

*Source:* Otto (2002).

Table 8.9 shows the impact of a 3 percent versus a 20 percent depreciation rate. The effect is considerable for the short-lived gold model mine, but there is less of an impact on the longer-lived copper model mine.

*Recommendation:*

▪ A longer period of depreciation (8 to 10 years) should be considered and the previous system of 20 percent depreciation should be reinstated for buildings; a 3 percent rate yields a depreciation period of over 33 years (longer than the life of most mines).

Peru has an exceptionally short loss carry forward time limit of four years. One of the most common tax incentives is to allow taxpayers the ability to carry forward losses from one year to offset taxable income in the succeeding years. For capital-intensive industries and for industries exceptionally prone to commodity price fluctuation, criteria that are no doubt met by the mining, loss carry forward is an important issue. For a sample of countries, a loss carry forward time limit as of 2000 shows that, of the 22 nations, all had a longer time limit than Peru (Table 8.10). Table 8.11 shows the effect of lengthening the loss carry forward time limit.

*Recommendation:*

▪ The loss carry forward time limit should be extended to at least 10 years, or preferably, no time limit should be imposed. While a short period is adequate for most small, short-lived mines, it is not conducive to attracting investment for larger mines.

**TABLE 8.8: DEPRECIATION APPLIED TO TYPICAL MINING EQUIPMENT IN SELECTED JURISDICTIONS**

| Country | Accelerated Method Available for Some Capital Equipment (Yes or No) | Example |
|---|---|---|
| Argentina | Yes | 3-year straight-line |
| Bolivia | Yes | 8-year straight-line |
| Burkina Faso | Yes | Useful life minus one year |
| Canada | Yes | Up to 100% in year incurred for new mine or 25% declining pool |
| Chile | Yes | 3-year straight-line |
| China | Yes | 10 years |
| Ghana | Yes | 75% in 1st year, then 50% declining balance |
| Greenland | Yes | The company may decide the rate and period |
| Indonesia | Yes | 10-year straight-line or 20% declining balance |
| Ivory Coast | Yes | Method of acceleration depends on life of equipment |
| Kazakhstan | Yes | 25% declining balance method |
| Mexico | No | |
| **Peru** | Yes | 5-year straight-line (20%), except for mine buildings |
| Philippines | Yes | Twice the normal straight-line rate |
| Poland | Yes | 5-year straight-line (20%) |
| South Africa | Yes | Expensed in 1st year of production |
| Sweden | Yes | 5-year straight-line (20%) |
| Tanzania | Yes | 12.5% straight-line |
| U.S. (Arizona) | No | |
| Uzbekistan | No | 8% straight-line |
| W. Australia | Yes | Prime cost or diminishing value methods (less than effective life) |
| Zimbabwe | Yes | Expensed in year incurred or 1st year of production |

Source: Otto (2002).

**TABLE 8.9: TAX SENSITIVITY TO BUILDING DEPRECIATION RATES**

| Loss Carry Forward Time Limit | Effective Tax Rate (%) | Investor IRR (%) | Government Revenue: All Taxes & Fees (US$ millions) |
|---|---|---|---|
| **Copper Model:** | | | |
| 3% rate (current system) | 47 | 11.7 | 471 |
| 20% rate | 46 | 11.9 | 461 |
| **Gold Model:** | | | |
| 3% rate (current system) | 43 | 14.7 | 76 |
| 20% rate | 41 | 15.2 | 72 |

Source: Otto (2002).

## TABLE 8.10: LOSS CARRY FORWARD/BACK POLICY IN SELECTED JURISDICTIONS

| Country | Loss Carry Forward | Loss Carry-Back Time Limit (yrs) | Available | Time Limit (yrs) |
|---|---|---|---|---|
| Argentina | Yes | 5 | No | – |
| Bolivia | Yes | None | No | – |
| Burkina Faso | Yes | 5 | No | – |
| Canada (Ontario) | Yes | 7 | Yes | 3 |
| Chile | Yes | None | Yes | None |
| China | Yes | 5 | No | – |
| Ghana | Yes | None | No | – |
| Greenland | Yes | None | Yes | 5 |
| Indonesia | Yes | 8 | No | – |
| Ivory Coast | Yes | 5 | No | – |
| Kazakhstan | Yes | 7 | No | – |
| Mexico | Yes | 10 | Yes | None |
| **Peru** | **Yes** | **4** | **No** | **–** |
| Philippines | Yes | 5 | No | – |
| Poland | Yes | 5 | No | – |
| South Africa | Yes | None | No | – |
| Sweden | Yes | None | No | – |
| Tanzania | Yes | None | No | – |
| U.S. (Arizona) | Yes | 15 | Yes | 3 |
| Uzbekistan | No | – | No | – |
| W. Australia | Yes | None | No | – |
| Zimbabwe | Yes | None | No | – |

Source: Otto (2002).

## TABLE 8.11: TAX SENSITIVITY TO LOSS CARRY FORWARD TIME LIMIT

| Loss Carry Forward Time Limit | Effective Tax Rate (%) | Investor IRR (%) | Government Revenue: All Taxes & Fees (U$ millions) |
|---|---|---|---|
| **Copper Model:** | | | |
| 4 years (current system) | 47 | 11.7 | 471 |
| 5 years | 45 | 12.1 | 451 |
| 7 years | 45 | 12.1 | 450 |
| No time limit | 45 | 12.1 | 450 |
| **Gold Model:** | | | |
| 4 years (current system) | 43 | 14.7 | 76 |
| 5 years | 43 | 14.7 | 76 |
| 7 years | 43 | 14.7 | 76 |
| No time limit | 43 | 14.7 | 76 |

Source: Otto (2002.)

Peru does not have a provision for mining closure. Of increasing concern to governments is the issue of mine reclamation and closure. These costs are primarily incurred by the miner late in the project at a time when production is falling off or close to nil. Thus, companies cannot recover the costs involved with closure unless the tax system is adjusted to take these into account while cash flows are still being generated. It is in the government's interest to see that the company does plan and set aside funds for this activity, because at the end of the mine life, funds will not be generated. One way to encourage companies to fund closure is to require an annual setaside over the life of the mine and to allow this setaside as a tax deduction. Table 8.12 indicates the effect of allowing a deduction for such costs spread equally over the life of the mine.

### Recommendation:

■ The tax system should be modified so that money set aside for this purpose can be deducted straight-line as amortization over the productive life of the mine.

Peru's current tax system recognizes the importance of mine contributions to local communities and infrastructure and allows a deduction for such expenditures. There is intense interest by many stakeholders in furthering the concept of sustainable development. One way to foster this is to invest in communities impacted by mining so that when the mine closes, the affected communities will be able to carry on with social and alternative economic activities. Deductions are allowed only if the expenditure is approved by the government, and companies have found it extremely difficult to get such approval from the relevant ministries.

### Recommendations:

■ The current practice of allowing government-approved, miner-paid-for investment in communities and infrastructure to be tax deductible should continue. Deductions should apply not only to hard investment (transport, power), but also to soft investment in local infrastructure/capacity building by community groups (training, education).

■ However, the current system of approval does not work well, if at all, and needs reform. Such approval authority should vest in a single ministry, not with the ministry responsible for the particular type of infrastructure.

■ The relevant law should also state that if the ministry does not give its approval for such tax status on the proposed investment within a reasonable time period, say 60 days, the request will be deemed to have been approved.

Until recently, Peru offered mining investors an incentive to increase the company's production with a reinvestment provision, but this benefit was eliminated in a recent tax reform. Before

| TABLE 8.12: TAX SENSITIVITY TO ANNUAL ALLOWED CLOSURE DEDUCTION OVER THE MINE LIFE | | | |
|---|---|---|---|
| Closure Deduction | Effective Tax Rate (%) | Investor IRR (%) | Government Revenue: All Taxes & Fees (US$ millions) |
| **Copper Model:** | | | |
| No deduction (current system) | 47 | 11.7 | 471 |
| Annual life of mine deduction | 46 | 11.8 | 463 |
| **Gold Model:** | | | |
| No deduction (current system) | 43 | 14.7 | 76 |
| Annual life of mine deduction | 42 | 15.1 | 73 |

*Source:* Otto (2002.)

## TABLE 8.13: TAX SENSITIVITY TO REINVESTMENT ALLOWANCE

| Scenario | Effective Tax Rate (%) | Investor IRR (%) | Government Revenue: All Taxes & Fees (US$ millions) |
|---|---|---|---|
| **Copper Model:** | | | |
| 20% expansion, no reinvestment allowance (current system) | 46 | 12.1 | 533 |
| 20% expansion, 80% reinvestment allowance | 44 | 12.5 | 506 |

*Source:* Otto (2002).

reform, the company was not subject to paying income tax on the profits it reinvested, provided these sums were in accordance with an investment program approved by the mining authority. The period of validity was four years, but could be extended for another three. However, the benefit was capped at 80 percent of the total profits, with the balance being subject to income tax. A reinvestment incentive such as this is extremely uncommon globally. Most governments use the "penalty" approach to encourage reinvestment rather than the "incentive" approach, that is, they impose a foreign-dividend withholding tax. To assess the impact of such an incentive, the copper mine model was modified (Table 8.13).[4]

A critical policy question when assessing a proposed tax incentive is whether the incentive (which, presumably, will lead to a short-term tax decrease) will lead to increased tax revenues over the long run. There are two ways to look at this: (a) will government returns from an individual project be increased over the life of the project, and (b) will government revenue increase because other potential investors (who would not have invested had there been no incentive) invest? With regard to (a), for the particular mine model used here, the table shows that the government will end up with less revenue. Even though there will be more metal sold over the life of the mine and various taxes will be applied to those sales, the additional revenue does not equal the amount of revenue lost in the four tax-incentive years. With regard to (b), it is doubtful that such an incentive would attract new investors. In practice, the incentive might further reduce government revenue if companies purposefully underbuild initial capacity in order to take advantage of the liberal capacity increase allowance in later years.

### Recommendation:

■ The decision to eliminate the reinvestment tax allowance should *not* be reversed.

Peru is one of the mining countries in the world that do not impose a traditional royalty-type tax. The theory of optimal taxation of nonrenewable natural resources states that, under suitable assumptions, a government can tax away the pure rents generated in the extraction of those resources with no loss of allocation efficiency. This justifies the imposition of special taxes on nonrenewable-resource producers over and beyond the taxes levied on firms operating in the other sectors of the economy. It is widely acknowledged that the simplest special tax to administer is the gross royalty, and this helps explain why 60 percent of the countries in the reference sample impose royalties on mining producers (Table 8.14).

---

4. It allows for a four-year, phased 20 percent mine capacity expansion commencing in the eighth year after production began. The cost was assumed to be $80 million for the expansion. It was assumed that an 80 percent profit exemption cap is applicable. The economic measures for the expanded project were assessed with and without the tax incentives to determine its effect on government revenue and company rate of return.

| TABLE 8.14: PRESENCE OF MINERAL ROYALTY TAX SYSTEMS IN SELECTED JURISDICTIONS | |
|---|---|
| **Country** | **Mineral Royalty Type Tax on Most Minerals?** |
| Argentina | Yes |
| Bolivia | Yes |
| Burkina Faso | Yes |
| Canada (Ontario) | No |
| Chile | No |
| China | Yes |
| Ghana | Yes |
| Greenland | No |
| Indonesia | Yes |
| Ivory Coast | Yes |
| Kazakhstan | Yes |
| Mexico | No |
| Papua New Guinea | Yes |
| Philippines | Yes |
| **Peru** | No |
| Poland | Yes |
| South Africa | No |
| Sweden | No |
| Tanzania | Yes |
| U.S. | No |
| Uzbekistan | Yes |
| W. Australia | Yes |
| Zimbabwe | No |

*Source:* Otto (2002).

In the Peruvian context, a decision on royalty taxes must be made taking into account the mining taxation system as a whole. One of the simpler forms of royalty is a tax-deductible gross sales revenue ad valorem tax. The impact of such a tax was assessed on the model mines (Table 8.15). Taking into account the rest of the system, it is relevant to point out that Peru already imposes substantial input taxes (import duty, VAT). On the other hand, whereas a royalty tax is assessed only in years during which there are commercial revenues, an input tax, such as import duty, entails collection during the project startup period, before there is any mine income. Companies would much prefer to pay taxes during years when production has begun rather than during construction.

*Recommendation:*

■ A reasonable royalty should be imposed, provided that the import duty is eliminated by exemption or zero-rating, or that workers' participation is modified in a process affecting the entire public sector.[5] The royalty tax should (a) be based on gross mineral sales revenues, (b) not exceed a rate of 3 percent, (c) have a uniform rate for all mineral types, and (d) be offset by the elimination of the import duty.

---

5. There is a negative impact on mining competitiveness of the 8 percent workers' participation since it increases the real income tax rate burden of firms from about 30 percent to about 38 percent. Authorities indicated that this participation could be diminished and unified across all similar activities in an upcoming initiative.

## TABLE 8.15: TAX SYSTEM SENSITIVITY TO A ROYALTY TAX

| Royalty Tax on Gross Sales Revenue | Effective Tax Rate (%) | Investor IRR (%) | Government Revenue: All Taxes & Fees (US$ millions) |
|---|---|---|---|
| **Copper Model** | | | |
| 0% (current) | 47 | 11.7 | 471 |
| 1% | 49 | 11.3 | 493 |
| 2% | 51 | 11.0 | 516 |
| 2.5% | 52 | 10.8 | 527 |
| 3% | 53 | 10.6 | 538 |
| **Gold Model:** | | | |
| 0% (current) | 43 | 14.7 | 76 |
| 1% | 47 | 13.9 | 82 |
| 2% | 51 | 13.0 | 88 |
| 2.5% | 53 | 12.5 | 92 |
| 3% | 54 | 12.1 | 95 |

*Source:* Otto (2002).

Peru does impose substantial import duties, and the rates vary according to the item. However, import duty is allowed as a depreciable deduction against income subject to income tax. Mining is capital intensive and uses specialized equipment that is usually imported. This means that an import duty on equipment has a direct impact on project economics in the project's early years. Project feasibility studies calculate various projections of profitability, such as discounted rate of return, and such measures are very sensitive to large costs in the early years of a project. Even modest levels of equipment import duties can sink a marginal project. Competition for mineral sector investment worldwide is fierce, and many countries have either eliminated import duties on mine equipment or have found ways to exempt projects or their equipment from such duties. The effect of eliminating the import duty is shown in Table 8.16. The impact of import duty is high on both government and taxpayer.

## TABLE 8.16: TAX SYSTEM SENSITIVITY TO IMPORT DUTY

| Representative Mining Equipment Import Duty Rate | Effective Tax Rate (%) | Investor IRR (%) | Government Revenue: All Taxes & Fees (US$ millions) |
|---|---|---|---|
| **Copper Model:** | | | |
| 15% | 48 | 11.2 | 484 |
| 12% (current) | 47 | 11.7 | 471 |
| 5% | 44 | 12.9 | 438 |
| 0% | 41 | 13.9 | 413 |
| **Gold Model:** | | | |
| 15% | 45 | 14.1 | 78 |
| 12% (current) | 43 | 14.7 | 76 |
| 5% | 40 | 16.3 | 69 |
| 0% | 37 | 17.5 | 65 |

*Source:* Otto (2002).

Recommendations:
- ▦ Peru should follow the lead of most other nations and eliminate import duty through either an exemption, or if duty category lists are sufficiently detailed to isolate most mining equipment, by zero rating such categories.
- ▦ However, if this recommendation is adopted, a royalty tax of 2 to 3 percent should be imposed on gross mineral sales revenues. The combined effect of eliminating import duty and adding a royalty tax is shown in Table 8.17.

Peru levies an 18 percent general sales tax (VAT) on goods and services purchased. It must be paid on goods and services, but in the case where a mine exports its output, it can be credited against the Income Tax up to a limit of 18 percent of such sales of exported minerals. Because the VAT is a "consumer" tax and export minerals must compete globally, almost all mineral-exporting nations have chosen to eliminate its impact on both export mineral sales and equipment purchases. Peru eliminates that impact through allowing the possibility that the VAT on export sales be reimbursed. The amount of VAT that may be credited is restricted to 18 percent of export sales, and any amount exceeding this may be carried forward as a credit against future export sales. Moreover, the VAT paid during exploration is refundable.

Recommendation:
- ▦ The current system of VAT as applied to mining should remain unchanged.

Additional recommendations for improving the use of intergovernmental transfers are:

- ▦ Transparent managing of mining tax revenue: The administration of the channeling and use of *canon minero* transfers need to be transparent. An important step forward is the Government of Peru's recent decision to publish the monthly revenue transfers to municipalities in the *Portal de Transparencia Económica*. This is not enough. In the Public Expenditure Tracking Surveys (PETS) developed (see Chapter IV), about 6 out of 10 municipalities

## TABLE 8.17: TAX SENSITIVITY TO ELIMINATING IMPORT DUTY AND IMPOSING A ROYALTY

| Scenario | Effective Tax Rate (%) | Investor IRR (%) | Government Revenue: All Taxes & Fees (US$ millions) |
|---|---|---|---|
| **Copper Model:** | | | |
| 12% import duty, 0% royalty (current system) | 47 | 11.7 | 471 |
| 0% import duty, 1% royalty | 43 | 13.5 | 436 |
| 0% import duty, 2% royalty | 46 | 13.1 | 460 |
| 0% import duty, 2.5% royalty | 47 | 12.8 | 472 |
| 0% import duty, 3% royalty | 48 | 12.6 | 484 |
| **Gold Model:** | | | |
| 12% import duty, 0% royalty (current system) | 43 | 14.7 | 76 |
| 0% import duty, 1% royalty | 41 | 16.6 | 71 |
| 0% import duty, 2% royalty | 45 | 15.6 | 78 |
| 0% import duty, 2.5% royalty | 46 | 15.2 | 86 |
| 0% import duty, 3% royalty | 48 | 14.7 | 84 |

*Source:* Otto (2002).

---

**BOX 8.2: CREATING MINING STABILIZATION FUNDS. THE ANCASH MODEL.**

Given the unpredictability of fiscal transfers, a Mining Stabilization Fund is desirable. It could be created with private sector participation and have a long-term view to finance: local infrastructure projects prepared by municipalities under participatory plans and capacity-building activities. The Fund could be supervised by a *Mesa de Concertación* and be subject to strengthened auditing procedures by the official authorities.

A pilot case, though not based on government transfers, has already been created with the Ancash Fund. This Fund contains about US$110 million of payments, which the firm Antamina still had to pay in the context of its privatization. Rather than paying those straight to the Treasury, the company and the involved mayors have proposed a "Fund model": The Treasury, upon collecting from Antamina, puts the entire revenue into this Fund, which then finances infrastructure projects in the region (13 projects making up about 60 percent of available funds are already identified, including roads, assessments, and electrification). Resources of the Fund could also regularly be replenished with part of *canon minero* transfers.

---

outside Lima claiming that they knew how their transfers were estimated, actually did not know, and in the poor and extremely poor municipalities, the number decreased to 3 out of 10. Transfers also show high volatility and unpredictability, and are subject to limited auditing capacity by the Central Government (Apoyo Institute 2002a). The emphasis of new regulations and their subsequent administration should be on ensuring that the local communities are well-trained and informed as to how and when these transfers are estimated.

- Ways to stabilize the annual flows of mining transfers (Stabilization Fund) should be explored,[6] because the cyclical behavior of international prices affect income tax revenue and, therefore, *canon minero* flows (Box 8.2).
- Local administration capacity needs to be strengthened. Municipalities should be supported in learning how to make optimal use of these resources. They should develop capacity for managing them: taking investment decisions, and eventually managing their new assets obtained. Local administration officials and local community representatives would need to be enabled to participate in local economic development programs that might be initiated together with or by mining companies.

## Improving Mining Environment Management

The mining environment is cause for heated social and political concern in Peru. Complex political debates have emerged around existing and newly planned mining operations, typically in the context of criticisms that local communities and regions do not gain much from mining operations, the marginal employment these mines create for unskilled indigenous workers, the often negative social consequences on the communities living close to the mines (import of prostitutes and alcoholism are often mentioned as major social concerns), and the lack of genuine interest of some mining companies in promoting regional development and respecting environmental provisions.

Three weaknesses in Peru's environmental management are conflicts of interest, credibility, and capacity concerns. The mining sector, in general, has complied better with the environmental institutional assessment requirements, and with territorial environmental assessments. However, there are several instances of potential conflicts of interest.

- A conflicting case occurs between core technical groups within the Ministry of Mines and Energy (MEM), that wish to promote mining, and the environmental unit within the MEM, the mandate of which is to prevent environmental damage.

---

6. Once the annual amount is defined, the monthly transfers of the *canon minero* are constant.

■ Another conflicting case is the inspection of the Environmental Compliance and Management Programs in the energy and mining sectors. Aside from potentially presenting technical deficiencies, such inspection is under the responsibility of the General Directorates (electricity, hydrocarbon, and mining) with the help of independent experts contracted by the respective enterprises being evaluated, again in a clear conflict of interest.

■ The reform of the early 1990s had approached the environmental issue from a sectoral perspective, that is, one where each sectoral ministry has a General Directorate of the Environment (in the case of the MEM it would be the GDE-MEM), which in effect regulates and monitors environmental compliance. The only entity resembling a national environmental authority—the National Environmental Council (CONAM)—is limited to a very weak, intersectoral coordinating role. This has resulted in a perception by local communities of a conflict of interest at the MEM, which plays a twofold role of promoting mining investment and implementing environmental control, and the fear that environmental control is too lax at the expense of the health of the locals. This situation is aggravated by the fact that GDE-MEM does not release environmental information to the public.

■ The institutional structure is geographically centralized at the Lima-based GDE-MEM as the only responsible entity (the regional offices of the GDE-MEM are quite weak). Local populations participate only in consultations and do not form part of the institutional structure of the process.

The mining industry's environmental record has begun to impede private sector investments, even if in practice it is better than in some other sectors. Even when controls exist on paper, they are seldom implemented. Social and political conflicts that have been mainly triggered by accidents impacting the environment or the social fabric of the local community, such as spills or resettlement issues, have threatened the ability of companies to pursue mining permits or to continue to run their already existing operations. For example, Tambogrande in Piura, a medium-sized gold mining project awarded to Canadian Manhatten Minerals, is unlikely to go ahead, because the "Tambogrande Defense Committee" has successfully mobilized public opinion, including the Catholic Church, staging demonstrations and boycotts serious enough to cause the company to abandon completion of its environmental impact analysis. Other examples of such conflicts causing interruptions of ongoing project development or operations are the mines of Yanacocha and Antamina. Both were involved in massive community protests, one in the context of a mercury spill, the other in the context of a resettlement program that halted their operations temporarily and threatened to stop further expansion.

Current enforcement by the State entities responsible for the environment is inadequate. The National Environmental Council is a small organization lacking political power. In practice, it is the Ministry of Energy and Mines that has most influence over investment decisions. However, the team at the ministry responsible for environmental controls lacks the personnel or budget to properly carry out its functions. Naturally, given its mandate, rather than impose burdensome environmental controls, the ministry's main priority is to maximize investment and eventual output.

### The Role of the Private Sector

From an environmental perspective, the worst offenders tend not to be the large multinational mining companies, but rather the (Peruvian) owners of older and smaller mines, less sensitive than multinationals to allegations of disregarding environmental norms. Most multinationals have made serious efforts to comply with the environmental code and invest in technologies to reduce pollution and to create a good working relationship with surrounding communities. Only legal obligations, enforced by competent and credible institutions, will be able to influence the large number of Peruvian-owned mining firms to control water pollution, spills, and air pollution, and to appropriately solve conflicts over land rights.

*Recommendations:*

- A new national and independent environmental authority that is structured geographically and supported by local monitoring needs to be created. Such authority should regulate all sectors and be integrated with future regional authorities, which will be responsible for the monitoring and control of all environmental aspects.

- As part of the decentralization process, an agreement on roles and responsibilities in the environmental provisions of the mining sector is also needed to foster further private investment. This agreement should define a certain level of inter- and intraprovincial coordination to organize environmental controls smoothly and to promote cooperation.

- New roles and responsibilities will require the buildup of institutional capacity, especially at the subnational level.

- The regulatory framework of environmental management also needs to be reviewed to ensure that stricter environmental regulations are well designed and introduced.

- Local interest groups, supported by nongovernmental organizations, should be integrated into environmental monitoring and consultation. These groups will certainly continue to pressure the government to protect community interests from mining projects.

# Annex A

# A PUBLIC
# DEBT SUSTAINABILITY
# ANALYSIS FOR PERU

We estimate the level of Peru's public debt that would improve its sustainability in the medium term.[1] Authorities have shown their intention to develop a prudent debt management strategy. The 2000 debt exchange with private creditors slightly worsened the maturity profile of debt payments,[2] but authorities believe that the present value of public debt fell. Our baseline medium-term scenario indicates some external vulnerability over the medium term, conditional on low inflation, and moderate real GDP growth (average 4 percent) per year, which in turn would depend on recovery of private sector and foreign investment, increased productivity, and sound macroeconomic policies. Our debt sustainability model assumes the absence of major terms of trade shocks that would negatively affect the current account deficit, and no private capital outflows that would require a tighter monetary policy to avoid currency depreciation.

We examine the sensitivity of key public debt ratios to alternative assumptions about financing terms and growth rates. Our central premise is that both foreign financing and adjustment to fiscal fundamentals are necessary to ensure more sustainable public debt ratios. The path toward sustainability is estimated, with annual target primary balances consistent with non-financial public sector (NFPS) debt and debt-servicing requirements. The analysis concludes that the Government of Peru (GOP) could reach a public-debt-to-GDP sustainable ratio of 40 percent in 2004 and 36.2 in 2010, provided it builds primary balances close to 0.9 percent of GDP in 2004 and 1.3 percent of GDP in 2010. Nonetheless, the government would face a sizable debt-service burden that would peak at about 36 percent of exports and 44 percent of tax revenue in 2004 and decrease thereafter,

---

1. This Annex was prepared with the research assistance of Rashmi Shankar, numerous comments on early drafts and data support from IMF staff, and a very timely suggestion from Sara Calvo, who motivated its extension to shocks and provided enthusiastic advise on its development.

2. New government 10-year bonds with bullet payment at maturity exchanged for front-loaded interest reduction Brady bonds or FLIRBs, which were selling at a discount of 28.5 percent, at end 2001. These carry low interest rates, and the principal is to be amortized gradually from 2005 to 2017.

the latter result being a direct reflection of the fiscal deficits and low tax ratios that Peru has featured in past years. Faster growth accompanied by tight control of expenditure and additional foreign financing would be essential to bring the GOP to a high case scenario, to channel more resources to a poverty-reduction strategy, while reducing its debt-servicing burden. A comprehensive tax reform is needed to improve such prospects.

This Annex is divided into two sections. The first section is a conventional debt sustainability analysis as described above. The second section considers the impact of two hypothetical shocks. The first shock consists of a slowing down of capital inflows (sudden stop) resulting in real exchange rate (RER) depreciation. The second shock reflects the materialization of the government's contingent liabilities, arising from an eventual failure of the private sector to fulfill its short-term external debt obligations.

## Peru's Macroeconomic Background

While economic activity remains weak, the macroeconomic situation has been stabilizing since 2000, with inflation decreasing from 7.3 percent in 1998 to 2 percent in 2001. The combined fiscal deficit reversed its upward trend, but still was significant at 2.5 percent of GDP. The current account as a percent of GDP improved significantly between 1998 and 2001, from −6.4 percent to −2.1 percent. Measures to strengthen the banking system are reflected in improvements in some indicators of bank soundness. Loan quality has improved, as measured by the ratio of nonperforming to total loans (excluding restructured and refinanced loans), and liquidity and capital adequacy ratios have risen.

While the total (public and private, short-, medium-, and long-term) debt-to-GDP ratio remains high at 52.3 percent, adverse developments in the region have had little effect on Peru's financial indicators. Yet, the external *public* debt represents around 70 percent of total debt, and virtually all is long term. Around 60 percent of this debt is with multilateral and bilateral creditors. Because of the high degree of dollarization of domestic debt, it is vulnerable to currency risk, making fiscal and monetary policy lose some degree of freedom.

For illustrative purposes, a comparison of Argentina's (before the crisis) and Peru's fiscal deficits, public-debt-to-GDP ratio, public debt-servicing-exports ratio, and current account balance is contained in Table A.1. Peru has a lower NFPS deficit and a lower current account deficit. Argentina's public debt and public debt-servicing burden is higher than Peru's, but the rising trend in the public debt service/exports ratio in the latter is worrisome. Strengthening of the export performance, the banking sector, and particularly the fiscal position, will play a significant role in keeping Peru's public debt manageable. In a base case, inflation remains low at approximately 2 percent, which would allow the government to relax somewhat monetary policy in the face of weak economic activity. A managed floating exchange rate regime is preserved and the international reserves position would remain comfortable.

## The Target Fiscal Adjustment Under a Baseline and Alternative Scenarios With No External Shocks

We present alternative scenarios of growth and interest rates, multilateral financing, and the sensitivity of key public debt ratios to the assumptions made. The dynamic is detailed in Table A.2. In each case, the target primary balance needed to sustain the public debt outcome is estimated.

### General Assumptions

- Receipts from privatization are US$600 million for 2002 and 2003, and fall to less than $50 million per year thereafter.
- Inflation in the GDP deflator (US$ terms) increases from 0.9 percent in 2002, to approximately 2 percent during 2003–10.
- Continued rollover of short-term debt during 2002–10.

TABLE A.1:  CURRENT MACROECONOMIC AND FINANCIAL TRENDS

| (% of GDP) | 1998 | | 1999 | | 2000 | | 2001* | |
|---|---|---|---|---|---|---|---|---|
| | Argentina | Peru | Argentina | Peru | Argentina | Peru | Argentina | Peru |
| Current Account | -4.80 | -6.37 | -4.30 | -3.50 | -3.20 | -3.00 | -2.80 | -2.10 |
| Public Debt Service (% of Exports) | 56.80 | 27.46 | 73.50 | 32.65 | 70.50 | 42.80 | 78.20 | 43.30 |
| Public Debt Service (% of Revenue) | 31.40 | 25.26 | 36.80 | 31.89 | 38.90 | 33.53 | 48.30 | 28.89 |
| Public Debt | 37.60 | 42.70 | 43.00 | 48.00 | 44.90 | 45.90 | 51.0 | 46.50 |
| NFPS Budget Deficit | -2.40 | -0.70 | -4.40 | -3.10 | -3.80 | -3.20 | -3.50 | -2.50 |

*Preswap estimate for Argentina.

Source:  World Bank staff estimates.

## TABLE A.2: DEBT DYNAMICS NON-FINANCIAL PUBLIC SECTOR: SCENARIO WITH NO EXTERNAL SHOCKS
(in percent of GDP)

| | 2000 | 2001 | 2002 | 2003 | 2004 | 2005 | 2006 | 2007 | 2008 | 2009 | 2010 |
|---|---|---|---|---|---|---|---|---|---|---|---|
| **1. Baseline: Scenario A** | | | | | | | | | | | |
| Primary balance | -0.5 | -0.6 | 0.2 | 0.4 | 0.9 | 1.1 | 1.1 | 1.2 | 1.3 | 1.3 | 1.3 |
| Public debt to GDP | 45.9 | 46.5 | 44.9 | 40.9 | 40.0 | 39.3 | 38.7 | 38.2 | 37.5 | 36.9 | 36.2 |
| Public external debt service/exports | 25.0 | 23.3 | 27.4 | 31.5 | 36.1 | 38.1 | 30.9 | 28.7 | 26.7 | 25.6 | 23.7 |
| Public debt service/GDP | 3.8 | 3.9 | 3.8 | 4.5 | 5.3 | 6.0 | 5.2 | 5.0 | 4.9 | 4.8 | 4.6 |
| Public debt service/tax revenue | 27.4 | 26.1 | 32.1 | 36.1 | 43.5 | 50.0 | 43.7 | 43.3 | 43.1 | 43.6 | 42.4 |
| *Memorandum items* | | | | | | | | | | | |
| Fiscal balance (percent of GDP) | -3.2 | -2.5 | -1.9 | -1.8 | -1.8 | -1.7 | -1.7 | -1.6 | -1.5 | -1.5 | -1.4 |
| GDP (millions of US$) | 53513 | 53983 | 56816 | 60068 | 63033 | 66800 | 70861 | 75170 | 79740 | 84671 | 89819 |
| Exports (millions of US$) | 7028 | 7132 | 7915 | 8525 | 9325 | 10548 | 11833 | 13107 | 14568 | 15984 | 17402 |
| **2. Scenario B** | | | | | | | | | | | |
| Primary balance | -0.5 | -0.6 | 0.2 | 0.4 | 0.8 | 1.0 | 1.0 | 1.0 | 1.0 | 1.0 | 1.0 |
| Public debt to GDP | 45.9 | 46.5 | 44.9 | 40.8 | 39.4 | 38.2 | 37.1 | 36.0 | 34.8 | 33.6 | 32.2 |
| Public external debt service/exports | 25.0 | 23.3 | 27.4 | 31.2 | 35.2 | 36.7 | 29.0 | 26.4 | 24.2 | 22.7 | 20.5 |
| Public debt service/GDP | 3.8 | 3.9 | 3.8 | 4.4 | 5.2 | 5.7 | 4.7 | 4.4 | 4.2 | 4.0 | 3.7 |
| Public debt service/tax revenue | 27.4 | 26.1 | 32.1 | 35.7 | 42.0 | 47.3 | 40.0 | 38.4 | 37.2 | 36.5 | 34.3 |
| *Memorandum items* | | | | | | | | | | | |
| Fiscal balance (percent of GDP) | -3.2 | -2.5 | -1.9 | -1.8 | -1.7 | -1.5 | -1.4 | -1.3 | -1.2 | -1.1 | -1.0 |
| GDP (millions of US$) | 53513 | 53983 | 56816 | 60068 | 63639 | 68091 | 72925 | 78103 | 83648 | 89675 | 96042 |
| Exports (millions of US$) | 7028 | 7132 | 7915 | 8525 | 9325 | 10548 | 11833 | 13107 | 14568 | 15984 | 17402 |
| **3. Scenario C** | | | | | | | | | | | |
| Primary balance | -0.5 | -0.6 | -0.3 | 0.0 | 0.7 | 1.1 | 1.3 | 1.6 | 1.9 | 2.1 | 2.2 |
| Public debt to GDP | 45.9 | 46.5 | 45.4 | 41.3 | 41.4 | 41.7 | 42.0 | 42.4 | 42.6 | 42.7 | 42.7 |
| Public external debt service/exports | 25.0 | 23.3 | 27.4 | 32.2 | 37.9 | 40.8 | 34.3 | 32.6 | 31.1 | 30.3 | 28.7 |
| Public debt service/GDP | 3.8 | 3.9 | 3.8 | 4.6 | 5.7 | 6.6 | 6.0 | 6.0 | 6.1 | 6.2 | 6.2 |
| Public debt service/tax revenue | 27.4 | 26.1 | 32.1 | 36.8 | 46.3 | 55.0 | 50.7 | 52.1 | 53.8 | 56.2 | 56.7 |
| *Memorandum items* | | | | | | | | | | | |
| Fiscal balance (percent of GDP) | -3.2 | -2.5 | -2.4 | -2.3 | -2.3 | -2.2 | -2.1 | -2.1 | -2.0 | -2.0 | -1.9 |
| GDP (millions of US$) | 53513 | 53983 | 56816 | 60068 | 62124 | 64887 | 67839 | 70926 | 74153 | 77603 | 81134 |
| Exports (millions of US$) | 7028 | 7132 | 7915 | 8525 | 9325 | 10548 | 11833 | 13107 | 14568 | 15984 | 17402 |

*Source:* World Bank staff estimates.

- The terms of new multilateral financing depend on Peru's classification as a Category IV country. The loan period is on average 17 years, with a five-year grace period, and the interest is the London Interbank Offered Rate (LIBOR) (World Bank forecast of 4 percent) plus a 70-basis-point spread, on average.
- The NFPS elasticities of revenues and expenditures with respect to GDP remain constant at 0.98 and 0.95, respectively. Elasticities are estimated for 1994–2002.

*Scenario A.* This is the *baseline* scenario. It incorporates the preliminary figures for the Brady buy-back under which all outstanding front-loaded interest reduced bonds (FLIRBs) have been exchanged. The baseline assumptions are:

- Moderate growth: 3.7 percent in 2002, followed by 4 percent during 2003–10;
- Moderate average international interest rates: 10 percent throughout the period;
- Moderate cut in fiscal deficits: tapering off from –1.9 percent of GDP to –1.4 percent of GDP over the period.

**Results:** Under the baseline assumptions, the public-debt-to-GDP ratio would fall to 36.2 percent in 2010, from 44.9 percent in 2002. The primary balance required to cover interest liabilities increases from 0.2 percent to 1.3 percent over the period. The public debt-servicing ratio would fall from 27.4 percent to 23.7 percent as a proportion of exports, would rise from 3.8 percent to 4.6 percent as a proportion of GDP, and would rise from 32.1 percent to 42.4 percent as a proportion of Central Government (CG) tax revenues, over the period. The assumption on mixed concessional-multilateral (reduced balance-of-payments support from 2003, partly offset by sector investment disbursements) and limited commercial borrowing, results in an implicit average interest rate on the total stock of NFPS debt between 6.7 percent and 7.9 percent during 2004–10.

*Scenario B.* This is the *best-case* scenario, which presents a sensitivity analysis of the public-debt-to-GDP ratio to higher growth and strengthened fiscal discipline. The assumptions are:

- High growth: 3.7 percent in 2002 followed by 5 percent during 2003–10;
- Low average international interest rates: the interest rate on new public debt is 7.5 percent over the period;
- Low fiscal deficits: tapering off, as a proportion of GDP, from –1.9 percent in 2002, to –1.8 percent in 2003, –1.3 percent in 2007, and –1 percent by 2010. This is based on the assumption of higher revenue, tighter expenditure, and faster growth. The revenue elasticity remains .98, but the expenditure elasticity is constrained to remain at .88, to cap expenditures at 18.3 percent of GDP in this scenario, in contrast to 18.7 percent of GDP in the baseline.

**Results:** Under this scenario, the public-debt-GDP ratio would fall lower, to 32.2 percent in 2010 from 44.9 percent in 2002. The primary balance required for reaching sustainability would also be lower than in the baseline, due to faster growth and better financial conditions. To cover debt-service liabilities it increases from –0.5 percent in 2000 to 1 percent in 2005, and remains stable at that proportion of GDP until the end of the forecast horizon. The public debt-servicing ratio falls from 27.4 percent in 2002 to 20.5 percent as a proportion of exports, remains constant at 3.7 percent as a proportion of GDP, and increases slightly from 32.1 percent to 34.3 percent as a proportion of CG tax revenue, over the same period. The assumption on mixed concessional-multilateral (full balance-of-payments support) and commercial borrowing results in an implicit average interest rate on total NFPS debt of around 6.4 percent during 2004–10, which is lower than in the baseline due to a higher share of multilateral financing and better placement conditions in international markets.

*Scenario C.* This is the *worst-case* scenario, reflecting the sensitivity of the public-debt-to-GDP ratio to low growth and poor fiscal discipline. The assumptions are:

- Low growth: growth rate of 2.5 percent is assumed over the entire period;
- High fiscal deficit: the fiscal deficit falls from 2.4 percent to only −1.9 percent of GDP over the entire period;
- High average international interest rate: the interest rate on public debt is 12 percent over the period.

**Results:** Under this scenario, the public-debt-to-GDP ratio would fall slightly, to 42.7 percent in 2010 from 45.4 percent in 2002. However, the primary balance required to cover debt-service liabilities increases to 2.2 percent in 2010 from −0.5 percent in 2000. The public-debt-servicing ratio increases from 27.4 percent to 28.7 percent as a proportion of exports, rises from 3.8 percent to 6.2 percent as a proportion of GDP, and rises from 32.1 percent to 56.7 percent as a proportion of CG tax revenue, during 2002–10. The implicit average interest rate on total NFPS debt increases to between 7.3 percent and 9.9 percent during 2004–2010 because of the increased reliance on commercial borrowing following from the previous assumption of reduced multilateral financing and worst bond placement conditions in international markets. Thus external financing is more expensive in this scenario. It is assumed that there is reduced multilateral financing and no fast-disbursing loans.

## Summary:

Table A.2 and the figures (Figure A.1) present details of the dynamics of public debt financing toward medium-term sustainability. It is important to note that in the worst-case scenario, the implication of a required government primary surplus of 2.2 percent of GDP merely reflects that a bigger fiscal effort would be required in a deteriorated scenario for Peru to honor its payments (see Tables A3–A.5).

## The Target Fiscal Adjustment Under a "Sudden Stop" Scenario: Accounting for a Real Exchange Rate and Contingent Liability Shocks
### Motivation

The recent literature on crises identifies a combination of fiscal sustainability and RER misalignment as a likely cause of rapidly growing public debt and a loss of access to international credit markets. One perspective stresses that unexpected stops in capital flows of a permanent nature can in itself generate substantial swings in the RER (Table A.6). Our purpose here is to identify the RER adjustment necessary to close the current account in the event of Peru being the victim of such a shock, that is, a sudden stop in capital inflows, and to assess its impact on debt sustainability.

### Computing the Real Exchange Rate Adjustment

A sudden stop in capital inflow is typically accompanied by large contractions in international reserves and a decline in the relative price of nontradables with respect to tradables (or a depreciation in the RER). This follows from the current account identity: a relative price adjustment is necessary to absorb the demand for tradables in order for the current account deficit to be reduced in line with the fall in capital flows. Calvo, Izquierdo, and Talvi (2002) demonstrate that the necessary RER adjustment is given by a percentage fall in the resource imbalance necessary to reduce the current account deficit to the required extent (current account deficit/imports), divided by the elasticity of demand for nontradables with respect to $p$ (the relative price of nontradables to that of tradables). Based on their model, we compute the following RER adjustments for Peru, Bolivia, and Ecuador:

It must be emphasized that these numbers are extreme values based on the assumption that capital flows will cease completely, and the current account deficit will have to be closed. A more reasonable assumption, that is, a 10-percent depreciation in the RER, would capture the idea that

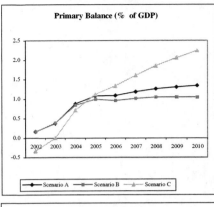

**Primary Balance (% of GDP)**

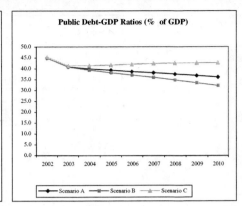

**Public Debt-GDP Ratios (% of GDP)**

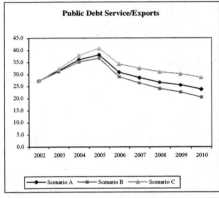

**Public Debt Service/Exports**

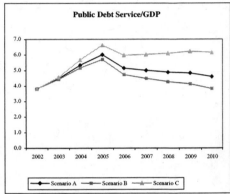

**Public Debt Service/GDP**

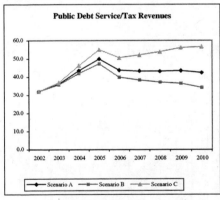

**Public Debt Service/Tax Revenues**

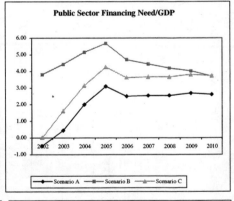

**Public Sector Financing Need/GDP**

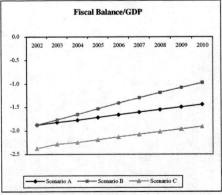

**Fiscal Balance/GDP**

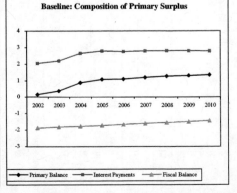

**Baseline: Composition of Primary Surplus**

*Source:* World Bank staff estimates.

TABLE A.3: SCENARIO WITHOUT SHOCKS
Scenario A: Baseline (in millions of US$)

| | 2002 Proj. | 2003 Proj. | 2004 Proj. | 2005 Proj. | 2006 Proj. | 2007 Proj. | 2008 Proj. | 2009 Proj. | 2010 Proj. |
|---|---|---|---|---|---|---|---|---|---|
| Nominal GDP | 56,816 | 60,068 | 63,033 | 66,800 | 70,861 | 75,170 | 79,740 | 84,671 | 89,819 |
| **Real Growth** | **3.7** | **4.0** | **4.0** | **4.0** | **4.0** | **4.0** | **4.0** | **4.0** | **4.0** |
| Deflator | | | 0.9 | 1.9 | 2.0 | 2.0 | 2.0 | 2.1 | 2.0 |
| **Average Interest Paid on New Debt** | | **10** | **10** | **10** | **10** | **10** | **10** | **10** | **10** |
| Primary balance | 94 | 225 | 551 | 719 | 773 | 892 | 1007 | 1106 | 1208 |
| **Primary Balance as % of GDP** | 0.16 | 0.37 | 0.87 | 1.08 | 1.09 | 1.19 | 1.26 | 1.31 | 1.35 |
| Interest payments | 1160 | 1318 | 1672 | 1868 | 1949 | 2098 | 2242 | 2370 | 2503 |
| Existing debt | 1160 | 1233 | 1439 | 1468 | 1357 | 1321 | 1267 | 1179 | 1080 |
| Domestic | 194 | 200 | 176 | 156 | 54 | 41 | 26 | 17 | 9 |
| Foreign (incl. new multi- and bilateral disbursements) | 966 | 1033 | 1263 | 1312 | 1303 | 1280 | 1241 | 1162 | 1071 |
| Newly issued commercial debt | 0 | 85 | 233 | 400 | 592 | 777 | 975 | 1191 | 1423 |
| Interest payments as % of GDP | 2.0 | 2.2 | 2.7 | 2.8 | 2.8 | 2.8 | 2.8 | 2.8 | 2.8 |
| Overall fiscal balance | -1066 | -1093 | -1121 | -1148 | -1177 | -1206 | -1235 | -1265 | -1295 |
| Revenues | 11376 | 11822 | 12286 | 12767 | 13268 | 13788 | 14328 | 14890 | 15474 |
| Revenues as % of GDP | 20.0 | 19.7 | 19.5 | 19.1 | 18.7 | 18.3 | 18.0 | 17.6 | 17.2 |
| Tax revenues (IMF projections for 2002–03) | 6761 | 7448 | 7740 | 8044 | 8359 | 8687 | 9027 | 9381 | 9749 |
| Expenditures | 12443 | 12916 | 13406 | 13916 | 14445 | 14993 | 15563 | 16155 | 16768 |
| Expenditures as % of GDP | 21.9 | 21.5 | 21.3 | 20.8 | 20.4 | 19.9 | 19.5 | 19.1 | 18.7 |
| **Overall Fiscal Balance as % of GDP** | **-1.9** | **-1.8** | **-1.8** | **-1.7** | **-1.7** | **-1.6** | **-1.5** | **-1.5** | **-1.4** |
| Privatization receipts | 600 | 600 | 400 | 47 | 45 | 45 | 40 | 40 | 40 |
| Privatization as % of GDP | 1.1 | 1.0 | 0.6 | 0.1 | 0.1 | 0.1 | 0.1 | 0.0 | 0.0 |
| Amortization of existing debt | 1009 | 1371 | 1693 | 2153 | 1706 | 1662 | 1653 | 1716 | 1629 |
| Domestic debt | 148 | 316 | 549 | 863 | 305 | 188 | 132 | 128 | 54 |
| Foreign debt | 873 | 1078 | 1179 | 1334 | 1445 | 1528 | 1575 | 1676 | 1696 |
| _Multilateral_ | 410 | 419 | 445 | 515 | 589 | 600 | 601 | 650 | 651 |
| _On new additional multilateral disbursements_ | 0 | 0 | 0 | 0 | 0 | 0 | 0 | 29 | 54 |
| Paris Club | 429 | 592 | 633 | 686 | 723 | 762 | 808 | 815 | 793 |

| | | | | | | | | | |
|---|---|---|---|---|---|---|---|---|---|
| *Brady Bonds* | 34 | 67 | 101 | 133 | 133 | 166 | 166 | 182 | 198 |
| *PDI* | 34 | 67 | 101 | 101 | 101 | 101 | 101 | 101 | 101 |
| *FLIRB* | 0 | 0 | 0 | 32 | 32 | 65 | 65 | 81 | 97 |
| New foreign disbursements | 1250 | 1096 | 1156 | 1174 | 1063 | 905 | 809 | 660 | 524 |
| Multilateral creditors | 1071 | 740 | 808 | 771 | 713 | 635 | 586 | 514 | 422 |
| Bilateral creditors | 229 | 356 | 348 | 403 | 350 | 270 | 223 | 146 | 102 |
| Financing need (issuance of new commercial debt) | -275 | 268 | 1258 | 2080 | 1775 | 1917 | 2039 | 2281 | 2360 |
| Domestic | 0 | | | | | | | | |
| Foreign (residual) | -275 | | | | | | | | |
| Total debt service | 2169 | 2689 | 3365 | 4021 | 3655 | 3760 | 3895 | 4087 | 4132 |
| Debt service/tax revenue | 32.08 | 36.10 | 43.47 | 49.98 | 43.73 | 43.28 | 43.14 | 43.56 | 42.39 |
| Total debt service as % of GDP | 3.8 | 4.5 | 5.3 | 6.0 | 5.2 | 5.0 | 4.9 | 4.8 | 4.6 |
| **Implicit Average Interest Rate** | **5.39** | **5.26** | **6.72** | **7.27** | **7.27** | **7.48** | **7.65** | **7.75** | **7.86** |
| Domestic | 6.20 | | | | | | | | |
| Foreign | 5.14 | | | | | | | | |
| **Total Debt as % of GDP** | **44.92** | **40.88** | **39.95** | **39.25** | **38.70** | **38.16** | **37.52** | **36.86** | **36.16** |
| Total debt | 25524 | 24557 | 25183 | 26222 | 27421 | 28685 | 29922 | 31208 | 32478 |
| Stock of new commercial debt | 1155 | 1698 | 2956 | 5036 | 6811 | 8728 | 10767 | 13048 | 15408 |
| Total existing debt | 24369 | 22859 | 22227 | 21186 | 20610 | 19957 | 19155 | 18160 | 17069 |
| **Existing Stock MLT External Debt of the Non-Financial Public Sector (A + D)** | 18576 | 17382 | 17299 | 17121 | 16850 | 16385 | 15715 | 14848 | 13811 |
| **Buy-Back Operation** | | | | | | | | | |
| Eurobond issue | 1430 | | | | | | | | |
| FLIRB Brady | | | | | | | | | |
| Outstanding principal (nominal) | 1212 | | | | | | | | |
| Discount rate | 77 | | | | | | | | |
| Market value in percent of nominal | 930 | | | | | | | | |
| Additional financing | 500 | | | | | | | | |
| Debt servicing | 2.17 | 2.69 | 3.36 | 4.02 | 3.66 | 3.76 | 3.89 | 4.09 | 4.13 |
| Exports | 7.92 | 8.53 | 9.33 | 10.55 | 11.83 | 13.11 | 14.57 | 15.98 | 17.40 |
| TDS/export | 0.27 | 0.32 | 0.36 | 0.38 | 0.31 | 0.29 | 0.27 | 0.26 | 0.24 |
| TDS/GDP | 0.04 | 0.04 | 0.05 | 0.06 | 0.05 | 0.05 | 0.05 | 0.05 | 0.05 |
| Financing need/GDP | 0.00 | 0.00 | 0.02 | 0.03 | 0.03 | 0.03 | 0.03 | 0.03 | 0.03 |
| Debt servicing/revenue | 19.07 | 22.74 | 27.39 | 31.49 | 27.55 | 27.27 | 27.18 | 27.44 | 26.70 |

*Source:* World Bank staff estimates.

TABLE A.4: SCENARIO WITH NO SHOCKS

Scenario B (in millions of US$)

| | 2002 Proj. | 2003 Proj. | 2004 Proj. | 2005 Proj. | 2006 Proj. | 2007 Proj. | 2008 Proj. | 2009 Proj. | 2010 Proj. |
|---|---|---|---|---|---|---|---|---|---|
| Nominal GDP | 56,816 | 60,068 | 63,639 | 68,091 | 72,925 | 78,103 | 83,648 | 89,675 | 96,042 |
| **Real growth** | **3.7** | **5.0** | **5.0** | **5.0** | **5.0** | **5.0** | **5.0** | **5.0** | **5.0** |
| Deflator | | | 0.9 | 1.9 | 2.0 | 2.0 | 2.0 | 2.1 | 2.0 |
| **Average interest paid on new debt** | **7.5** | **7.5** | **7.5** | **7.5** | **7.5** | **7.5** | **7.5** | **7.5** | **7.5** |
| Primary balance | 94 | 230 | 535 | 679 | 701 | 793 | 877 | 941 | 1005 |
| **Primary balance as % of GDP** | **0.2** | **0.4** | **0.8** | **1.0** | **1.0** | **1.0** | **1.0** | **1.0** | **1.0** |
| Interest payments | 1160 | 1291 | 1589 | 1721 | 1730 | 1804 | 1867 | 1905 | 1939 |
| Existing debt | 1160 | 1240 | 1453 | 1489 | 1385 | 1357 | 1310 | 1229 | 1136 |
| Domestic | 194 | 200 | 176 | 156 | 54 | 41 | 26 | 17 | 9 |
| Foreign (incl. new multi- and bilateral disbursements) | 966 | 1040 | 1277 | 1333 | 1331 | 1316 | 1284 | 1212 | 1127 |
| Newly issued commercial debt | 0 | 51 | 136 | 232 | 345 | 448 | 557 | 676 | 803 |
| Interest payments as % of GDP | 2.0 | 2.1 | 2.5 | 2.5 | 2.4 | 2.3 | 2.2 | 2.1 | 2.0 |
| Overall fiscal balance | -1066 | -1061 | -1054 | -1043 | -1029 | -1011 | -989 | -964 | -933 |
| Revenues | 11376 | 11934 | 12519 | 13132 | 13775 | 14450 | 15158 | 15901 | 16680 |
| Revenues as % of GDP | 20.0 | 19.9 | 19.7 | 19.3 | 18.9 | 18.5 | 18.1 | 17.7 | 17.4 |
| Tax revenues (IMF projections for 2002–03) | 6761 | 7448 | 7813 | 8196 | 8598 | 9019 | 9461 | 9925 | 10411 |
| Expenditures | 12443 | 12995 | 13572 | 14175 | 14804 | 15461 | 16148 | 16865 | 17614 |
| Expenditures as % of GDP | 21.9 | 21.6 | 21.3 | 20.8 | 20.3 | 19.8 | 19.3 | 18.8 | 18.3 |
| **Overall fiscal balance as % of GDP** | **-1.9** | **-1.8** | **-1.7** | **-1.5** | **-1.4** | **-1.3** | **-1.2** | **-1.1** | **-0.97** |
| Privatization receipts | 600 | 600 | 400 | 47 | 45 | 45 | 40 | 40 | 40 |
| Privatization as % of GDP | 1.1 | 1.0 | 0.6 | 0.1 | 0.1 | 0.1 | 0.0 | 0.0 | 0.0 |
| Amortization of existing debt | 1009 | 1371 | 1693 | 2153 | 1706 | 1662 | 1653 | 1716 | 1629 |
| Domestic debt | 148 | 316 | 549 | 863 | 305 | 188 | 132 | 128 | 54 |
| Foreign debt | 873 | 1078 | 1179 | 1334 | 1445 | 1528 | 1575 | 1694 | 1732 |
| *Multilateral* | 410 | 419 | 445 | 515 | 589 | 600 | 601 | 650 | 651 |
| *On new additional multilateral disbursements* | 0 | 0 | 0 | 0 | 0 | 0 | 0 | 47 | 90 |
| *Paris Club* | 429 | 592 | 633 | 686 | 723 | 762 | 808 | 815 | 793 |

| | | | | | | | | | |
|---|---|---|---|---|---|---|---|---|---|
| Brady Bonds | 34 | 67 | 101 | 133 | 133 | 166 | 166 | 182 | 198 |
| PDI | 34 | 67 | 101 | 101 | 101 | 101 | 101 | 101 | 101 |
| FLIRB | 0 | 0 | 0 | 32 | 32 | 65 | 65 | 81 | 97 |
| New foreign disbursments | 1250 | 1396 | 1456 | 1474 | 1363 | 1205 | 1109 | 960 | 824 |
| Multilateral creditors | 1071 | 1040 | 1108 | 1071 | 1013 | 935 | 886 | 814 | 722 |
| Bilateral creditors | 229 | 356 | 348 | 403 | 350 | 270 | 223 | 146 | 102 |
| Financing need (issuance of new commercial debt) | -275 | -64 | 891 | 1675 | 1327 | 1423 | 1493 | 1680 | 1699 |
| Domestic | 0 | | | | | | | | |
| Foreign (residual) | -275 | | | | | | | | |
| Total debt service | 2169 | 2662 | 3282 | 3874 | 3436 | 3466 | 3520 | 3621 | 3568 |
| Debt service/tax revenue | 32.08 | 35.74 | 42.00 | 47.27 | 39.96 | 38.43 | 37.20 | 36.49 | 34.27 |
| Total debt service as % of GDP | 3.8 | 4.4 | 5.2 | 5.7 | 4.7 | 4.4 | 4.2 | 4.0 | 3.7 |
| **Implicit average interest rate** | **5.39** | **5.16** | **6.41** | **6.74** | **6.52** | **6.54** | **6.52** | **6.43** | **6.35** |
| Domestic | 6.20 | | | | | | | | |
| Foreign | 5.14 | | | | | | | | |
| **Total debt as % of GDP** | **44.92** | **40.83** | **39.42** | **38.21** | **37.12** | **36.03** | **34.82** | **33.56** | **32.25** |
| Total debt | 25524 | 24525 | 25084 | 26018 | 27068 | 28138 | 29130 | 30097 | 30970 |
| Stock of new commercial debt | 1155 | 1366 | 2257 | 3932 | 5258 | 6681 | 8175 | 9855 | 11553 |
| Total existing debt | 24369 | 23159 | 22827 | 22086 | 21810 | 21457 | 20955 | 20242 | 19417 |
| **Existing domestic debt stock (incl. BR)** | 5793 | 5477 | 4928 | 4065 | 3760 | 3572 | 3440 | 3312 | 3258 |
| **Existing stock MLT External Debt of the Non-Financial Public Sector (A + D)** | 18576 | 17682 | 17899 | 18021 | 18050 | 17885 | 17515 | 16930 | 16159 |
| **Buy-Back Operation** | | | | | | | | | |
| Eurobond issue | 1430 | | | | | | | | |
| FLIRB Brady | | | | | | | | | |
| Outstanding principal (nominal) | 1212 | | | | | | | | |
| Discount rate | 77 | | | | | | | | |
| Market value in percent of nominal | 930 | | | | | | | | |
| Additional financing | 500 | | | | | | | | |
| Debt servicing | 2.17 | 2.66 | 3.28 | 3.87 | 3.44 | 3.47 | 3.52 | 3.62 | 3.57 |
| Exports | 7.92 | 8.53 | 9.33 | 10.55 | 11.83 | 13.11 | 14.57 | 15.98 | 17.4 |
| TDS/export | 0.27 | 0.31 | 0.35 | 0.37 | 0.29 | 0.26 | 0.24 | 0.23 | 0.21 |
| TDS/GDP | 0.04 | 0.04 | 0.05 | 0.06 | 0.05 | 0.04 | 0.04 | 0.04 | 0.04 |
| Financing need/GDP | 0.00 | 0.00 | 0.01 | 0.02 | 0.02 | 0.02 | 0.02 | 0.02 | 0.02 |
| Debt servicing/revenue | 19.1 | 22.3 | 26.2 | 29.5 | 24.9 | 24.0 | 23.2 | 22.8 | 21.4 |

*Source:* World Bank staff estimates.

TABLE A.5: SCENARIO WITH NO SHOCKS
Scenario C (in millions of US$)

| | 2002 Proj. | 2003 Proj. | 2004 Proj. | 2005 Proj. | 2006 Proj. | 2007 Proj. | 2008 Proj. | 2009 Proj. | 2010 Proj. |
|---|---|---|---|---|---|---|---|---|---|
| Nominal GDP | 56,816 | 60,068 | 62,124 | 64,887 | 67,839 | 70,926 | 74,153 | 77,60? | 81,134 |
| **Real growth** | **3.7** | **2.5** | **2.5** | **2.5** | **2.5** | **2.5** | **2.5** | **2.5** | **2.5** |
| Deflator | | | 0.9 | 1.9 | 2.0 | 2.0 | 2.0 | 2.1 | 2.0 |
| **Average interest paid on new debt** | **12** | **12** | **12** | **12** | **12** | **12** | **12** | **12** | **12** |
| Primary balance | -190 | -1 | 441 | 728 | 904 | 1143 | 1377 | 1597 | 1822 |
| **Primary balance as % of GDP** | **-0.3** | **0.0** | **0.7** | **1.1** | **1.3** | **1.6** | **1.9** | **2.1** | **2.2** |
| Interest payments | 1160 | 1373 | 1839 | 2151 | 2351 | 2614 | 2874 | 3120 | 3371 |
| Existing debt | 1160 | 1229 | 1434 | 1461 | 1347 | 1306 | 1246 | 1151 | 1042 |
| Domestic | 194 | 200 | 176 | 156 | 54 | 41 | 26 | 17 | 9 |
| Foreign (incl. new multi- and bilateral disbursements) | 966 | 1029 | 1258 | 1305 | 1293 | 1265 | 1220 | 1134 | 1033 |
| Newly issued commercial debt | 0 | 144 | 406 | 689 | 1004 | 1308 | 1628 | 1969 | 2329 |
| Interest payments as % of GDP | 2.0 | 2.3 | 3.0 | 3.3 | 3.5 | 3.7 | 3.9 | 4.0 | 4.2 |
| Overall fiscal balance | -1350 | -1374 | -1398 | -1422 | -1447 | -1472 | -1497 | -1523 | -1549 |
| Revenues | 11376 | 11934 | 12519 | 13132 | 13775 | 14450 | 15158 | 15901 | 16680 |
| Revenues as % of GDP | 20.0 | 19.9 | 19.7 | 19.3 | 18.9 | 18.5 | 18.1 | 17.7 | 17.4 |
| Tax revenues (IMF projections 2002–03) | 6761 | 7448 | 7813 | 8196 | 8598 | 9019 | 9461 | 9925 | 10411 |
| Expenditures | 12443 | 12995 | 13572 | 14175 | 14804 | 15461 | 16148 | 16865 | 17614 |
| Expenditures as % of GDP | 21.9 | 21.6 | 21.3 | 20.8 | 20.3 | 19.8 | 19.3 | 18.8 | 18.3 |
| **Overall fiscal balance as % of GDP** | **-2.4** | **-2.3** | **-2.3** | **-2.2** | **-2.1** | **-2.1** | **-2.0** | **-2.0** | **-1.9** |
| Privatization receipts | 600 | 600 | 400 | 47 | 45 | 45 | 40 | 40 | 40 |
| Privatization as % of GDP | 1.1 | 1.0 | 0.6 | 0.1 | 0.1 | 0.1 | 0.1 | 0.1 | 0.0 |
| Amortization of existing debt | 1009 | 1371 | 1693 | 2153 | 1706 | 1662 | 1653 | 1716 | 1629 |
| Domestic debt | 148 | 316 | 549 | 863 | 305 | 188 | 132 | 128 | 54 |
| Foreign debt | 873 | 1078 | 1179 | 1334 | 1445 | 1528 | 1575 | 1666 | 1684 |
| Multilateral | 410 | 419 | 445 | 515 | 589 | 600 | 601 | 650 | 651 |
| On new additional multilateral disbursements | 0 | 0 | 0 | 0 | 0 | 0 | 0 | 19 | 41 |
| Paris Club | 429 | 592 | 633 | 686 | 723 | 762 | 808 | 815 | 793 |

| | | | | | | | | | |
|---|---|---|---|---|---|---|---|---|---|
| Brady Bonds | 34 | 67 | 101 | 133 | 133 | 166 | 166 | 182 | 198 |
| PDI | 34 | 67 | 101 | 101 | 101 | 101 | 101 | 101 | 101 |
| FLIRB | 0 | 0 | 0 | 32 | 32 | 65 | 65 | 81 | 97 |
| New foreign disbursements | 1250 | 674 | 734 | 752 | 641 | 483 | 387 | 238 | 102 |
| Multilateral creditors | 1071 | 318 | 386 | 349 | 291 | 213 | 164 | 92 | 0 |
| Bilateral creditors | 229 | 356 | 348 | 403 | 350 | 270 | 223 | 146 | 102 |
| Financing need (issuance of new commercial debt) | 9 | 971 | 1957 | 2776 | 2467 | 2606 | 2723 | 2961 | 3036 |
| Domestic | 0 | | | | | | | | |
| Foreign (residual) | 9 | | | | | | | | |
| Total debt service | 2169 | 2744 | 3532 | 4304 | 4057 | 4276 | 4527 | 4836 | 5000 |
| Debt service/tax revenue | 32.08 | 36.83 | 46.29 | 55.05 | 50.65 | 52.11 | 53.85 | 56.15 | 56.67 |
| Total debt service as % of GDP | 3.8 | 4.6 | 5.7 | 6.6 | 6.0 | 6.0 | 6.1 | 6.2 | 6.2 |
| Implicit average interest rate | 5.39 | 5.42 | 7.27 | 8.15 | 8.46 | 8.93 | 9.33 | 9.65 | 9.95 |
| Domestic | 6.20 | | | | | | | | |
| Foreign | 5.14 | | | | | | | | |
| Total debt as % of GDP | 45.42 | 41.35 | 41.43 | 41.69 | 42.04 | 42.37 | 42.55 | 42.66 | 42.70 |
| Total debt | 25808 | 24838 | 25741 | 27054 | 28522 | 30053 | 31552 | 33107 | 34643 |
| Stock of new commercial debt | 1439 | 2401 | 4358 | 7134 | 9601 | 12206 | 14929 | 17890 | 20926 |
| Total existing debt | 24369 | 22437 | 21383 | 19920 | 18922 | 17847 | 16623 | 15217 | 13717 |
| Existing domestic debt stock (incl. BR) | 5793 | 5477 | 4928 | 4065 | 3760 | 3572 | 3440 | 3312 | 3258 |
| Existing stock MLT External Debt of the Non-Financial Public Sector (A + D) | 18576 | 16960 | 16455 | 15855 | 15162 | 14275 | 13183 | 11905 | 10459 |
| **Buy-Back Operation** | | | | | | | | | |
| Eurobond issue | 1430 | | | | | | | | |
| FLIRB Brady | | | | | | | | | |
| Outstanding principal (nominal) | 1212 | | | | | | | | |
| Discount rate | 77 | | | | | | | | |
| Market value in percent of nominal | 930 | | | | | | | | |
| Additional financing | 500 | | | | | | | | |
| Debt servicing | 2.17 | 2.74 | 3.53 | 4.30 | 4.06 | 4.28 | 4.53 | 4.83 | 5.00 |
| Exports | 7.92 | 8.53 | 9.33 | 10.55 | 11.83 | 13.11 | 14.57 | 15.98 | 17.40 |
| TDS/export | 0.27 | 0.32 | 0.38 | 0.41 | 0.34 | 0.33 | 0.31 | 0.30 | 0.29 |
| TDS/GDP | 0.04 | 0.05 | 0.06 | 0.07 | 0.06 | 0.06 | 0.06 | 0.06 | 0.06 |
| Financing need/GDP | 0.00 | 0.02 | 0.03 | 0.04 | 0.04 | 0.04 | 0.04 | 0.04 | 0.04 |
| Debt servicing/revenue | 19.07 | 23.54 | 29.58 | 35.18 | 32.37 | 33.30 | 34.41 | 35.89 | 36.21 |

*Source:* World Bank staff estimates.

**TABLE A.6:  REAL EXCHANGE RATE ADJUSTMENT IN THE EVENT OF A "SUDDEN STOP"**

|  | Peru | Bolivia | Ecuador |
|---|---|---|---|
| Elasticity of demand for nontradables with respect to p (x) | 0.40 | 0.40 | 0.40 |
| w = 1   (current account deficit/imports) | 0.79 | 0.72 | 0.68 |
| Real exchange rate depreciation | 34% | 41% | 45% |

*Source:* World Bank staff calculations based on Calvo, Izquierdo, and Talvi (2002).

in the event of a shock, capital inflows may slow down, but not cease completely. Figure A.2 presents a graphic representation of the implication of 10-percent RER adjustments for public debt sustainability in Peru. In the sensitivity exercises (based on the same assumptions as in the previous section), we are therefore accounting for a shock that leads to a slowing down, but not complete cessation, of capital inflows.

Additionally, we account for the impact on public debt dynamics of the contingent liabilities arising from a possible failure of the private sector to meet its *short-term* contractual debt obligations. We

**FIGURE A.2:  SCENARIO WITH SHOCKS**

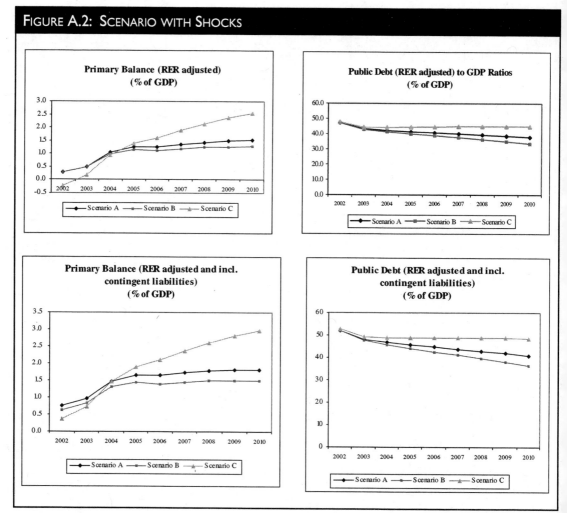

*Source:* World Bank staff estimates.

compute contingent liabilities as the share of foreign credit to the private sector that is allocated to nontradable activities. In Peru's case, the nontradables share is roughly two thirds of the economy (that is, $1 - (\text{trade}/\text{GDP}) = .67$). Short-term private sector liabilities are roughly US\$3.9 billion, that is, nearly 45 percent of the total private sector debt, reported to be US\$8.7 billion.

## Sensitivity Analysis and the Target Fiscal Adjustment (if the RER adjusts by 10 percent and contingent liabilities are accounted for)

**Scenario A:** Under the baseline scenario, incorporating an RER adjustment of 10 percent (assumed to occur in 2002) results in a higher public-debt-to-GDP ratio of 37.8 percent in 2010, compared to the unadjusted figure of 36.2 percent. Similarly, the required primary balance rises to 1.5 percent of GDP from 1.3 percent. Once we add the contingent liabilities, the public-debt-to-GDP ratio increases to 40.8 percent in 2010, while the required primary surplus increases to 1.8 percent of GDP.

**Scenario B:** Under the best-case scenario, incorporating an RER adjustment of 10 percent (assumed to occur in 2002) results in a higher public-debt-to-GDP ratio of 33.5 percent in 2010, compared to the unadjusted figure of 32.2 percent. Similarly, the required primary balance rises to 1.3 percent of GDP from 1 percent. Once we add the contingent liabilities, public-debt-to-GDP ratio increases to 36.4 percent in 2010, while the required primary surplus increases to 1.5 percent of GDP.

**Scenario C:** Under the worst-case scenario, incorporating an RER adjustment of 10 percent (assumed to occur in 2003) results in a higher public-debt-to-GDP ratio of 44.9 percent in 2010, compared to the unadjusted figure of 42.7 percent. Similarly, the required primary balance rises to 2.6 percent of GDP from 2.2 percent. Once we add the contingent liabilities, the public-debt-to-GDP ratio increases to 48.4 percent in 2010, while the required primary surplus increases to 3.0 percent of GDP.

## Summary:

Figure A.3 presents a comparison of public-debt-to-GDP ratios and required primary surplus as a percent of GDP, under the three scenarios with and with no shocks. Table A.7 presents a summary of these results under alternative assumptions (see Tables A.8–A.10).

# Figure A.3:  Peru Debt Dynamics: Comparison of Scenarios With and With No Shocks

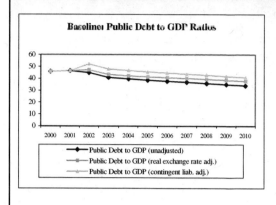

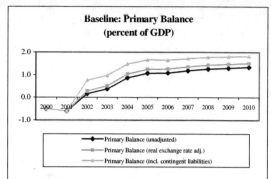

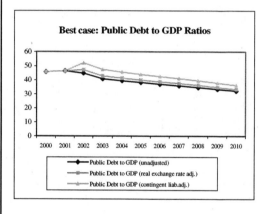

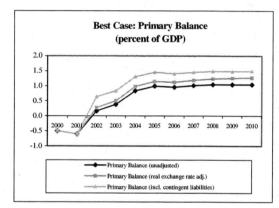

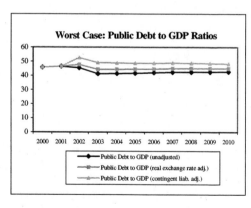

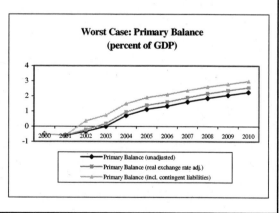

*Source:*  World Bank staff estimates.

## TABLE A.7: PUBLIC SECTOR DEBT SUSTAINABILITY WITH AND WITH NO SHOCKS
(in percent of GDP)

| | 2000 | 2001 | 2002 | 2003 | 2004 | 2005 | 2006 | 2007 | 2008 | 2009 | 2010 |
|---|---|---|---|---|---|---|---|---|---|---|---|
| **1. Baseline: Scenario A** | | | | | | | | | | | |
| Primary balance (unadjusted) | –0.5 | –0.6 | 0.2 | 0.4 | 0.9 | 1.1 | 1.1 | 1.2 | 1.3 | 1.3 | 1.3 |
| Primary balance (real exchange rate adj.) | –0.5 | –0.6 | 0.3 | 0.5 | 1.0 | 1.3 | 1.3 | 1.4 | 1.4 | 1.5 | 1.5 |
| Primary balance incl. contingent liabilities | –0.5 | –0.6 | 0.8 | 1.0 | 1.5 | 1.7 | 1.7 | 1.7 | 1.8 | 1.8 | 1.8 |
| Public debt to GDP (unadjusted) | 45.9 | 46.5 | 44.9 | 40.9 | 40.0 | 39.3 | 38.7 | 38.2 | 37.5 | 36.9 | 36.2 |
| Public debt to GDP (real exchange rate adj.) | 45.9 | 46.5 | 47.3 | 43.3 | 42.2 | 41.4 | 40.7 | 40.1 | 39.3 | 38.6 | 37.8 |
| Public debt to GDP (contingent liab.adj.) | 45.9 | 46.5 | 52.1 | 47.9 | 46.6 | 45.5 | 44.6 | 43.8 | 42.8 | 41.8 | 40.8 |
| **2. Scenario B** | | | | | | | | | | | |
| Primary balance (unadjusted) | –0.5 | –0.6 | 0.2 | 0.4 | 0.8 | 1.0 | 1.0 | 1.0 | 1.0 | 1.0 | 1.0 |
| Primary balance (real exchange rate adj.) | –0.5 | –0.6 | 0.3 | 0.5 | 1.0 | 1.2 | 1.1 | 1.2 | 1.2 | 1.3 | 1.3 |
| Primary balance incl. contingent liabilities | –0.5 | –0.6 | 0.6 | 0.8 | 1.3 | 1.5 | 1.4 | 1.5 | 1.5 | 1.5 | 1.5 |
| Public debt to GDP (unadjusted) | 45.9 | 46.5 | 44.9 | 40.8 | 39.4 | 38.2 | 37.1 | 36.0 | 34.8 | 33.6 | 32.2 |
| Public debt to GDP (real exchange rate adj.) | 45.9 | 46.5 | 47.3 | 42.9 | 41.3 | 40.0 | 38.8 | 37.6 | 36.3 | 34.9 | 33.5 |
| Public debt to GDP (contingent liab.adj.) | 45.9 | 46.5 | 52.1 | 47.5 | 45.6 | 44.0 | 42.5 | 41.1 | 39.5 | 38.0 | 36.4 |
| **3. Scenario C** | | | | | | | | | | | |
| Primary balance (unadjusted) | –0.5 | –0.6 | –0.3 | 0.0 | 0.7 | 1.1 | 1.3 | 1.6 | 1.9 | 2.1 | 2.2 |
| Primary balance (real exchange rate adj.) | –0.5 | –0.6 | –0.2 | 0.2 | 0.9 | 1.4 | 1.6 | 1.9 | 2.2 | 2.4 | 2.6 |
| Primary balance incl. contingent liabilities | –0.5 | –0.6 | 0.4 | 0.7 | 1.5 | 1.9 | 2.1 | 2.4 | 2.6 | 2.8 | 3.0 |
| Public debt to GDP (unadjusted) | 45.9 | 46.5 | 45.4 | 41.3 | 41.4 | 41.7 | 42.0 | 42.4 | 42.6 | 42.7 | 42.7 |
| Public debt to GDP (real exchange rate adj.) | 45.9 | 46.5 | 47.8 | 44.4 | 44.3 | 44.4 | 44.7 | 44.9 | 45.0 | 45.0 | 44.9 |
| Public debt to GDP (contingent liab.adj.) | 45.9 | 46.5 | 52.6 | 49.1 | 48.9 | 48.8 | 48.8 | 48.9 | 48.8 | 48.6 | 48.4 |

*Source:* World Bank staff estimates.

TABLE A.8: SCENARIOS WITH SHOCKS (10% DEPRECIATION IN REAL EXCHANGE RATE AND ADJUSTMENT FOR CONTINGENT LIABILITIES)
Scenario A: Baseline (in millions of lcu)

| | 2002 Proj. | 2003 Proj. | 2004 Proj. | 2005 Proj. | 2006 Proj. | 2007 Proj. | 2008 Proj. | 2009 Proj. | 2010 Proj. |
|---|---|---|---|---|---|---|---|---|---|
| lcu$ | 3.77 | 3.77 | 3.77 | 3.77 | 3.77 | 3.77 | 3.77 | 3.77 | 3.77 |
| Nominal GDP | 203,280 | 213,314 | 223,843 | 237,220 | 251,643 | 266,943 | 283,173 | 300,684 | 318,966 |
| **Real growth** | **3.7** | **4.0** | **4.0** | **4.0** | **4.0** | **4.0** | **4.0** | **4.0** | **4.0** |
| Deflator | 0.9 | 0.9 | 0.9 | 1.9 | 2.0 | 2.0 | 2.0 | 2.1 | 2.0 |
| **Average interest paid on new debt** | **10** | **10** | **10** | **10** | **10** | **10** | **10** | **10** | **10** |
| Primary balance incl. cont. liab. % of GDP | 0.8 | 1.0 | 1.5 | 1.7 | 1.7 | 1.7 | 1.8 | 1.8 | 1.8 |
| **Primary balance as % of GDP** | **0.28** | **0.51** | **1.04** | **1.25** | **1.26** | **1.36** | **1.44** | **1.48** | **1.52** |
| Interest payments including cont. liab | 5362.56 | 5957.89 | 7292.80 | 8032.01 | 8340.58 | 8901.37 | 9444.04 | 9928.14 | 10429.15 |
| Newly issued commercial debt | 0 | 320 | 878 | 1508 | 2235 | 2931 | 3678 | 4493 | 5368 |
| Interest payments as % of GDP incl. cont. liab. | 2.6 | 2.8 | 3.3 | 3.4 | 3.3 | 3.3 | 3.3 | 3.3 | 3.3 |
| **Overall fiscal balance as % of GDP** | **−1.9** | **−1.8** | **−1.8** | **−1.7** | **−1.7** | **−1.6** | **−1.5** | **−1.5** | **−1.4** |
| Privatization receipts | 2264 | 2264 | 1509 | 177 | 170 | 170 | 151 | 151 | 151 |
| Amortization of existing debt | 3807 | 5173 | 6387 | 8123 | 6437 | 6270 | 6236 | 6476 | 6148 |
| Domestic debt | 558 | 1192 | 2071 | 3256 | 1151 | 709 | 498 | 483 | 204 |
| Foreign debt | 3292 | 4068 | 4447 | 5034 | 5453 | 5764 | 5941 | 6325 | 6401 |
| Multilateral | 1547 | 1581 | 1679 | 1943 | 2222 | 2264 | 2268 | 2452 | 2456 |
| On new additional multilateral disbursements | 0 | 0 | 0 | 0 | 0 | 0 | 0 | 111 | 205 |
| Paris Club | 1619 | 2234 | 2388 | 2588 | 2728 | 2875 | 3049 | 3075 | 2992 |
| Brady Bonds | 127 | 253 | 380 | 503 | 503 | 625 | 625 | 686 | 748 |
| PDI | 127 | 253 | 380 | 380 | 380 | 380 | 380 | 380 | 380 |
| FLIRB | 0 | 0 | 0 | 123 | 123 | 245 | 245 | 306 | 368 |

| | | | | | | | | |
|---|---|---|---|---|---|---|---|---|
| New foreign disbursements | 4716 | 4135 | 4362 | 4430 | 4011 | 3415 | 3052 | 2490 | 1977 |
| Multilateral creditors | 4041 | 2792 | 3049 | 2909 | 2690 | 2396 | 2211 | 1939 | 1592 |
| Bilateral creditors | 864 | 1343 | 1313 | 1521 | 1321 | 1019 | 841 | 551 | 385 |
| Financing need (issuance of new commercial debt) | –1244 | 769 | 4496 | 7595 | 6435 | 6967 | 7418 | 8326 | 8617 |
| Domestic | 0 | | | | | | | | |
| Foreign (residual) | –1244 | | | | | | | | |
| Total debt service | 8184 | 10145 | 12694 | 15169 | 13792 | 14186 | 14695 | 15418 | 15591 |
| Total debt service as % of GDP | 4.0 | 4.8 | 5.7 | 6.4 | 5.5 | 5.3 | 5.2 | 5.1 | 4.9 |
| Implicit average interest rate | 5.39 | 5.28 | 6.75 | 7.31 | 7.33 | 7.56 | 7.75 | 7.87 | 7.99 |
| Domestic | 6.20 | | | | | | | | |
| Foreign | 5.14 | | | | | | | | |
| Total debt as % of GDP (RER adjusted) | 47.27 | 43.32 | 42.23 | 41.39 | 40.71 | 40.07 | 39.32 | 38.55 | 37.75 |
| Total debt as % of GDP (RER adjusted + contingent liab.) | 52.12 | 47.94 | 46.63 | 45.55 | 44.63 | 43.76 | 42.80 | 41.83 | 40.84 |
| Total debt | 96095 | 92411 | 94524 | 98190 | 102451 | 106956 | 111349 | 115919 | 120422 |
| Stock of new commercial debt | 4151 | 6165 | 10661 | 18256 | 24691 | 31658 | 39076 | 47402 | 56019 |
| Total existing debt | 91944 | 86246 | 83863 | 79934 | 77760 | 75298 | 72273 | 68517 | 64403 |
| Existing domestic debt stock (incl. BR) | 21857 | 20665 | 18593 | 15337 | 14186 | 13477 | 12979 | 12496 | 12292 |
| Existing contingent liab. (1998) | 9859 | 9859 | 9859 | 9859 | 9859 | 9859 | 9859 | 9859 | 9859 |
| Existing stock MLT External Debt of the Non-Financial Public Sector (A + D) | 70087 | 65582 | 65270 | 64597 | 63574 | 61820 | 59294 | 56021 | 52111 |

*Source:* World Bank staff estimates.

TABLE A.9: SCENARIOS WITH SHOCKS (10% DEPRECIATION IN REAL EXCHANGE RATE AND ADJUSTMENT FOR CONTINGENT LIABILITIES)
Scenario B (in millions of lcu)

| | 2002 Proj. | 2003 Proj. | 2004 Proj. | 2005 Proj. | 2006 Proj. | 2007 Proj. | 2008 Proj. | 2009 Proj. | 2010 Proj. |
|---|---|---|---|---|---|---|---|---|---|
| lcu$ | 3.77 | 3.77 | 3.77 | 3.77 | 3.77 | 3.77 | 3.77 | 3.77 | 3.77 |
| Nominal GDP | 203,280 | 215,365 | 228,168 | 244,129 | 261,462 | 280,026 | 299,908 | 321,516 | 344,344 |
| **Real growth** | **3.7** | **5.0** | **5.0** | **5.0** | **5.0** | **5.0** | **5.0** | **5.0** | **5.0** |
| Deflator | 0.9 | 0.9 | 0.9 | 1.9 | 2.0 | 2.0 | 2.0 | 2.1 | 2.0 |
| **Average interest paid on new debt** | **7.5** | **7.5** | **7.5** | **7.5** | **7.5** | **7.5** | **7.5** | **7.5** | **7.5** |
| Primary balance % of GDP incl. cont. liab. | **0.6** | **0.8** | **1.3** | **1.5** | **1.4** | **1.5** | **1.5** | **1.5** | **1.5** |
| **Primary balance as % of GDP** | **0.28** | **0.50** | **0.98** | **1.15** | **1.12** | **1.19** | **1.24** | **1.26** | **1.28** |
| Interest payments incl. cont. liab. | 5116.09 | 5616.71 | 6757.11 | 7285.79 | 7361.52 | 7699.34 | 8008.82 | 8243.33 | 8480.38 |
| Interest payments as % of GDP | 2.2 | 2.3 | 2.6 | 2.7 | 2.5 | 2.5 | 2.4 | 2.3 | 2.2 |
| Interest payments as % of GDP incl. cont. liab. | 2.5 | 2.6 | 3.0 | 3.0 | 2.8 | 2.7 | 2.7 | 2.6 | 2.5 |
| **Overall fiscal balance as % of GDP** | **−1.9** | **−1.8** | **−1.7** | **−1.5** | **−1.4** | **−1.3** | **−1.2** | **−1.1** | **−1.0** |
| Privatization receipts | 2264 | 2264 | 1509 | 177 | 170 | 170 | 151 | 151 | 151 |
| Amortization of existing debt | 3807 | 5173 | 6387 | 8123 | 6437 | 6270 | 6236 | 6476 | 6148 |
| Domestic debt | 558 | 1192 | 2071 | 3256 | 1151 | 709 | 498 | 483 | 204 |
| Foreign debt | 3292 | 4068 | 4447 | 5034 | 5453 | 5764 | 5941 | 6391 | 6534 |
| Multilateral | 1547 | 1581 | 1679 | 1943 | 2222 | 2264 | 2268 | 2452 | 2456 |
| On new additional multilateral disbursements | 0 | 0 | 0 | 0 | 0 | 0 | 0 | 178 | 338 |
| Paris Club | 1619 | 2234 | 2388 | 2588 | 2728 | 2875 | 3049 | 3075 | 2992 |
| Brady Bonds | 127 | 253 | 380 | 503 | 503 | 625 | 625 | 686 | 748 |
| PDI | 127 | 253 | 380 | 380 | 380 | 380 | 380 | 380 | 380 |
| FLIRB | 0 | 0 | 0 | 123 | 123 | 245 | 245 | 306 | 368 |

| | | | | | | | | |
|---|---|---|---|---|---|---|---|---|
| New foreign disbursements | 4716 | 5267 | 5493 | 5561 | 5143 | 4546 | 4184 | 3622 | 3109 |
| Multilateral creditors | 4041 | 3924 | 4180 | 4041 | 3822 | 3528 | 3343 | 3071 | 2724 |
| Bilateral creditors | 864 | 1343 | 1313 | 1521 | 1321 | 1019 | 841 | 551 | 385 |
| Financing need (issuance of new commercial debt) | -1244 | -439 | 3162 | 6123 | 4813 | 5179 | 5449 | 6158 | 6234 |
| Domestic | 0 | | | | | | | | |
| Foreign (residual) | -1244 | | | | | | | | |
| Total debt service | 8184 | 10050 | 12405 | 14670 | 13059 | 13230 | 13506 | 13980 | 13889 |
| Total debt service as % of GDP | 4.0 | 4.7 | 5.4 | 6.0 | 5.0 | 4.7 | 4.5 | 4.3 | 4.0 |
| Implicit average interest rate | 5.39 | 5.18 | 6.45 | 6.83 | 6.66 | 6.74 | 6.80 | 6.79 | 6.80 |
| Domestic | 6.20 | | | | | | | | |
| Foreign | 5.14 | | | | | | | | |
| **Total debt as % of GDP** | **47.27** | **42.87** | **41.30** | **39.97** | **38.76** | **37.56** | **36.26** | **34.90** | **33.49** |
| **Total debt as % of GDP (RER adjusted + contingent liab.)** | **52.12** | **47.45** | **45.63** | **44.01** | **42.53** | **41.09** | **39.55** | **37.97** | **36.36** |
| Total debt | 96095 | 92334 | 94245 | 97572 | 101342 | 105190 | 108746 | 112214 | 115332 |
| Stock of new commercial debt | 4151 | 4956 | 8118 | 14242 | 19054 | 24233 | 29682 | 35840 | 42074 |
| Total existing debt | 91944 | 87378 | 86127 | 83330 | 82288 | 80957 | 79064 | 76374 | 73259 |
| **Existing domestic debt stock (incl. BR)** | 21857 | 20665 | 18593 | 15337 | 14186 | 13477 | 12979 | 12496 | 12292 |
| **Existing contingent liab. (1998)** | 9859 | 9859 | 9859 | 9859 | 9859 | 9859 | 9859 | 9859 | 9859 |
| **Existing stock MLT External Debt of the Non-Financial Public Sector (A + D)** | 70087 | 66714 | 67533 | 67993 | 68101 | 67480 | 66085 | 63878 | 60966 |

Source: World Bank staff estimates.

TABLE A.10: SCENARIOS WITH SHOCKS (10% DEPRECIATION IN REAL EXCHANGE RATE AND ADJUSTMENT FOR CONTINGENT LIABILITIES)
Scenario C (in millions of lcu)

| | 2002 Proj. | 2003 Proj. | 2004 Proj. | 2005 Proj. | 2006 Proj. | 2007 Proj. | 2008 Proj. | 2009 Proj. | 2010 Proj. |
|---|---|---|---|---|---|---|---|---|---|
| lcu$ | 3.77 | 3.77 | 3.77 | 3.77 | 3.77 | 3.77 | 3.77 | 3.77 | 3.77 |
| Nominal GDP | 203,280 | 210,237 | 217,433 | 227,103 | 237,436 | 248,239 | 259,534 | 271,609 | 283,967 |
| **Real growth** | **3.7** | **2.5** | **2.5** | **2.5** | **2.5** | **2.5** | **2.5** | **2.5** | **2.5** |
| Deflator | 0.9 | 0.9 | 0.9 | 1.9 | 2.0 | 2.0 | 2.0 | 2.1 | 2.0 |
| **Average interest paid on new debt** | **12** | **12** | **12** | **12** | **12** | **12** | **12** | **12** | **12** |
| Primary balance % of GDP incl. cont. liab. | **0.4** | **0.7** | **1.5** | **1.9** | **2.1** | **2.4** | **2.6** | **2.8** | **3.0** |
| **Primary balance as % of GDP** | +0.22 | 0.18 | 0.94 | 1.38 | 1.60 | 1.90 | 2.16 | 2.37 | 2.57 |
| Interest payments incl. cont. liab. | 5559.74 | 6361.91 | 8122.52 | 9296.92 | 10053.35 | 11047.14 | 12026.63 | 12953.96 | 13900.42 |
| Interest payments as % of GDP incl. cont. liab. | 2.7 | 3.0 | 3.7 | 4.1 | 4.2 | 4.5 | 4.6 | 4.8 | 4.9 |
| **Overall fiscal balance as % of GDP** | **-2.4** | **-2.3** | **-2.3** | **-2.2** | **-2.1** | **-2.1** | **-2.0** | **-2.0** | **-1.9** |
| Privatization receipts | 2264 | 2264 | 1509 | 177 | 170 | 170 | 151 | 151 | 151 |
| Amortization of existing debt | 3807 | 5173 | 6387 | 8123 | 6437 | 6270 | 6236 | 6476 | 6148 |
| Domestic debt | 558 | 1192 | 2071 | 3256 | 1151 | 709 | 498 | 483 | 204 |
| Foreign debt | 3292 | 4068 | 4447 | 5034 | 5453 | 5764 | 5941 | 6284 | 6352 |
| Multilateral | 1547 | 1581 | 1679 | 1943 | 2222 | 2264 | 2268 | 2452 | 2456 |
| On new additional multilateral disbursements | 0 | 0 | 0 | 0 | 0 | 0 | 0 | 0 | 156 |
| Paris Club | 1619 | 2234 | 2388 | 2588 | 2728 | 2875 | 3049 | 3075 | 2992 |
| Brady Bonds | 127 | 253 | 380 | 503 | 503 | 625 | 625 | 686 | 748 |
| PDI | 127 | 253 | 380 | 380 | 380 | 380 | 380 | 380 | 380 |
| FLIRB | 0 | 0 | 0 | 123 | 123 | 245 | 245 | 306 | 368 |

| | | | | | | | | | |
|---|---|---|---|---|---|---|---|---|---|
| New foreign disbursements | 4716 | 2543 | 2769 | 2837 | 2418 | 1822 | 1460 | 898 | 385 |
| Multilateral creditors | 4041 | 1200 | 1456 | 1317 | 1098 | 804 | 619 | 347 | 0 |
| Bilateral creditors | 864 | 1343 | 1313 | 1521 | 1321 | 1019 | 841 | 551 | 385 |
| Financing need (issuance of new commercial debt) | −228 | 3288 | 7001 | 10086 | 8912 | 9429 | 9865 | 10757 | 11032 |
| Domestic | 0 | | | | | | | | |
| Foreign (residual) | −228 | | | | | | | | |
| Total debt service | 8184 | 10351 | 13327 | 16237 | 15307 | 16134 | 17080 | 18247 | 18865 |
| Total debt service as % of GDP | 4.0 | 4.9 | 6.1 | 7.1 | 6.4 | 6.5 | 6.6 | 6.7 | 6.6 |
| Implicit average interest rate | 5.39 | 5.44 | 7.32 | 8.23 | 8.57 | 9.07 | 9.51 | 9.86 | 10.19 |
| Domestic | 6.20 | | | | | | | | |
| Foreign | 5.14 | | | | | | | | |
| Total debt as % of GDP | 47.77 | 44.40 | 44.32 | 44.44 | 44.67 | 44.90 | 44.96 | 44.97 | 44.91 |
| Total debt as % of GDP (RER adjusted + contingent liab.) | 52.62 | 49.09 | 48.85 | 48.78 | 48.83 | 48.87 | 48.76 | 48.60 | 48.38 |
| Total debt | 97112 | 93338 | 96363 | 100929 | 106075 | 111449 | 116697 | 122146 | 127520 |
| Stock of new commercial debt | 5167 | 8684 | 15685 | 25771 | 34683 | 44112 | 53977 | 64734 | 75766 |
| Total existing debt | 91944 | 84654 | 80678 | 75158 | 71391 | 67337 | 62720 | 57412 | 51754 |
| Existing domestic debt stock (incl. BR) | 21857 | 20665 | 18593 | 15337 | 14186 | 13477 | 12979 | 12496 | 12292 |
| Existing contingent liab. (1998) | 9859 | 9859 | 9859 | 9859 | 9859 | 9859 | 9859 | 9859 | 9859 |
| Existing stock MLT External Debt of the Non-Financial Public Sector (A + D) | 70087 | 63989 | 62085 | 59820 | 57205 | 53859 | 49740 | 44916 | 39462 |

Source:  World Bank staff estimates.

# Annex B

# THE FISCAL EFFORT REQUIRED FOR A SUSTAINED STRUCTURAL DEFICIT

We estimate the required fiscal adjustment that is necessary to achieve the more sustainable debt-to-GDP ratios calculated in Annex A.[1] Fears of excessive fiscal deficits stem from the likelihood that they might be unsustainable in the long run. The fiscal effort in question is calculated in terms of the path that the *structural* deficit (as opposed to the *actual* deficit that incorporates a cyclically adjusted component) must follow to be consistent with debt and debt-service sustainability. Therefore, first, a structural primary balance is calculated, consistent with maintaining and even reducing the overall non-financial public sector (NFPS) debt as a ratio of GDP, in terms of both principal and servicing requirements. Second, we estimate the fiscal adjustment required to achieve sustainability on the assumption that the cyclical component of the primary balance will approach zero over the 10-year forecast period. The fiscal effort is estimated under three alternative scenarios and its sensitivity is analyzed according to alternative interest rate, financing, and output growth assumptions. The underlying assumptions, target debt-to-GDP and primary-surplus-to-GDP ratios, and the implicit average interest rates on total debt follow from the analysis in Annex A.

## Rationale for Using the Structural Balance and Methodology to Calculate It

It has long been recognized[2] that the nominal budget balance is an imperfect indicator of the government's true fiscal stance. The problem is that, in general, the fiscal balance depends not only on officials' tax and expenditure decisions, but also on the extent to which autonomous spending decisions by the private sector reflect themselves on the country's output and national income levels, and thereby on tax collection. Thus, if the economy enters a recession because of, say, a reduction in private investment, tax revenue automatically declines, irrespective of the officials' fiscal stance, and the fiscal balance worsens. Conversely, if an autonomous increase in private spending leads to an

---

1. This Annex was prepared with technical assistance from Rashmi Shankar.
2. See, for instance, Dornbusch and Fischer (1990).

increase in national income, tax revenue increases and the fiscal balance improves. These changes in the fiscal balance take place automatically for a given tax structure. This implies that, as its stands, the nominal fiscal balance is a distorted measure of whether government fiscal policy is expansionary or contractionary. A given fiscal stance is consistent with a worsening or an improvement in the nominal balance, depending on whether private spending decreases or increases.

To address the issue of the need to have a measure of fiscal policy that is independent of the particular position of the economy in the business cycle, the concept of cyclically adjusted or structural budget balance has been developed in the macroeconomics literature.[3] The basic idea is to carry out a simple decomposition of the nominal budget balance (B) into two unobservable components—the structural component ($SB$) and the cyclical component ($CB$)—in such a way that the following equation holds for period t:

$$B(t) = SB(t) + CB(t) \qquad (B.1)$$

Under the admittedly inaccurate, simplifying assumption that government spending is not a function of the state of the business cycle, the structural component is defined by:

$$SB(t) = SR(t) - G(t) \qquad (B.2)$$

where $SR(t)$, the structural revenue, is the fiscal revenue that would be collected if actual output in t were the level of output determined by the long-run trend, which will be called trend output. $G(t)$ is total government spending. $SR$ is estimated by means of the following equation:

$$SR(t) = R(t)[TY(t)/Y(t)]^{\beta} \qquad (B.3)$$

where $R(t)$ is the observed value for the government revenue; $TY(t)$ is the economy's trend output, $Y(t)$ the actual level of output, and ß is the income elasticity of total government revenue. Completion of the calculations implied by equations (B2) and (B3) requires that estimates for both trend output and the income elasticity of revenue be generated. These two issues are addressed below.

The revenue elasticity of the cyclical component during 1970–2001 was estimated. It was found to be 1.14.[4]

For the purpose of estimation trend output, the estimation method proposed by Hodrick and Prescott (1997) is used. In terms of this method, if the logarithm of $Y(t)$ is denoted $y(t)$, the time series for $y(t)$ can be decomposed in its trend component $ty(t)$ and its cyclical component $cy(t)$:

$$y(t) = ty(t) + cy(t); \text{ for } t = 1, \dots, T \qquad (B.4)$$

then the Hodrick-Prescott (HP) trend output, $hpy(t)$, is the series that minimizes the expression:

$$\sum cy(t)^2 + \lambda \sum \{[ty(t) - ty(t-1)] - [ty(t-1) - ty(t-2)]\}^2 \qquad (B.5)$$

where the sums are carried out from t = 1 to t = T and $\lambda$ is a parameter that determines how smooth the trend line will be. The method's idea is to minimize the sum of two terms where the first term is the sum of squares of the cyclical component and the second term is the sum of squares of the trend component's second differences. While the first term in (B.5) penalizes large residuals

---

3. See, for instance, Brown (1956); de Leeuw and others (1980); and Hagemann (1999). For a criticism of this approach, see Fellner (1982).

4. This is different from the revenue elasticity of 0.98 assumed for the main debt sustainability analysis for a shorter period, since what is considered here is the elasticity of *cyclical* tax revenues with respect to *cyclical* output.

(that is, poor fit),[5] the second term penalizes lack of smoothness in the trend. If λ is zero, the trend will simply equal the original series for all t; but, if λ is very large, changes in the slope of the trend are avoided, and, in the limit, the trend will simply be a straight line. For quarterly data there is a consensus among practitioners around the value of λ = 1600, originally proposed by Hodrick and Prescott (1980). There is no consensus, however, for data of other frequencies, and originally Dolado, Sebastián, and Vallés (1993) used λ = 400, and Backus and Kehoe (1992), Giorno and others (1995), and the European Central Bank (2002) use λ = 100 for the structural deficit of the European Union countries. Econometric software like Eviews also uses the latter value. Hence, a value of λ = 100 is assumed.

Figure 2.12 (see Chapter II) shows actual output and estimated structural or cyclically adjusted output for Peru during 1990–2002. Figure 2.13 shows actual and estimated fiscal balance.

Calculation of the structural balance allows us to carry out the next steps in the simulation exercise. They are:

1. Estimation of the required primary surplus consistent with the target debt-to-GDP ratio in period "*t+n*" where *n* is the number of forecast periods. This requires a forecast of future real interest and growth rates.
2. Estimation of the structural primary surplus in "*t+n*", the present value of which must equal the present value of the primary surpluses over the *n* periods in the forecast horizon.
3. Estimation of the fiscal effort required: Here a time horizon of nine years is assumed since the purpose of the exercise is to capture the transition dynamics in terms of the permanent, or long-run, fiscal adjustment required. The issue is then explored of how the debt-to-GDP ratio would evolve under alternative assumptions on interest rates, growth, and financing. The purpose is to capture the impact of changes in the assumptions regarding the values taken by key parameters on the target permanent primary surplus that is consistent with sustainable debt and debt servicing.

## Scenarios and Assumptions

Following the above indicated methodological steps, three simulation scenarios are run for 2002–10. The assumptions defining each scenario are similar to those in Annex A and are summarized in what follows.[6]

The *baseline* scenario assumes a moderate growth rate of 4.0 percent, which is slightly higher than the average growth rate of Peru's economy in the 1990s (3.6 percent). This scenario incorporates the preliminary figures for the Brady buy-back under which all outstanding front-loaded interest reduced Brady bonds have been exchanged. It is assumed that maintains moderate levels. The average interest rate on new debt is fixed at 10 percent throughout the period. It is also assumed that there will be reduced balance-of-payment support from the multilaterals (being phased out in 2003), but that this reduction will be partly offset by sector investment. There is limited resort to commercial borrowing. The financing mix is such that the implicit average interest rate on the total stock of NFPS debt grows gradually from 5.4 percent to 7.9 percent during 2002–10.

---

5. The *cy*(t) values are deviations from trend and the conceptual framework implies that, for a good fit to exist, their average over long time periods must be close to zero.

6. There is a set of assumptions common to all scenarios. They are (a) by 2010, automatic stabilizers will ensure that the cyclical component of the primary balance is close to zero; (b) the permanent primary balance is –43 percent in 2001; (c) receipts from privatization will be US$600 million for 2002 and 2003, and will fall to less than $50 million per year thereafter; (d) inflation in the GDP deflator (US$ terms) will increase from 0.9 percent in 2002 to approximately 2 percent during 2006–10; (e) continued rollover of short-term debt over the entire period 2002–10; (f) the permanent primary surplus grows "smoothly" to the required level; and (g) the NFPS elasticities of actual unadjusted revenues and expenditures with respect to GDP remain constant at 0.98 and 0.95, respectively. Elasticities are estimated for 1994–2002.

## TABLE B.1: REQUIRED FISCAL EFFORT FOR DEBT SUSTAINABILITY

| Diagonal Elements Corresponding to Main DSA (as a percentage of GDP) | Est. | | | | Projections | | | | | |
|---|---|---|---|---|---|---|---|---|---|---|
| | 2001 | 2002 | 2003 | 2004 | 2005 | 2006 | 2007 | 2008 | 2009 | 2010 |
| Primary surplus | −0.6 | | | | | | | | | |
| Permanent primary surplus | −0.4 | | | | | | | | | |
| Cyclical component of primary surplus | −0.3 | | | | | | | | | |
| **Scenario A: Baseline** | | | | | | | | | | |
| Interest rate (implicit average on NFPS debt) | 6.6 | 5.4 | 5.3 | 6.7 | 7.3 | 7.3 | 7.5 | 7.7 | 7.8 | 7.9 |
| Rate of growth of potential output (annual, %) | 3.7 | 4.0 | 4.0 | 4.0 | 4.0 | 4.0 | 4.0 | 4.0 | 4.0 | 4.0 |
| Target debt stock (% of GDP) | | | | | | | | | | **36.2** |
| Target permanent primary surplus (% of GDP) | −0.4 | −0.2 | 0.0 | 0.2 | 0.4 | 0.5 | 0.7 | 0.9 | 1.1 | 1.2 |
| Fiscal correction (% of GDP) | | | | | | | | | | 1.6 |
| **Scenario B: Best Case** | | | | | | | | | | |
| Interest rate (implicit average on NFPS debt) | 6.6 | 5.4 | 5.1 | 6.3 | 6.6 | 6.4 | 6.4 | 6.3 | 6.2 | 6.1 |
| Rate of growth of potential output (annual, %) | 3.7 | 5.0 | 5.0 | 5.0 | 5.0 | 5.0 | 5.0 | 5.0 | 5.0 | 5.0 |
| Target debt stock (% of GDP) | | | | | | | | | | **34.0** |
| Target permanent primary surplus (% of GDP) | −0.4 | −0.3 | −0.2 | −0.1 | 0.0 | 0.0 | 0.1 | 0.2 | 0.3 | 0.3 |
| Fiscal correction (% of GDP) | | | | | | | | | | 0.7 |
| **Scenario C: Worst Case** | | | | | | | | | | |
| Interest rate (implicit average on NFPS debt) | 6.6 | 5.4 | 5.4 | 7.3 | 8.2 | 8.5 | 9.0 | 9.4 | 9.7 | 10.1 |
| Rate of growth of potential output (annual, %) | 3.7 | 2.5 | 2.5 | 2.5 | 2.5 | 2.5 | 2.5 | 2.5 | 2.5 | 2.5 |
| Target debt stock (% of GDP) | | | | | | | | | | **42.7** |
| Target permanent primary surplus (% of GDP) | −0.4 | 0.0 | 0.4 | 0.7 | 1.1 | 1.4 | 1.8 | 2.2 | 2.5 | 3.0 |
| Fiscal correction (% of GDP) | | | | | | | | | | 3.3 |

Source: World Bank staff estimates.

A second, optimistic *best-case* scenario assumes a higher average growth rate of GDP (5.0 percent). The interest rate on new debt will be 7.5 percent over the simulation period. The multilaterals are assumed to provide full balance-of-payments support. The mix of multilateral financing and (limited) commercial borrowing is such that the implicit average interest rate on total NFPS debt stays at lower levels than in the other two scenarios, growing slowly from 5.4 percent to 6.1 percent during 2002–10.

Finally, a pessimistic *worst-case* scenario assumes both a low average growth rate (2.5 percent) and an even higher implicit interest rate on debt. The latter is the result of (a) reduced multilateral financing (no fast-disbursing loans and reduced new commitments from 2003 onward), and (b) the interest rate on new commercial debt is assumed to be 12.0 percent and the country has to rely more on this type of debt.

## Results

For the baseline scenario a substantial fiscal effort is required. The primary balance will have to be steadily increased from the 2001 deficit of –0.4 percent of GDP to a surplus of 1.2 percent of GDP by 2010, for a net fiscal correction of 1.6 percent of GDP (Table B.1).

In the optimistic scenario a lighter but still considerable fiscal effort in its own right will be required. The goal would be to reach a surplus of 0.3 percent of GDP by 2009–10, for a net fiscal correction of 0.7 percent of GDP. This is consistent with higher growth and fiscal discipline.

Not surprisingly, the pessimistic scenario would entail an extremely demanding fiscal effort. The (structural) primary balance would have to be reduced to zero immediately. With no delay, increasingly high primary surpluses would have to be attained and the net fiscal correction in the nine-year period through 2010 would amount to 3.4 percent of GDP.

# Annex C

# QUESTIONNAIRE ON PUBLIC FINANCIAL MANAGEMENT

*NOTE: Nelson Shack, Budget General Director, and Oscar Pajuelo, Accountant General of Peru, responded to this questionnaire.*

## Aggregate Fiscal Discipline
### *Budget Preparation and Approval*

**1a. Are there formal constraints (constitutional or legislatively mandated) on aggregate spending and/or deficits?** Yes. The objective of the Law of Fiscal Prudence and Transparency is to establish the guidelines for better management of the public finances in order to contribute to the economic stability, an essential condition to obtaining sustained economic growth and social welfare. At the same time, the Law establishes macro fiscal rules for the General Government, the Consolidated Public Sector, and it creates the Fiscal Stabilization Fund. Besides discipline on the expenditure side, the support of the fiscal equilibrium needs to generate fiscal savings in booms in order to face negative internal or external situations. It is necessary to establish fiscal goals for the medium term. In this way, the law contributes to the formation of expectations for the economic agents, in a period of three years. For that reason, the Law establishes ceilings for the levels of expenditures and debt.

**1b. Is the government required to publish actual figures relative to these constraints?** Yes. The Ministry of Economy and Finance (MEF) is in charge of the elaboration of the Multiyear Macroeconomic Framework (MMM) and the evaluation of its execution and publication. The MMM includes the Declaration of Principles of Fiscal Policy, the goals of fiscal policy over the next three years, and the targets for macroeconomic indicators in the next three years. It also contains the projection of fiscal revenue and expenditure, the sum of public investment, and the level of public debt.

**1c. Are these constraints imposed and monitored by donors?** No, they are not, but all economic agents observe the fiscal performance.

**2a. Are there formal constraints (constitutional or legislatively mandated) on public debt and domestic/external borrowing by (a) the Central Government, (b) subnational governments, and (c) public enterprises?** The Law mandates that the public debt in the medium term should be consistent with the principle of fiscal equilibrium. It is necessary to establish limits to the levels of expenditures and debt. There are no formal restrictions on the components of public debt, but there are limits under the Annual Law of Public Debt.

**2b. Is this monitored by the Central Bank?** Yes. Debt ceilings are established in the projections of the MMM and are coordinated with the General Direction of Public Credit at the MEF.

**2c. Are these constraints imposed and monitored by donors?** No, but all economic agents observe fiscal performance.

**2d. Is the government required to publish actual figures relative to these borrowing constraints?** Yes. They are in the MMM.

**3a. Is there a medium-term expenditure framework that projects an aggregate expenditure ceiling over a three-to-five-year horizon, consistent with the macroeconomic targets?** The MMM has a horizon of three years and the Sector Strategy Plans (SEPs) have a horizon of five years.

**3b. Is this published?** Yes, the MMM and the SEPs are published in *El Diario Oficial* and in the MEF's *Portal de Transparencia* website.

**3c. What is the percent difference between the aggregate spending in the projection and the annual budget?** It is very small, because the annual budget is elaborated as a function of the levels of expenses and incomes, consistent with the revised fiscal projections that the MMM realizes every year.

**4a. What is the percent deviation between the aggregate spending in the budget as proposed by the central agencies (that is, Ministry of Finance in the Budget Call Circular) and that approved by cabinet at the end of budget discussions?** No response.

**4b. What is the percent deviation between aggregate spending proposed by the Cabinet and the Legislature?** There is no deviation. Congress cannot alter the level of aggregate expenditure proposed by the Executive.

### Budget Execution and Monitoring

**1a. Are there formal rules that guard against overspending by agencies relative to budgeted amounts (for example, central agencies, chief accountants, or banks having the authority to refuse expenditures if there are insufficient funds in the ministerial account)?** Yes. No agency can spend more than the budget authorized by the National Directorate of the Public Budget (DNPP). Moreover, the Integrated Financial Management System (SIAF) contributes to respect for those rules.

**1b. Is there a published reconciliation of actual expenditures versus budgeted amounts?** Yes. The monthly Treasury report, the quarterly and annual reports from the DNPP, and the annual report from the General Office of Economic and Social Affairs (DGAES). All are available on the website.

**1c. Is there punitive action taken against overspending by agencies?** Yes, but on a case-by-case basis. There are administrative, civil, and penal responsibilities. The system of authorization in the SIAF allows a permanent and continuing evaluation of the authorizations of commitments and payments of checks. In this way, there is an efficient control of expenditure.

**2a. Is there a formal or informal requirement to report on aggregate fiscal outcomes relative to targets?** Yes. The report about the MMM's execution must be published semiannually. The

MEF goes to Congress annually to report about the execution of the budget. On the other hand, it is legally consistent with the revised fiscal projections that the MMM realizes every year.

2b. **Are these published?** Yes, on the website.

2c. **With what lags?** The access of information in the SIAF is virtual and has information aggregated up to the last month.

2d. **What is the percent deviation between the aggregate spending in the annual budget and the total amount actually spent at the end of the fiscal year?** No response.

## Expenditure Priorization and Allocative Efficiency
*Budget Preparation and Approval Breadth of Consultations*
1a. **What percent of expenditures is allocated by the Central Government (as opposed to subnational governments)?** Approximately 90 percent.

1b. **Which of these activities do subnational governments have constitutional responsibility for in allocating their budgetary expenditures: (a) primary education, (b) secondary education, (c) university education, (d) hospitals, (e) health clinics? Check only those that apply.** There exist the Transitory Councils of the Regional Administration (CTARs), in which one can find the Regional Offices of Health and Education. The local government, at the provincial or district levels, does not have the responsibility of providing education and health services.

2a. **Are there explicit pre-budget consultations about budgetary priorities between the government and the following groups in the private sector: (a) the business community, (b) public interest groups (for example, NGOs), (c) labor unions, and (d) farmers associations? Check only those that apply.** The budget is formulated internally in the public sector. There is not a framework that involves the participation of other sectors of the society yet.

2b. **How large a change vis-à-vis existing priorities in the current budget have emerged from such consultations: negligible, modest, or large?** It is not applicable but incoming pilot participatory budgeting will address investment expenditure.

2c. **Are there post-budget consultations with the same group, which attempt to reconcile pre-budget understandings with actual allocations?** No, there are not.

3a. **At the start of budget preparation, is there a session in the Legislature about budget priorities?** No.

3b. **How large a change vis-à-vis existing priorities in the current budget have emerged from such a session: negligible, modest, or large?** Not applicable.

4a. **Rank the following in terms of relative influence in deciding on broad priorities for the composition of expenditures: (a) Ministry of Finance/Planning, (b) the Cabinet, (c) the Legislature, (d) Donors, (e) private sector–government consultation committees.** That ranking is okay.

4b. **What is the average percent deviation in the allocation for the major sectors and programs between (a) the budget as proposed by the central ministries and that by the Cabinet, and (b) the budget as proposed by the Cabinet and that approved by the legislature? Range: negligible (0 to 10 percent), modest (10 to 30 percent), high (more than 30 percent).** Negligible (0 to 10 percent).

5a. **Does the government publish expenditure priorities corresponding to the following levels of disagreegation: (a) sector expenditures, (b) programs, (c) projects? Check only those that apply.** Yes, it does, but at the level of sectors and programs. These priorites are included in the MMM.

5b. **If so, are these expressed in terms of outcomes (that is, impact on beneficiaries, such as infant mortality) or outputs (that is, goods and services produced, such as number of health clinics or immunizations provided)?** No, they are not.

5c. **Are actual achievements of sector expenditures published?** Yes, on the website

5d. **If so, is there a public or published reconciliation with the targets?** Yes.

6a. **What percentage of public spending is financed by donors?** It is less than 2 percent of the budget.

6b. **Is there a prior agreement among donors about the composition of expenditures that are being collectively financed?** No.

6c. **If so, is this agreement induced by the leadership of a central donor?** Not applicable.

## Budget Preparation and Approval Allocation Rules and Criteria

1a. **Are expenditure allocations across ministries and programs increased or decreased in the same proportion across-the-board?** The variations, which could happen in the different assignments of expenses, are not proportional. They depend on the level of the expenditure priority.

1b. **Are there formulas or rules that earmark funds for specific expenditures? What proportion of total expenditures do they constitute?** No.

2a. **Are there formal or informal rules that require explicit consideration of whether individual programs or projects that are to be funded by the budget can be undertaken by the private sector?** No.

2b. **For which sectors is this done? For what percentage of programs/projects is this actually done (100 percent, 50 to 99 percent, 20 to 49 percent, less than 20 percent)?** Not applicable.

3a. **Is there a requirement to conduct an ex ante quantitative analysis of costs and benefits before a new program/project is initiated?** Yes, in the case of projects, the Law of National System of Public Inversion requires such analysis.

3b. **For which sectors is this done? Indicate the percentage of programs/projects for which this is actually done (100 percent, 50 to 99 percent, 20 to 49 percent, less than 20 percent)?** Since 2001, it is 100 percent.

4a. **Is the distributional impact of public spending explicitly quantified and considered in allocating resources among programs and projects?** No.

4b. **For which sectors is this done? Indicate the percentage of programs/projects for which this is actually done (100 percent, 50 to 99 percent, 20 to 49 percent, less than 20 percent)?** Not applicable.

## Budgeting Preparation and Approval Norms

1a. **Is there a system of forward estimates that projects the future cost implications of existing and proposed programs and projects?** No.

1b. **Are these automatically rolled over into the next budget, adjusted only for key national parameters such as inflation rate?** Not applicable.

1c. **Are these forward estimates published?** Not applicable.

1d. **Does the government publish a reconciliation statement explaining any significant deviations in the composition of expenditures between the original forward estimates and the annual budget?** Not applicable.

2a.  Are line agencies required to identify cuts in their existing programs to match new spending proposals? No.

2b.  Are various new spending proposals and offsetting cuts discussed systematically at a Cabinet or sub-Cabinet level? Yes.

## Budgeting Preparation and Approval of Capital/Recurrent Budgeting

1a.  Are there separate budgets for capital and recurrent expenditures? Yes.

1b.  Is there a requirement to estimate the recurrent cost implications of new capital investments? Yes.

1c.  Are there different ministries responsible for preparing capital budgets (for example, Ministry of Planning) and recurrent budgets (for example, MEF)? The investment office (ODI) at MEF does it.

1d.  What percent of public investments is donor financed? Not available.

## Budget Preparation and Approval of Donor Rules

1a.  Is there a donor conditionality on the overall composition of expenditures? No.

1b.  Has expenditure composition been changed in accordance with this conditionality? Not applicable.

1c.  What percent of donor-financed expenditures is earmarked for particular programs and projects? Not available.

## Budgeting Execution and Monitoring

1a.  What is the average percent deviation between the composition of expenditures as approved in the annual budget and the actual allocation at the end of the budget year? Not available.

1b.  On what basis was the composition changed: (a) arbitrary/ad hoc, (b) related to specific problems? It was changed in relation of specific problems such as internal shocks of natural character (*El Niño* phenomenon), and political and external shocks (financial crisis and the world recession).

1c.  What was the relative role of the following in inducing these changes: (a) Ministry of Finance/Planning, (b) the Cabinet, (c) the Legislature, (d) private sector–government consultation committees? Rank these in order of importance, with 1 for the least influence and 4 for the most. Not available.

2a.  Is there a requirement for carrying out ex post evaluation of programs/projects? By whom: central agencies, line agencies, or by independent external agencies? Check all those that apply. They are done by the ODI, Special Programs, MEF.

2b.  Are the results used in expenditure allocations for the next budget? Yes.

3.  Are client surveys routinely carried out as part of these evaluations? No.

## Accountability

1a.  Is there a clear specification of the output to be produced by (a) a ministry, (b) a department within a ministry, and (c) a division, program, or project unit within a department? Yes, there is, financially for the ministry ruled by the norms issued by the Nation Public Auditor's Office and they are in agreement with the Principles of "Generally Accepted Accounting," which includes, according to the case, the development of the International Norms.

**1b. If so, are these outputs published?** They are published, with limited distribution to the Executive and the Legislative bodies. They are available at the National Public Accountant's Office website.

**2a. Are performance indicators specifically linked to senior manager (a) tenure, (b) promotion, and (c) compensation?** No.

**2b. Are these performance indicators based on the achievement of outputs (that is, goods and services produced, such as number of immunizations of health clinics) or outcomes (that is, impact of beneficiaries, such as lower infant mortality)?** They are collected by the National Office of Public Budget with few details.

**2c. Have chief executives been fired on account of nonperformance?** No.

**3a. What is the percentage deviation between public and private pay for different grade levels?** It is 5 to 1 in proportion to staff.

**3b. Is there an explicit link between pay and performance?** No.

**4a. Is competitive bidding required for the procurement of major expenditure items?** Yes, procedures are under standard. The Superior Council of Contractings and Procurements from the State (CONSUCODE) supervises the process.

**4b. Are the rules for bidding made public?** Yes. When the bidding amount is larger, the publication is larger, too.

**5a. When are financial accounts of line agencies prepared: (a) quarterly during the budget year, (b) semestral during the budget year, (c) within six months from the end of the fiscal year, (d) more than six months but less than one year, (e) between one and three years, (f) more than three years.** Yes, for (a) and (b). Yes. The budget program is reconciled with the numbers rendered by the entities of accounts, the National Office of Public Budget, and the Nation Public Auditor's Office. No for (c) (d) (e) and (f).

**5b. Are there punitive actions taken against (a) delays, and (b) discrepancies?** Under the law, there are actions, but in practice it depends on the actions of the Republic General Auditor's Office, which is the entity in charge of that. It is not frequent to see actions by the General Account of the Republic.

**5c. Are these accounts tabled before a separate session of the Legislature?** The procedure dictates that the General Account of the Republic is forwarded to the Republic General Auditor's Office in order to create the Auditor's report. After that, it is forwarded to the Presidency of the Republic, to the MEF, and to the Review Commission of the General Accounts of Congress.

**5d. Are they made public?** They are distributed to the Executive and Congress. They are on the Public Auditor's Office website for the fiscal year. They are divulged in the training, local, domestic, or international competitions.

**6a. Are the agency accounts audited?** In the majority of cases, especially those of public enterprise entities of the Central Government, the Republic General Auditor's Office is in charge of auditing the General Account from the Republic.

**6b. If so, by whom: internal agency auditor, the government auditor within the Executive, independent auditor?** No response.

**6c. When are audits of agency accounts undertaken: (a) quarterly during the budget year, (b) semestral during the budget year, (c) within six months from the end of the fiscal year, (d) more than six months but less than one year, (e) between one and three years, (f) more than three years.** Once per year.

6d.  **What percent of programs have been audited in the last five years?** As a percentage of the number of entities, approximately 20 percent. In budget amounts, approximately 80 percent.

6e.  **What percent are financial audits as opposed to performance audits?** Approximately 35 percent.

6f.  **Are the results published?** No.

6g.  **Has there been punitive action or promotion based on these audits?** Yes, there has been. The Republic General Auditor Office, with the help of the Attorney General's Office, is in charge of that.

7a.  **Are there client surveys undertaken?** Depends on each case. Part of the control of procedures includes actions with the providers and clients.

7b.  **How frequently?** There is not an established schedule. It depends on the Control Plans.

7c.  **Are the results published?** No.

7d.  **Do these surveys measure satisfaction with service delivery (that is, outputs), or with success of the program (that is, outcomes), or both?** No.

8a.  **How many major donors provide project financing?** There are no data available.

8b.  **Do these projects specify the amount and type of expenditures on which project resources will be spent?** There are no data available.

8c.  **Does each donor have its own rules about disbursement, procurement, accounting, and auditing of projects funds?** Yes. We are working on adapting those requirements with the Integrated Financial Management System in the area of functional and operational competence.

8d.  **Do these rules match those of the government?** Yes.

# Annex D

# A PUBLIC EXPENDITURE TRACKING SURVEY: METHODOLOGICAL ISSUES

## Sample Design

Measuring leakages in transfers to subnational governments, local organizations, and program beneficiaries is not an easy task since it involves two central problems. First, none of the parties affected by the leak have an interest in having it revealed. Second, leakages can occur at so many levels that tracing them all requires a complex methodology. Those are the two challenges that this report faced and, to a considerable degree, overcame.

The core of our methodology was to collect data at each stage in the transference of public funds from the top of the chain, the Central Government (CG), to the bottom of the chain, the beneficiary. In order to gather data on each of these levels, the study carried out in Peru involved an extensive amount of fieldwork based on a series of questionnaires. The questionnaires themselves are attached to Apoyo Institute (2002a). In this Annex, we briefly describe how we went about gathering the data.

The project began with a pilot study in Lima, Peru. The objectives of the pilot included an assessment of the duration of the fieldwork and a test of its effectiveness for the purposes of the study (for example, to explore whether the information collected in the fieldwork would be sufficient to rigorously estimate leakages). The pilot consisted of 20 districts of the department of Lima (out of a total of 177 districts). Each district included a survey for the municipality; 3, 4, or 5 surveys[1] for the *Vaso de Leche* (VDL) mother's committees; and 16 surveys for beneficiary households[2]

---

1. For the pilot the following rule was established: 3 *Vaso de Leche* committees if there were less than 30 committees total, 4 if the number of committees were between 30 and 70, and 5 if there were more than 70 committees.

2. When the pilot was carried out, the project had not yet formally included surveys to household beneficiaries. A tentative instrument was tested on households to evaluate the importance and viability of including beneficiaries. Therefore, the pilot survey was shorter than and different from the survey applied to beneficiaries during the final fieldwork.

(4 per VDL committee). Additionally, Lima was selected for the pilot because it differs considerably from the rest of the country and needs separate treatment. The advantage of doing it this way was that we were able to report comparisons between Lima and the rest of the country, which in many cases were quite large.

Based on the experience of the Lima sample, and after a thorough process of consultation, and with guidance from the National Institute of Statistics and Information (INEI), a national sample selection methodology was agreed upon. The following departments were chosen to be representative of Peru (excluding Lima and Callao): Ancash, Arequipa, Cajamarca, Cusco, Loreto, and Piura. These departments gave us the broadest range of geography, population density, and poverty distribution, while reducing our field costs to reasonable levels (that is, we did not have the resources to include municipalities from all of Peru's provinces). We then selected a total of 100 municipalities in which the surveys were carried out. Our method of selecting the municipalities was focused on poverty as a central stratification variable since the VDL program was meant to deal directly with poverty. The sample, then, represents Peru (when the Lima sample is included), and the 100 municipalities selected are stratified by level of poverty so that the efficiency of the sample would be maximized (stratification reduces sampling error). The sample is self-weighting, making it easy to work with when complex multivariate programs are employed. Our method of municipality selection follows.

## Stratification According to Poverty

A database consisting of the entire universe of districts in Peru, excluding Lima and Callao (total of 1,651 districts) was used as a starting point.

- The Ministry of Economy and Finance's (MEF's) continuous index of poverty, FGT2,[3] was used to calculate poverty population deciles.
- The deciles were arranged into three groups such that group 1 consisted of deciles 1 to 3, group 2 of deciles 4 to 7, and group 3 of deciles 8 to 10. These three groups approximate the categories of "not poor," "poor," and "extreme poor," and were used to stratify the districts of our subpopulation (Ancash and Piura) into three strata.
- The three strata represent 14 percent, 41 percent, and 45 percent of the districts in Peru (excluding Lima and Callao), respectively.
- In order for the sample to be self-weighted 14, 41, and 45 municipalities (total of 100) were chosen from each stratum respectively (from the subpopulation of six departments). The selection for each stratum was done using Probability Proportional to Size (PPS)[4] relative to district population.

Once the above procedure was carried out, individual municipalities were selected according to PPS criteria, using a complete listing of all districts selected that were ordered within the stratums by geographic order to allow a systematic selection that ensured geographic heterogeneity.

Within each municipality, the field used the roster of *Vaso de Leche* committees and systematic sampling to select four of those, unless there were fewer than four in a given municipality, in which case all were selected. The only restriction was that if travel time to a given committee would have required more than 24 hours, a substitute was used. This means that the sample slightly underrepresented remote areas within the neighborhoods of the selected committees; the field team

---

3. $FGT_2 = \dfrac{1}{N} \sum_{i=1}^{Q} \left( \dfrac{PL - EXPpc_i}{PL} \right)^2$ where PL = poverty line, EXPpc = per capita household expenditures, Q = number of poor, and N = population.

4. PPS is a method used in sample selection whereby the probability that a given element enters the sample is proportional to some quantity (in our particular case, the district's total population).

selected four households from the beneficiary lists that are maintained by each committee. Recalls were not made, but the next household on the list was used as a substitute when blanks were encountered.

The survey was conducted February 3–17, 2002. Descriptive statistics for the samples are provided in the full report. Within each municipality we interviewed the mayor, obtained municipal-level data from him or her, and also obtained the municipal roster of committees participating in the *Vaso de Leche* program. The committees were selected from the roster using a systematic selection. Once we met with at least one committee member and interviewed that individual with our survey instrument, we obtained from that member a list of individual beneficiary households and interviewed four households in each committee catchments area, using the survey instrument intended for households.

## Description of Transfers from Central Government to Municipalities and Downward

Municipal resources come from two primary sources: Central Government (CG) transfers and local revenues. CG transfers are a very important source of revenue, particularly for small and rural municipalities, which have very little income-collection capacity. CG transfers include *Fondo de Compensación Municipal* (FONCOMUN) and *Vaso de Leche* (VDL) for all municipalities, and *Canon Minero* and *Canon/Sobrecanón Petrolero* for some of them. CG transfers represent an important percentage of total district-level income, (for the districts outside of Lima in our sample, transfers, on average, represent 72 percent of total income, and among the districts of the extreme poor stratum they can represent over 90 percent of total income).

In 2001, these four major CG transfers totaled, at the national level, NS/1.9 billion (roughly $560 million) (Table D.1).[5] For these reasons the leakages, delays, volatilities, and inefficiencies associated with the execution process of these transfers have considerable impact on municipal-level finances, and their understanding is, consequently, of paramount importance.

Of these four transfers, only the *Canon Minero* is not variable month to month. In theory, the VDL transfer should not be variable month to month either, but as Table D.2 shows, this is not true in practice. FONCOMUN and the *Canon/Sobrecanon Petrolero* are percentages of a variable quantity (primarily the national sales tax in the case of FONCOMUN and the ad valorem tax on petroleum production in the case of the *Canon/Sobrecanon Petrolero*). The implicit volatility in these two transfers is a source of hardship for municipalities, the budgets of which depend heavily on them.

Month-to-month percentage changes in amounts for each of the four major transfers were calculated. The volatility of the transfers was defined as the standard deviation of these month-to-month changes. Table D.2 details the volatilities of FONCOMUN, *Canon/Sobrecanon Petrolero,* and *Vaso de Leche* in 2001.[6] The measure of dispersion is the degree to which the volatilities vary within each of these subclassified categories. The volatility of the *Canon/Sobrecanon Petrolero* transfers is the combination of the variations in world petroleum prices and the variability of local production, and is, on average, twice as high as that of the FONCOMUN transfer. FONCOMUN's volatility is not considerably different between urban/rural districts or between poverty strata, but is twice as high in larger districts (as measured by their projected 2001 populations). The volatility of the *Canon/Sobrecanon Petrolero*, on the other hand, is quite a bit higher in poor, rural, remote districts of Peru. The former finding is quite interesting given that the assignment formula does not vary within the year.

Therefore, a percentage change in the sales tax revenue (and/or any other component of the FONCOMUN) should imply an equal percentage change in the amounts allocated to the districts across the board. However, we see that the standard deviations of the monthly percentage changes are not equivalent. This is partly due to the fact that these transfers have a built-in floor (NS/15,600) and therefore their variations are asymmetrical. Surprisingly, the VDL transfer also suffered from

---

5. Using MEF statistics at the national level.

6. The volatilities are estimated by calculating the standard deviation of the rate of change of the monthly amounts for each of the three transfers.

## TABLE D.1: TOTAL TRANSFERS TO MUNICIPALITIES IN 2001
(in U.S. dollars)

| | FONCOMUN | Canon Minero | Canon/ Sobrecanon Petrolero | Vaso de Leche | TOTAL |
|---|---|---|---|---|---|
| Peru | 400,023,180 | 23,765,654 | 37,461,817 | 97,148,245 | 558,398,895 |
| Lima | 72,466,783 | 714,003 | N.A. | 33,753,411 | 106,934,197 |
| Urban | 69,482,021 | 691,650 | N.A. | 33,359,639 | 103,533,311 |
| Rural | 2,984,762 | 22,353 | N.A. | 393,772 | 3,400,887 |
| No. Observations | 177 | 171 | N.A. | 177 | N.A. |
| Rest of Peru | 327,556,397 | 23,051,651 | 37,461,817 | 63,394,833 | 451,464,698 |
| Not Poor | 76,066,085 | 5,692,301 | 9,924,653 | 15,642,446 | 107,325,483 |
| Poor | 132,062,598 | 8,603,523 | 17,670,749 | 24,705,129 | 183,041,999 |
| Extreme Poor | 119,427,714 | 8,755,827 | 9,866,416 | 23,047,259 | 161,097,216 |
| Urban | 152,245,705 | 9,629,748 | 20,840,016 | 30,939,959 | 213,655,428 |
| Rural | 175,310,692 | 13,421,902 | 16,621,801 | 32,454,874 | 237,809,270 |
| Small | 65,758,919 | 3,206,004 | 3,916,796 | 8,990,266 | 81,871,986 |
| Medium | 50,188,784 | 3,515,896 | 5,744,644 | 10,333,395 | 69,782,718 |
| Large | 211,608,694 | 16,329,751 | 27,800,377 | 44,071,173 | 299,809,994 |
| More Accessible | 239,125,681 | 17,287,765 | 22,227,123 | 46,727,882 | 325,368,452 |
| Less Accessible | 88,430,716 | 5,763,885 | 15,234,694 | 16,666,951 | 126,096,246 |
| Nonprovincial Capital | 188,468,161 | 11,999,547 | 18,319,805 | 41,422,875 | 260,210,387 |
| Provincial Capital | 139,088,236 | 11,052,104 | 19,142,013 | 21,971,958 | 191,254,311 |
| No. Observations | 1,641 | 1,296 | 142 | 1,641 | N.A. |

Note: Information based on national official statistics.
Source: MEF.

considerable volatility in 2001 in the districts outside the department of Lima. The poorest districts were the most affected, with a standard deviation of percentage changes on the order of 15 percent for the year. This figure is in sharp contrast to the average volatility of 0.3 percent experienced by the 177 districts of Lima and Callao (Table D.2).

## FONCOMUN

The *Fondo de Compensación Municipal* (FONCOMUN) is mentioned in subsection 4 of article 193 of the Constitution of the Republic of Peru. It is comprised of 2 percent of the federal sales tax (the VAT), 8 percent of gasoline sales, 5 percent of recreational embarkations, and 25 percent of the net income generated by casinos and other gambling establishments. The contribution from the VAT accounts for approximately 93 percent of FONCOMUN revenues, and therefore constitutes its main source of variability. The law that permits the redirection of a portion of the VAT under the name of *Impuesto de Promoción Municipal* is dictated by Article 86 of Legislative Decree 776 of the Law of Municipal Taxes.

The Fund is calculated on a monthly basis and is distributed monthly to all the municipalities, based on a predefined allocation formula of the Ministry of Economy and Finance (MEF). The process for disbursing the transfer from the CG to the municipalities is the following. The collection of funds is centralized at the *Banco de la Nación* (BN, the Treasury). Within the first five days of each month, the BN informs the National Directorate for the Public Budget (DNPP) of the MEF regarding the amount collected. This office in turn informs the General Directorate of Fiscal Policy (DGPF) of the MEF, which is in charge of estimating the amount to be distributed to each

| TABLE D.2: VOLATILITY OF TRANSFERS TO MUNICIPALITIES[1] (in percent) | | | | | | |
|---|---|---|---|---|---|---|
| | FONCOMUN | | Canon/Sobrecanon Petrolero | | Vaso de Leche | |
| | Volatility | Dispersion | Volatility | Dispersion | Volatility | Dispersion |
| *Lima* | 4.9 | 4.1 | N.A.[2] | N.A. | 0.3 | 1.6 |
| Urban | 5.5 | 4.2 | N.A. | N.A. | 0.2 | 1.2 |
| Rural | 2.9 | 3.2 | N.A. | N.A. | 0.5 | 2.6 |
| *No. Observations* | 177 | | N.A. | | 177 | |
| *Rest of Peru* | 6.3 | 3.4 | 13.4 | 6.9 | 11.6 | 30.3 |
| Not Poor | 6.1 | 3.8 | 9.2 | 3.1 | 10.0 | 56.8 |
| Poor | 6.0 | 3.6 | 11.6 | 4.7 | 8.1 | 22.2 |
| Extreme Poor | 6.5 | 3.2 | 18.8 | 8.4 | 15.4 | 23.9 |
| Urban | 5.7 | 3.8 | 10.4 | 4.1 | 5.2 | 19.5 |
| Rural | 6.5 | 3.2 | 15.7 | 7.7 | 14.7 | 33.9 |
| Small | 4.0 | 3.1 | 13.2 | 5.0 | 10.7 | 34.9 |
| Medium | 8.2 | 1.7 | 15.5 | 9.4 | 15.3 | 26.3 |
| Large | 9.4 | 0.8 | 12.4 | 5.7 | 10.5 | 21.7 |
| More Accessible | 6.8 | 3.3 | 10.3 | 5.0 | 9.5 | 27.5 |
| Less Accessible | 5.5 | 3.5 | 16.4 | 7.2 | 14.2 | 33.3 |
| Nonprovincial Capital | 5.8 | 3.4 | 13.4 | 6.8 | 12.1 | 28.9 |
| Provincial Capital | 9.6 | 0.5 | 13.8 | 7.4 | 7.7 | 39.7 |
| *No. Observations* | 1,642 | | 142 | | 1,642 | |

1. Standard deviation of the percent changes month-over-month 2001.
2. The department of Lima does not receive Canon/Sobrecanon Petrolero.

*Source:* National Official Statistics, MEF.

municipality. Once the distribution is determined, the DGFP informs the DNPP, which issues the transfer order to the BN. Finally, the BN deposits the money in the account of each municipality on the 13th to 15th day of the month (Figure D.1).

According to the MEF personnel our team interviewed, the process is automatic and should take no longer than the terms established.[7] The distribution criteria do not change frequently, although there are certain minimums established which require a complicated reallocation if there is a downturn in resources for a given month. Nonetheless, as the results of the fieldwork indicate, the municipalities do face some delays. In principle, the transfer process funds from the CG to the municipalities is straightforward and does not suggest ex ante that there will exist a leakage in this segment of the chain. At this stage, the process is quite systematic and the BN serves a limited function—that of electronically transferring funds from one account to another and issuing arrival notifications.

The DGFP office of the MEF uses a formula to calculate the way it will distribute the total amount of funds to each municipality. For the districts outside of Lima and Callao, the formula allocates amounts to each province based on the infant mortality rate and the total population of the province. The formula further assigns amounts to the districts based on district-level populations, with a bias toward rural populations (rural inhabitants count twice as much as urban inhabitants do).

---

7. The FONCOMUN transfer, and the other municipality transfers and finances in general, are still not incorporated into the SIAF. At the time this report was being prepared, the SIAF was working with a pilot sample of at least 25 municipalities to integrate them (see Chapter III).

## FIGURE D.1: FONCOMUN TRANSFER PROCESS

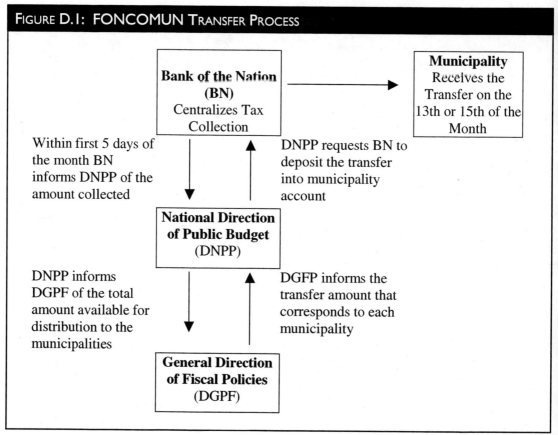

Source: MEF.

For Lima and Callao the objective is to prioritize urban marginal districts. The allocation criteria considered are the following: population, illiteracy rate for those older than age 15, households with at least one child attending school, households without a water connection in the home, households without sewerage, households without electricity, households that occupy makeshift homes, and households with three or more inhabitants per room. All these indicators are provided by the INEI and are based on the 1993 census. Until December 2001 (December 29th), the law established that only up to 30 percent of FONCOMUN could be used for current expenditures. At least 70 percent of the fund had to go toward capital expenditures. Since January 2002, the FONCOMUN no longer has been subject to the 70 to 30 ratio, and can be freely used as the municipalities best see fit.

### Canon Minero

Dictated by supreme decrees 88-95-EF and 041-97-EF, the *Canon Minero* is a CG transfer that distributes a portion of the mining sales to the localities in which the mineral ore was extracted. Twenty percent of the income tax paid by the mining companies is distributed among the municipalities in the following manner: 40 percent for provinces and districts in the region or regions[8] in which the ore was extracted or in which the mining company's economic headquarters are located; and 60 percent for provinces and districts in the department or departments in which the ore was extracted or in which the mining company's economic headquarters are located (in addition to the 40 percent).

---

8. Under the administration of President Alan Garcia regions (several adjacent departments) were created.

The total amount allocated to a set of municipalities is then distributed by the MEF according to a formula similar to the one used for FONCOMUN. Within a region, the allocation to provinces is based on the infant mortality rate and the total population of the province. Of that amount, 20 percent remains at the provincial municipality (provincial capital) and the remaining 80 percent is distributed among the municipalities of the province based on their respective populations (once again giving a two-to-one preference to rural populations). For Lima and Callao, where the objective is to give priority to the urban-marginal districts, the additional criteria used in the distribution of the FONCOMUN are also used for the *Canon Minero*. The process of disbursement of the *Canon Minero* is simple. The tax agency, SUNAT, deposits the taxes collected in a special account at the BN. The DNPP then distributes the total amount among municipalities (following the criteria mentioned above) in 12 equal monthly installments made by the BN through electronic deposits. There is a restriction in place governing the usage of the *Canon Minero* funds: municipalities are authorized to use the resources obtained through this transfer only to cover capital expenditures.

## Canon y Sobrecanon Petrolero

These transfers were established by Law Decree 21678 in November 1976 and are comprised of a percentage of the ad valorem petroleum production. The *Canon* is 10 percent of the ad valorem petroleum production and is distributed among the districts within the department where the petroleum was extracted. The *Sobrecanon* is 5 percent of ad valorem petroleum production and is distributed among the districts that are not within a department that produces petroleum, but are within the same region. The *Canon/Sobrecanon* is distributed equally among the provinces[9] in the department, and then distributed to the district level based on criteria such as[10] population, geographic area, whether it is a provincial or departmental capital, and whether the population is greater than 100,000.

## Vaso de Leche Program

The *Vaso de Leche* (Glass of Milk, VDL) program was started by the Mayor of Lima in 1984 for the metropolitan area, and as its name reflects, it originally consisted of distributing glasses of milk to school-aged children. Since then, the program has grown to national coverage (in 1985), and is not restricted to milk products. It has become one of the most significant transfers from the central to local governments (second only to FONCOMUN). It achieved its current form under Law 24059 and Article 7 of Law 27470 (2001). Although the spirit of the program remains the same, its organization has undergone considerable changes due to increased coverage. By Law, the intended primary beneficiaries are children aged 6 or younger, and pregnant and breastfeeding mothers. Priority is given to those showing clear signs of malnutrition or tuberculosis. The Law also establishes that if there are resources left over after attending to the needs of the primary beneficiaries, then attention may be provided to secondary beneficiaries, that is, children aged 7 and 13, the elderly, and those suffering from tuberculosis.

The main goal of the program is to improve the nutritional level of infants, small children, and pregnant or breastfeeding mothers, and to improve the quality of life of the poorest segments of the population. Given the empirical evidence, which identifies milk as an important nutritional source, a decision was made to distribute milk and milk-related products. Unfortunately, organizational hurdles, inefficiencies, leakages, and low nutritional value of the products chosen for distribution are aspects that limit the ability of the VDL program to achieve its original goals. Because of the program's flawed design organization and the way in which it functions, there are no effective mechanisms that enforce its priorities.

---

9. For the departments of Loreto and Ucayali, the distribution at the province level is in proportion to their share of production. In Piura and Tumbes the distribution makes no distinction between the provinces.

10. In the case of the province of Puerto Inca, Huánuco, the distribution among districts is simply in equal parts.

Currently, the MEF makes monthly transfers to municipalities for use in the VDL program. The transfer amounts are calculated by the MEF using distribution indexes that are based primarily on poverty and demographic indicators supplied by the National Institute of Statistics. Local governments are solely responsible for the operation of the VDL program in their jurisdiction, and have autonomy, except for the definition of the beneficiaries, from the CG as far as the product they wish to distribute and other operational details. However, three additional restrictions are placed on the municipalities by the CG. First, 100 percent of the VDL funds must go toward the purchase of the product(s) to be distributed. Second, the product(s) should have a minimum of 90 percent of national inputs (up to 100 percent in the areas in which the local supply can cover the entire demand). The products distributed can be milk in any form and/or milk substitutes, and/or other products such as soybean, oatmeal, quinua, and kiwicha.[11] Third, the CG requires that each municipality create an Administrative Committee with a certain membership composition: the mayor, a municipal employee, a representative from the Ministry of Health, three representatives of the Mother's Associations (elected by the mothers following the rules established in their own statutes), and a representative of the local agriculture/farming association duly accredited by the Ministry of Agriculture.

By law, the municipalities or committees cannot charge the beneficiaries for the products distributed. However, some municipalities and many committees charge some money (or require that in-kind contributions be made) to cover some of the expenses that the program incurs. Requests for contributions are more common in poor municipalities that need to cover distribution expenses, and in committees that prepare the product onsite and need to pay for things such as fuel and other inputs. In general, larger districts have an entire office dedicated to the VDL program, including a director and other full-time employees. Often, in smaller districts, the mayor himself or one of his *regidores* (municipal council members) administers and directs the program. It is noteworthy that beneficiaries (the mothers) organize themselves into *Comités/Clubs de Madres* (Mother's Associations), which have noticeably increased the social capital of the communities. These Mothers' Associations span the entire country, including the most remote areas, and together form a huge national network. The social network that results from the Mother's Associations has become a way for these rural and impoverished communities to gain a voice at the local level even on matters unrelated to the VDL program.

Details of the transfer process are:

- The municipality receives the transfer from the CG. A monthly transfer is deposited in the BN local branch office and the municipality is notified. The monthly amount does not vary in a given year, except in very particular situations, and the transfer usually arrives around the same day each month.
- The product is chosen and, in most cases, a public bidding process is used to select a provider, normally for a year and for the whole municipality jurisdiction. The selection of the product or products is done differently in different districts. In some cases, mothers have a direct say in the choice of product via surveys or direct vote. In other cases, the Administrative Committee makes the decision. Finally, in some cases it is the mayor's decision.
- A roster of all direct beneficiaries in each committee by category (children aged 0 to 6 years and pregnant or breastfeeding mothers) is prepared. The mothers' committees normally conduct this process, which is supposedly closely supervised by the municipality. This roster should also be frequently revised. However, in most cases these rosters are not updated and the municipality does not supervise the process. Using these registers, the municipality determines the product allocation to each of the mothers' committees in its jurisdiction.

11. Recently, a new law was passed that requires that distributed products have a minimum of 207 calories. Mothers, however, are not pleased with this requirement because it implies that milk substitutes will be distributed, and they do not like them. Mothers protested in the streets, demanding evaporated or fresh milk.

■ The municipality (or the provider) distributes the product to the Mothers' Associations. These usually cover a given neighborhood and can have a variable number of beneficiaries. A president, a vice-president, treasurer, and secretary usually lead them. The officers are voted into office for extended periods of time, and they are rarely voted out of office unless problems arise. Depending normally on the size of the municipality, the products are directly distributed to the committees or to intermediate entities: groups of committees or *centros de acopio* (special locations where the products are collected by areas and from where the committees pick up their allocations). The mothers' committees should follow the rosters of beneficiaries to determine the allocation per household or beneficiary, but in most cases, rosters are only "referential" and follow other criteria.

■ The mothers (or the intended beneficiary) pick up their ration(s) at the Mothers' Association headquarters. Usually the headquarters is the house of the president of the Mothers' Association and there is a certain time of the day/week/month that the distribution is made depending on the frequency with which the product is distributed. The committees distribute to the beneficiaries a product already prepared or in its raw form. The decision may depend on the type of product, the resources' availability, or the geographic dispersion of the beneficiaries. In the cases in which the products are not prepared by the committee, mothers use them at theirs home at their total discretion (usually distributing the products among all children or household members).

## Technical Definitions of Leakages in the Vaso de Leche Program

**Leak 1. From the Central Government to the Municipalities.** Leak 1 is defined as the percentage of the transfer reported by the MEF that is unaccounted for by the municipality. We compare the amount the MEF reports as outgoing with the amount the municipality reports to have received. This leakage is estimated with municipal-level data of December 2001.

$$\text{Leak}^1 = 1 - \left[ \frac{\text{Amt. Municipality Reported}}{\text{Amt. MEF Reported}} \right]$$

**Leak 2. Within Municipality.** Leak 2 is defined as the percentage of the amount transferred to the municipality "i" from the CG for the month of December 2001 that is unaccounted for by the total expenses of the municipality for that month (in terms of products purchased for the VDL program). Leak 2 is zero if the municipality spends the entirety of the resources available in December 2001 under the VDL program on products to be distributed by the program. This leakage is estimated based on municipal-level data.

$$\text{Leak}^2_{\text{MUN}} = 1 - \left[ \frac{\sum_i (\text{Quantity}_i \times \text{Price}_i)}{\text{Transfer Amount}_{\text{MUN}}} \right]$$

**Leak 3. From Municipality to VDL Committees.** Leak 3 is defined as the percentage of the amount listed in the municipality not accounted for by the VDL committee. This leakage is estimated using municipal and committee data and is computed at the committee level. This leakage indicates how much is lost in this segment of distribution, but does not allow one to attribute it to one of the two parties involved at this stage. In other words, we estimate the leakage from the municipality to the individual VDL committees, but do not know if the leakage is a result of misappropriation or inefficiencies of the municipality, the Advisory Committee, or both.

$$\text{Leak}^3_{\text{COM}} = 1 - \left[ \frac{\text{Amount Received}_{\text{COM}}}{\text{Amount listed in Municipal Roster}_{\text{COM}}} \right]$$

**Leak 4: From VDL Committees to Beneficiaries/Households.** Leak 4 is the loss due to the difference between what VDL committees receive according to beneficiaries registered and what they actually distribute to households. The estimation of the leakage at this level is done by calculating the monetary value of each of the products (using municipal price figures) and adding these up. This allows a comparison of the monetary value of the amount of all the products received by the VDL committee per beneficiary with the monetary value of the amount received by the individual households per beneficiary (excluding the committees that distribute prepared products). The first variable is obtained from the quantities declared by the mothers' committee representative in the VDL committee survey (in the four committees surveyed in each municipality). The second variable is obtained from the quantities declared by the beneficiaries' household representative in a beneficiary household survey (on four households surveyed for each VDL committee).

$$\text{Leak}^4 = 1 - \left[ \frac{\left(\frac{\sum_i (\text{Quantity}_i \times \text{Price}_i)}{\text{Beneficiary}}\right)_{\text{HH}}}{\left(\frac{\sum_i (\text{Quantity}_i \times \text{Price}_i)}{\text{Beneficiary}}\right)_{\text{COM}}} \right]$$

**Leak 5: Inside the Household.** Leak 5 is attributed to beneficiary dilution at the household level. It is defined as one minus the percentage of household members who consume *Vaso de Leche* products, who are direct beneficiaries. This leakage is estimated using household-level data.

$$\text{Leak}^5_{\text{HH}} = 1 - \left[ \frac{\text{Beneficiaries}_{\text{HH}}}{\text{Consumers}_{\text{HH}}} \right]$$

# Annex E

## PUBLIC ENTERPRISE REFORM IN PERU: INTRODUCING MANAGEMENT CONTRACTS AT FONAFE

In 1999, as part of several isolated efforts of state modernization in Peru, the National Fund for Financing Government Enterprise Activity (FONAFE), an institution with no more than 30 employees, became a useful instrument to increase public savings and improve the efficiency and effectiveness of public enterprises.[1] FONAFE is the public entity assigned to the Ministry of Economy and Finance (MEF), which is in charge of directing the entrepreneurial activity of the State. It has temporarily extended its management instruments to regulatory and revenue-collecting agencies in Peru's public sector. Enterprises under FONAFE's control include those in which the State owns either the total of the social capital or the majority of shares. In those cases in which the state is a minor partner, FONAFE exercises only stockholder options corresponding to its shares. Its main functions are to (a) approve the consolidated budget of the enterprises in which it holds the majority of shares, (b) approve management norms for those enterprises, (c) exercise stockholder options and administer resources resulting from its shareholder status, and (d) name representatives to the boards of those enterprises in which it is a shareholder (in those cases in which the State holds all the shares, FONAFE names a board of five members).

Upon introducing reform, FONAFE developed and implemented four basic management tools:

- An *Integrated Expenditure on Personnel*, which sets a global amount that enterprises and other public entities under its supervision are authorized to use for this purpose, while allowing management flexibility within that limit.
- A *Maximum Salary Limit*, which establishes the maximum annual salary any employee can receive, excluding the productivity bonus.
- A *Productivity Bonus*, an annual monetary incentive to personnel, which can add up to 6 percent of the payroll and that is granted only if 90 percent or more of the annual objectives are achieved.

---

1. This Annex was prepared by Gabriel Ortiz de Zevallos.

■ A *Management Contract* that establishes the specific terms of the agreement between FONAFE and the enterprise or public entity under its supervision.

These instruments have shifted management from being focused on inputs and procedures to outcomes and results.

A key element of the system is the capability to develop adequate indicators in the areas of cost, quality, coverage, and internal efficiency. FONAFE's approach has been to let each enterprise develop its own indicators based on its strategic planning processes, which are then analyzed and validated by FONAFE. According to its key officials, this allows for greater legitimacy and applicability. Indicators proposed by each entity need to fulfill usually recommended requirements:

■ *Appropriateness.* They should be the expression of the processes and products of the institution in order to properly reflect the fulfillment of the institutional objectives.

■ *Independence.* They should be independent of each other and respond to the actions developed by the institution. When possible, indicators depending on external factors should be avoided (such as situation of the country, demand variations, third-party decisions, tariff changes, and so forth).

■ *Measurement.* Availability of data and methodological issues should be considered in the proposal.

■ *Control.* Basic data should be part of a system that can be audited.

■ *Cost.* Information for the management indicators should be collected and processed within reasonable limits of cost and time.

Introducing these instruments has not been easy. Preliminary results have been very positive (see Table E.1). However, some difficulties encountered are:

■ Reactions to implementing change have been uneven and diverse. Enterprises under FONAFE operate in different sectors, can be old or relatively new, may or may not have data easily available, have different levels of managerial capabilities, and their personnel may not have the same willingness to be part of this kind of change.

## TABLE E.1: PUBLIC ENTERPRISES TARGET INDICATORS

| Characteristics | | Year | | | Goal |
|---|---|---|---|---|---|
| | | 1999 | 2000 | 2001 | 2002 |
| **Enterprise** | **SEDAPAL (Lima's Water and Sewerage Service)** | | | | |
| Indicator: | Service continuity (in hours) | 15.9 | 17.6 | 19.3 | 22.0 |
| **Enterprise** | **SEAL (South-West Electricity Society)** | | | | |
| Indicator: | Energy loses in the distribution system | 21.7% | 21.25% | 18.12% | 16.40% |
| **Entity** | **OSIPTEL (Telecommunications Regulation Agency)** | | | | |
| Indicator: | Supervision in the delivery of the telecommunications public service (supervision actions) | 364 | 524 | – | – |

*Note:* Starting in 2001, OSIPTEL is no longer under the scope of FONAFE, but management instruments continue to be negotiated directly with the MEF.

*Source:* FONAFE.

▨ Managers have often started with unrealistic goals. In the first year of their implementation, most enterprises overestimated the results they would be able to achieve. After the first year, during which most targets were not met, managers changed to more modest, realistic goals.

Besides political will, leadership and a strong technical team, two factors have been key to success:

▨ Its legal and administrative status has allowed FONAFE not to be burdened by administrative procedures. FONAFE was created as a line unit of the MEF budget, so its budget does not have to be approved by Congress, but by the Council of Ministers. It has sufficient authority to dictate its norms, including budgetary issues, and the legal capacity to control management of the enterprises under its supervision.

▨ Its approach to transition has been incremental and case by case, enabling it to adapt to specific difficulties. For instance, FONAFE's 1999 agreement with the *Empresa de Gas Sociedad Anonima* (EGASA), the electricity-generating company of Arequipa, established as its initial performance indicator the development of a strategic plan for the next decade. Subsequent goals and indicators have been based on the implementation of new systems and plans.

FONAFE has extended management contracts to other public agencies, both regulatory and revenue collecting. Although desirable, extending them to the Central Government (CG) implies new difficulties:

▨ *Productivity bonuses come from savings, but generating surpluses to finance bonuses through the improvement of management is easier in State-owned enterprises than in ministries.* The Ministry of Education, for example, spends almost 90 percent of its budget on payroll, making it much harder to maneuver and generate savings to reward thousands of teachers. However, the current administration is barely tackling the very difficult issue of identifying how many "ghosts" are currently part of the teacher payroll.

▨ *Different personnel regimes coexist within the public sector.* While in public enterprises there are very few cases of workers not registered in the payroll, CG agencies tend to have large numbers of employees contracted as professional service staff outside the payroll. Legally, it is hard to justify a bonus in those cases.

▨ *Reliable data are fundamental, but extremely scare.* The need for quality administrative systems that generate and constantly update data is central for the success of management contracts. A recent study of 20 social programs that implied a budget of US$ 770 million in 2000, found that only 3 of those programs, accounting for US$17 million, have institutionalized proper monitoring and evaluation systems in manuals.

# Annex F

# A METHODOLOGY FOR FUNCTIONAL REVIEWS AND FOR ANALYZING FUNCTIONAL PROSPECTS

The absence of an *implementation strategy* in the Framework Law for Modernization may result in rather haphazard efforts to apply it to specific ministerial or sectoral contexts. Such an implementation strategy is imperative. Below, Moore (2002) proposes some initial elements for conducting functional reviews as part of this implementation strategy. The basic question that guides the methodology is how are these functions currently organized in the structure of the ministry or sector, and how can or should they be organized in the future—by units or by levels of the ministry? Its central premise is that to be efficient, any organization must fulfill seven basic functional subsystems. The strategic management of the organization requires an analysis of how these are structured and how they interact. Each of these functions consists of sets of activities that can be identified, and several levels of the organization may exercise each of these activities either exclusively or concurrently. A matrix for identifying functions, activities, levels, and exclusivity can be designed for application to the organizational structure. These subsystems include:

- The *programmatic function* that provides the *why* of the organization and its vision and mission. This function defines the substance of the institution and explains its purpose and linkages to other sectors or institutions.
- The *planning function* that provides the *how* for carrying out the institutional vision and combines activities related to policy formulation and planning, and their budgetary expression. At the same time, the function incorporates those activities related to investigation (for strategic planning).
- The *financial administration function* that provides for the identification of the processes related to *what resources* (financial) are needed and used to carry out the how. This function is delimited by financial analysis, the administration of resource generation, budget execution, and the control of the use of financial resources.
- The *human resources administration function* that provides for the management of *what resources* (human) are necessary to carry out the activities of the institution and relates to

the various subsystems of human resource management (recruitment, selection, promotion, development, evaluation, and so forth).

■ The *management control, supervision, and evaluation function(s)* that determine how the institution is regulated, how supervision takes place, and how resource execution of projects and plans is carried out to assure accountability in policy execution.

■ The *administrative support function* that guarantees the acquisition of goods and services, assures the capacity to carry out institutional actions, and includes those activities related to acquisition, maintenance, construction, and their organization.

■ The *information function* for producing, processing, distributing, and consolidating the information requirements to guarantee opportune and efficient decisionmaking, management and execution, and the appropriate diffusion of information.

Each of these consists of activities that can be identified (current, future) by units and levels in the form of a matrix of activities. Such an initial matrix for identification was recently used in Ecuador's Ministry of Education.[1] In real terms, the carrying out of the exercise is organized in a series of workshops or seminars of relevant (primarily internal) persons to arrive at the completed matrix. The matrix is then applied to a reorganization strategy.

---

1. See Annex 3 in Moore (2002) for a full description of details of the Ecuadorian experience.

# Annex G

# LIST OF BACKGROUND PAPERS

Alcazar, Lorena and Erik Wachtenheim. "A PETS in Central Government Transfers to Municipalities in Peru: A Detailed Look at the Vaso de Leche Program."

Alcazar, Lorena and Erik Wachtenheim. "Public Expenditure Tracking Surveys (PETS)—Executive Summary."

Alcazar, Lorena and Erik Wachtenheim. "Public Expenditure Tracking Surveys (PETS)—The Education Sector in Peru."

Apoyo Institute. "Seguimiento del Desembolso de Recursos en el Sistema Educativo."

Díaz, Juvenal. "Grado de Focalización de Algunos Programas Sociales, 1998–2000."

Eduardo Fernández. "La Deuda Corriente de los Municipios Peruanos."

Gregory, Peter. "Public Sector Employment in Peru."

López-Cálix, José R. and Rashmi Shankar. "Peru: Fiscal Trends and the Fiscal Sustainability Issue."

Moore, Richard. "Applying a Functional Analysis to Ministries' Decentralization, An Example."

Moore, Richard. "Prospects for the Decentralization of Health and Education in Peru."

Mostajo, Rossana. "¿Protección Presupuestaria? Los Programas Sociales Protegidos En El Perú."

Otto, James. "Position of the Peruvian Taxation System as Compared to Mining Taxation Systems in Other Nations."

Recanatini, Francesca. "Voices of the Misgoverned and Misruled: An Empirical Diagnostic Study on Governance, Rule of Law and Corruption for Peru."

Schenone, Osvaldo. "Exoneraciones y Regímenes Tributarios Especiales en Perú."

Valderrama, José. "Perú—Propuesta de Reforma a las Reglas Fiscales."

Wodon, Quentin. "The Efficiency of Public Spending in Peru."

# STATISTICAL APPENDIX

## TABLE SA.1: COMBINED PUBLIC SECTOR OPERATION
(millions of Nuevo Soles)

| | 1991 | 1992 | 1993 | 1994 | 1995 | 1996 | 1997 | 1998 | 1999 | 2000 | 2001 1/ |
|---|---|---|---|---|---|---|---|---|---|---|---|
| I. Current Revenues | 4 115 | 7 485 | 11 474 | 17 025 | 21 470 | 25 288 | 29 712 | 31 261 | 30 653 | 33 077 | 32 382 |
| II. Non-financial expenditures | 3 682 | 7 268 | 10 915 | 16 824 | 21 335 | 24 136 | 27 795 | 29 728 | 32 956 | 34 425 | 33 620 |
| 1. Current expenditures | 2 932 | 5 475 | 7 903 | 11 671 | 15 289 | 17 813 | 20 523 | 22 614 | 25 396 | 27 610 | 27 755 |
| 2. Capital expenditures | 750 | 1 794 | 3 011 | 5 153 | 6 046 | 6 323 | 7 272 | 7 115 | 7 560 | 6 815 | 5 864 |
| III. Others | 33 | 57 | -28 | 357 | 329 | 613 | 224 | 571 | 577 | 554 | 316 |
| IV. Primary Balance | 466 | 273 | 531 | 558 | 463 | 1 765 | 2 141 | 2 104 | -1 726 | -793 | -922 |
| V. Interest | 1 042 | 2 007 | 2 908 | 3 588 | 4 064 | 3 332 | 2 844 | 3 174 | 3 729 | 4 120 | 4 122 |
| VI. Overall Balance | -577 | -1 734 | -2 377 | -3 031 | -3 601 | -1 567 | -704 | -1 070 | -5 455 | -4 913 | -5 044 |
| VII. Net Financing | 577 | 1 734 | 2 377 | 3 031 | 3 601 | 1 567 | 704 | 1 070 | 5 455 | 4 913 | 5 044 |
| 1. External | 954 | 1 426 | 2 141 | 2 453 | 2 878 | 1 081 | 12 | 561 | -313 | 2 097 | 1 980 |
| 2. Domestic | -379 | 239 | -64 | -4 454 | -1 428 | -4 792 | -800 | -255 | 4 449 | 1 389 | 1 930 |
| 3. Privatization | 1 | 69 | 300 | 5 032 | 2 151 | 5 279 | 1 492 | 764 | 1 318 | 1 427 | 1 134 |

1/ Preliminary.

Source: MEF, Banco de la Nación, BCRP, Sunat, Aduanas, ESSALUD, public beneficiary societies, local government and public institutions.

## TABLE SA.2: COMBINED PUBLIC SECTOR OPERATIONS
(percent of GDP)

| | 1991 | 1992 | 1993 | 1994 | 1995 | 1996 | 1997 | 1998 | 1999 | 2000 | 2001 1/ |
|---|---|---|---|---|---|---|---|---|---|---|---|
| I. Current Revenues | 15.4 | 16.7 | 16.6 | 17.3 | 17.8 | 18.5 | 18.9 | 18.8 | 17.5 | 17.7 | 17.1 |
| II. Non-financial expenditures | 13.8 | 16.2 | 15.8 | 17.1 | 17.7 | 17.6 | 17.7 | 17.9 | 18.9 | 18.4 | 17.7 |
| 1. Current expenditures | 11.0 | 12.2 | 11.4 | 11.8 | 12.7 | 13.0 | 13.0 | 13.6 | 14.5 | 14.8 | 14.6 |
| 2. Capital expenditures | 2.8 | 4.0 | 4.3 | 5.2 | 5.0 | 4.6 | 4.6 | 4.3 | 4.3 | 3.6 | 3.1 |
| III. Others | 0.1 | 0.1 | 0.0 | 0.4 | 0.3 | 0.4 | 0.1 | 0.3 | 0.3 | 0.3 | 0.2 |
| IV. Primary Balance | 1.7 | 0.6 | 0.8 | 0.6 | 0.4 | 1.3 | 1.4 | 1.3 | -1.0 | -0.4 | -0.5 |
| V. Interest | 3.9 | 4.5 | 4.2 | 3.6 | 3.4 | 2.4 | 1.8 | 1.9 | 2.1 | 2.2 | 2.2 |
| VI. Overall Balance | -2.2 | -3.9 | -3.4 | -3.1 | -3.0 | -1.1 | -0.4 | -0.6 | -3.1 | -2.6 | -2.7 |
| VII. Net Financing | 2.2 | 3.9 | 3.4 | 3.1 | 3.0 | 1.1 | 0.4 | 0.6 | 3.1 | 2.6 | 2.7 |
| 1. External | 3.6 | 3.2 | 3.1 | 2.5 | 2.4 | 0.8 | 0.0 | 0.3 | -0.2 | 1.1 | 1.0 |
| 2. Domestic | -1.4 | 0.5 | -0.1 | -4.5 | -1.2 | -3.5 | -0.5 | -0.2 | 2.5 | 0.7 | 1.0 |
| 3. Privatization | 0.0 | 0.2 | 0.4 | 5.1 | 1.8 | 3.9 | 0.9 | 0.5 | 0.8 | 0.8 | 0.6 |
| GDP (Million soles) | 26,686 | 44,953 | 69,262 | 98,577 | 120,858 | 136,929 | 157,274 | 166,514 | 174,719 | 186,756 | 189,532 |

1/ Preliminary

Source: Statistical Appendix, Table SA.1

TABLE SA.3: COMBINED PUBLIC SECTOR OPERATIONS
(millions of 1994 Nuevo Soles)

| | 1991 | 1992 | 1993 | 1994 | 1995 | 1996 | 1997 | 1998 | 1999 | 2000 | 2001 1/ |
|---|---|---|---|---|---|---|---|---|---|---|---|
| I. Current Revenues | 13127 | 13761 | 14197 | 17025 | 19319 | 20399 | 22081 | 21661 | 20527 | 21348 | 20495 |
| II. Non-financial expenditures | 11746 | 13363 | 13505 | 16824 | 19198 | 19470 | 20656 | 20599 | 22069 | 22218 | 21278 |
| 1. Current expenditures | 9352 | 10065 | 9779 | 11671 | 13758 | 14370 | 15252 | 15669 | 17007 | 17819 | 17567 |
| 2. Capital expenditures | 2394 | 3298 | 3726 | 5153 | 5441 | 5101 | 5404 | 4930 | 5062 | 4398 | 3712 |
| III. Others | 105 | 104 | -35 | 357 | 296 | 495 | 167 | 395 | 387 | 358 | 200 |
| IV. Primary Balance | 1486 | 502 | 657 | 558 | 417 | 1424 | 1591 | 1458 | -1156 | -512 | -583 |
| V. Interest | 3326 | 3689 | 3598 | 3588 | 3657 | 2688 | 2114 | 2199 | 2497 | 2659 | 2609 |
| VI. Overall Balance | -1839 | -3187 | -2941 | -3031 | -3240 | -1264 | -523 | -741 | -3653 | -3171 | -3192 |
| VII. Net Financing | 1839 | 3187 | 2941 | 3031 | 3240 | 1264 | 523 | 741 | 3653 | 3171 | 3192 |
| 1. External | 3045 | 2621 | 2649 | 2453 | 2590 | 872 | 9 | 389 | -209 | 1354 | 1253 |
| 2. Domestic | -1210 | 439 | -80 | -4454 | -1285 | -3866 | -595 | -177 | 2979 | 896 | 1222 |
| 3. Privatization | 5 | 127 | 371 | 5032 | 1935 | 4258 | 1109 | 529 | 883 | 921 | 717 |
| Average CPI Deflator | 31 | 54 | 81 | 100 | 111 | 124 | 135 | 144 | 149 | 155 | 158 |

1/ Preliminary.

Source: Statistical Appendix, Table SA.1.

## TABLE SA.4: CENTRAL GOVERNMENT OPERATIONS
Millions of Nuevos Soles

| | 1991 | 1992 | 1993 | 1994 | 1995 | 1996 | 1997 | 1998 | 1999 | 2000 | 2001 1/ | 2002 2/ |
|---|---|---|---|---|---|---|---|---|---|---|---|---|
| I. Current revenues | 3 193 | 6 059 | 9 424 | 14 386 | 18 319 | 21 522 | 25 001 | 26 174 | 25 334 | 27 515 | 26 733 | 28 341 |
| I.a. TAX REVENUES | 2 958 | 5 416 | 8 478 | 12 866 | 16 212 | 19 036 | 22 122 | 22 995 | 21 873 | 22 663 | 23 383 | 23 919 |
| 1. Income tax | 250 | 749 | 1 406 | 2 526 | 3 462 | 4 981 | 5 710 | 5 861 | 5 072 | 5 130 | 5 630 | 6 030 |
| 2. Property tax | 177 | 201 | 254 | 85 | 30 | 3 | 3 | 1 | 11 | 0 | | |
| 3. Export tax | | | | | | | | | | | | |
| 4. Import tax | 336 | 650 | 1 228 | 1 700 | 2 144 | 2 308 | 2 471 | 2 891 | 2 848 | 2 913 | 2 738 | 3 015 |
| 5. Value added tax | 765 | 1 702 | 3 534 | 5 954 | 7 646 | 8 578 | 10 344 | 11 040 | 11 029 | 11 996 | 11 806 | 12 462 |
| - Domestic | 437 | 911 | 1 992 | 3 563 | 4 217 | 4 723 | 5 929 | 6 384 | 6 470 | 7 004 | 6 866 | 7 035 |
| - Imports | 328 | 791 | 1 543 | 2 391 | 3 429 | 3 856 | 4 415 | 4 655 | 4 559 | 4 993 | 4 940 | 5 427 |
| 6. Excise tax | 1 196 | 1 743 | 1 611 | 2 267 | 2 486 | 2 761 | 3 365 | 3 427 | 3 446 | 3 421 | 3 533 | 3 417 |
| - Fuel | 781 | 995 | 991 | 1 288 | 1 493 | 1 599 | 1 931 | 2 000 | 2 092 | 2 118 | 2 318 | 2 211 |
| - Others | 415 | 748 | 620 | 979 | 993 | 1 162 | 1 434 | 1 426 | 1 354 | 1 303 | 1 215 | 1 206 |
| 7. Other tax revenues | 312 | 442 | 528 | 834 | 1 160 | 1 268 | 1 737 | 1 569 | 1 568 | 1 873 | 2 507 | 2 412 |
| 8. Tax refund | -78 | -71 | -84 | -499 | -715 | -863 | -1 509 | -1 794 | -2 101 | -2 669 | -2 832 | -3 417 |
| I.b. NON-TAX REVENUES | 236 | 643 | 946 | 1 520 | 2 108 | 2 485 | 2 879 | 3 179 | 3 460 | 4 851 | 3 350 | 4 342 |
| II. Non-interest expenditures | 2 842 | 5 839 | 8 992 | 14 270 | 18 575 | 20 729 | 23 729 | 25 379 | 27 697 | 28 989 | 28 253 | 29 426 |
| 1. Current expenditures | 2 319 | 4 401 | 6 448 | 9 929 | 13 545 | 15 680 | 17 934 | 19 756 | 21 797 | 23 757 | 23 857 | 25 004 |
| a. Wages and salaries | 911 | 1 770 | 2 659 | 3 866 | 5 098 | 5 433 | 6 397 | 6 979 | 7 774 | 8 180 | 8 389 | 8 643 |
| b. Goods and services | 552 | 966 | 1 413 | 2 570 | 3 928 | 5 129 | 5 319 | 6 022 | 6 210 | 7 068 | 7 068 | 7 236 |
| c. Transfers | 856 | 1 665 | 2 375 | 3 493 | 4 518 | 5 118 | 6 217 | 6 756 | 7 813 | 8 508 | 8 400 | 9 045 |
| 2. Capital expenditures | 523 | 1 438 | 2 544 | 4 341 | 5 031 | 5 048 | 5 795 | 5 623 | 5 900 | 5 232 | 4 396 | 4 422 |
| a. Capital formation | 504 | 1 115 | 2 150 | 3 342 | 3 955 | 3 921 | 4 448 | 4 964 | 5 652 | 4 749 | 3 901 | 4 221 |
| b. Transfers | 4 | 122 | 45 | 4 | 109 | 16 | 0 | 0 | 0 | 254 | | |
| c. Others | 15 | 200 | 349 | 995 | 967 | 1 111 | 1 347 | 659 | 248 | 229 | 494 | 201 |
| III. Others 3/ | 23 | 28 | -58 | 324 | 274 | 578 | 192 | 533 | 539 | 530 | 291 | 503 |

(continued)

## TABLE SA.4: CENTRAL GOVERNMENT OPERATIONS (CONTINUED)
### Millions of Nuevos Soles

| | 1991 | 1992 | 1993 | 1994 | 1995 | 1996 | 1997 | 1998 | 1999 | 2000 | 2001 1/ | 2002 2/ |
|---|---|---|---|---|---|---|---|---|---|---|---|---|
| **IV. Primary balance** | 375 | 248 | 373 | 440 | 18 | 1 371 | 1 465 | 1 327 | -1 825 | - 944 | -1 229 | -603 |
| **V. Interest** | 1 035 | 1 998 | 2 888 | 3 560 | 4 023 | 3 289 | 2 789 | 3 119 | 3 674 | 4 074 | 4 062 | 3 819 |
| 1. Domestic debt | 86 | 91 | 61 | 107 | 90 | 76 | 116 | 176 | 238 | 543 | 466 | 3 417 |
| 2. External debt | 949 | 1 907 | 2 827 | 3 453 | 3 933 | 3 213 | 2 673 | 2 944 | 3 436 | 3 532 | 3 596 | 603 |
| **VI. Overall balance** | -660 | -1 750 | -2 515 | -3 120 | -4 005 | -1 918 | -1 324 | -1 792 | -5 499 | -5 019 | -5 291 | -4 422 |
| **VII. Net financing** | 660 | 1 750 | 2 515 | 3 120 | 4 005 | 1 918 | 1 324 | 1 792 | 5 499 | 5 019 | 5 291 | 4 422 |
| 1. External | 954 | 1 426 | 2 141 | 2 453 | 2 878 | 1 077 | 12 | 561 | -313 | 2 097 | 1 980 | 1 407 |
| 2. Domestic | -296 | 256 | 74 | -4 365 | -1 023 | -4 438 | -180 | 467 | 4 493 | 1 494 | 2 177 | 603 |
| 3. Privatization | 1 | 69 | 300 | 5 032 | 2 151 | 5 279 | 1 492 | 764 | 1 318 | 1 427 | 1 134 | 2 412 |

1/ Preliminary.

2/ Estimate.

3/ Less payments to American International Group and Convenio Perú-Alemania.

*Source:* MEF, Banco de la Nación, BCRP, Sunat, Customs, Empresa Nacional de Comercialización de Insumos S.A. (Enci). Empresa Comercializadora de Alimentos S.A. (Ecasa); and Petroperú. IMF and World Bank staff estimates for 2002.

## TABLE SA.5: CENTRAL GOVERNMENT OPERATIONS
Percent of GDP

| | 1991 | 1992 | 1993 | 1994 | 1995 | 1996 | 1997 | 1998 | 1999 | 2000 | 2001 1/ | 2002 2/ |
|---|---|---|---|---|---|---|---|---|---|---|---|---|
| **I. Current revenues** | 12.0 | 13.5 | 13.6 | 14.6 | 15.2 | 15.7 | 15.9 | 15.7 | 14.5 | 14.7 | 14.1 | 14.1 |
| I.a. TAX REVENUES | 11.1 | 12.0 | 12.2 | 13.1 | 13.4 | 13.9 | 14.1 | 13.8 | 12.5 | 12.1 | 12.3 | 11.9 |
| 1. Income tax | 0.9 | 1.7 | 2.0 | 2.6 | 2.9 | 3.6 | 3.6 | 3.5 | 2.9 | 2.7 | 3.0 | 3.0 |
| 2. Property tax | 0.7 | 0.4 | 0.4 | 0.1 | 0.0 | 0.0 | 0.0 | 0.0 | 0.0 | 0.0 | 0.0 | 0.0 |
| 3. Export tax | | | | | | | | | | | | |
| 4. Import tax | 1.3 | 1.4 | 1.8 | 1.7 | 1.8 | 1.7 | 1.6 | 1.7 | 1.6 | 1.6 | 1.4 | 1.5 |
| 5. Value added tax | 2.9 | 3.8 | 5.1 | 6.0 | 6.3 | 6.3 | 6.6 | 6.6 | 6.3 | 6.4 | 6.2 | 6.2 |
| - Domestic | 1.6 | 2.0 | 2.9 | 3.6 | 3.5 | 3.4 | 3.8 | 3.8 | 3.7 | 3.8 | 3.6 | 3.5 |
| - Imports | 1.2 | 1.8 | 2.2 | 2.4 | 2.8 | 2.8 | 2.8 | 2.8 | 2.6 | 2.7 | 2.6 | 2.7 |
| 6. Excise tax | 4.5 | 3.9 | 2.3 | 2.3 | 2.1 | 2.0 | 2.1 | 2.1 | 2.0 | 1.8 | 1.9 | 1.7 |
| - Fuel | 2.9 | 2.2 | 1.4 | 1.3 | 1.2 | 1.2 | 1.2 | 1.2 | 1.2 | 1.1 | 1.2 | 1.1 |
| - Others | 1.6 | 1.7 | 0.9 | 1.0 | 0.8 | 0.8 | 0.9 | 0.9 | 0.8 | 0.7 | 0.6 | 0.6 |
| 7. Other tax revenues | 1.2 | 1.0 | 0.8 | 0.8 | 1.0 | 0.9 | 1.1 | 0.9 | 0.9 | 1.0 | 1.3 | 1.2 |
| 8. Tax refund | -0.3 | -0.2 | -0.1 | -0.5 | -0.6 | -0.6 | -1.0 | -1.1 | -1.2 | -1.4 | -1.5 | -1.7 |
| I.b. NON-TAX REVENUES | 0.9 | 1.4 | 1.4 | 1.5 | 1.7 | 1.8 | 1.8 | 1.9 | 2.0 | 2.6 | 1.8 | 2.2 |
| **II. Non-interest expenditures** | 10.6 | 13.0 | 13.0 | 14.5 | 15.4 | 15.1 | 15.1 | 15.2 | 15.9 | 15.5 | 14.9 | 14.6 |
| 1. Current expenditures | 8.7 | 9.8 | 9.3 | 10.1 | 11.2 | 11.5 | 11.4 | 11.9 | 12.5 | 12.7 | 12.6 | 12.4 |
| a. Wages and salaries | 3.4 | 3.9 | 3.8 | 3.9 | 4.2 | 4.0 | 4.1 | 4.2 | 4.4 | 4.4 | 4.4 | 4.3 |
| b. Goods and services | 2.1 | 2.1 | 2.0 | 2.6 | 3.3 | 3.7 | 3.4 | 3.6 | 3.6 | 3.8 | 3.7 | 3.6 |
| c. Transfers | 3.2 | 3.7 | 3.4 | 3.5 | 3.7 | 3.7 | 4.0 | 4.1 | 4.5 | 4.6 | 4.4 | 4.5 |
| 2. Capital expenditures | 2.0 | 3.2 | 3.7 | 4.4 | 4.2 | 3.7 | 3.7 | 3.4 | 3.4 | 2.8 | 2.3 | 2.2 |
| a. Capital formation | 1.9 | 2.5 | 3.1 | 3.4 | 3.3 | 2.9 | 2.8 | 3.0 | 3.2 | 2.5 | 2.1 | 2.1 |
| b. Transfers | 0.0 | 0.3 | 0.1 | 0.0 | 0.1 | 0.0 | 0.0 | 0.0 | 0.0 | 0.1 | | |
| c. Others | 0.1 | 0.4 | 0.5 | 1.0 | 0.8 | 0.8 | 0.9 | 0.4 | 0.1 | 0.1 | 0.3 | 0.1 |
| **III. Others 3/** | 0.1 | 0.1 | -0.1 | 0.3 | 0.2 | 0.4 | 0.1 | 0.3 | 0.3 | 0.3 | 0.2 | 0.3 |

(continued)

## TABLE SA.5:    CENTRAL GOVERNMENT OPERATIONS (CONTINUED)
Percent of GDP

| | 1991 | 1992 | 1993 | 1994 | 1995 | 1996 | 1997 | 1998 | 1999 | 2000 | 2001 / | 2002 2/ |
|---|---|---|---|---|---|---|---|---|---|---|---|---|
| IV. Primary balance | 1.4 | 0.6 | 0.5 | 0.4 | 0.0 | 1.0 | 0.9 | 0.8 | -1.0 | -0.5 | -0.6 | -0.3 |
| V. Interest | 3.9 | 4.4 | 4.2 | 3.6 | 3.3 | 2.4 | 1.8 | 1.9 | 2.1 | 2.2 | 2.1 | 1.9 |
| 1. Domestic debt | 0.3 | 0.2 | 0.1 | 0.1 | 0.1 | 0.1 | 0.1 | 0.1 | 0.1 | 0.3 | 0.2 | 1.7 |
| 2. External debt | 3.6 | 4.2 | 4.1 | 3.5 | 3.3 | 2.3 | 1.7 | 1.8 | 2.0 | 1.9 | 1.9 | 0.3 |
| VI. Overall balance | -2.5 | -3.9 | -3.6 | -3.2 | -3.3 | -1.4 | -0.8 | -1.1 | -3.1 | -2.7 | -2.8 | -2.2 |
| VII. Net Financing | 2.5 | 3.9 | 3.6 | 3.2 | 3.3 | 1.4 | 0.8 | 1.1 | 3.1 | 2.7 | 2.8 | 2.2 |
| 1. External | 3.6 | 3.2 | 3.1 | 2.5 | 2.4 | 0.8 | 0.0 | 0.3 | -0.2 | 1.1 | 1.0 | 0.7 |
| 2. Domestic | -1.1 | 0.6 | 0.1 | -4.4 | -0.8 | -3.2 | -0.1 | 0.3 | 2.6 | 0.8 | 1.1 | 0.3 |
| 3. Privatization | 0.0 | 0.2 | 0.4 | 5.1 | 1.8 | 3.9 | 0.9 | 0.5 | 0.8 | 0.8 | 0.6 | 1.2 |
| GDP (Million soles) | 26,686 | 44,953 | 69,262 | 98,577 | 120,858 | 136,929 | 157,274 | 166,514 | 174,719 | 186,756 | 189,532 | 201,000 |

1/ Preliminary.

2/ Estimate.

3/ Less payments to American International Group and Convenio Perú-Alemania.

*Source:* MEF, Banco de la Nación, BCRP, Sunat, Customs, Empresa Nacional de Comercialización de Insumos S.A. (Enci). Empresa Comercializadora de Alimentos S.A. (Ecasa); and Petroperú. IMF and World Bank staff estimates for 2002.

## TABLE SA.6: CENTRAL GOVERNMENT OPERATIONS
In Millions 1994 Soles

| | 1991 | 1992 | 1993 | 1994 | 1995 | 1996 | 1997 | 1998 | 1999 | 2000 | 2001 1/ | 2002 2/ |
|---|---|---|---|---|---|---|---|---|---|---|---|---|
| **I. Current revenues** | 10187 | 11139 | 11661 | 14386 | 16485 | 17361 | 18580 | 18136 | 16965 | 17758 | 16920 | 17620 |
| I.a. TAX REVENUES | 9435 | 9957 | 10491 | 12866 | 14588 | 15356 | 16440 | 15933 | 14648 | 14627 | 14799 | 14871 |
| 1. Income tax | 796 | 1377 | 1740 | 2526 | 3115 | 4018 | 4243 | 4061 | 3396 | 3311 | 3564 | 3749 |
| 2. Property tax | 565 | 370 | 315 | 85 | 27 | 2 | 2 | 1 | 7 | 0 | | |
| 3. Export tax | | | | | | | | | | | | |
| 4. Import tax | 1070 | 1195 | 1520 | 1700 | 1929 | 1862 | 1836 | 2003 | 1907 | 1880 | 1733 | 1874 |
| 5. Value added tax | 2441 | 3128 | 4373 | 5954 | 6880 | 6920 | 7688 | 7649 | 7386 | 7742 | 7472 | 7748 |
| - Domestic | 1395 | 1674 | 2465 | 3563 | 3795 | 3810 | 4406 | 4424 | 4333 | 4520 | 4346 | 4374 |
| - Imports | 1045 | 1454 | 1909 | 2391 | 3085 | 3110 | 3281 | 3226 | 3053 | 3222 | 3127 | 3374 |
| 6. Excise tax | 3816 | 3205 | 1994 | 2267 | 2237 | 2228 | 2501 | 2374 | 2308 | 2208 | 2236 | 2124 |
| - Fuel | 2493 | 1829 | 1227 | 1288 | 1343 | 1290 | 1435 | 1386 | 1401 | 1367 | 1467 | 1375 |
| - Others | 1323 | 1375 | 767 | 979 | 893 | 937 | 1066 | 988 | 907 | 841 | 769 | 750 |
| 7. Other tax revenues | 996 | 813 | 654 | 834 | 1044 | 1023 | 1291 | 1087 | 1050 | 1209 | 1587 | 1500 |
| 8. Tax refund | -249 | -131 | -104 | -499 | -643 | -696 | -1121 | -1243 | -1407 | -1723 | -1792 | -2124 |
| I.b. NON-TAX REVENUES | 752 | 1182 | 1170 | 1520 | 1897 | 2005 | 2140 | 2203 | 2317 | 3131 | 2120 | 2699 |
| **II. Non-interest expenditures** | 9066 | 10734 | 11127 | 14270 | 16715 | 16721 | 17634 | 17585 | 18548 | 18710 | 17882 | 18295 |
| 1. Current expenditures | 7398 | 8092 | 7978 | 9929 | 12188 | 12649 | 13328 | 13689 | 14597 | 15333 | 15100 | 15546 |
| a. Wages and salaries | 2906 | 3254 | 3291 | 3866 | 4587 | 4383 | 4754 | 4835 | 5206 | 5280 | 5310 | 5374 |
| b. Goods and services | 1761 | 1776 | 1749 | 2570 | 3535 | 4137 | 3953 | 4172 | 4159 | 4562 | 4474 | 4499 |
| c. Transfers | 2731 | 3061 | 2939 | 3493 | 4066 | 4129 | 4620 | 4681 | 5232 | 5491 | 5316 | 5623 |
| 2. Capital expenditures | 1667 | 2643 | 3148 | 4341 | 4527 | 4072 | 4307 | 3896 | 3951 | 3377 | 2782 | 2749 |
| a. Capital formation | 1609 | 2050 | 2661 | 3342 | 3559 | 3163 | 3305 | 3439 | 3785 | 3065 | 2469 | 2624 |
| b. Transfers | 12 | 224 | 55 | 4 | 98 | 13 | 0 | 0 | 0 | 164 | 0 | |
| c. Others | 47 | 369 | 432 | 995 | 870 | 896 | 1001 | 456 | 166 | 148 | 313 | 125 |
| **III. Others 3/** | 75 | 51 | -72 | 324 | 246 | 466 | 143 | 369 | 361 | 342 | 184 | 312 |

(continued)

## TABLE SA.6: CENTRAL GOVERNMENT OPERATIONS (CONTINUED)
In Millions 1994 Soles

| | 1991 | 1992 | 1993 | 1994 | 1995 | 1996 | 1997 | 1998 | 1999 | 2000 | 2001 1/ | 2002 2/ |
|---|---|---|---|---|---|---|---|---|---|---|---|---|
| IV. Primary balance | 1196 | 455 | 462 | 440 | 16 | 1106 | 1089 | 920 | -1222 | -609 | -778 | -375 |
| V. Interest | 3302 | 3673 | 3573 | 3560 | 3620 | 2653 | 2073 | 2161 | 2460 | 2630 | 2571 | 2374 |
| 1. Domestic debt | 275 | 166 | 75 | 107 | 81 | 62 | 86 | 122 | 159 | 350 | 295 | 2124 |
| 2. External debt | 3027 | 3507 | 3498 | 3453 | 3539 | 2592 | 1987 | 2040 | 2301 | 2279 | 2276 | 375 |
| VI. Overall balance | -2106 | -3218 | -3111 | -3120 | -3604 | -1547 | -984 | -1242 | -3682 | -3239 | -3349 | -2749 |
| VII. Net financing | 2106 | 3218 | 3111 | 3120 | 3604 | 1547 | 984 | 1242 | 3682 | 3239 | 3349 | 2749 |
| 1. External | 3045 | 2621 | 2649 | 2453 | 2590 | 869 | 9 | 389 | -209 | 1354 | 1253 | 875 |
| 2. Domestic | -944 | 471 | 91 | -4365 | -921 | -3580 | -134 | 323 | 3009 | 964 | 1378 | 375 |
| 3. Privatization | 5 | 127 | 371 | 5032 | 1935 | 4258 | 1109 | 529 | 883 | 921 | 717 | 1500 |
| CPI Deflator | 31 | 54 | 81 | 100 | 111 | 124 | 135 | 144 | 149 | 155 | 158 | 161 |

1/ Preliminary.
2/ Estimate.
3/ Less payments to American International Group and Convenio Perú-Alemania.

Source: MEF, Banco de la Nación, BCRP, Sunat, Customs, Empresa Nacional de Comercialización de Comercialización de Insumos S.A. (Enci). Empresa Comercializadora de Alimentos S.A. (Ecasa); and Petroperú. IMF and World Bank staff estimates for 2002.

TABLE SA.7A: STRUCTURE OF CENTRAL GOVERNMENT'S FIXED CAPITAL FORMATION
Millions of Nuevo Soles

| | 1991 | 1992 | 1993 | 1994 | 1995 | 1996 | 1997 | 1998 | 1999 | 2000 |
|---|---|---|---|---|---|---|---|---|---|---|
| **ECONOMIC SECTORS** | 364 | 865 | 1344 | 1942 | 2169 | 2222 | 2810 | 2434 | 3220 | 2563 |
| 1. Agriculture | 233 | 373 | 544 | 589 | 580 | 510 | 615 | 809 | 1089 | 911 |
| 2. Transport and communications | 116 | 360 | 568 | 904 | 1152 | 1096 | 1688 | 1194 | 1596 | 1132 |
| 3. Energy and mining | 2 | 63 | 151 | 380 | 365 | 544 | 463 | 420 | 494 | 483 |
| 4. Industry, commerce, tourism | 3 | 3 | 11 | 20 | 20 | 19 | 22 | 11 | 21 | 16 |
| 5. Fishing | 10 | 66 | 71 | 49 | 52 | 53 | 22 | 0 | 19 | 21 |
| **SOCIAL SECTORS** | 59 | 122 | 489 | 738 | 994 | 751 | 684 | 939 | 1065 | 910 |
| 1. Education | 34 | 41 | 166 | 368 | 509 | 356 | 377 | 416 | 608 | 496 |
| 2. Health | 15 | 25 | 37 | 88 | 186 | 271 | 159 | 323 | 271 | 260 |
| 3. Housing and construction | 4 | 6 | 0 | 0 | 0 | 0 | 0 | 0 | 0 | 0 |
| 4. Employment and others | 7 | 49 | 285 | 282 | 299 | 125 | 148 | 200 | 187 | 154 |
| **OTHER SECTORS** 1/ | 28 | 90 | 231 | 411 | 371 | 726 | 571 | 902 | 728 | 702 |
| **MULTISECTORAL PROGRAMS** 2/ | 53 | 38 | 86 | 251 | 421 | 222 | 383 | 690 | 639 | 573 |
| **TOTAL** | 504 | 1115 | 2150 | 3342 | 3955 | 3921 | 4448 | 4964 | 5652 | 4749 |

1/ Includes Ministry of the President, Ministries of Justice, Interior, Exterior Relations, Economy and Finance, Ministerio Público, Jurado Nacional de Elecciones, and Instituto Nacional de Planificación.

2/ Includes projects with diverse sectoral scopes. The latest periods incorporate expenditures in the microregions.

Source:  MEF, WB staff estimates.

TABLE SA.7B: STRUCTURE OF CENTRAL GOVERNMENT'S FIXED CAPITAL FORMATION
Percent of Total

| | 1991 | 1992 | 1993 | 1994 | 1995 | 1996 | 1997 | 1998 | 1999 | 2000 |
|---|---|---|---|---|---|---|---|---|---|---|
| **ECONOMIC SECTORS** | **72.1** | **77.6** | **62.5** | **58.1** | **54.8** | **56.7** | **63.2** | **49.0** | **57.0** | **54.0** |
| 1. Agriculture | 46.1 | 33.4 | 25.3 | 17.6 | 14.7 | 13.0 | 13.8 | 16.3 | 19.3 | 19.2 |
| 2. Transport and communications | 23.1 | 32.3 | 26.4 | 27.0 | 29.1 | 28.0 | 37.9 | 24.1 | 28.2 | 23.8 |
| 3. Energy and mining | 0.3 | 5.7 | 7.0 | 11.4 | 9.2 | 13.9 | 10.4 | 8.5 | 8.7 | 10.2 |
| 4. Industry, commerce, tourism | 0.5 | 0.3 | 0.5 | 0.6 | 0.5 | 0.5 | 0.5 | 0.2 | 0.4 | 0.3 |
| 5. Fishing | 2.0 | 5.9 | 3.3 | 1.5 | 1.3 | 1.3 | 0.5 | 0.0 | 0.3 | 0.4 |
| **SOCIAL SECTORS** | **11.8** | **10.9** | **22.7** | **22.1** | **25.1** | **19.2** | **15.4** | **18.9** | **18.8** | **19.2** |
| 1. Education | 6.7 | 3.7 | 7.7 | 11.0 | 12.9 | 9.1 | 8.5 | 8.4 | 10.8 | 10.4 |
| 2. Health | 3.0 | 2.2 | 1.7 | 2.6 | 4.7 | 6.9 | 3.6 | 6.5 | 4.8 | 5.5 |
| 3. Housing and Construction | 0.8 | 0.6 | 0.0 | 0.0 | 0.0 | 0.0 | 0.0 | 0.0 | 0.0 | 0.0 |
| 4. Employment and others | 1.4 | 4.4 | 13.3 | 8.4 | 7.5 | 3.2 | 3.3 | 4.0 | 3.3 | 3.2 |
| **OTHER SECTORS 1/** | **5.6** | **8.1** | **10.7** | **12.3** | **9.4** | **18.5** | **12.8** | **18.2** | **12.9** | **14.8** |
| **MULTISECTORAL PROGRAMS 2/** | **10.5** | **3.4** | **4.0** | **7.5** | **10.7** | **5.7** | **8.6** | **13.9** | **11.3** | **12.1** |
| **TOTAL** | **100** | **100** | **100** | **100** | **100** | **100** | **100** | **100** | **100** | **100** |

1/ Includes Ministry of the President, Ministries of Justice, Interior, Exterior Relations, Economy and Finance, Ministerio Público, Jurado Nacional de Elecciones, and Instituto Nacional de Planificación.

2/ Includes projects with diverse sectoral scopes. The latest periods incorporate expenditures in the microregions.

Source: MEF, WB staff estimates.

TABLE SA.8A: OPERATIONS OF THE NON-FINANCIAL PUBLIC SECTOR
Millions of Nuevo Soles

| | 1991 | 1992 | 1993 | 1994 | 1995 | 1996 | 1997 | 1998 | 1999 | 2000 | 2001 1/ |
|---|---|---|---|---|---|---|---|---|---|---|---|
| **I. Primary Balance** | **480** | **546** | **1 038** | **972** | **461** | **2 113** | **3 210** | **1 946** | **−1 675** | **−1 706** | **−593** |
| **1. Primary Balance of the CG** | **375** | **248** | **373** | **440** | **18** | **1 371** | **1 465** | **1 327** | **−1 825** | **−944** | **−1 229** |
| a. Current revenues | 3 193 | 6 059 | 9 424 | 14 386 | 18 319 | 21 522 | 25 001 | 26 174 | 25 334 | 27 515 | 26 733 |
| i. Tax revenues | 2 958 | 5 416 | 8 478 | 12 866 | 16 212 | 19 036 | 22 122 | 22 995 | 21 873 | 22 663 | 23 383 |
| ii. Non-tax revenues | 236 | 643 | 946 | 1 520 | 2 108 | 2 485 | 2 879 | 3 179 | 3 460 | 4 851 | 3 350 |
| b. Non-financial expenditures | 2 842 | 5 839 | 8 992 | 14 270 | 18 575 | 20 729 | 23 729 | 25 379 | 27 697 | 28 989 | 28 253 |
| i. Current | 2 319 | 4 401 | 6 448 | 9 929 | 13 545 | 15 680 | 17 934 | 19 756 | 21 797 | 23 757 | 23 857 |
| ii. Capital | 523 | 1 438 | 2 544 | 4 341 | 5 031 | 5 048 | 5 795 | 5 623 | 5 900 | 5 232 | 4 396 |
| c. Others 2/ | 23 | 28 | −58 | 324 | 274 | 578 | 192 | 533 | 539 | 530 | 291 |
| **2. Primary Balance of the Rest** | **105** | **299** | **665** | **532** | **443** | **743** | **1 745** | **618** | **150** | **−762** | **636** |
| a. Rest of Central Government | 75 | 57 | 97 | 107 | 371 | 409 | 679 | 659 | 233 | 109 | 143 |
| b. Local Governments | 16 | −32 | 61 | 11 | 74 | −15 | −3 | 117 | −134 | 42 | 154 |
| c. State Enterprises | 14 | 273 | 507 | 414 | −2 | 349 | 1 069 | −158 | 51 | −913 | 377 |
| **II. Interest** | **1 225** | **2 302** | **3 159** | **3 727** | **4 261** | **3 507** | **2 957** | **3 275** | **3 807** | **4 236** | **4 231** |
| a. External debt | 956 | 1 919 | 2 844 | 3 486 | 3 946 | 3 220 | 2 697 | 2 972 | 3 469 | 3 582 | 3 666 |
| b. Domestic debt | 269 | 383 | 314 | 241 | 314 | 287 | 259 | 302 | 338 | 654 | 564 |
| **III. Overall Balance (I-II)** | **−745** | **−1 755** | **−2 121** | **−2 756** | **−3 800** | **−1 394** | **253** | **−1 329** | **−5 482** | **−5 942** | **−4 823** |
| **IV. Net Financing** | **745** | **1 755** | **2 121** | **2 756** | **3 800** | **1 394** | **−253** | **1 329** | **5 482** | **5 942** | **4 823** |
| a. External Net Financing | 1 106 | 1 447 | 2 107 | 2 383 | 3 048 | 1 092 | −591 | 642 | −111 | 2 280 | 1 755 |
| (Millons of US$) | 1372 | 1052 | 1063 | 1090 | 1341 | 443 | −229 | 224 | −21 | 654 | 498 |
| i. Disbursements 3/ | 874 | 320 | 1388 | 496 | 628 | 382 | 1566 | 657 | 812 | 1299 | 1318 |
| ii. Amortizations 3/ | 1032 | 770 | 931 | 941 | 832 | 842 | 735 | 799 | 883 | 635 | 778 |
| iii. Others 3/ | 1531 | 1502 | 606 | 1535 | 1545 | 904 | −1060 | 365 | 50 | −10 | −43 |
| b. Net Domestic Financing | −363 | 239 | −286 | −4 660 | −1 398 | −4 976 | −1 155 | −77 | 4 274 | 2 235 | 1 935 |
| c. Privatization Revenues | 1 | 69 | 300 | 5 032 | 2 151 | 5 279 | 1 492 | 764 | 1 318 | 1 427 | 1 134 |

1/ Preliminary.
2/ Less payment to American International Group and to Convenio Perú-Alemania.
3/ Includes exceptional and short-term financing.

Source: MEF, Banco de la Nación, BCRP, Sunat, Customs, ESSALUD, public beneficiary societies, local government, state enterprises and public institutions.

## TABLE SA.8B: OPERATIONS OF THE NON-FINANCIAL PUBLIC SECTOR
Percent of GDP

| | 1991 | 1992 | 1993 | 1994 | 1995 | 1996 | 1997 | 1998 | 1999 | 2000 | 2001 1/ |
|---|---|---|---|---|---|---|---|---|---|---|---|
| **I. Primary Balance** | 1.8 | 1.2 | 1.5 | 1.0 | 0.4 | 1.5 | 2.0 | 1.2 | -1.0 | -0.9 | -0.3 |
| **1. Primary Balance of the CG** | 1.4 | 0.6 | 0.5 | 0.4 | 0.0 | 1.0 | 0.9 | 0.8 | -1.0 | -0.5 | -0.6 |
| a. Current revenues | 12.0 | 13.5 | 13.6 | 14.6 | 15.2 | 15.7 | 15.9 | 15.7 | 14.5 | 14.7 | 14.1 |
| i. Tax revenues | 11.1 | 12.0 | 12.2 | 13.1 | 13.4 | 13.9 | 14.1 | 13.8 | 12.5 | 12.1 | 12.3 |
| ii. Non-tax revenues | 0.9 | 1.4 | 1.4 | 1.5 | 1.7 | 1.8 | 1.8 | 1.9 | 2.0 | 2.6 | 1.8 |
| b. Non-financial expenditures | 10.6 | 13.0 | 13.0 | 14.5 | 15.4 | 15.1 | 15.1 | 15.2 | 15.9 | 15.5 | 14.9 |
| i. Current | 8.7 | 9.8 | 9.3 | 10.1 | 11.2 | 11.5 | 11.4 | 11.9 | 12.5 | 12.7 | 12.6 |
| ii. Capital | 2.0 | 3.2 | 3.7 | 4.4 | 4.2 | 3.7 | 3.7 | 3.4 | 3.4 | 2.8 | 2.3 |
| c. Others 2/ | 0.1 | 0.1 | -0.1 | 0.3 | 0.2 | 0.4 | 0.1 | 0.3 | 0.3 | 0.3 | 0.2 |
| **2. Primary Balance of the Rest** | 0.4 | 0.7 | 1.0 | 0.5 | 0.4 | 0.5 | 1.1 | 0.4 | 0.1 | -0.4 | 0.3 |
| a. Rest of Central Government | 0.3 | 0.1 | 0.1 | 0.1 | 0.3 | 0.3 | 0.4 | 0.4 | 0.1 | 0.1 | 0.1 |
| b. Local Governments | 0.1 | -0.1 | 0.1 | 0.0 | 0.1 | 0.0 | 0.0 | 0.1 | -0.1 | 0.0 | 0.1 |
| c. State Enterprises | 0.1 | 0.6 | 0.7 | 0.4 | 0.0 | 0.3 | 0.7 | -0.1 | 0.0 | -0.5 | 0.2 |
| **II. Interest** | 4.6 | 5.1 | 4.6 | 3.8 | 3.5 | 2.6 | 1.9 | 2.0 | 2.2 | 2.3 | 2.2 |
| a. External debt | 3.6 | 4.3 | 4.1 | 3.5 | 3.3 | 2.4 | 1.7 | 1.8 | 2.0 | 1.9 | 1.9 |
| b. Domestic debt | 1.0 | 0.9 | 0.5 | 0.2 | 0.3 | 0.2 | 0.2 | 0.2 | 0.2 | 0.4 | 0.3 |
| **III. Overall Balance (I-II)** | -2.8 | -3.9 | -3.1 | -2.8 | -3.1 | -1.0 | 0.2 | -0.8 | -3.1 | -3.2 | -2.5 |
| **IV. Net Financing** | 2.8 | 3.9 | 3.1 | 2.8 | 3.1 | 1.0 | -0.2 | 0.8 | 3.1 | 3.2 | 2.5 |
| a. External Net Financing | 4.1 | 3.2 | 3.0 | 2.4 | 2.5 | 0.8 | -0.4 | 0.4 | -0.1 | 1.2 | 0.9 |
| i. Disbursements 3/ | 3.3 | 0.7 | 2.0 | 0.5 | 0.5 | 0.3 | 1.0 | 0.4 | 0.5 | 0.7 | 0.7 |
| ii. Amortizations 3/ | 3.9 | 1.7 | 1.3 | 1.0 | 0.7 | 0.6 | 0.5 | 0.5 | 0.5 | 0.3 | 0.4 |
| iii. Others 3/ | 5.7 | 3.3 | 0.9 | 1.6 | 1.3 | 0.7 | -0.7 | 0.2 | 0.0 | 0.0 | 0.0 |
| b. Net Domestic Financing | -1.4 | 0.5 | -0.4 | -4.7 | -1.2 | -3.6 | -0.7 | 0.0 | 2.4 | 1.2 | 1.0 |
| c. Privatization Revenues | 0.0 | 0.2 | 0.4 | 5.1 | 1.8 | 3.9 | 0.9 | 0.5 | 0.8 | 0.8 | 0.6 |
| GDP (Million soles) | 26,686 | 44,953 | 69,262 | 98,577 | 120,858 | 136,929 | 157,274 | 166,514 | 174,719 | 186,756 | 189,532 |

1/ Preliminary.
2/ Less payment to American International Group and to Convenio Perú-Alemania.
3/ Includes exceptional and short-term financing.

Source: MEF, Banco de la Nación, BCRP, Sunat, Customs, ESSALUD, public beneficiary societies, local government, state enterprises and public institutior s.

## TABLE SA.8C: OPERATIONS OF THE NON-FINANCIAL PUBLIC SECTOR
In Millions 1994 Soles

| | 1991 | 1992 | 1993 | 1994 | 1995 | 1996 | 1997 | 1998 | 1999 | 2000 | 2001 1/ |
|---|---|---|---|---|---|---|---|---|---|---|---|
| **I. Primary Balance** | 1531 | 1004 | 1284 | 972 | 415 | 1705 | 2385 | 1348 | -1122 | -1101 | -375 |
| **1. Primary Balance of the CG** | 1196 | 455 | 462 | 440 | 16 | 1106 | 1089 | 920 | -1222 | -609 | -778 |
| a. Current revenues | 10187 | 11139 | 11661 | 14386 | 16485 | 17361 | 18580 | 18136 | 16965 | 17758 | 16920 |
| i. Tax revenues | 9435 | 9957 | 10491 | 12866 | 14588 | 15356 | 16440 | 15933 | 14648 | 14627 | 14799 |
| ii. Non-tax revenues | 752 | 1182 | 1170 | 1520 | 1897 | 2005 | 2140 | 2203 | 2317 | 3131 | 2120 |
| b. Non-financial expenditures | 9066 | 10734 | 11127 | 14270 | 16715 | 16721 | 17634 | 17585 | 18548 | 18710 | 17882 |
| i. Current | 7398 | 8092 | 7978 | 9929 | 12188 | 12649 | 13328 | 13689 | 14597 | 15333 | 15100 |
| ii. Capital | 1667 | 2643 | 3148 | 4341 | 4527 | 4072 | 4307 | 3896 | 3951 | 3377 | 2782 |
| c. Others 2/ | 75 | 51 | -72 | 324 | 246 | 466 | 143 | 369 | 361 | 342 | 184 |
| **2. Primary Balance of the Rest** | 335 | 549 | 823 | 532 | 399 | 599 | 1297 | 428 | 100 | -492 | 403 |
| a. Rest of Central Government | 238 | 106 | 120 | 107 | 334 | 330 | 504 | 457 | 156 | 70 | 91 |
| b. Local Governments | 52 | -58 | 75 | 11 | 67 | -12 | -2 | 81 | -90 | 27 | 97 |
| c. State Enterprises | 45 | 502 | 627 | 414 | -2 | 281 | 794 | -110 | 34 | -589 | 239 |
| **II. Interest** | 3907 | 4232 | 3908 | 3727 | 3834 | 2829 | 2197 | 2269 | 2549 | 2734 | 2678 |
| a. External debt | 3051 | 3528 | 3520 | 3486 | 3551 | 2598 | 2005 | 2059 | 2323 | 2312 | 2321 |
| b. Domestic debt | 857 | 704 | 389 | 241 | 283 | 232 | 193 | 209 | 226 | 422 | 357 |
| **III. Overall Balance (I-II)** | -2376 | -3227 | -2624 | -2756 | -3419 | -1124 | -188 | -921 | -3671 | -3835 | -3053 |
| **IV. Net Financing** | 2376 | 3227 | 2624 | 2756 | 3419 | 1124 | -188 | 921 | 3671 | 3835 | 3053 |
| a. External Net Financing | 3530 | 2661 | 2607 | 2383 | 2742 | 881 | -439 | 445 | -74 | 1471 | 1111 |
| i. Disbursements 3/ | 2787 | 589 | 1718 | 496 | 566 | 308 | 1164 | 455 | 544 | 838 | 834 |
| ii. Amortizations 3/ | 3292 | 1416 | 1152 | 941 | 749 | 679 | 546 | 554 | 591 | 410 | 492 |
| iii. Others 3/ | 4883 | 2761 | 749 | 1535 | 1390 | 729 | -788 | 253 | 33 | -7 | -27 |
| b. Net Domestic Financing | -1158 | 440 | -354 | -4660 | -1258 | -4014 | -858 | -53 | 2862 | 1443 | 1225 |
| c. Privatization Revenues | 5 | 127 | 371 | 5032 | 1935 | 4258 | 1109 | 529 | 883 | 921 | 717 |
| Average CPI Deflator | 31 | 54 | 81 | 100 | 111 | 124 | 135 | 144 | 149 | 155 | 158 |

1/ Preliminary.
2/ Less payment to American International Group and to Convenio Perú-Alemania.
3/ Includes exceptional and short-term financing.

Source: MEF, Banco de la Nación, BCRP, Sunat, Customs, ESSALUD, public beneficiary societies, local government, state enterprises and public institutions.

TABLE SA.9: LOCAL GOVERNMENT OPERATIONS
Millions of Nuevo Soles

| | 1991 | 1992 | 1993 | 1994 | 1995 | 1996 | 1997 | 1998 | 1999 | 2000 | 2001 |
|---|---|---|---|---|---|---|---|---|---|---|---|
| I. Current Revenues | 495 | 825 | 1 338 | 1 713 | 2 170 | 2 539 | 3 144 | 3 454 | 3 279 | 3 549 | 3 754 |
| II. Non-financial expenditures | 488 | 886 | 1 307 | 1 735 | 2 151 | 2 588 | 3 175 | 3 374 | 3 451 | 3 784 | 3 832 |
| 1. Current expenditures | 317 | 582 | 920 | 1 086 | 1 285 | 1 483 | 1 840 | 2 022 | 2 079 | 2 239 | 2 289 |
| 2. Capital expenditures | 172 | 303 | 387 | 649 | 866 | 1 106 | 1 335 | 1 352 | 1 372 | 1 545 | 1 543 |
| III. Others | 9 | 29 | 30 | 33 | 55 | 35 | 28 | 38 | 38 | 273 | 233 |
| IV. Primary Balance | 16 | −32 | 61 | 11 | 74 | −15 | −3 | 117 | −134 | 42 | 154 |
| V. Interest | 2 | 9 | 19 | 28 | 40 | 42 | 53 | 53 | 54 | 45 | 59 |
| VI. Overall Balance | 14 | −40 | 42 | −17 | 34 | −56 | −56 | 64 | −188 | −2 | 95 |

Source: Local governments and Contaduría Pública de la Nación.

## TABLE SA.10: OPERATIONS OF THE NON-FINANCIAL STATE ENTERPRISES
Millions of Nuevo Soles

| | 1991 | 1992 | 1993 | 1994 | 1995 | 1996 | 1997 | 1998 | 1999 | 2000 | 2001 |
|---|---|---|---|---|---|---|---|---|---|---|---|
| **I. Current Revenues** | **4 083** | **6 105** | **8 917** | **11 272** | **12 486** | **12 304** | **11 388** | **9 524** | **10 700** | **12 914** | **11 581** |
| 1. Petroperú | 1 691 | 2 716 | 3 867 | 5 154 | 5 861 | 6 187 | 5 216 | 4 285 | 5 370 | 7 724 | 6 797 |
| 2. Electroperú | 238 | 356 | 618 | 869 | 1 108 | 1 390 | 1 386 | 1 450 | 1 265 | 1 214 | 1 221 |
| 3. Regionales de Electricidad | na | na | na | na | 736 | 825 | 975 | 1 197 | 1 454 | 1 568 | 1 339 |
| 4. Sedapal | 66 | 133 | 208 | 356 | 418 | 507 | 621 | 581 | 626 | 643 | 665 |
| 5. Centromin | 311 | 515 | 738 | 1018 | 1336 | 1440 | 1554 | 603 | 546 | 258 | 202 |
| 6. Others | 1 778 | 2 386 | 3 486 | 3 875 | 3 027 | 1 953 | 1 635 | 1 408 | 1 438 | 1 507 | 1 358 |
| **II. Non-financial Current Expenditures** | **3 833** | **5 503** | **7 826** | **9 985** | **11 575** | **10 932** | **9 450** | **8 308** | **9 047** | **12 588** | **10 495** |
| 1. Petroperú | 1 694 | 2 685 | 3 754 | 4 878 | 5 774 | 5 828 | 4 782 | 4 212 | 5 344 | 7 823 | 6 343 |
| 2. Electroperú | 124 | 254 | 391 | 591 | 755 | 899 | 1 019 | 1 126 | 675 | 782 | 858 |
| 3. Regionales de Electricidad | na | na | na | na | 608 | 619 | 652 | 893 | 1 122 | 1 509 | 958 |
| 4. Sedapal | 55 | 116 | 136 | 246 | 300 | 331 | 391 | 379 | 357 | 447 | 400 |
| 5. Centromin | 333 | 456 | 684 | 899 | 1205 | 1323 | 1169 | 606 | 365 | 507 | 203 |
| 6. Otros | 1 628 | 1 992 | 2 861 | 3 371 | 2 934 | 1 932 | 1 436 | 1 092 | 1 184 | 1 520 | 1 732 |
| **III. Gastos de Capital** | **280** | **459** | **684** | **954** | **1 115** | **1 367** | **1 571** | **2 025** | **1 711** | **1 312** | **785** |
| 1. Petroperú | 35 | 48 | 124 | 150 | 449 | 182 | 23 | 41 | 29 | 32 | 40 |
| 2. Electroperú | 95 | 106 | 127 | 157 | 77 | 450 | 101 | 528 | 533 | 453 | 150 |
| 3. Regionales de Electricidad | na | na | na | na | 96 | 114 | 229 | 204 | 426 | 367 | 244 |
| 4. Sedapal | 24 | 38 | 91 | 124 | 88 | 170 | 371 | 426 | 453 | 264 | 196 |
| 5. Centromin | 21 | 7 | 28 | 23 | 39 | 61 | 65 | 46 | 28 | 42 | 8 |
| 6. Others | 105 | 260 | 315 | 500 | 366 | 389 | 783 | 779 | 241 | 154 | 147 |
| **IV. Others** | **44** | **129** | **100** | **82** | **202** | **344** | **703** | **650** | **108** | **73** | **75** |
| **V. Primary Balance (I-II-III+IV)** | **14** | **273** | **507** | **414** | **-2** | **349** | **1 069** | **-158** | **51** | **-913** | **377** |
| **VI. Interest** | **182** | **295** | **251** | **139** | **197** | **175** | **112** | **101** | **78** | **115** | **107** |
| **VII. Overall Balance** | **-168** | **-22** | **256** | **275** | **-199** | **173** | **957** | **-259** | **-27** | **-1 028** | **270** |
| 1. Petroperú | -87 | -59 | -53 | 97 | -464 | 90 | 385 | 7 | -18 | -154 | 398 |
| 2. Electroperú | -1 | -36 | 99 | 102 | 263 | 22 | 241 | -220 | 56 | -21 | 214 |
| 3. Regionales de Electricidad | na | na | na | na | 26 | 86 | 88 | 182 | -96 | -333 | 182 |
| 4. Sedapal | -8 | -9 | -20 | -19 | 48 | 37 | -56 | -64 | -157 | -109 | 27 |
| 5. Centromin | -57 | 35 | -7 | 80 | 69 | 41 | 308 | -60 | 144 | -298 | -15 |
| 6. Others | -15 | 46 | 236 | 14 | -141 | -103 | -9 | -103 | 44 | -114 | -536 |

na: not available.

Source: State enterprises, Fondo Nacional de Financiamiento de la Actividad Empresarial del Estado (FONAFE).

TABLE SA.11: OPERATIONS OF THE REST OF THE CENTRAL GOVERNMENT 1/
Millions of Nuevo Soles

| | 1991 | 1992 | 1993 | 1994 | 1995 | 1996 | 1997 | 1998 | 1999 | 2000 | 2001 |
|---|---|---|---|---|---|---|---|---|---|---|---|
| **I. Current Revenues** | **707** | **1 147** | **1 558** | **2 314** | **3 070** | **3 731** | **4 715** | **5 169** | **6 090** | **6 557** | **6 667** |
| 1. Contributions to ESSALUD and ONP 2/ | 539 | 933 | 1 335 | 1 748 | 2 194 | 2 378 | 2 804 | 2 795 | 2 945 | 3 112 | 3 166 |
| 2. Others | 169 | 214 | 222 | 565 | 875 | 1 354 | 1 911 | 2 374 | 3 145 | 3 446 | 3 501 |
| **II. Non-financial Expenditures** | **633** | **1 090** | **1 461** | **2 207** | **2 807** | **3 324** | **4 040** | **4 510** | **5 857** | **6 449** | **6 524** |
| 1. Current | 577 | 1 037 | 1 381 | 2 045 | 2 549 | 3 155 | 3 898 | 4 370 | 5 569 | 6 157 | 6 396 |
| 2. Capital | 56 | 53 | 80 | 162 | 258 | 169 | 142 | 140 | 287 | 291 | 129 |
| **III. Others** | **0** | **0** | **0** | **0** | **109** | **1** | **4** | **0** | **0** | **0** | **0** |
| **IV. Primary Balance (I-II+III)** | **75** | **57** | **97** | **107** | **371** | **409** | **679** | **659** | **233** | **109** | **143** |
| **V. Interest** | **5** | **0** | **0** | **0** | **0** | **1** | **2** | **1** | **—** | **—** | **—** |
| **VI. Overall Balance** | **70** | **57** | **97** | **106** | **371** | **407** | **677** | **658** | **232** | **108** | **141** |
| 1. ESSALUD 3/ | 65 | 11 | 98 | 211 | 179 | 338 | 531 | 414 | 142 | –100 | 92 |
| 2. ONP 3/ | 0 | 0 | 0 | –126 | 142 | –2 | –34 | 10 | –39 | 65 | 19 |
| 3. FCR | 0 | 0 | 0 | 0 | 0 | 0 | 112 | 72 | 26 | 97 | 53 |
| 4. FONAHPU | 0 | 0 | 0 | 0 | 0 | 0 | 0 | 42 | 42 | 103 | –53 |
| 5. Others | 4 | 46 | –1 | 22 | 50 | 72 | 67 | 119 | 62 | –57 | 30 |

1/ Includes ESSALUD, Oficina de Normalización Previsional (ONP), public beneficiary societies, Fondo Consolidado de Reservas (FCR), el Fondo Nacional de Ahorro Público (FONAHPU), regulated organizations, and registries.

2/ ONP receives the revenues corresponding to the collections of the Sistema Nacional de Pensiones (SNP).

3/ Up to 1993, it shows the operations of IPSS in ESSALUD, consolidating the provisional pension and health regimes.

Source: MEF, Sunat, Aduanas, ESSALUD, public beneficiary societies, and regulated organizations.

# TABLE SA.12A: FUNCTIONAL CLASSIFICATION OF CENTRAL GOVERNMENT BUDGET EXPENDITURES
Millions of Nuevos Soles

| | 1997 | 1998 | 1999 | 2000 | 2001 | 2002 1/ |
|---|---|---|---|---|---|---|
| Planning and Administration | 8,847 | 6,601 | 8,246 | 9,253 | 8,701 | 9,514 |
| Pensions and Social Assistance | 5,593 | 5,885 | 7,149 | 7,717 | 7,931 | 8,196 |
| Pensions | 4,041 | 4,575 | 5,330 | 6,127 | 6,294 | 6,480 |
| Social Assistance | 1,552 | 1,310 | 1,819 | 1,590 | 1,637 | 1,716 |
| Education | 4,172 | 4,529 | 5,230 | 5,403 | 5,323 | 6,067 |
| Pre-primary | 303 | 382 | 455 | 448 | 415 | 612 |
| Primary | 1,518 | 1,598 | 1,910 | 1,957 | 1,818 | 2,048 |
| Secondary | 1,130 | 1,134 | 1,308 | 1,400 | 1,424 | 1,676 |
| Tertiary | 743 | 836 | 970 | 955 | 965 | 1,039 |
| Others | 478 | 579 | 587 | 642 | 700 | 692 |
| Defense and National Security | 4,523 | 4,858 | 4,958 | 5,366 | 4,709 | 4,189 |
| Health and Water | 2,258 | 2,465 | 2,709 | 2,914 | 3,052 | 3,328 |
| Water and Sewage | 283 | 271 | 269 | 333 | 207 | 159 |
| Healthcare | 1,975 | 2,194 | 2,440 | 2,581 | 2,845 | 3,169 |
| Transportation | 1,709 | 1,532 | 1,752 | 1,383 | 1,286 | 1,318 |
| Agriculture | 968 | 1,205 | 1,289 | 1,255 | 1,049 | 961 |
| Justice | 556 | 621 | 678 | 703 | 733 | 862 |
| Energy and Natural Resources | 269 | 311 | 338 | 266 | 257 | 297 |
| Other 2/ | 691 | 808 | 1,008 | 1,109 | 1,034 | 1,039 |
| **TOTAL** | 29,586 | 28,815 | 33,357 | 35,369 | 34,075 | 35,772 |
| *Memorandum items:* | | | | | | |
| Total Social Expenditure + Pensions | 14,937 | 15,451 | 17,667 | 18,835 | 18,972 | 20,286 |
| Total Social Expenditure | 10,896 | 10,876 | 12,337 | 12,708 | 12,678 | 13,806 |
| Budget Social Expenditure 3/ | 7,982 | 8,304 | 9,758 | 9,907 | 10,012 | 11,111 |
| ESSALUD 4/ | 1,735 | 2,025 | 2,489 | 2,801 | 2,666 | 2,695 |
| FONAVI 5/ | 1,179 | 547 | 90 | | | |
| Exchange Rate | | | | 3.49 | 3.43 | 3.54 |

1/ Budget.
2/ Includes foreign relations, legislative, housing and urban development, industry, commerce and services, fishing, communications, and employment.
3/ Includes education, health, and sanitation and other social assistance.
4/ Total expenditure by Essalud, the public health insurance administration
5/ Includes net operations of the national housing fund (FONAVI)—loan disbursements and amortizations received.

Source: MEF, IMF.

TABLE SA.12B: FUNCTIONAL CLASSIFICATION OF CENTRAL GOVERNMENT BUDGET EXPENDITURES
Percent of GDP

| | 1997 | 1998 | 1999 | 2000 | 2001 | 2002 /1 |
|---|---|---|---|---|---|---|
| Planning and Administration | 5.6 | 4.0 | 4.7 | 5.0 | 4.6 | 4.7 |
| Pensions and Social Assistance | 3.6 | 3.5 | 4.1 | 4.1 | 4.2 | 4.1 |
| Pensions | 2.6 | 2.7 | 3.1 | 3.3 | 3.3 | 3.2 |
| Social Assistance | 1.0 | 0.8 | 1.0 | 0.9 | 0.9 | 0.9 |
| Education | 2.7 | 2.7 | 3.0 | 2.9 | 2.8 | 3.0 |
| Pre-primary | 0.2 | 0.2 | 0.3 | 0.2 | 0.2 | 0.3 |
| Primary | 1.0 | 1.0 | 1.1 | 1.0 | 1.0 | 1.0 |
| Secondary | 0.7 | 0.7 | 0.7 | 0.7 | 0.8 | 0.8 |
| Tertiary | 0.5 | 0.5 | 0.6 | 0.5 | 0.5 | 0.5 |
| Others | 0.3 | 0.3 | 0.3 | 0.3 | 0.4 | 0.3 |
| Defense and National Security | 2.9 | 2.9 | 2.8 | 2.9 | 2.5 | 2.1 |
| Health and Water | 1.4 | 1.5 | 1.6 | 1.6 | 1.6 | 1.7 |
| Water and Sewage | 0.2 | 0.2 | 0.2 | 0.2 | 0.1 | 0.1 |
| Healthcare | 1.3 | 1.3 | 1.4 | 1.4 | 1.5 | 1.6 |
| Transportation | 1.1 | 0.9 | 1.0 | 0.7 | 0.7 | 0.7 |
| Agriculture | 0.6 | 0.7 | 0.7 | 0.7 | 0.6 | 0.5 |
| Justice | 0.4 | 0.4 | 0.4 | 0.4 | 0.4 | 0.4 |
| Energy and Natural Resources | 0.2 | 0.2 | 0.2 | 0.1 | 0.1 | 0.1 |
| Other /2 | 0.4 | 0.5 | 0.6 | 0.6 | 0.5 | 0.5 |
| TOTAL | 18.8 | 17.3 | 19.1 | 18.9 | 18.0 | 17.8 |
| *Memorandum items:* | | | | | | |
| Total Social Expenditure | 6.9 | 6.5 | 7.1 | 6.8 | 6.7 | 6.9 |
| Budget Social Expenditure /3 | 5.1 | 5.0 | 5.6 | 5.3 | 5.3 | 5.5 |
| ESSALUD /4 | 1.1 | 1.2 | 1.4 | 1.5 | 1.4 | 1.3 |
| FONAVI /5 | 0.7 | 0.3 | 0.1 | | | |
| Exchange Rate | | | | 3.49 | 3.43 | 3.54 |

1/ Budget.
2/ Includes foreign relations, legislative, housing and urban development, industry, commerce and services, fishing, communications, and employment.
3/ Includes education, health, and sanitation and other social assistance.
4/ Total expenditure by Essalud, the public health insurance administration
5/ Includes net operations of the national housing fund (FONAVI)—loan disbursements and amortizations received.

Source: MEF, IMF

TABLE SA.13: CENTRAL GOVERNMENT SPENDING BY MINISTRY OR INSTITUTION
Millions of Nuevos Soles

| Sectors | 1999 | | | 2000 | | | 2001 | | |
|---|---|---|---|---|---|---|---|---|---|
| | Budgeted | Actual | Diff. % | Budgeted | Actual | Diff. % | Budgeted | Actual | Diff. % |
| Presidency of the Council of Ministers | 268 | 292 | 8.8 | 360 | 399 | 10.9 | 368 | 279 | −24.2 |
| Judicial Power | 413 | 454 | 9.9 | 459 | 477 | 3.8 | 471 | 482 | 2.4 |
| Justice | 307 | 269 | −12.7 | 310 | 392 | 26.6 | 381 | 362 | −4.8 |
| Interior | 2,424 | 2,891 | 19.3 | 2,776 | 3,029 | 9.1 | 2,931 | 2,888 | −1.5 |
| Exterior Relations | 293 | 346 | 18.1 | 341 | 382 | 12.0 | 366 | 374 | 2.3 |
| Economy and Finance | 10,362 | 10,009 | −3.4 | 12,126 | 12,533 | 3.4 | 13,382 | 12,741 | −4.8 |
| Education | 2,713 | 3,040 | 12.1 | 2,534 | 2,625 | 3.6 | 2,478 | 2,154 | −13.1 |
| Health | 1,623 | 1,664 | 2.5 | 1,828 | 1,728 | −5.5 | 1,859 | 1,939 | 4.3 |
| Labor and Social Assistance | 126 | 51 | −59.3 | 25 | 50 | 98.9 | 36 | 38 | 5.4 |
| Agriculture | 648 | 827 | 27.6 | 749 | 810 | 8.1 | 664 | 787 | 18.5 |
| Industry, Tourism, Integration and International Commercial Negotiations | 79 | 81 | 2.7 | 93 | 95 | 1.4 | 103 | 85 | −16.8 |
| Transport, Communications, Housing and Construction | 1,817 | 1,793 | −1.4 | 1,599 | 1,348 | −15.7 | 1,496 | 1,196 | −20.1 |
| Energy and Mining | 490 | 325 | −33.7 | 359 | 259 | −27.9 | 281 | 254 | −9.7 |
| Fisheries | 90 | 150 | 66.6 | 83 | 97 | 16.6 | 102 | 110 | 8.1 |
| General Comptroller | 52 | 49 | −6.0 | 52 | 48 | −7.4 | 48 | 49 | 3.3 |
| Office of the People's Ombudsperson | 12 | 19 | 52.1 | 16 | 22 | 33.9 | 17 | 21 | 25.9 |
| National Council of the Magistrate | 3 | 3 | −6.8 | 3 | 4 | 15.9 | 5 | 7 | 44.8 |
| Ministry of the Public | 156 | 158 | 1.2 | 160 | 152 | −4.8 | 157 | 179 | 13.8 |
| Constitutional Tribunal | 7 | 7 | 3.2 | 8 | 8 | −0.9 | 9 | 8 | −2.9 |
| Ministry of the Presidency | 6,384 | 6,698 | 4.9 | 5,961 | 6,122 | 2.7 | 6,075 | 5,802 | −4.5 |
| Defense | 2,773 | 3,398 | 22.5 | 3,228 | 3,684 | 14.1 | 3,486 | 3,148 | −9.7 |
| Congress | 247 | 236 | −4.4 | 282 | 288 | 2.0 | 299 | 304 | 1.9 |
| National Election Body | 12 | 15 | 28.0 | 10 | 26 | 157.0 | 11 | 41 | 272.9 |
| National Office of the Electoral Process | 9 | 34 | 290.0 | 12 | 141 | 1060.3 | 14 | 281 | 1857.1 |
| National Registry of Identification and Civil State | 112 | 72 | −36.0 | 75 | 113 | 49.5 | 87 | 79 | −9.2 |
| Advancement of Women and Human Development | 524 | 474 | −9.5 | 597 | 539 | −9.8 | 588 | 466 | −20.7 |
| TOTAL | 31,947 | 33,357 | 4.4 | 34,046 | 35,368 | 3.9 | 35,712 | 34,075 | −4.6 |

Source: MEF, SIAF for 2001.

TABLE SA.14: SOCIAL SPENDING BY TYPE
Millions of Nuevos Soles

| | 1991 | 1992 | 1993 | 1994 | 1995 | 1996 | 1997 | 1998 | 1999 | 2000 |
|---|---|---|---|---|---|---|---|---|---|---|
| Education | 578 | 1,037 | 1,944 | 3,310 | 4,255 | 4,287 | 5,011 | 5,300 | 4,827 | 5,657 |
| Social Security | 403 | 827 | 1,524 | 1,933 | 3,161 | 3,430 | 4,712 | 5,300 | 4,603 | 5,305 |
| Nutrition | 44 | 76 | 155 | 359 | 677 | 587 | 817 | 843 | 776 | 964 |
| Health | 264 | 459 | 634 | 1,037 | 1,547 | 1,814 | 2,200 | 2,372 | 2,215 | 2,143 |
| Justice | 37 | 70 | 170 | 194 | 194 | 374 | 547 | 498 | 586 | 622 |
| Other Social Investment | 90 | 243 | 815 | 1,111 | 1,281 | 1,480 | 1,682 | 2,144 | 2,132 | 1,783 |
| Total | 1,416 | 2,712 | 5,242 | 7,944 | 11,116 | 11,971 | 14,968 | 16,457 | 15,139 | 16,474 |
| Percent of GDP | 5.3% | 6.0% | 7.6% | 8.1% | 9.2% | 8.7% | 9.5% | 9.9% | 8.7% | 8.8% |

Source: MEF. Note: this table has minor inconsistencies with the other tables.

## TABLE SA.15: COMPOSITION OF SOCIAL EXPENDITURES
(Millions of Nuevo Soles)

| | 1999 | 2000 | 2001 1/ | 2002 2/ |
|---|---|---|---|---|
| **I. UNIVERSAL SOCIAL EXPENDITURE** | **6 821** | **7 207** | **7 448** | **8 439** |
| EDUCATION | 4 552 | 4 812 | 5 042 | 5 797 |
| HEALTH | 2 268 | 2 395 | 2 405 | 2 643 |
| **II. EXTREME POVERTY PROGRAMS** | **3 257** | **3 043** | **2 979** | **3 531** |
| FONCODES | 758 | 469 | 350 | 537 |
| Apoyo Social 2/ | 232 | 184 | 19 | |
| Strengthening Social Programs | 42 | 56 | 32 | 38 |
| Social Investment/Productive Development | 483 | 228 | 207 | 179 |
| Programa de Emergencia Social Productiva | na | na | 92 | 320 |
| EDUCATION | 377 | 315 | 163 | 355 |
| Improving Primary Education | 260 | 219 | 102 | 55 |
| Improving Education at Other Levels | 116 | 96 | 61 | 271 |
| Literacy | | | | 29 |
| HEALTH | 126 | 136 | 205 | 291 |
| Lucha Contra Epidemias | 8 | 39 | 42 | 43 |
| Family Planning | 32 | 11 | 20 | 9 |
| Seguro Escolar/Materno Infantil (Prog. Apoyo Reforma Sector Salud—SALUD) | 87 | 86 | 143 | 239 |
| AGRICULTURE | 317 | 293 | 416 | 276 |
| Agricultural Support in Emergency Zones | 62 | 74 | 257 | 40 |
| Pronamachs 1/ | 191 | 185 | 143 | 219 |
| Land Titling | 64 | 34 | 15 | 17 |
| PRONAA | 237 | 258 | 221 | 216 |
| Food Assistance/Support in Emergency Cases | 211 | 233 | 201 | 195 |
| Proyectos de Asistencia Alimentaria | 26 | 25 | 20 | 21 |
| PROG. APOYO REPOBLACION Y DESARROLLO ZONA DE EMERG. | 22 | 29 | 21 | 17 |
| Programa de Apoyo a la Repoblación | 22 | 29 | 21 | 17 |
| ECONOMY AND FINANCE | 338 | 350 | 357 | 363 |
| Vaso de Leche (Gobiernos Locales) | 305 | 325 | 332 | 343 |
| Apoyo Social—PL 480 | 33 | 25 | 25 | 20 |
| ENERGY AND MINING | 77 | 96 | 108 | 111 |
| Distribution Infrastructure for Energy | 77 | 96 | 108 | 111 |
| TRANSPORT AND COMMUNICATIONS | 190 | 112 | 59 | 160 |
| Rural Roads | 190 | 112 | 59 | 160 |
| MIPRE | 102 | 336 | 312 | 329 |
| Prog. Nacional de Agua Potable y Alcantarillado | 92 | 63 | 89 | 102 |
| Targeted Investment to Reduce Extreme Poverty | 10 | 8 | 14 | 20 |
| Prog. Equipamiento Básico Municipal | na | 256 | 209 | 207 |
| Water for All | na | 9 | | |
| COOPOP | 8 | 6 | 12 | 9 |
| Multisectoral Projects | 8 | 6 | 12 | 9 |
| INIED/INFES | 77 | 50 | 31 | 50 |
| Education Infrastructure | 77 | 50 | 31 | 50 |

(continued)

## TABLE SA.15: COMPOSITION OF SOCIAL EXPENDITURES (CONTINUED)
### (Millions of Nuevo Soles)

|  | 1999 | 2000 | 2001 1/ | 2002 2/ |
|---|---|---|---|---|
| COMISION DE FORMALIZACIÓN DE LA PROP. INFORMAL | 86 | 76 | 19 | 61 |
| PROMUDEH | 70 | 84 | 68 | 42 |
| Literacy/Educational Development | 70 | 84 | 68 | 42 |
| BASIC SOCIAL EXPENDITURE | 472 | 433 | 606 | 713 |
| Education | 39 | 34 | 33 | 59 |
| Health | 305 | 264 | 255 | 316 |
| Instituto Nacional de Salud | 83 | 93 | 268 | 300 |
| Others | 45 | 42 | 50 | 38 |
| **III NON-TARGETED SOCIAL PROGRAMS** | **9,466** | **10,526** | **10,625** | **10,906** |
| ESSALUD | 2489 | 2801 | 2666 | 2695 |
| FONAVI | 90 |  |  |  |
| Tertiary and Other Education | 1557 | 1597 | 1665 | 1731 |
| Pensions | 5330 | 6127 | 6294 | 6480 |
| **TOTAL** | **19 544** | **20 775** | **21 051** | **22 877** |
| *Memo items:* |  |  |  |  |
| Total budgeted social expenditure as (% of GDP) 3/ | 6.7% | 6.3% | 6.4% | 6.8% |
| Total social expenditure and pensions as (% of GDP) | 11.2% | 11.1% | 11.1% | 11.4% |
| Total poverty-reduction programs (% of GDP) | 5.8% | 5.5% | 5.5% | 6.0% |
| Poverty reduction (% of total budgeted social expenditure) | 86.6% | 86.5% | 86.2% | 87.4% |
| Non-targeted social programs (% of total social expenditure and pension) | 48.4% | 50.7% | 50.5% | 47.7% |

1/ Preliminary.
2/ Estimated.
3/ Budgeted social expenditure excludes ESSALUD, FONAVI, and pensions.

*Source:* MEF.

## TABLE SA.16:  PESEM: PROJECTED SOCIAL SPENDING BY INSTITUTION, 2002–06

| | 2002 | 2003 | 2004 | 2005 | 2006 |
|---|---|---|---|---|---|
| **Nominal Million NS** | | | | | |
| Social Sectors | 11898 | 12554 | 13224 | 14307 | 15260 |
| Education | 6068 | 6662 | 7457 | 8232 | 9062 |
| Justice | 356 | 386 | 416 | 452 | 491 |
| Health | 3224 | 3377 | 3580 | 3776 | 3978 |
| President | 1788 | 1653 | 1223 | 1256 | 1093 |
| Woman and Human Development | 462 | 476 | 548 | 592 | 636 |
| Defense and Interior | 5346 | 5573 | 5573 | 5720 | 5881 |
| **Total** | **35991** | **38034** | **39026** | **40861** | **42781** |
| **Percent of Budget** | | | | | |
| Social Sectors | 33.1 | 33.0 | 33.9 | 35.0 | 35.7 |
| Education | 16.9 | 17.5 | 19.1 | 20.1 | 21.2 |
| Justice | 1.0 | 1.0 | 1.1 | 1.1 | 1.1 |
| Health | 9.0 | 8.9 | 9.2 | 9.2 | 9.3 |
| President | 5.0 | 4.3 | 3.1 | 3.1 | 2.6 |
| Woman and Human Development | 1.3 | 1.3 | 1.4 | 1.4 | 1.5 |
| Defense and Interior | 14.9 | 14.7 | 14.3 | 14.0 | 13.7 |
| **Total** | **100.0** | **100.0** | **100.0** | **100.0** | **100.0** |
| **Percent of GDP** | | | | | |
| Social Sectors | 5.9 | 5.8 | 5.7 | 5.8 | 5.7 |
| Education | 3.0 | 3.1 | 3.2 | 3.3 | 3.4 |
| Justice | 0.2 | 0.2 | 0.2 | 0.2 | 0.2 |
| Health | 1.6 | 1.6 | 1.5 | 1.5 | 1.5 |
| President | 0.9 | 0.8 | 0.5 | 0.5 | 0.4 |
| Woman and Human Development | 0.2 | 0.2 | 0.2 | 0.2 | 0.2 |
| Defense and Interior | 2.7 | 2.6 | 2.4 | 2.3 | 2.2 |
| **Total** | **17.9** | **17.6** | **16.8** | **16.4** | **16.1** |
| *GDP Nominal* | 201000 | 216300 | 232523 | 248799 | 266215 |

*Source:* MEF and World Bank staff estimates, based on multiyear sectoral programs (PESEM).

## TABLE SA.17: PLEDGES AT THE 2002 CONSULTATIVE GROUP FOR PERU

| Country | Grants | Pledges Concessional | Debt Swaps | Loans | Total |
|---|---|---|---|---|---|
| Spain | 49.6 | 212.4 | 9.0 | – | 271.0 |
| Belgium | 20.5 | – | – | – | 20.5 |
| Canada | 32.7 | – | – | – | – |
| Denmark | – | – | – | – | – |
| Finland | 1.4 | – | – | – | 1.4 |
| France | – | – | – | – | – |
| Germany | 13.6 | – | 22.5 | – | 36.1 |
| Italy | 10.0 | 14.0 | 127.0 | – | – |
| Japan | – | – | – | – | – |
| Luxemburg | – | – | – | – | – |
| Norway | – | – | – | – | – |
| Sweden | – | – | – | – | – |
| Switzerland | 20.0 | – | – | – | – |
| TheNetherlands | 10.0 | – | – | – | – |
| UnitedKingdom | 21.0 | | | | – |
| UnitedStates | 330.0 | – | – | – | – |
| **TOTAL** | **508.8** | **226.4** | **158.5** | **–** | **329.0** |
| **Institution:** | | | | | |
| IADB | – | – | – | 400.0 | – |
| WorldFoodProg | 15.0 | – | – | – | – |
| EuropeanCommission | 90.0 | – | – | – | 90.0 |
| WB | – | – | – | 120.0 | – |
| EuropeanInvestBank | – | – | – | 20.0 | – |
| IFAD | – | – | – | 25.0 | – |
| CAF | 1.5 | – | – | 321.0 | – |
| **TOTAL** | **106.5** | **–** | **–** | **886.0** | **90.0** |
| **GRAND TOTAL** | **615.3** | **226.4** | **158.5** | **886.0** | **419.0** |

Source: IDB.

## TABLE SA.18: PRIVATIZATIONS AND CONCESSIONS, 2001–04
### Millions of US$

| | 2001 | 2002 | 2003 | 2004 |
|---|---|---|---|---|
| **Sale of Participatory Stocks** | 145 | 100 | 0 | 0 |
| Edelnor stocks (36%) | | 80 | | |
| Relapasa stocks (32%) | 88 | | | |
| Iscaycruz stocks (25%) | 18 | | | |
| Elevensa stocks (38%) | 39 | | | |
| Emp. Electrica Piura stocks (40%) | | 20 | | |
| **Electric Distributors** | 0 | 220 | 160 | 0 |
| EE RR Electricity (JORBSA) | | 220 | | |
| Other distributors (100%): Puno, Oriente, Sur, etc. | | | 160 | |
| **Electric Generators** | 220 | 0 | 350 | 300 |
| Complete Mantaro (CH 1008 Mw): Concession (up front) | | | | 300 |
| ElectroAndes (CH 183 Mw) | 220 | | | |
| Egasa (CT 154 Mw and CH 165 Mw) | | | 200 | |
| Egesur (CT 28.6 Mw and CH 35 Mw) | | | 30 | |
| Egemsa (CH 70 Mw) | | | 60 | |
| San Gaban (CH 110) | | | 60 | |
| **Electric Transmission: Etecen and Etesur** | 0 | 330 | 0 | 0 |
| Elecen (LT 3000 km) | | 240 | | |
| Etesur (LT 880 km) | | 90 | | |
| **Petroperu** | 0 | 0 | 35 | 0 |
| Talara refinery (62 TBD): Concession (up front) | | | 15 | |
| Conchan refinery (12 TDB) and Iquitos (10.5 TBD) | | | 20 | |
| **Concessions** | 10 | 0 | 55 | 0 |
| Telephone: Fixed lines | 10 | | | |
| Regional ports and from Callao | | | 45 | |
| Telephonia Multimedios (other bands) | | | 10 | |
| **Sale of Buildings** | 0 | 0 | 45 | 0 |
| **Earlier Sales and Other Privatizations** | 85 | 50 | 55 | 50 |
| **TOTAL** | 460 | 700 | 700 | 350 |
| *Memo 1: Revenues of the Public Treasury and Fonahpu* | | | | |
| A. Public Treasury | 328 | 600 | 316 | 350 |
| Privatization revenues | 90 | 50 | 201 | 50 |
| Deducted for the assumption of debt | 238 | 550 | 115 | 300 |
| B. FONAHPU | 127 | 100 | 0 | 0 |
| C. Revenue FEF | 5 | 0 | 384 | 0 |
| **TOTAL** | 460 | 700 | 700 | 350 |
| *Memo 2: Deduction for assuming debt* | | | | |
| Iscaycruz (by Minero Peru) | 18 | | | |
| Electro Andes (by Centromin) | 220 | | | |
| EE RR Electricidad: JORBSA (by Electroperu) | | 220 | | |
| Etecen and Etesur (by Electroperu) | | 330 | | |
| Complejo Mantaro (by Electroperu) | | | | 300 |
| Egasa and Egesur (by Electroperu) | | | 80 | |
| Cochan and Iquitos Refineries (by Electroperu) | | | 35 | |
| **TOTAL[1/]** | 238 | 550 | 115 | 300 |

*Notes:* CT = Central Térmica, CH = Central Hidraúlica, Mw = Megawatts, LT = Transmission line, TBD = thous. barrels a day.

1/ The deductions for debt assumed from and capitalization of Electroperu are for a total of $930 mln.

*Source:* Copri (August 2001).

## TABLE SA.19:   CURRENT REVENUES BY AWARDED CONCESSIONS
### Millions of US$

|  | 2001 | 2002 | 2003 | 2004 |
|---|---|---|---|---|
| Jorge Chavez airport 1/ | 0 | 35 | 40 | 50 |
| Camisea | 0 | 0 | 0 | 90 |
| Complejo Mantaro (15%) 2/ | 0 | 0 | 0 | 40 |
| Ports (15%) | 0 | 0 | 0 | 15 |
| **TOTAL** | 0 | 35 | 40 | 195 |
| Government | 0 | 23 | 40 | 155 |
| Enterprises | 0 | 12 | 0 | 0 |
| FONAHPU | 0 | 0 | 0 | 40 |
| **TOTAL** | 0 | 35 | 40 | 195 |

1/ In 2002, $12 mln was destined to Coipac and $23 mln to the government.
2/ Revenues of FONAHPU.

*Source:* Copri (August 2001).

## TABLE SA.20:   COMPARATIVE PERFORMANCE IN SOCIAL INDICATORS

|  | Life Expectancy | | | Net Primary Enrollment | | |
|---|---|---|---|---|---|---|
|  | Country-Level Efficiency | Divided by Region Avg. | Divided by World Avg. | Country-Level Efficiency | Divided by Region Avg. | Divided by World Avg. |
| **Latin America/Caribbean** | **83.5** |  | **103.2** | **76.4** |  | **103.1** |
| Argentina | 85.3 | 102.2 | 105.5 | 84.8 | 110.9 | 114.4 |
| Bahamas, The | 85.0 | 101.8 | 105.1 |  |  |  |
| Bolivia | 73.6 | 88.1 | 91.0 | 80.6 | 105.5 | 108.8 |
| Brazil | 80.6 | 96.6 | 99.7 | 76.8 | 100.5 | 103.7 |
| Chile | 89.3 | 106.9 | 110.4 | 72.2 | 94.5 | 97.5 |
| Colombia | 84.1 | 100.7 | 104.0 | 65.7 | 85.9 | 88.6 |
| Costa Rica | 91.0 | 109.0 | 112.5 | 72.6 | 95.0 | 98.0 |
| Ecuador | 82.1 | 98.4 | 101.6 | 77.7 | 101.7 | 104.8 |
| El Salvador | 83.6 | 100.1 | 103.3 | 69.8 | 91.3 | 94.2 |
| Guatemala | 79.1 | 94.8 | 97.9 | 69.6 | 91.1 | 93.9 |
| Guyana | 76.2 | 91.3 | 94.3 |  |  |  |
| Haiti | 69.4 | 83.1 | 85.8 |  |  |  |
| Honduras | 84.7 | 101.5 | 104.8 | 83.5 | 109.3 | 112.7 |
| Jamaica | 90.3 | 108.2 | 111.7 | 83.2 | 108.9 | 112.3 |
| Mexico | 86.0 | 104.0 | 106.3 | 85.5 | 111.9 | 115.4 |
| Nicaragua | 83.1 | 99.5 | 102.7 | 74.1 | 97.0 | 100.0 |
| Panama | 88.3 | 105.7 | 109.2 | 77.5 | 101.3 | 104.5 |
| Paraguay | 83.2 | 99.7 | 102.9 | 77.0 | 100.7 | 103.9 |
| **Peru** | **81.6** | **97.7** | **100.9** | **77.1** | **100.9** | **104.1** |
| Trinidad & Tobago | 86.5 | 103.6 | 107.0 |  |  |  |
| Uruguay | 86.8 | 104.0 | 107.4 | 75.3 | 98.5 | 101.6 |
| Venezuela, RB | 87.0 | 104.2 | 107.5 | 72.8 | 95.3 | 98.2 |

*Source:* Wodon et al. (2001).

# TABLE SA.21: MAIN TAX BREAKS

| Sector | Types of Tax Breaks | Estimated Cost (% of GDP) |
|---|---|---|
| Mining | Reinvestment of profits; accelerated depreciation; agreements on tax stability; advanced recovery of IGV/IVM; reduced tariffs extended on capital good imports. | 0.4 |
| Hydrocarbons | Accelerated depreciation; agreements on tax stability; advance recovery of IGV/IVM; exemption of IGV/IPM and ISC for imports of inputs during exploration; exemption of IGV/IPM and ISC on fuel in three regions in the country. | 0.1 |
| Agriculture | Exemption of IR for small producers (50 UIT) and reduced tariffs of 15% for the sector; reinvestment of profits (up to 20%); accelerated depreciation for irrigation infrastructure; exoneration from IES; issuance of documents cancelling taxes for the imports of certain inputs and capital goods for agro-industry; IGV of 5% for rice producers. | 0.4 |
| Industry (forest and frontier) | Exoneration from IR for industrial enterprises; reinvestment of profits; exoneration from IGV/IPM and Peru-Colombia protocol duties; agreements on tax stability; reduced tariffs on capital good imports. | <0.05 |
| Housing | Exoneration of IGV/IPM on the first housing sale of less than $35,000; exemption of IGV on construction contracts and housing sales in the Amazonia. | <0.05 |
| Tourism and Hotels | Accelerated depreciation; exemption from IGV/IPM for services borrowed in favor of external operators. | <0.05 |
| Public Works and Concessions | Agreements on tax stability; advanced recovery of IGV/IPM; exemption from IES. | <0.05 |
| Education | Reinvestment of profits (up to 50%); accelerated depreciation; exemption from IGV/IPM; exemption from IES. | <0.05 |
| CETICOS | Exoneration of IR, IGV/IPM, ISC, tariffs; duties of 8% for local commercialization; exoneration of IES and other national and municipal taxes and tariffs. | 0.1 |
| Amazonia | Reduced IR tarif (0, 5, and 10%); reinvestment of profits; exemption from IGV/IPM; fiscal credit of 25 and 50% for IGV on sales in the interior; IES exemption. | 0.9 |
| Other Sectors | Agreements on tax stability. | <0.05 |
| **TOTAL** | | **2.0** |

*Source:* SUNAT, IMF calculations, IMF (2000).

# TABLE SA.22: ALTERNATIVE MEASURES FOR TAX REFORM BY SECTOR OR REGION

| Proposed Measures | Collection Impact (% of GDP) | Sector or Region the Privileges of which Will Be Affected |
|---|---|---|
| Eliminate exemption of goods in Appendix 1, of the IGV law | 0.25 | Agriculture |
| Eliminate exoneration to financial profits | 0.27 | Financial |
| Eliminate zero-rate tax regime in the Amazonia | 0.25 | Amazonia |
| Eliminate exoneration of IGV and ISC to fuels | 0.10 | Amazonia |
| Eliminate CETICOS regime | 0.13 | CETICOS |
| Unify income tax rates | 0.05 | Agriculture and Amazonia |

*Source:* Schenone (2002).

## TABLE SA.23A: LATIN AMERICA GENERAL GOVERNMENT'S TAX REVENUES, 1998 1/
Percent of GDP

| | Uruguay | Brazil | Argentina | Chile | Mexico | Colombia | Venezuela | Ecuador | Peru |
|---|---|---|---|---|---|---|---|---|---|
| TOTAL | 27.8 | 24.5 | 23.5 | 20.4 | 20.3 | 18.8 | 18.4 | 18.1 | 14.8 |
| Resources | 0 | na | na | 1.1 | 4.3 | 1.6 | 7.6 | 4.5 | 0.1 |
| Non-renewable 2/ | | | | | | | | | |
| Rest of Tax Revenues | 27.8 | 24.5 | 23.5 | 19.3 | 16 | 17.2 | 10.8 | 13.6 | 14.7 |
| Direct Taxes 3/ | 5.1 | 4.8 | 3.4 | 3.9 | 4.6 | 5.0 | 2.0 | 1.8 | 3.5 |
| Social Security | 6.5 | 5.1 | 4 | 1.5 | 1.7 | 3.4 | 0.7 | 2.2 | 1.7 |
| VAT | 8.5 | 8.4 | 7.1 | 8.9 | 3.3 | 4.5 | 4.3 | 4.2 | 6.1 |
| Special Taxes | 4 | 1.8 | 2.3 | 2.2 | 2.3 | 3.1 | 1.2 | 0.6 | 1.9 |
| Trade Taxes | 1.2 | 0.7 | 1.0 | 1.8 | 0.6 | 1.2 | 2 | 3.1 | 1.4 |
| Other Revenues | 2.5 | 3.7 | 5.7 | 1.0 | 3.5 | 0 | 0.6 | 1.7 | 0.1 |
| Memorandum: | | | | | | | | | |
| Productivity of VAT 4/ | 0.37 | na | 0.34 | 0.49 | 0.22 | 0.28 | 0.26 | 0.42 | 0.34 |

na = not applicable.
1/ Includes tax revenues and non-tax revenues of non-renewable resources. For Mexico and Peru, data is for 1999.
2/ Excludes VAT, tariffs, and special taxes on petrol derivatives. In Chile includes payments net of taxes by CODELCO (the state enterprise that extracts and exports copper) which is 0.4% of GDP; the estimated payments of the rest of the mining companies is about 0.7% of GDP.
3/ In Peru includes taxes a la planilla (IES).
4/ Collection as a percentage of GDP, divided by the legal rate.

Source: IMF.

## TABLE SA.23B: LATIN AMERICAN ECONOMIES: OUTLINE OF FISCAL POLICY RULES[1]

| Rule/Country | Effective Date | Coverage[2] | Basic Rule[3] | Escape Clause[3] | Additional Rule[3] | Statute[4] | Sanction[5] |
|---|---|---|---|---|---|---|---|
| **Budget Rule** | | | | | | | |
| Argentina | 2000 | NG[6] | OB/DL | CF | EL | L | J |
| Brazil | 2001 | NG, SG | CB | | WL | C, L | J |
| Colombia | 2001 | SG | CB | | WL | L | J |
| Ecuador | proposal | NG | OB | CF/MY | | L | J |
| Mexico | 1917 | SG | CB | | | C | R |
| Mexico | proposal | NG | OB | MY | | C | J |
| Peru | 2000 | NG | OB/DL | CF | EL | L | J |
| Venezuela | 2000 | NG | CB | CF/MY | TL | C, L | R |
| **Debt Rule** | | | | | | | |
| Brazil | 2001 | NG, SG | SL | | | C, L | J |
| Colombia | 1997 | SG | FL | | | L | F |
| Ecuador | proposal | NG, SG | PL | | | L | J |

1/ Encompasses permanent restrictions on aggregate fiscal performance indicators. Table excludes prohibition or limits on financing from specific sources, notably from the Central Bank.
2/ General government (GG), or limited to national (central, federal) government (NG) or subnational (including local) government (SG).
3/ Budget rules consist of overall balance (OB) or current balance (CB), subject to a prescribed limit on deficit (DL) as a proportion of GDP. An alternative rule calls for prohibition on domestic financing of deficits (DF). All these rules are applied on an annual basis, except if specified on a multiyear (MY) basis; alternatively, a contingency fund (CF) is provided in some cases. Additional rules consist of limits on total expenditure (TL), primary expenditure (EL), or wage bill (WL). Debt rules are specified as a debt limit for a given year (SL), permanently (PL), or on debt service (FL), as a proportion of GDP or of government revenue.
4/ Constitution (C), legal provision (L), or policy guideline (P).
5/ Sanctions for noncompliance: reputational (R), judicial (J), or financial (F).
6/ Refers to the national nonfinancial public sector.

*Source:* Kopits (2002).

TABLE SA.24:   ELASTICITIES OF SOCIAL SPENDING TO TOTAL SPENDING OF THE CONSOLIDATED PUBLIC SECTOR IN PERU (1997–2002) 1/

| Spending Category | Average Share of Total Spending | Elasticity to a Change in Total Public Spending | Level of Significance | Elasticity to an Increase in Total Public Spending (1998–2000) | Level of Significance | Point of Elasticity in 1998 | Point of Elasticity in 2001 |
|---|---|---|---|---|---|---|---|
| Planning and Administration | 25.7 | 2.05** | 0.05 | 1.82** | 0.05 | 3.76 | 1.43 |
| Pensions and Social Assistance | 21.46 | 1.37 | 0.16 | 1.43*** | 0.01 | 0.20 | -0.14 |
| Pensions | 16.57 | 1.32 | 0.31 | 1.44 | 0.17 | -0.56 | -0.13 |
| Social Assistance | 4.89 | 1.41 | 0.16 | 1.36 | 0.54 | 2.48 | -0.17 |
| Education | 15.56 | 0.92 | 0.22 | 0.84 | 0.13 | -0.13 | 0.61 |
| Pre-primary | 1.32 | 1.12 | 0.55 | 0.81 | 0.36 | -1.68 | 1.68 |
| Primary | 5.5 | 1.03* | 0.08 | 1.02 | 0.17 | 0.19 | 1.64 |
| Secondary | 4.08 | 1.21 | 0.18 | 0.99*** | 0.01 | 0.69 | 0.05 |
| Tertiary | 2.79 | 0.56 | 0.41 | 0.60 | 0.46 | -0.50 | 0.16 |
| Others | 1.86 | 0.68 | 0.94 | 0.15 | 0.75 | -1.26 | -1.17 |
| Health and Water | 8.47 | 0.74 | 0.36 | 0.67 | 0.13 | -0.18 | -0.47 |
| Water and Sewage | 0.78 | -0.24 | 0.94 | 0.55 | 0.71 | 1.18 | 8.73 |
| Healthcare | 7.69 | 0.77 | 0.51 | 0.64*** | 0.01 | -0.36 | -1.37 |
| Other /2 | 2.87 | 1.38 | 0.27 | 1.69** | 0.05 | -0.90 | 1.57 |
| **Total Social Expenditure** | **37.21** | **0.73**** | **0.04** | **0.63** | **0.19** | **0.75** | **0.39** |

* indicates significance at 10%; ** indicates significance at 5%; *** indicates significance at 1%.

1/ Estimate.

2/ Includes foreign relations, legislative, housing and urban development, industry commerce and services, fishing, communications, and employment.

*Source:*  Table SA.12a and WB Staff estimates.

## TABLE SA.25: DEGREE OF TRANSPARENCY IN THE PUBLICATION OF INSTITUTIONAL INFORMATION

| Type of Information | Published |
|---|---|
| **MEF** | |
| Consolidated Public Sector Balance | Available from 2002 |
| Revenues and Expenditures of the Central Government and Decentralized requests | Yes |
| Plans of the Budgetary Law, Indebtedness and Financial Equilibrium | Yes |
| Balance and Profile of the Domestic and External Public Debt | Yes |
| Disbursements and Amortizations of the Domestic and External Debt | Yes |
| Major Public Investment Plans of the 1,200 UITs | Yes |
| Balance of the Fiscal Stabilization Fund | Available from 2002 |
| Evaluation Results of Applicable Indicators | Available from 2002 |
| **FONAFE** | |
| Consolidated Budget | Yes |
| General Balance | Yes |
| Statement of Financial Audits | Available from 2002 |
| Progress Indicators to be applied | Yes |
| Results of the Evaluation of the Progress Indicators | Available from 2002 |
| **ONP** | |
| Financial Statement of the Fondo Consolidado de Reserva Previsional (FRC) audited by 2001 | Available from 2002 |
| Financial Statement of the Fondo Nacional de Ahorro Publico (FONAHPU) audited by 2001 | Available from 2002 |
| Financial Assets of FONAHPU and FRC invested | Yes |
| **CONSUCODE** | |
| Major Acquisitions and Contracting of the 50 UITs | Yes |

*Source:* MEF.


## TABLE SA.26: PUBLISHED INFORMATION OF THE BUDGET IN 2002

| | Ministries | CTARS | Superintendencies | Public Enterprises |
|---|---|---|---|---|
| Original Budget | 100% | 100% | 83% | 100% |
| Executed Budget | 100% | 100% | 83% | 100% |
| Economic Information on Investment Plans | 100% | 100% | 33% | 100% |
| Info on Contracting and Acquisitions | 63% | 88% | 33% | 25% |
| Strategic Plans | 100% | 0% | 83% | 100% |

*Source:* MEF.

TABLE SA.27:   COMPOSITE GOVERNANCE INDICATORS, INTERNATIONAL COMPARISONS, 1998
(Global rankings—lower is more positive)

| | Voice and Accountability | | Political Instability | | Government Effectiveness | | Regulatory Quality | | Rule of Law | | Corruption | |
|---|---|---|---|---|---|---|---|---|---|---|---|---|
| | 1998 | 2001 | 1998 | 2001 | 1998 | 2001 | 1998 | 2001 | 1998 | 2001 | 1998 | 2001 |
| **Peru** | **125** | **70** | **112** | **95** | **54** | **93** | **37** | **61** | **111** | **109** | **74** | **72** |
| Argentina | 59 | 56 | 48 | 51 | 48 | 66 | 38 | 70 | 59 | 66 | 81 | 88 |
| Bolivia | 63 | 67 | 88 | 122 | 84 | 101 | 22 | 39 | 98 | 100 | 96 | 119 |
| Brazil | 57 | 57 | 96 | 57 | 83 | 89 | 88 | 84 | 88 | 87 | 56 | 70 |
| Chile | 54 | 52 | 51 | 30 | 23 | 23 | 18 | 13 | 24 | 24 | 25 | 17 |
| Colombia | 91 | 112 | 141 | 149 | 74 | 95 | 69 | 93 | 129 | 132 | 103 | 89 |
| Ecuador | 66 | 92 | 109 | 131 | 111 | 129 | 61 | 95 | 122 | 130 | 125 | 140 |
| Mexico | 90 | 73 | 101 | 81 | 52 | 59 | 42 | 46 | 108 | 101 | 82 | 82 |
| Venezuela | 68 | 106 | 93 | 100 | 133 | 124 | 92 | 115 | 118 | 136 | 116 | 107 |
| *No. of Countries* | *173* | *173* | *155* | *161* | *156* | *159* | *166* | *169* | *166* | *170* | *155* | *161* |
| **LAC Median** | **64** | **60** | **91** | **69** | **84** | **87** | **46** | **66** | **105** | **98** | **87** | **86** |
| Peru Rank in LAC | 25/26 | 17/26 | 20/24 | 17/25 | 8/24 | 16/25 | 10/26 | 13/26 | 15/26 | 16/26 | 10/24 | 9/25 |

*Source:* Kaufmann, Kraay, and Zoido-Lobáton (January 2002).

## TABLE SA.28: VOLATILITY IN LATIN AMERICA
### (Standard deviations of growth rates by decade, percent)

| Country | GDP | | PRIVATE | |
|---|---|---|---|---|
| | 1980s | 1990s | 1980s | 1990s |
| Argentina | 5.6 | 5.5 | 5.9 | 5.7 |
| Bolivia | 2.9 | 1.0 | 3.3 | 0.5 |
| Brazil | 4.6 | 3.0 | 4.4 | 4.9 |
| Chile | 6.4 | 3.5 | 9.4 | 3.4 |
| Colombia | 1.5 | 3.3 | 1.2 | 1.9 |
| Costa Rica | 4.5 | 2.4 | 6.1 | 3.2 |
| Dominican Republic | 2.7 | 4.4 | 4.5 | 8.7 |
| Ecuador | 4.5 | 3.4 | 2.5 | 0.3 |
| El Salvador | 5.7 | 1.9 | 6.0 | 6.9 |
| Guatemala | 2.7 | 0.8 | 2.4 | 1.0 |
| Honduras | 2.5 | 2.5 | 3.1 | 1.9 |
| Haiti | 2.9 | 6.4 | 4.4 | – |
| Jamaica | 4.3 | 2.2 | 7.6 | 16.5 |
| Mexico | 4.4 | 3.6 | 4.9 | 5.1 |
| Nicaragua | 5.4 | 2.3 | 15.8 | 14.4 |
| Panama | 6.5 | 2.6 | 11.3 | 10.2 |
| **Peru** | **8.4** | **5.2** | **8.3** | **4.6** |
| Paraguay | 5.3 | 1.5 | 11.2 | 12.5 |
| Trinidad and Tobago | 5.7 | 6.8 | 14.0 | 17.6 |
| Uruguay | 6.6 | 2.8 | 9.4 | 5.4 |
| Venezuela | 4.8 | 5.0 | 3.5 | 4.7 |
| Unweighted average | 4.7 | 3.3 | 6.6 | 6.5 |
| Overall median | 4.6 | 3.0 | 5.9 | 5.0 |
| Weighted average | 4.6 | 3.5 | 4.9 | 4.7 |

Source: WB staff estimates.

# TABLE SA.29: ECONOMIC DISTRIBUTION OF GENERAL GOVERNMENT REVENUE AND EXPENDITURE, SELECTED COUNTRIES

| | Bolivia (1998) | Argentina (1998) | Brazil (1997) | Chile (1997) | Colombia (1997) | Costa Rica (1997) | Guatemala (1997) | Mexico (1997) | Panama (1997) | Paraguay (1997) | Peru (2001) | Venezuela (1997) | LAC (85–99) |
|---|---|---|---|---|---|---|---|---|---|---|---|---|---|
| **Percent of GDP** | | | | | | | | | | | | | |
| Total Revenue | 24.0 | 19.4 | 29.2 | 25.6 | 27.4 | 24.8 | 11.5 | na | na | 18.7 | 14.2 | 32.2 | |
| Tax revenue | 19.0 | 17.8 | 24.5 | 19.7 | 19.7 | 23.5 | 8.9 | na | 16.1 | 11.8 | 11.8 | 10.2 | |
| Total Expenditure | 27.4 | 21.9 | 29.3 | 23.4 | 26.7 | 28.0 | 12.9 | 22.8 | 26.8 | 20.2 | 16.8 | 30.3 | 20.4 |
| Current Expenditure | 21.7 | 20.2 | 26.8 | 19.0 | 18.6 | 25.6 | 8.1 | 19.1 | 23.0 | 14.8 | 14.6 | 21.8 | 17.6 |
| Interest | 1.9 | 1.9 | 2.5 | 0.6 | 3.0 | 5.3 | 0.9 | 4.3 | 3.1 | 0.5 | 2.1 | 2.9 | 3.6 |
| Other | 7.1 | 1.6 | 8.4 | 8.4 | 2.1 | 0.8 | 1.8 | – | – | 2.0 | 3.7 | 0.8 | 3.7 |
| Transfers | 4.1 | 4.4 | 1.0 | 5.3 | 6.9 | 3.4 | 2.1 | 6.7 | 1.7 | 0.5 | 3.3 | 3.2 | 4.0 |
| Wages and Salaries | 8.3 | 7.3 | 11.9 | 4.5 | 6.6 | 5.8 | 3.4 | 2.6 | 10.2 | 8.5 | 6.6 | 4.2 | 6.3 |
| Capital Expenditure | 6.0 | 1.7 | 2.5 | 4.4 | 7.8 | 2.4 | 4.8 | 3.7 | 3.8 | 5.4 | 2.2 | 8.5 | 3.0 |
| **Percent of total** | | | | | | | | | | | | | |
| Total Revenue | 100.0 | 100.0 | 100.0 | 100.0 | 100.0 | 100.0 | 100.0 | 100.0 | 100.0 | 100.0 | 100.0 | 100.0 | 100.0 |
| Tax revenue | 79.2 | 91.8 | 83.9 | 77.0 | 71.8 | 94.8 | 77.4 | – | – | 63.1 | 87.4 | 31.7 | |
| Total Expenditure | 100.0 | 100.0 | 100.0 | 100.0 | 100.0 | 100.0 | 100.0 | 100.0 | 100.0 | 100.0 | 100.0 | 100.0 | 100.0 |
| Current Expenditure | 79.2 | 92.2 | 91.5 | 81.2 | 69.5 | 91.4 | 62.8 | 83.9 | 85.8 | 73.3 | 84.5 | 71.9 | 86.3 |
| Interest | 6.9 | 8.7 | 8.5 | 2.6 | 11.4 | 18.9 | 7.0 | 18.9 | 11.7 | 2.5 | 10.9 | 9.6 | 15.6 |
| Other | 25.9 | 7.2 | 28.7 | 35.9 | 8.1 | 2.9 | 14.0 | – | – | 9.9 | 21.5 | 2.6 | 16.1 |
| Transfers | 15.0 | 20.1 | 3.4 | 22.6 | 25.7 | 12.1 | 15.9 | 29.4 | 6.3 | 2.5 | 13.0 | 10.6 | 16.1 |
| Wages and Salaries | 30.3 | 33.3 | 40.6 | 19.2 | 24.7 | 20.7 | 26.0 | 11.6 | 38.1 | 42.1 | 39.1 | 13.9 | 33.6 |
| Capital Expenditure | 21.9 | 7.8 | 8.5 | 18.8 | 29.3 | 8.6 | 37.2 | 16.1 | 14.2 | 26.7 | 13.6 | 28.1 | 14.3 |

Note: Data corresponds to the central government

Source: World Bank Bolivia PER, Staff estimates.

TABLE SA.30: DISTRIBUTION OF SOCIAL INVESTMENT BY DIFFERENT SOCIAL PROGRAMS AND BY DECILE OF POVERTY SEVERITY

| Decile | Population 2001 | Investment (S/.), 2001 | | | Amount US$ | Assigned |
| --- | --- | --- | --- | --- | --- | --- |
| | | PRONAA | FONCODES* | VASO DE LECHE | RURAL ROADS** | PESP-URBANO |
| Poorest | 2,636,584 | 21,976,075 | 93,159,772 | 39,915,361 | 53,932,215 | 0.035 |
| Decile 2 | 2,616,108 | 20,682,281 | 69,530,728 | 37,123,636 | 40,256,685 | 0.018 |
| Decile 3 | 2,645,999 | 18,493,705 | 39,663,491 | 33,902,357 | 34,483,305 | 0.049 |
| Decile 4 | 2,645,123 | 12,976,223 | 16,299,443 | 31,566,264 | 21,225,735 | 0.178 |
| Decile 5 | 2,631,770 | 12,823,801 | 8,013,721 | 30,507,673 | 8,081,100 | 0.190 |
| Decile 6 | 2,655,524 | 19,120,704 | 3,451,029 | 35,518,612 | 1,785,900 | 0.150 |
| Decile 7 | 2,655,539 | 18,153,031 | 1,974,642 | 38,062,931 | 240,000 | 0.143 |
| Decile 8 | 2,607,142 | 13,421,899 | 1,577,795 | 39,703,391 | 160,200 | 0.118 |
| Decile 9 | 2,616,694 | 9,699,637 | 3,983,925 | 29,057,248 | 1,528,755 | 0.085 |
| Least poor | 2,636,362 | 6,675,466 | 3,025,690 | 16,889,527 | – | 0.035 |
| TOTAL | 26,346,845 | 154,022,822 | 240,680,236 | 332,247,000 | 161,693,895 | 1.000 |
| **Percent** | | | | | | |
| Poorest | 10 | 14.27 | 38.71 | 12.01 | 33.35 | 3.50 |
| Decile 2 | 10 | 13.43 | 28.89 | 11.17 | 24.90 | 1.80 |
| Decile 3 | 10 | 12.01 | 16.48 | 10.20 | 21.33 | 4.85 |
| Decile 4 | 10 | 8.42 | 6.77 | 9.50 | 13.13 | 17.75 |
| Decile 5 | 10 | 8.33 | 3.33 | 9.18 | 5.00 | 19.00 |
| Decile 6 | 10 | 12.41 | 1.43 | 10.69 | 1.10 | 15.00 |
| Decile 7 | 10 | 11.79 | 0.82 | 11.46 | 0.15 | 14.30 |
| Decile 8 | 10 | 8.71 | 0.66 | 11.95 | 0.10 | 11.80 |
| Decile 9 | 10 | 6.30 | 1.66 | 8.75 | 0.95 | 8.50 |
| Least poor | 10 | 4.33 | 1.26 | 5.08 | – | 3.50 |
| TOTAL | 100 | 100 | 100 | 100 | 100 | 100 |

*Includes the PESP-RURAL.
**Accumulated to 2001. Preliminary date. (Estimation based on US$ 15,000/km.)

Source: INEI.

**TABLE SA.31A:  AVERAGE MONTHLY PER CAPITA INCOME OF HOUSEHOLDS, 2000 (US$)**

| Geographic Area | Total | I | II | III | IV | V | VI | VII | VIII | XI | X |
|---|---|---|---|---|---|---|---|---|---|---|---|
| TOTAL | 95.8 | 13.7 | 25.0 | 34.7 | 44.6 | 53.9 | 64.3 | 81.1 | 103.9 | 151.6 | 385.4 |
| Urban | 129.1 | 18.6 | 35.7 | 48.1 | 60.7 | 72.9 | 86.3 | 108.4 | 139.9 | 203.2 | 518.2 |
| Rural | 38.1 | 4.5 | 7.9 | 11.5 | 16.4 | 20.6 | 25.9 | 33.3 | 42.2 | 61.6 | 156.8 |

*Source:* Diaz (2001) based on ENAHO 2000-II.

**TABLE SA.31B:  HOUSEHOLD ACCESS TO SOCIAL PROGRAMS BY INCOME PER CAPITA DECILES, 2000**
Percent of Total

| Geographic Area | Total | I | II | III | IV | V | VI | VII | VIII | XI | X |
|---|---|---|---|---|---|---|---|---|---|---|---|
| Total | 5,632,815 | 7.4 | 8.6 | 8.9 | 9.1 | 9.0 | 9.6 | 9.8 | 11.0 | 12.1 | 14.5 |
| Beneficiaries | 3,330,760 | 10.6 | 12.2 | 11.9 | 11.1 | 10.0 | 10.6 | 9.9 | 8.7 | 8.3 | 6.8 |
| Non-beneficiaries | 2,302,055 | 2.7 | 3.4 | 4.6 | 6.4 | 7.5 | 8.1 | 9.6 | 14.3 | 17.7 | 25.6 |
| Urban | 3,607,764 | 7.8 | 8.5 | 9.0 | 9.3 | 8.9 | 9.5 | 10.4 | 11.3 | 12.2 | 13.1 |
| Beneficiaries | 184,157 | 12.2 | 13.9 | 13.6 | 11.6 | 10.8 | 10.2 | 10.7 | 7.3 | 6.1 | 3.7 |
| Non-beneficiaries | 1,773,607 | 3.2 | 2.9 | 4.1 | 7.0 | 7.0 | 8.7 | 10.1 | 15.4 | 18.6 | 22.9 |
| Rural | 2,025,051 | 6.7 | 8.8 | 8.8 | 8.8 | 9.1 | 9.8 | 8.6 | 10.5 | 12.0 | 16.8 |
| Beneficiaries | 1,496,602 | 8.7 | 10.1 | 9.8 | 10.4 | 9.0 | 11.2 | 8.9 | 10.4 | 10.9 | 10.5 |
| Non-beneficiaries | 528,449 | 1.0 | 5.1 | 6.0 | 4.3 | 9.2 | 6.1 | 7.8 | 10.6 | 14.9 | 34.8 |

*Source:* Diaz (2001) based on ENAHO 2000-II.

**TABLE SA.31C:  HOUSEHOLD ACCESS TO SOCIAL PROGRAMS BY INCOME PER CAPITA DECILES, 2000**
Percent of Subtotal

| Geographic Area | Total | I | II | III | IV | V | VI | VII | VIII | XI | X |
|---|---|---|---|---|---|---|---|---|---|---|---|
| Monthly Income/ Capita US$ | 95.8 | 13.7 | 25.0 | 34.7 | 44.6 | 53.9 | 64.3 | 81.1 | 103.9 | 151.6 | 385.4 |
| Total | 100.0 | 100.0 | 100.0 | 100.0 | 100.0 | 100.0 | 100.0 | 100.0 | 100.0 | 100.0 | 100.0 |
| Beneficiaries | 59.1 | 85.2 | 83.8 | 79.1 | 71.6 | 65.8 | 65.4 | 59.8 | 46.8 | 40.2 | 27.6 |
| Non-beneficiaries | 40.9 | 14.8 | 16.2 | 20.9 | 28.4 | 34.2 | 34.6 | 40.2 | 53.2 | 59.8 | 72.4 |
| Urban | 100.0 | 100.0 | 100.0 | 100.0 | 100.0 | 100.0 | 100.0 | 100.0 | 100.0 | 100.0 | 100.0 |
| Beneficiaries | 50.8 | 79.9 | 83.2 | 77.3 | 63.3 | 61.4 | 54.6 | 52.2 | 32.8 | 25.3 | 14.3 |
| Non-beneficiaries | 49.2 | 20.1 | 16.8 | 22.7 | 36.7 | 38.6 | 45.4 | 47.8 | 67.2 | 74.7 | 85.7 |
| Rural | 100.0 | 100.0 | 100.0 | 100.0 | 100.0 | 100.0 | 100.0 | 100.0 | 100.0 | 100.0 | 100.0 |
| Beneficiaries | 73.9 | 96.0 | 84.8 | 82.3 | 87.2 | 73.4 | 83.7 | 76.2 | 73.6 | 67.5 | 46.1 |
| Non-beneficiaries | 26.1 | 4.0 | 15.2 | 17.7 | 12.8 | 26.6 | 16.3 | 23.8 | 26.4 | 32.5 | 53.9 |

*Source:* Diaz (2001) based on ENAHO 2000-II.

### TABLE SA.32: MISTARGETING BY TYPES OF FOOD ASSISTANCE, 2000

| Social Program | No. of Beneficiaries | Total | Poverty Extreme | Not Extreme | Total | Non-Poor |
|---|---|---|---|---|---|---|
| **TOTAL** | | | | | | |
| Desayuno Escolar | 2,972,859 | 100.0 | 51.1 | 18.7 | 69.8 | 30.2 |
| Vaso de Leche | 2,283,919 | 100.0 | 40.1 | 24.1 | 64.2 | 35.8 |
| Comedor Popular | 746,134 | 100.0 | 40.2 | 14.5 | 54.7 | 45.3 |
| **URBAN** | | | | | | |
| Desayuno Escolar | 1,000,349 | 100.0 | 21.3 | 34.5 | 55.9 | 44.1 |
| Vaso de Leche | 1,104,018 | 100.0 | 15.7 | 34.6 | 50.2 | 49.8 |
| Comedor Popular | 363,769 | 100.0 | 18.3 | 18.6 | 36.9 | 63.1 |
| **RURAL** | | | | | | |
| Desayuno Escolar | 1,972,510 | 100.0 | 66.2 | 10.7 | 76.9 | 23.1 |
| Vaso de Leche | 1,179,901 | 100.0 | 63.0 | 14.2 | 77.2 | 22.8 |
| Comedor Popular | 382,365 | 100.0 | 61.1 | 10.6 | 71.7 | 28.3 |

*Source:* Diaz (2001) based on ENAHO 2000-II.

### TABLE SA.33: MISTARGETING BY TYPES OF HEALTH PROGRAMS, 2000

| Social Program | No. of Beneficiaries | Total | Poverty Extreme | Not Extreme | Total | Non-Poor |
|---|---|---|---|---|---|---|
| **TOTAL** | | | | | | |
| Regulating child growth | 1,729,899 | 100.0 | 33.7 | 18.4 | 52.1 | 47.9 |
| School health insurance | 1,157,912 | 100.0 | 36.8 | 20.6 | 57.4 | 42.6 |
| Family planning | 870,947 | 100.0 | 22.1 | 24.8 | 46.8 | 53.2 |
| **URBAN** | | | | | | |
| Regulating child growth | 908,742 | 100.0 | 9.2 | 24.5 | 33.7 | 66.3 |
| School health insurance | 636,888 | 100.0 | 15.8 | 31.6 | 47.4 | 52.6 |
| Family planning | 585,964 | 100.0 | 11.7 | 26.0 | 37.7 | 62.3 |
| **RURAL** | | | | | | |
| Regulating child growth | 821,157 | 100.0 | 60.8 | 11.8 | 72.5 | 27.5 |
| School health insurance | 521,024 | 100.0 | 62.5 | 7.1 | 69.6 | 30.4 |
| Family planning | 284,984 | 100.0 | 43.4 | 22.3 | 65.6 | 34.4 |

*Source:* Diaz (2001) based on ENAHO 2000-II.

## TABLE SA.34: MISTARGETING BY TYPES OF EDUCATION PROGRAMS, 2000

| Social Program | No. of Beneficiaries | Total | Poverty Extreme | Not Extreme | Total | Non-Poor |
|---|---|---|---|---|---|---|
| TOTAL | | | | | | |
| Regulating child growth | 1,729,899 | 100.0 | 33.7 | 18.4 | 52.1 | 47.9 |
| TOTAL | | | | | | |
| School text and materials | 2,970,567 | 100.0 | 44.4 | 19.7 | 64.1 | 35.9 |
| URBAN | | | | | | |
| School text and materials | 1,513,755 | 100.0 | 22.3 | 28.7 | 51.0 | 49.0 |
| RURAL | | | | | | |
| School text and materials | 1,456,812 | 100.0 | 67.3 | 10.4 | 77.6 | 22.4 |

Source: Diaz (2001) based on ENAHO 2000-II.

## TABLE SA.35: EVOLUTION OF HOUSEHOLD ACCESS TO SOCIAL PROGRAMS, 1998–2000

| | 1998 thousands | 1999 thousands | 2000 thousands | Var. % 99/98 | 2000/99 | 2000/98 |
|---|---|---|---|---|---|---|
| TOTAL | 5,408 | 5,490 | 5,633 | 1.5 | 2.6 | 4.2 |
| Beneficiaries | 2,848 | 3,279 | 3,331 | 15.1 | 1.6 | 17.0 |
| One program | 1,004 | 937 | 755 | −6.7 | −19.3 | −24.8 |
| More than one | 1,843 | 2,342 | 2,575 | 27.1 | 10.0 | 39.7 |
| Non-beneficiaries | 2,561 | 2,211 | 2,302 | −13.6 | 4.1 | −10.1 |
| URBAN | 3,546 | 3,572 | 3,608 | 0.7 | 1.0 | 1.7 |
| Beneficiaries | 1,624 | 1,915 | 1,834 | 17.9 | −4.2 | 12.9 |
| One program | 669 | 633 | 536 | −5.4 | −15.3 | −19.8 |
| More than one | 955 | 1,282 | 1,298 | 34.2 | 1.2 | 35.8 |
| Non-beneficiaries | 1,921 | 1,657 | 1,774 | −13.7 | 7.0 | −7.7 |
| RURAL | 1,863 | 1,918 | 2,025 | 3.0 | 5.6 | 8.7 |
| Beneficiaries | 1,223 | 1,364 | 1,497 | 11.5 | 9.7 | 22.3 |
| One program | 335 | 304 | 219 | −9.4 | −27.9 | −34.7 |
| More than one | 888 | 1,060 | 1,278 | 19.4 | 20.5 | 43.9 |
| Non-beneficiaries | 639 | 554 | 528 | −13.3 | −4.6 | −17.3 |

Source: Diaz (2001) based on ENAHO 2000-II.

## TABLE SA.36: ANNUAL PRIVATE EXPENDITURE ON EDUCATION BY PER CAPITA INCOME DECILE, 2000
By type and level of education attending, Millions of US$

| Education Level | Total | Deciles of Per Capita Income | | | | | | | | | |
|---|---|---|---|---|---|---|---|---|---|---|---|
| | | I | II | III | IV | V | VI | VII | VIII | XI | X |
| TOTAL | 4445.4 | 2.0 | 2.4 | 2.5 | 3.6 | 5.7 | 5.5 | 7.6 | 10.3 | 16.8 | 43.5 |
| Initial | 459.7 | 0.9 | 1.6 | 0.9 | 2.5 | 3.9 | 1.1 | 1.3 | 7.4 | 14.6 | 65.8 |
| Primary | 967.1 | 4.5 | 3.5 | 5.2 | 4.7 | 3.6 | 6.4 | 7.2 | 13.4 | 10.5 | 41.0 |
| Secondary | 762.1 | 3.3 | 3.0 | 4.1 | 3.7 | 9.0 | 11.9 | 8.7 | 12.6 | 15.1 | 28.5 |
| Bachillerato | 6.1 | 24.8 | 7.9 | 5.8 | 10.2 | 4.9 | | 11.9 | 8.4 | 26.1 | 0.0 |
| Supplemental Non-Univ. | 588.4 | 1.3 | 3.0 | 2.9 | 6.0 | 3.6 | 5.7 | 19.7 | 11.3 | 23.6 | 23.0 |
| Supplemental Univ. | 1476 | 0.4 | 1.8 | 0.7 | 2.8 | 4.6 | 3.6 | 5.4 | 8.5 | 21.1 | 51.2 |
| Post-graduate | 185.9 | | | | | 23.5 | | | 3.6 | 6.1 | 66.8 |
| PUBLIC | 1099 | 5.3 | 5.7 | 7.0 | 8.1 | 6.5 | 10.1 | 9.5 | 10.3 | 17.5 | 20.0 |
| Initial | 53.6 | 3.5 | 13.4 | 4.3 | 6.9 | 9.7 | 5.0 | 7.0 | 14.8 | 18.9 | 16.6 |
| Primary | 298.7 | 11.0 | 10.8 | 11.3 | 9.2 | 7.1 | 9.7 | 8.3 | 13.9 | 8.3 | 10.4 |
| Secondary | 260.8 | 7.7 | 6.3 | 11.3 | 7.2 | 10.5 | 15.2 | 9.5 | 10.8 | 13.2 | 8.5 |
| Bachillerato | 6.1 | 24.8 | 7.9 | 5.8 | 10.2 | 4.9 | | 11.9 | 8.4 | 26.1 | 0.0 |
| Supplemental Non-Univ. | 98.6 | 2.3 | 2.3 | 5.1 | 10.7 | 8.0 | 10.2 | 31.0 | 15.2 | 12.6 | 2.5 |
| Supplemental Univ. | 286.8 | | 1.4 | 2.1 | 9.8 | 3.2 | 10.5 | 6.9 | 4.6 | 37.2 | 24.3 |
| Post-graduate | 94.5 | | | | | | | | 7.0 | 3.0 | 90.0 |
| PRIVATE | 3346.3 | 0.9 | 1.4 | 1.1 | 2.2 | 5.5 | 4.0 | 7.0 | 10.3 | 16.5 | 51.2 |
| Initial | 406.1 | 0.6 | 0.0 | 0.4 | 1.9 | 3.1 | 0.6 | 0.6 | 6.5 | 14.0 | 72.3 |
| Primary | 668.4 | 1.6 | 0.2 | 2.5 | 2.7 | 2.1 | 4.9 | 6.7 | 13.2 | 11.5 | 54.7 |
| Secondary | 501.3 | 1.1 | 1.3 | 0.4 | 2.0 | 8.2 | 10.1 | 8.4 | 13.6 | 16.0 | 38.9 |
| Supplemental Univ. | 489.8 | 1.0 | 3.1 | 2.4 | 5.1 | 2.7 | 4.8 | 17.5 | 10.4 | 25.8 | 27.2 |
| Supplemental Non-Univ. | 1189.3 | 0.5 | 1.9 | 0.4 | 1.1 | 4.9 | 1.9 | 5.1 | 9.4 | 17.2 | 57.7 |
| Post-graduate | 91.4 | | | | | 47.9 | | | | 9.4 | 42.8 |

Note: Exchange rate of US$1=Nuevo Soles 3.50.
Source: Diaz (2001) based on ENAHO 2000-II.

## TABLE SA.37: ANNUAL EXPENDITURE ON HEALTH BY PER CAPITA INCOME DECILE
By place of consultation, Millions of US$ and respective percentage of total

| Place of Treatment | Total | I | II | III | IV | V | VI | VII | VIII | XI | X |
|---|---|---|---|---|---|---|---|---|---|---|---|
| Total Expenditure | 742 | 2.6 | 5.7 | 8.8 | 6.0 | 7.0 | 7.6 | 10.9 | 11.2 | 13.2 | 27.1 |
| Puesto, Central Minsa | 137 | 5.4 | 16.5 | 8.7 | 11.3 | 9.6 | 9.0 | 11.7 | 11.4 | 13.4 | 3.0 |
| Posta, Policlinico IPSS | 16 | 0.2 | 20.3 | 5.5 | 1.9 | 0.7 | 7.9 | 0.4 | 48.3 | 9.0 | 5.9 |
| Hospital MINSA | 196 | 3.4 | 6.5 | 21.5 | 4.7 | 10.5 | 8.9 | 15.9 | 10.1 | 4.3 | 14.3 |
| Hospital ESSALUD | 58 | 0.3 | 0.9 | 4.1 | 5.4 | 5.2 | 13.6 | 5.0 | 8.2 | 23.1 | 34.2 |
| Hospital FF.AA. Policia Nac. | 27 | 3.0 | 0.2 | 0.7 | 1.0 | 0.2 | 4.4 | 0.0 | 15.0 | 18.7 | 56.7 |
| Consultorio Medico Part. | 148 | 0.7 | 8.0 | 0.5 | 5.3 | 5.1 | 6.1 | 15.3 | 13.0 | 20.2 | 25.8 |
| Various clinics | 146 | 1.1 | 0.4 | 2.6 | 3.1 | 3.4 | 0.6 | 2.5 | 9.3 | 11.1 | 65.8 |
| Pharmacy | 18 | 6.0 | 7.6 | 14.6 | 13.1 | 9.8 | 8.6 | 16.8 | 6.3 | 7.5 | 9.6 |
| Home | 23 | 2.7 | 2.2 | 8.5 | 0.1 | 1.4 | 9.3 | 21.5 | 22.9 | 18.2 | 13.1 |
| Indigenous treatment | 12 | 2.9 | 7.0 | 7.6 | 2.4 | 15.8 | 9.9 | 6.6 | 9.0 | 34.1 | 4.7 |
| Others | 20 | 0.7 | 5.6 | 1.9 | 23.4 | 11.0 | 13.2 | 17.5 | 3.8 | 8.3 | 14.7 |
| Self-treatment | 38 | 1.1 | 7.5 | 5.6 | 1.4 | 17.0 | 10.7 | 7.4 | 4.6 | 27.6 | 17.1 |

Source: Diaz (2001) based on ENAHO 2000-II.

## TABLE SA.38: DEFINITIONS OF THE CONSOLIDATED PUBLIC SECTOR (CPS)

**Consolidated Public Sector**

| | |
|---|---|
| Ministries, Regional Governments, Public Institutions, Universities and ONP (without funds) | General Government |
| Organized Supervisors of Special Funds (FCR, FEF, FONAHPU and Fondo Mivivienda), Beneficiary Societies | |
| ESSALUD, Public companies, Regulatory bodies | Rest of Public Sector |
| Local government and their companies | Local Government |

Source: MEF.

## TABLE SA.39: CENTRAL GOVERNMENT NATIONAL AND REGIONAL BUDGET COMPOSITION, 2002

| I. Current and Capital Expenditures | | | 61% |
|---|---|---|---|
| **National** | **Mln NS** | **Regional** | **Mln NS** |
| Congress | 265 | Amazonas | 250 |
| CNM | 9 | Ancash | 637 |
| General Comptroller | 53 | Apurimac | 448 |
| Defense | 2,226 | Arequipa | 583 |
| Public Defense | 18 | Ayacucho | 411 |
| Economy and Finance | 1,688 | Cajamarca | 618 |
| Interior | 2,117 | Callao | 225 |
| JNE | 12 | Cusco | 666 |
| Justice | 341 | Huancavelica | 322 |
| Public Ministry | 228 | Huánuco | 381 |
| ONPE | 13 | Ica | 325 |
| Judicial Power | 467 | Junín | 526 |
| PCM | 260 | La Libertad | 530 |
| RENIEC | 90 | Lambayeque | 397 |
| Exterior Relations | 616 | Lima | 2,408 |
| Constitutional Tribunal | 10 | Loreto | 520 |
| National Administration | 1,220 | Madre de Dios | 100 |
| | | Moquegua | 121 |
| | | Pasco | 160 |
| | | Piura | 739 |
| | | Puno | 713 |
| | | San Martín | 452 |
| | | Tacna | 200 |
| | | Tumbes | 167 |
| | | Ucayali | 256 |
| **TOTAL** | **9633** | **TOTAL** | **12,152** |
| | **Mlns US$** | | **Mlns US$** |
| Current expenditure | 2,468 | Current expenditure | 2,342 |
| Capital expenditure | 253 | Capital expenditure | 1,091 |
| | 44% | | 56% |
| **II. Structural Obligation** | **Mlns US$** | | **39%** |
| Debt Service | 2,200 | | |
| Previsional obligations | 1,752 | | |

*Source:* MEF.

## TABLE SA.40: MAIN REVENUE SOURCES FOR MUNICIPALITIES, 2002

| | NS | Percent |
|---|---|---|
| **Total General** | 1865 | 100 |
| **Current Revenues** | 1835 | 90 |
| **Taxes** | 520 | 28 |
| Capital | 433 | |
| Production/Consumption | 41 | |
| Others | 45 | |
| **Rates** | 834 | 45 |
| General Administration | 34 | |
| Education | 6 | |
| Health | 308 | |
| Housing and Construction | 131 | |
| Agroindustry and Mineral Resources | 1 | |
| Industry, Mining, and Commerce | 67 | |
| Tranport and Communications | 149 | |
| Others | 138 | |
| **Contributions** | 12 | 1 |
| For Pensions | 1 | |
| For Public Works | 7 | |
| Others | 3 | |
| **Sale of Goods** | 56 | 3 |
| Agroindustry and Mineral Resources | 25 | |
| Industries | 22 | |
| Transport, Communication and Storage | 0.1 | |
| Education, Recreation, and Culture | 0.1 | |
| Health | 2 | |
| Others | 7 | |
| **Service Contributions** | 115 | 6 |
| Transport, Communication and Storage | 10 | |
| Education, Recreation, and Culture | 3 | |
| Health | 15 | |
| Others | 86 | |
| **Property Income** | 99 | 5 |
| Real Estate | 90 | |
| Financial | 1 | |
| Others | 8 | |
| **Fines, Sanctions and Others** | 199 | 11 |
| Fines | 135 | |
| Sanctions | 54 | |
| Others | 11 | |
| **Capital Revenues** | 30 | 2 |
| **Sale of Assets** | 30 | 2 |
| Buildings (except land) | 7 | |
| Urban and rural land | 15 | |
| Vehicles, Equipment and Machines (used) | 0.3 | |
| Others | 8 | |

*Source:* MEF.

## TABLE SA.41: DEPARTMENTAL BUDGET—EDUCATION AND HEALTH BY EXPENDITURE CATEGORY, 2002
Millions of NS

| Department | Education | Health |
|---|---|---|
| **Regional Distribution (Percent)** | | |
| Lima | 34.4 | 50.9 |
| Puno | 4.9 | 3.9 |
| Piura | 4.7 | 3.8 |
| Loreto | 4.4 | 3.6 |
| La Libertad | 4.3 | 3.6 |
| Cusco | 4.3 | 3.5 |
| Cajamarca | 4.3 | 2.9 |
| Arequipa | 4.2 | 2.8 |
| Ancash | 4.2 | 2.7 |
| Junin | 4.1 | 2.6 |
| Lambayeque | 3.0 | 2.3 |
| Ayacucho | 2.8 | 2.0 |
| Ica | 2.8 | 1.9 |
| San Martin | 2.5 | 1.9 |
| Huanuco | 2.5 | 1.7 |
| Ucayali | 1.8 | 1.6 |
| Huancavelica | 1.8 | 1.4 |
| Apurimac | 1.6 | 1.4 |
| Amazonas | 1.4 | 1.2 |
| Pasco | 1.4 | 1.1 |
| Tacna | 1.4 | 0.9 |
| Tumbes | 1.3 | 0.7 |
| Moquegua | 0.8 | 0.6 |
| Callao | 0.7 | 0.5 |
| Madre de Dios | 0.4 | 0.5 |
| TOTAL | 100 | 100 |
| **By Expenditure Category (Mlns NS)** | | |
| Goods and Services | 892.1 | 1510.0 |
| Investment | 576.6 | 461.6 |
| Personal and Social Obligations | 4388.4 | 1076.7 |
| Others | 210.0 | 279.8 |
| TOTAL | 6067.2 | 3328.1 |
| **By Expenditure Category (Percent)** | | |
| Goods and Services | 14.7 | 45.4 |
| Investment | 9.5 | 13.9 |
| Personal and Social Obligations | 72.3 | 32.4 |
| Others | 3.5 | 8.4 |
| TOTAL | 100.0 | 100.0 |

Source: MEF.

## TABLE SA.42: INDEXES ON CORRUPTION

| Agency | Trans-parency | Rules | Enforce-ment | Merit | Political | Wage Satis-faction | Voice | Mission |
|---|---|---|---|---|---|---|---|---|
| Consejo Sup. | 69.5 | 71.7 | 72.0 | 60.4 | 16.4 | 60.4 | 79.1 | 68.2 |
| Corte Suprema | 41.4 | 56.5 | 69.7 | 58.5 | 33.7 | 19.3 | 67.3 | 68.7 |
| Corte Superior | 42.2 | 57.4 | 55.2 | 53.9 | 46.9 | 25.0 | 70.3 | 60.8 |
| Juzgados | 41.6 | 54.4 | 61.3 | 60.6 | 41.6 | 19.4 | 60.6 | 69.7 |
| Jueces de Paz | 21.0 | 68.5 | 75.3 | 67.8 | 34.2 | 57.1 | 59.4 | 83.1 |
| Sede Min. de Ju | 62.0 | 65.0 | 71.0 | 74.6 | 30.2 | 22.2 | 65.9 | 70.9 |
| Inst. Nac. Pen. | 45.4 | 61.1 | 64.1 | 65.1 | 39.0 | 17.9 | 62.3 | 74.7 |
| Inst. Nac. de Des. | 57.3 | 69.7 | 62.4 | 57.0 | 16.9 | 25.0 | 63.2 | 78.4 |
| Comisión de For. | 67.2 | 76.5 | 78.4 | 71.9 | 26.4 | 50.0 | 78.3 | 87.0 |
| Registro Pred. | 51.1 | 70.9 | 73.5 | 74.7 | 24.5 | 36.9 | 76.4 | 75.4 |
| Sup. Nac. de Reg. | 76.1 | 75.6 | 82.8 | 74.9 | 13.3 | 63.0 | 74.7 | 86.5 |
| Ministerio del Int | 53.3 | 67.7 | 70.3 | 66.2 | 28.9 | 27.9 | 71.6 | 87.0 |
| Sede Min. de Econ. | 51.4 | 55.7 | 72.1 | 16.6 | 35.8 | 12.5 | 85.7 | 43.4 |
| Programa del Vaso | 62.9 | 69.2 | 72.7 | 63.4 | 36.9 | 26.1 | 67.7 | 80.2 |
| Comedor popular | 85.4 | 94.4 | 96.5 | 76.3 | 30.5 | 33.7 | 89.5 | 91.1 |
| ONP | 86.7 | 78.4 | 93.3 | 94.3 | 3.3 | 75.0 | 82.8 | 88.2 |
| SUNAT | 66.2 | 72.1 | 79.7 | 66.9 | 20.9 | 73.8 | 68.9 | 85.6 |
| Sup. Nac. de Adua | 60.0 | 74.2 | 79.8 | 66.4 | 29.5 | 59.3 | 79.3 | 85.2 |
| OSIPTEL | 75.0 | 73.4 | 82.5 | 83.6 | 3.8 | 40.0 | 87.6 | 90.2 |
| Gobiernos loc. | 54.9 | 61.8 | 59.2 | 64.4 | 34.7 | 36.9 | 58.2 | 65.8 |
| SEDAPAL | 65.1 | 71.8 | 75.0 | 70.9 | 27.9 | 41.1 | 74.6 | 85.4 |
| Sede Min. de Edu | 59.7 | 70.5 | 71.8 | 74.5 | 39.9 | 41.3 | 65.6 | 71.7 |
| DRE | 73.5 | 78.2 | 82.3 | 81.8 | 19.0 | 18.5 | 75.3 | 81.4 |
| USE/ADE | 49.6 | 68.3 | 77.6 | 70.2 | 41.3 | 13.2 | 69.2 | 80.5 |
| Colegios | 56.3 | 62.4 | 64.2 | 64.9 | 35.7 | 23.1 | 56.6 | 70.5 |
| Inst. Nac. de Cul | 46.8 | 59.1 | 59.6 | 73.5 | 45.4 | 15.6 | 63.2 | 47.6 |
| Univer. Publicas | 50.5 | 66.2 | 64.1 | 59.6 | 45.6 | 26.6 | 59.5 | 71.1 |
| Sede Min. de Salud | 13.7 | 48.6 | 45.7 | 40.3 | 76.6 | 0.0 | 33.2 | 41.4 |
| Hospitales | 35.0 | 58.8 | 60.5 | 56.8 | 51.6 | 19.0 | 59.4 | 71.6 |
| Postas médicas | 36.0 | 57.6 | 53.9 | 48.4 | 40.0 | 30.0 | 66.1 | 76.8 |
| ESSALUD | 56.8 | 70.3 | 73.2 | 66.0 | 44.2 | 34.3 | 70.9 | 76.4 |
| Min. de Trabajo | 69.2 | 66.8 | 73.3 | 73.2 | 25.6 | 27.9 | 73.8 | 82.0 |
| Min. de agricul | 53.2 | 62.0 | 65.9 | 63.9 | 30.8 | 22.9 | 59.0 | 63.3 |
| Inst. de Recurso | 57.9 | 56.9 | 69.2 | 67.4 | 33.6 | 37.5 | 57.9 | 69.7 |
| MITINCI | 45.6 | 66.6 | 65.3 | 53.8 | 29.3 | 39.3 | 50.3 | 70.4 |
| Indecopi | 75.3 | 84.2 | 85.4 | 80.5 | 9.9 | 47.7 | 93.1 | 91.1 |
| Min. de Transp | 50.3 | 67.4 | 66.8 | 59.7 | 45.2 | 42.1 | 67.9 | 74.7 |
| Consejo Nacional | 78.3 | 91.3 | 93.6 | 86.7 | 5.6 | 42.5 | 91.3 | 91.5 |
| Min. de Energia | 58.8 | 68.2 | 70.4 | 70.5 | 28.5 | 34.6 | 68.4 | 81.0 |
| Reg. Púb. de Mineria | 56.2 | 75.8 | 74.5 | 65.9 | 28.6 | 68.1 | 83.4 | 84.9 |
| Min. de Pesqueria | 51.6 | 65.5 | 81.6 | 60.7 | 41.4 | 47.9 | 61.7 | 78.4 |
| Caja de Beneficios | 57.9 | 72.4 | 71.1 | 68.6 | 35.1 | 41.7 | 79.0 | 89.0 |
| Defensoria del Pueb | 63.3 | 63.9 | 62.9 | 69.6 | 14.6 | 55.0 | 85.9 | 84.5 |

| Quality of Service | Access | Resource | Audit | State Capture | Corruption in Personnel Policy | Corruption in Budget Mgmt | Overall Corruption |
|---|---|---|---|---|---|---|---|
| 65.3 | 50.0 | 60.2 | 88.4 | 87.6 | 17.0 | 0.0 | 49.3 |
| 60.2 | 46.6 | 49.2 | 55.4 | 80.8 | 42.6 | 33.8 | 60.7 |
| 55.8 | 46.1 | 44.5 | 51.9 | 75.5 | 25.4 | 27.1 | 50.8 |
| 50.8 | 31.3 | 36.4 | 54.2 | 72.0 | 44.9 | 50.0 | 58.2 |
| 57.7 | 67.9 | 35.6 | 52.6 | 83.0 | 40.4 | 25.0 | 60.9 |
| 64.5 | 68.1 | 52.2 | 56.2 | 61.6 | 14.8 | 20.8 | 37.0 |
| 54.1 | 60.1 | 36.9 | 57.1 | 79.5 | 38.4 | 41.4 | 58.1 |
| 74.7 | 80.0 | 55.1 | 64.8 | 71.8 | 9.1 | 3.1 | 39.3 |
| 78.4 | 90.6 | 69.0 | 79.4 | 76.8 | 21.3 | 13.0 | 46.6 |
| 69.7 | 78.6 | 59.2 | 72.2 | 70.9 | 24.6 | 22.3 | 45.1 |
| 76.0 | 64.6 | 74.8 | 79.8 | 74.0 | 18.5 | 3.8 | 44.0 |
| 69.5 | 85.4 | 42.4 | 62.9 | 66.3 | 38.7 | 21.5 | 50.4 |
| 66.7 | 87.5 | 74.7 | 77.2 | 60.2 | 19.6 | 12.5 | 42.4 |
| 66.4 | 79.3 | 47.6 | 71.1 | 73.3 | 46.2 | 30.8 | 57.5 |
| 77.0 | 93.0 | 49.0 | 92.1 | 85.2 | 28.2 | 24.2 | 53.9 |
| 70.4 | 91.7 | 70.8 | 91.7 | 65.6 | 3.3 | 0.0 | 32.7 |
| 66.6 | 69.0 | 73.3 | 64.7 | 67.8 | 19.1 | 9.9 | 40.4 |
| 73.1 | 63.0 | 70.2 | 70.5 | 77.4 | 22.6 | 22.2 | 48.8 |
| 73.1 | 67.5 | 74.1 | 86.9 | 53.1 | 9.7 | 0.0 | 26.6 |
| 57.0 | 58.3 | 50.1 | 62.5 | 69.6 | 31.5 | 28.6 | 50.0 |
| 73.8 | 78.6 | 55.5 | 78.5 | 69.8 | 10.7 | 16.4 | 40.5 |
| 61.7 | 61.4 | 61.5 | 68.9 | 69.1 | 29.2 | 30.0 | 48.2 |
| 66.7 | 74.0 | 66.3 | 81.4 | 61.0 | 11.2 | 14.1 | 36.0 |
| 60.9 | 74.3 | 50.0 | 65.2 | 70.8 | 32.2 | 28.8 | 50.2 |
| 61.6 | 77.8 | 45.0 | 62.1 | 86.2 | 41.2 | 34.6 | 61.8 |
| 55.2 | 59.4 | 32.2 | 54.5 | 90.6 | 41.5 | 31.3 | 65.0 |
| 65.1 | 58.6 | 50.9 | 62.0 | 79.5 | 29.6 | 34.8 | 54.8 |
| 48.4 | 18.8 | 59.5 | 21.1 | 90.7 | 15.2 | 50.0 | 59.9 |
| 64.5 | 58.8 | 46.8 | 43.7 | 83.1 | 35.7 | 47.9 | 59.9 |
| 56.0 | 58.8 | 33.8 | 49.8 | 74.6 | 45.5 | 41.3 | 58.4 |
| 62.9 | 52.9 | 58.3 | 74.0 | 75.9 | 39.9 | 19.3 | 54.2 |
| 70.9 | 82.0 | 55.1 | 68.3 | 63.4 | 22.8 | 10.5 | 40.3 |
| 57.3 | 68.8 | 45.6 | 61.5 | 80.2 | 25.0 | 20.8 | 51.8 |
| 60.3 | 47.5 | 52.3 | 68.9 | 70.6 | 21.1 | 12.5 | 43.5 |
| 66.4 | 53.6 | 55.7 | | 67.2 | 18.2 | 25.0 | 41.8 |
| 77.3 | 79.0 | 63.1 | 87.1 | 79.7 | 16.8 | 1.2 | 45.2 |
| 59.9 | 52.7 | 61.1 | 60.2 | 70.6 | 32.8 | 27.1 | 50.9 |
| 76.0 | 78.1 | 73.5 | 90.6 | 70.2 | 24.6 | 3.1 | 44.1 |
| 69.9 | 78.6 | 59.1 | 65.5 | 69.0 | 20.7 | 21.2 | 44.0 |
| 75.1 | 65.3 | 80.8 | 75.9 | 82.7 | 26.9 | 14.1 | 51.2 |
| 70.9 | 62.5 | 74.6 | 68.8 | 62.2 | 23.1 | 65.0 | 45.2 |
| 58.1 | 52.1 | 59.5 | 69.4 | 87.0 | 49.6 | 31.3 | 65.3 |
| 71.6 | 88.8 | 56.2 | 75.4 | 78.6 | 18.1 | 7.9 | 45.3 |

(continued)

## TABLE SA.42:  INDEXES ON CORRUPTION (CONTINUED)

| Agency | Trans-parency | Rules | Enforce-ment | Merit | Political | Wage Satis-faction | Voice | Mission |
|---|---|---|---|---|---|---|---|---|
| Ministerio publico | 53.4 | 69.8 | 72.1 | 70.3 | 25.5 | 38.8 | 74.8 | 77.7 |
| FONCODES | 67.4 | 76.3 | 79.1 | 81.3 | 29.8 | 70.5 | 86.4 | 86.5 |
| Insts Nac. de desar | 91.1 | 88.6 | 93.6 | 97.4 | 11.6 | 62.5 | 81.7 | 89.0 |
| Inst. de Infraestr | 75.9 | 72.8 | 88.0 | 79.3 | 18.5 | 31.9 | 78.5 | 79.0 |
| Corporacion de Desar | 45.2 | 68.1 | 74.1 | 55.1 | 51.5 | 34.2 | 62.7 | 73.4 |
| Ministerio de Defensa | 55.8 | 75.5 | 66.4 | 72.1 | 27.8 | 24.0 | 79.2 | 85.8 |
| Consejo de Just. Mil | 65.8 | 79.4 | 79.0 | 73.1 | 12.6 | 27.5 | 80.9 | 83.7 |
| Congreso de la Repub | 55.0 | 56.3 | 40.9 | 57.3 | 58.3 | 37.5 | 74.0 | 74.2 |
| RENIEC | 74.7 | 83.7 | 88.0 | 89.4 | 10.4 | 59.2 | 79.2 | 88.9 |
| Promudeh | 27.1 | 61.6 | 62.5 | 40.0 | 44.0 | 41.7 | 71.3 | 67.7 |
| INABIF | 50.3 | 62.2 | 67.0 | 58.6 | 34.0 | 46.3 | 60.4 | 72.4 |
| PRONAA | 34.3 | 74.1 | 84.4 | 39.5 | 55.2 | 56.4 | 74.6 | 82.9 |
| Programa de Apoyo | 49.3 | 58.8 | 63.9 | 55.3 | 47.9 | 31.3 | 59.0 | 71.2 |
| Oficina Nac. de Coop | 50.1 | 71.3 | 73.2 | 49.9 | 39.7 | 37.5 | 76.9 | 80.9 |
| **Averages:** | | | | | | | | |
| National | 57.9 | 68.1 | 71.5 | 66.6 | 30.3 | 39.0 | 71.1 | 75.8 |
| Municipal | 51.8 | 69.9 | 71.4 | 65.7 | 34.8 | 36.0 | 70.0 | 78.8 |
| Judiciary | 46.2 | 62.1 | 66.9 | 63.0 | 34.6 | 31.6 | 66.4 | 70.9 |

*Source:*  World Bank (2001c).

## TABLE SA.43:  CORRUPTION IN THE JUDICIARY, NATIONAL AND MUNICIPAL AGENCIES
Based on public officials' responses

| Variable | National Agencies Mean | Municipal Agencies Mean | Judiciary Mean |
|---|---|---|---|
| Index of Corruption | 47.3 | 55.1 | 53.6 |
| Index of State Capture | 73.1 | 79.2 | 77.2 |
| Index of Corruption in Personnel Administration | 24.0 | 34.3 | 31.9 |
| Index of Corruption in Budget Administration | 20.5 | 28.9 | 28.3 |
| Index of Transparency | 57.9 | 51.8 | 46.2 |
| Index of Quality of Rules | 68.1 | 69.9 | 62.1 |
| Index of Enforcement | 71.5 | 71.4 | 66.9 |
| Extent of Meritocracy | 66.6 | 65.7 | 63.0 |
| Degree of Politicization | 30.3 | 34.8 | 34.6 |
| Wage Satisfaction | 39.0 | 36.0 | 31.6 |
| Index of Voice | 71.1 | 70.0 | 66.4 |
| Index of Mission | 75.8 | 78.8 | 70.9 |
| (Perceived) Quality of Service | 66.3 | 64.3 | 58.3 |
| Service Access | 68.2 | 69.7 | 52.9 |
| Availability of Resources | 60.6 | 50.1 | 45.0 |
| Existence of Internal Audit Mechanisms | 68.6 | 65.5 | 59.4 |

*Source:*  World Bank (2001c).

| Quality of Service | Access | Resource | Audit | State Capture | Corruption in Personnel Policy | Corruption in Budget Mgmt | Overall Corruption |
|---|---|---|---|---|---|---|---|
| 70.6 | 79.4 | 63.8 | 58.6 | 77.7 | 28.0 | 20.3 | 51.2 |
| 72.2 | 96.8 | 79.1 | 86.2 | 85.4 | 13.0 | 17.7 | 48.7 |
| 70.4 | 84.4 | 74.9 | 98.6 | 57.6 | 35.7 | 0.0 | 41.0 |
| 69.6 | 94.4 | 81.6 | 90.3 | 68.4 | 4.1 | 6.9 | 36.7 |
| 63.7 | 73.0 | 58.4 | 63.3 | 72.9 | 30.0 | 32.4 | 50.2 |
| 63.8 | 71.6 | 63.7 | 63.8 | 70.0 | 36.5 | 36.4 | 51.6 |
| 61.5 | 78.1 | 70.2 | 76.1 | 77.5 | 13.8 | 0.0 | 43.5 |
| 80.1 | 62.5 | 57.6 | 64.9 | 75.5 | 10.8 | 12.5 | 42.7 |
| 81.2 | 87.5 | 76.4 | 84.4 | 82.1 | 18.9 | 5.8 | 47.5 |
| 58.3 | 65.3 | 45.1 | 44.0 | 67.7 | 26.6 | 48.2 | 48.2 |
| 62.8 | 74.4 | 56.6 | 59.9 | 77.6 | 29.1 | 30.2 | 52.7 |
| 63.9 | 84.1 | 67.9 | 56.0 | 77.5 | 29.3 | 42.6 | 53.5 |
| 57.7 | 72.9 | 54.7 | 59.8 | 68.0 | 33.2 | 32.5 | 50.1 |
| 60.7 | 84.4 | 55.4 | 53.4 | 80.3 | 34.9 | 35.9 | 56.0 |
| | | | | | | | |
| 66.3 | 68.2 | 60.6 | 68.6 | 73.1 | 24.0 | 20.5 | 47.3 |
| 64.3 | 69.7 | 50.1 | 65.5 | 79.2 | 34.3 | 28.9 | 55.1 |
| 58.3 | 52.9 | 45.0 | 59.4 | 77.2 | 31.9 | 28.3 | 53.6 |

# TABLE SA.44: EXPENDITURE BY DEPARTMENT, 2001

Millions of Nuevo Soles

| | Departments | No. of UEs | Population | TOTAL EXPENDITURES | | | CAPITAL INVESTMENTS | | | GOODS AND SERVICES | | |
|---|---|---|---|---|---|---|---|---|---|---|---|---|
| | | | | Budgeted | Executed | Executed/Budgeted | Budgeted | Executed | Executed/Budgeted | Budgeted | Executed | Executed/Budgeted |
| 1 | Amazonas | 12 | 420,606 | 228.7 | 215.3 | 94.1 | 97.4 | 85.6 | 87.8 | 30.1 | 23.7 | 78.8 |
| 2 | Ancash | 27 | 1,092,662 | 619.2 | 591.4 | 95.5 | 166.2 | 127.3 | 76.6 | 78.5 | 62.8 | 80.0 |
| 3 | Apurimac | 14 | 455,637 | 300.1 | 299.0 | 99.6 | 127.8 | 125.6 | 98.3 | 41.9 | 33.5 | 79.9 |
| 4 | Arequipa | 19 | 1,067,469 | 811.5 | 913.8 | 112.6 | 208.0 | 248.1 | 119.3 | 102.8 | 101.1 | 98.3 |
| 5 | Ayacucho | 20 | 541,427 | 413.8 | 465.1 | 112.4 | 139.8 | 188.8 | 135.0 | 66.8 | 49.9 | 74.8 |
| 6 | Cajamarca | 20 | 1,480,690 | 522.9 | 547.0 | 104.6 | 141.3 | 154.7 | 109.5 | 63.8 | 51.2 | 80.3 |
| 7 | Callao | 13 | 774,604 | 421.7 | 547.0 | 129.7 | 124.9 | 63.6 | 50.9 | 119.6 | 120.1 | 100.4 |
| 8 | Cusco | 17 | 1,194,275 | 702.9 | 716.6 | 101.9 | 250.1 | 250.7 | 100.2 | 115.2 | 90.6 | 78.7 |
| 9 | Huancavelica | 11 | 435,596 | 227.1 | 215.6 | 94.9 | 63.2 | 59.9 | 94.8 | 40.7 | 28.9 | 70.9 |
| 10 | Huánuco | 12 | 800,543 | 346.3 | 322.0 | 93.0 | 110.2 | 79.6 | 72.2 | 46.9 | 39.3 | 83.9 |
| 11 | Ica | 14 | 676,249 | 448.2 | 464.6 | 103.7 | 60.9 | 43.5 | 71.3 | 54.3 | 47.3 | 87.1 |
| 12 | Junín | 20 | 1,232,343 | 898.3 | 660.2 | 73.5 | 181.5 | 108.5 | 59.8 | 257.9 | 72.3 | 28.0 |
| 13 | La Libertad | 32 | 1,483,681 | 686.7 | 741.1 | 107.9 | 93.9 | 87.7 | 93.4 | 84.0 | 71.2 | 84.7 |
| 14 | Lambayeque | 14 | 1,110,129 | 518.2 | 553.5 | 106.8 | 72.8 | 65.3 | 89.6 | 72.3 | 58.6 | 81.0 |
| 15 | Lima | 194 | 7,617,193 | 24,829.0 | 23,747.2 | 95.6 | 1,696.4 | 1,291.8 | 76.2 | 4,643.7 | 4,672.7 | 100.6 |
| 16 | Loreto | 18 | 894,307 | 506.4 | 511.7 | 101.0 | 127.8 | 115.8 | 90.6 | 83.1 | 72.7 | 87.6 |
| 17 | Madre de Dios | 8 | 96,703 | 88.9 | 80.0 | 90.0 | 39.4 | 27.6 | 70.0 | 15.4 | 14.4 | 93.3 |
| 18 | Moquegua | 6 | 153,383 | 139.8 | 147.7 | 105.6 | 49.6 | 51.3 | 103.4 | 15.7 | 13.9 | 88.4 |
| 19 | Pasco | 8 | 259,137 | 191.7 | 172.7 | 90.1 | 31.4 | 23.3 | 74.3 | 29.3 | 22.6 | 77.1 |
| 20 | Piura | 16 | 1,611,573 | 798.3 | 788.1 | 98.7 | 267.9 | 216.2 | 80.7 | 109.3 | 00.1 | 91.6 |
| 21 | Puno | 33 | 1,247,494 | 648.3 | 651.2 | 100.4 | 182.2 | 170.2 | 93.4 | 93.2 | 74.1 | 79.5 |
| 22 | San Martín | 23 | 746,202 | 405.2 | 445.1 | 109.9 | 148.8 | 185.9 | 125.0 | 58.2 | 40.2 | 69.0 |
| 23 | Tacna | 9 | 286,539 | 227.1 | 222.2 | 97.9 | 63.6 | 51.6 | 81.2 | 32.0 | 28.1 | 87.7 |
| 24 | Tumbes | 8 | 197,605 | 171.3 | 179.1 | 104.6 | 58.5 | 58.2 | 99.4 | 18.2 | 17.9 | 98.6 |
| 25 | Ucayali | 16 | 450,693 | 237.4 | 225.6 | 95.1 | 66.0 | 57.5 | 87.1 | 46.0 | 35.2 | 76.4 |
| | **Total** | **584** | **26,326,740** | **35,389.3** | **34,422.7** | **97.3** | **4,569.7** | **3,938.2** | **86.2** | **6,319.0** | **5,942.5** | **94.0** |
| | Total w/o Lima | 390 | 18,709,547 | 10,560.2 | 10,675.5 | 101.1 | 2,873.3 | 2,646.4 | 92.1 | 1,675.3 | 1,269.8 | 75.8 |

Source: MEF.

TABLE SA.45:  EXPENDITURE COEFFICIENTS BY DEPARTMENT, 2001

| | Department | No. of UEs | Population | Expenditure (Mlns of NS) | Coefficient of Expenditure by UEs | Coefficient of Expenditure by Population | Poverty Rate | Extreme Poverty Rate | Poverty Rankings by Definition | | |
|---|---|---|---|---|---|---|---|---|---|---|---|
| | | | | | | | | | MEF | INEI Poverty | INEI Extreme Poverty |
| 1 | Amazonas | 12 | 420,606 | 215.29 | 17.9 | 51.2 | 74.5 | 41.1 | 9 | 7 | 10 |
| 2 | Ancash | 27 | 1,092,662 | 591.41 | 21.9 | 54.1 | 61.1 | 33.3 | 3 | 15 | 12 |
| 3 | Apurimac | 14 | 455,637 | 298.97 | 21.4 | 65.6 | 78.0 | 47.4 | 5 | 4 | 5 |
| 4 | Arequipa | 19 | 1,067,469 | 913.80 | 48.1 | 85.6 | 44.1 | 14.5 | 15 | 19 | 18 |
| 5 | Ayacucho | 20 | 541,427 | 465.12 | 23.3 | 85.9 | 72.5 | 45.4 | 4 | 8 | 8 |
| 6 | Cajamarca | 20 | 1,480,690 | 546.98 | 27.3 | 36.9 | 77.4 | 50.8 | 6 | 5 | 4 |
| 7 | Callao | 13 | 774,604 | 546.98 | 42.1 | 70.6 | | | | | |
| 8 | Cusco | 17 | 1,194,275 | 716.58 | 42.2 | 60.0 | 75.3 | 51.3 | 11 | 6 | 3 |
| 9 | Huancavelica | 11 | 435,596 | 215.58 | 19.6 | 49.5 | 88.0 | 74.4 | 2 | 1 | 1 |
| 10 | Huánuco | 12 | 800,543 | 321.97 | 26.8 | 40.2 | 78.9 | 61.9 | 7 | 2 | 2 |
| 11 | Ica | 14 | 676,249 | 464.60 | 33.2 | 68.7 | 41.7 | 8.6 | 20 | 20 | 20 |
| 12 | Junín | 20 | 1,232,343 | 660.23 | 33.0 | 53.6 | 57.5 | 24.3 | 10 | 16 | 14 |
| 13 | La Libertad | 32 | 1,483,681 | 741.07 | 23.2 | 49.9 | 52.1 | 18.3 | 8 | 17 | 17 |
| 14 | Lambayeque | 14 | 1,110,129 | 553.50 | 39.5 | 49.9 | 63.0 | 19.9 | 17 | 14 | 16 |
| 15 | Lima | 194 | 7,617,193 | 23,747.19 | 122.4 | 311.8 | 33.4 | 3.1 | 16 | 22 | 24 |
| 16 | Loreto | 18 | 894,307 | 511.69 | 28.4 | 57.2 | 70.0 | 47.2 | 13 | 10 | 6 |
| 17 | Madre de Dios | 8 | 96,703 | 79.99 | 10.0 | 82.7 | 36.7 | 11.5 | 23 | 21 | 19 |
| 18 | Moquegua | 6 | 153,383 | 147.72 | 24.6 | 96.3 | 29.6 | 7.6 | 21 | 24 | 21 |
| 19 | Pasco | 8 | 259,137 | 172.66 | 21.6 | 66.6 | 66.1 | 33.2 | 18 | 12 | 13 |
| 20 | Piura | 16 | 1,611,573 | 788.08 | 49.3 | 48.9 | 63.3 | 21.4 | 14 | 13 | 15 |
| 21 | Puno | 33 | 1,247,494 | 651.20 | 19.7 | 52.2 | 78.0 | 46.1 | 1 | 3 | 7 |
| 22 | San Martín | 23 | 746,202 | 445.11 | 19.4 | 59.7 | 66.9 | 36.2 | 12 | 11 | 11 |
| 23 | Tacna | 9 | 286,539 | 222.24 | 24.7 | 77.6 | 32.8 | 5.2 | 24 | 23 | 23 |
| 24 | Tumbes | 8 | 197,605 | 179.08 | 22.4 | 90.6 | 46.8 | 7.4 | 22 | 18 | 22 |
| 25 | Ucayali | 16 | 450,693 | 225.65 | 14.1 | 50.1 | 70.5 | 44.9 | 19 | 9 | 9 |
| | **Total** | **584** | **26,326,740** | **34,422.69** | **58.9** | **130.8** | | | | | |
| | Total w/o Lima | 390 | 18,709,547 | 10,675.50 | 27.4 | 57.1 | | | | | |

Source: MEF.

## TABLE SA.46: DECENTRALIZATION IN LAC

| | Political | Functional | Fiscal |
|---|---|---|---|
| **FEDERAL COUNTRIES** | | | |
| Argentina | Federal country reverts to type | Secondary education and health transferred to provinces | Minor adjustments in revenue sharing |
| Brazil | Federal country reverts to type, with new constitutional guarantees for municipalities | No explicit reallocation of functions | Increase in revenue sharing to municipalities |
| Colombia | Introduces election of mayors and governors | Transfers primary education, health to provinces | Increases earmarked transfers for social service expenditures in provinces, general revenue sharing to municipalities |
| Venezuela | Introduces election of governors, direct election of mayors | Introduces optional decentralization of social services, infrastructure to states | Increase in funding is to follow decentralization of functions |
| Mexico | Concedes opposition victories in states, municipalities | Transfers education and health to states; water supply, paving, public security to municipalities | Increases earmarked transfers for social services in states |
| **UNITARY COUNTRIES** | | | |
| Chile | Reverts to elected mayors in small municipalities, introduces election of mayors in cities | Transfers primary education, health to municipalities | Increases earmarked transfers for social services to municipalities |
| Bolivia | Introduces election of mayors | Transfers primary schools, clinics (physical assets only) to municipalities | Increases general revenue sharing to municipalities |
| Guatemala | Reverts to elected mayors | — | Increases general revenue sharing |

*Source:* Burki, Perry, and Dillinger (1999).

## TABLE SA.47: PRINCIPAL REVENUE SOURCES OF SUBNATIONAL GOVERNMENTS

| | Municipal Government |
|---|---|
| Argentina | Varying shares of provincial taxes and transfer revenues, fees |
| Brazil | Fixed shares of state VAT and central income and excise taxes, property and service taxes |
| Colombia | Fixed shares of total Central Government taxes; property tax; industry and commerce tax; gasoline surcharges |
| Mexico | Fixed shares of federal taxes (passed through states), property tax, business licenses |
| Peru | Shares of Central Government revenues, property tax, mining cannon |
| Venezuela | Fixed shares of state revenue-sharing receipts, taxes on property, vehicle tax |
| Chile | Earmarked capitation grants for education, health, property tax |
| Ecuador | Fixed shares of Central Government oil revenue, taxes on property, business assets, vehicles, business registration |
| Guatemala | Fixed shares of total Central Government revenue, miscellaneous local taxes |
| Bolivia | Fixed shares of total central government revenues, taxes on vehicles and property |

*Source:* Burki, Perry, and Dillinger (1999).

TABLE SA.48: SUMMARY OF MINING TAXATION AUTHORITY FOR SELECTED TAXES AND FEES

| Country | Corporate Income Tax | | | Mineral Royalty | | | Dividend Withholding Tax | | | Excise/Sales Tax on Equip. and Services | | | VAT on Imported Equipment | | | Property Tax | | | Fee Based on Land Area | | | Stamp Tax | | |
|---|---|---|---|---|---|---|---|---|---|---|---|---|---|---|---|---|---|---|---|---|---|---|---|---|
| | N | P | L | N | P | L | N | P | L | N | P | L | N | P | L | N | P | L | N | P | L | N | P | L |
| Argentina | X | | | | X | | X | | | | X | | X | | | | | | | X | | | X | |
| Bolivia | X | | | | X | | X | | | | | | X | | | | | | | — | | | | |
| Burkina Faso | X | | | X | | | X | | | | | | X | | | | | | X | | | X | | |
| Canada (Ont.) | X | X | | | | | X | | | | | | X | | | | | | | | | | | |
| Chile | X | | | X | | | X | | | X | | | X | | | X | | | X | | | X | | |
| China | X | X | | X | | | X | | | | | | | | | | | | X | | | X | | |
| Ghana | X | | | X | | | X | | | X | | | X | | | | | | X | | | X | | |
| Greenland | X | | | X | | | X | | | | | | | | | | | | | | | | | |
| Indonesia 2/ | X | | | X | | | X | | | | | | X | | | 3 | | | X | | | X | | |
| Ivory Coast | X | | | X | | | X | | | | | | X | | | X | | | X | | | | | |
| Kazakhstan | X | | | X | | | X | | | | | | X | | | | | X | | | X | | | |
| Mexico | X | | | | | | X | | | | | | X | | | 4 | 4 | 4 | 4 | 4 | 4 | | | |
| Papua NG 5/ | X | | | X | | | X | | | X | X | | | | | X | | | X | | | X | | |
| **Peru** | **X** | | | | | | **X** | | | | | | **X** | | | | | | | | | | | |
| Philippines | X | | | X | 6 | | X | | | | | | X | | | | | X | | | X | X | | |
| Poland | X | | | | | 7 | X | | | | | | | | X | | | X | | | | | | |

(continued)

TABLE SA.48: SUMMARY OF MINING TAXATION AUTHORITY FOR SELECTED TAXES AND FEES (CONTINUED)

| Country | Corporate Income Tax | | | Mineral Royalty | | | Dividend Withholding Tax | | | Excise/Sales Tax on Equip. and Services | | | VAT on Imported Equipment | | | Property Tax | | | Fee Based on Land Area | | | Stamp Tax | | |
|---|---|---|---|---|---|---|---|---|---|---|---|---|---|---|---|---|---|---|---|---|---|---|---|---|
| | N | P | L | N | P | L | N | P | L | N | P | L | N | P | L | N | P | L | N | P | L | N | P | L |
| South Africa | X | | | 8 | | | X | | | X | | | X | | | | | | | | | | | |
| Sweden | X | | | | | | | | | X | | | X | | | X | | | X | | | X | | |
| Tanzania | X | | | X | | | X | | | | | | | | | | X | | X | | | X | | |
| USA | X | X | | 9 | 9 | | X | | | X | X | | | | | | X | | | | | | | |
| Uzbekistan | X | | | X | | | X | | | | | | X | | | | X | | | | X | | | |
| West. Australia | X | | | | X | | X | | | X | | | X | | | | X | | | X | | | | |
| Zimbabwe | X | | | | | | X | | | | | | | | | | | | X | | | | X | |

N - National government; P - Provincial government; L - Local government

*Notes:* Where an X is given, the tax exists although a project may sometimes be exempted; where there is a blank the tax does not apply to a typical mine; where a number is given, refer to that attached note with that number.

1/ Bolivia: 70% to national government, 30% to provincial.

2/ Indonesia: 6th generation contract, taxes under later COWs may differ.

3/ Indonesia: Status of property tax is unclear from author's data sources.

4/ Mexico: This tax may go to the national, provincial, or local government depending on ownership.

5/ Papua New Guinea: For larger mines specially negotiated revenue sharing agreements between national, provincial, and affected communities may apply.

6/ Philippines: If minerals are located on "ancestral lands," a special royalty is assessed.

7/ Poland: If a "basic" mineral, paid to the national government; if a common mineral (industrial mineral), paid to local government.

8/ South Africa: A royalty is paid to national government for mineral in federal lands. Most minerals are privately owned.

9/ USA: Royalties are not assessed for most minerals unless they are found in special types of land.

*Source:* Otto (2002).

## TABLE SA.49: MINING FISCAL METHODS AND THEIR AMENABILITY TO FISCAL DECENTRALIZATION

| Tax type | National Government | Provincial Government | Local Government |
|---|:---:|:---:|:---:|
| Income or profits-based tax | Y | P | N |
| Import duty | Y | N | N |
| Export duty | Y | N | N |
| Royalty (profits-based type) | Y | P | N |
| Royalty (ad valorem type) | Y | Y | P |
| Royalty tax (unit type) | Y | Y | Y |
| Royalty tax collected nationally and % distributed | Y | Y | Y |
| Licensing fees | Y | Y | Y |
| Surface rental or land use fees | Y | Y | Y |
| Withholding taxes on loan interest, dividends, services | Y | N | N |
| VAT on goods and services | Y | P | N |
| Sales & excise tax | Y | P | P |
| Stamp duty | Y | Y | Y |
| Property tax (on book or assessed value) | Y | Y | Y |
| Payroll-based taxes | Y | P | N |
| Surtaxes | Y | Y | Y |
| User fees | Y | Y | Y |

Source: Otto (2002).

## TABLE SA.50: TOTAL TRANSFERS IN SOLES
(by poverty quantile)

| Poverty quantile | Vaso de Leche | Canon Minero | FONCOMUN |
|---|---:|---:|---:|
| Poorest | 20,740,034 | 4,506,219 | 106,413,060 |
| 19 | 19,067,753 | 5,411,235 | 103,179,580 |
| 18 | 18,685,593 | 7,590,344 | 100,253,079 |
| 17 | 18,545,614 | 8,705,941 | 88,758,658 |
| 16 | 18,320,393 | 10,719,708 | 99,828,182 |
| 15 | 17,343,102 | 8,497,593 | 94,686,509 |
| 14 | 15,464,843 | 8,564,754 | 86,423,873 |
| 13 | 14,205,007 | 3,133,694 | 70,217,236 |
| 12 | 14,694,335 | 2,562,790 | 71,139,439 |
| 11 | 17,086,913 | 4,805,701 | 78,724,575 |
| 10 | 15,225,805 | 1,599,191 | 58,443,408 |
| 9 | 19,317,850 | 536,952 | 55,406,923 |
| 8 | 18,394,082 | 2,992,030 | 38,575,661 |
| 7 | 14,362,596 | 613,003 | 46,552,702 |
| 6 | 20,370,958 | 899,337 | 47,543,907 |
| 5 | 24,174,523 | 1,432,527 | 32,616,105 |
| 4 | 13,518,762 | 2,052,245 | 44,596,654 |
| 3 | 15,839,307 | 1,833,122 | 33,461,090 |
| 2 | 11,384,530 | 849,128 | 82,591,765 |
| Richest | 5,504,997 | 3,973,021 | 28,666,869 |
| **TOTAL** | **332,246,997** | **81,278,535** | **1,368,079,275** |

Source: Apoyo Institute (2002).

# BIBLIOGRAPHY

Altobelli, L. 2001. "Decentralization to Improve Health Care for the Poor." Background Paper for World Bank (2001a).

Apel, M., J. Hansen, and H. Lindberg. 1996. "Potential Output and Output Gap." *Quarterly Review of the Bank of Sweden*, 3 :24–35.

Apoyo Institute. 2002a. "A Public Expenditure Tracking Survey (PETS): Central Government Transfers to Municipalities in Peru." Background Paper for the *Public Expenditure Review*.

_____. 2002b. "PETS-The Education Sector in Peru." Background Paper for the *Public Expenditure Review*.

Arcia, Gustavo, and Humberto Belli. 1999. "Rebuilding the Social Contract: School Autonomy in Nicaragua." LCSHD Working Paper Series, Department of Human Development. Washington, D.C.: World Bank, April.

Arias, Luis, and others. 2000. "Ajuste Fiscal Ex-Ante o Ex-Post: Déficit Cíclicos en Perú." In E. Talvi and C. Vega, *Como Armar el Rompecabezas Fiscal*. Washington, D.C.: Inter-American Development Bank.

Backus, D. K., and P. J. Kehoe. 1992. "International Evidence on the Historical Properties of Business Cycles." *The American Economic Review*, 82 :864–88.

Banco Central de la República de Perú. 2002. "Sostenibilidad de la Política Fiscal." Jorge Estrella, Seminar on Fiscal Rules, Lima.

Brown, E. Cary. 1956. "Fiscal Policies in the Thirties: A Reappraisal." *The American Economic Review*, 46 :857–79.

Burki, S., G. Perry, and W. Dillinger. 1999. *Beyond the Center: Decentralizing the State.* Washington, D.C.: World Bank.

Calvo, Guillermo, Alejandro Izquierdo, and Ernesto Talvi. 2002. "Sudden Stops, the Real Exchange Rate and Fiscal Sustainability: Argentina's Lessons." Inter-American Development Bank Research Department. Washington, D.C.

Central Bank of Peru. 2002. "Estimando el Balance Estructural de Perú." Presentación al Seminario sobre Reglas Fiscales, Lima.

CEPAL. 1998. "La Descentralización de la Educación y la Salud." Santiago de Chile.

_____. 2001. *Decentralización en América Latina: Teoría y Práctica*. Iván Finot (CEPAL LC/L 1521), Santiago de Chile.

Cortez, R. 1998. "Equidad y Calidad de los servicios de Salud: El Caso de los CLAS." Universidad del Pacífico/Ministerio de Salud, Lima.

_____. 2001. "Capítulo de Salud." Universidad del Pacífico, Lima.

De Ferranti, David, Guillermo E. Perry, Indermit S. Gill, and Luis Servén. 2000. *Securing Our Future in a Global Economy*. Washington D.C.: World Bank.

De Leeuw, Frank, Thomas M. Holloway, Darwin G. Johnson, David S. McClain, and Charles A. Waite. 1980. "The High Employment Budget: New Estimates, 1955–80." *Survey of Current Business,* 60 :13–43.

Deutsche Bank. 2001. "Public Debt Sustainability in Selected Emerging Markets."

Díaz, J. 2001. "Grado de Focalización de Algunos Programas Sociales, 1998–2000." Ministerio de Economía y Finanzas, Dirección de Asuntos Económicos y Financieros, Lima.

Dolado, J. J., M. Sebastián, and J. Vallés. 1993. "Cyclical Patterns of the Spanish Economy." *Investigaciones Económicas,* XVII :445–73.

Dornbusch, R., and S. Edwards. 1991. *The Macroeconomics of Populism*. National Bureau of Economic Research. Chicago: The University of Chicago Press.

Dornbusch, R., and S. Fischer. 1990. *Macroeconomics*. New York: McGraw-Hill.

European Central Bank. 2000. "Potential Output Growth and Output Gaps: Concept, Uses and Estimates." *ECB Monthly Bulletin,* October :37–47.

Fellner, William. 1982. "The High Employment Budget and Potential Output: A Critique." *Survey of Current Business,* 62 November :25–33.

Fernández, E. 2002. "La Deuda Corriente de los Municipios Peruanos." Background Paper for the Performance Expenditure Review. Washington, D.C.

Finot, Ivan. 2001. "Descentralización en América Latina: teoría y práctica." Instituto Latinoamericano y del Caribe de Planificación Económica y Social–ILPES.

Giorno, C., P. Richardson, D. Roseveare, and P. van den Noord. 1995. "Estimating Potential Output, Ouput, Output Gaps, and Structural Budget Balances." Organization for Economic Cooperation and Development Economics Department, Working Papers, No. 152. Paris.

Gonzalez C., D. Rosenblatt, and S. Webb. 2002. "Stabilizing Intergovernmental Transfers in Latin America: A Complement to National/Subnational Fiscal Rules." Paper for the Seminar on Fiscal Rules, Lima.

Gregory P. 2002. "Public Sector Employment in Perú." Background Paper for the Performance Expenditure Review, Washington, D.C.

Gupta, Sanjeev, Marijn Venhoeven, and Erwin Tiongson. 1999. "Does Higher Governance Spending Buy Better Results in Education and Health Care?" International Monetary Fund Working Papers WP/99/21, Fiscal Affairs Department. Washington, D.C.

Hagemann, Robert. 1999. "The Structural Budget Balance: The IMF's Methodology." Working Paper. International Monetary Fund, Washington, D.C., July.

Hodrick, Robert, and Edward Prescott. 1997. "Postwar U.S. Business Cycles." *Journal of Money, Credit and Banking,* 29(1) :1–16.

IMF (International Monetary Fund). 2000. "Peru: Racionalización del Sistema Tributario." G. Kopits, J. P. Ley, and J. Córdova. Departament of Public Finance. Washington, D.C.

IMF/WB. 2001. "Tracking of Poverty Reducing Spending in Heavily Indebted Poor Countries (HIPC)." Washington, D.C: International Monetary Fund.

_____. 2002. "Actions to Strengthen the Tracking of Poverty Reducing Spending in Heavily Indebted Poor Countries (HIPC)." Washington, D.C.: International Monetary Fund.

Instituto Apoyo. 2002. "Central Government Transfers to Municipalities in Peru: A Detailed Look at the Vaso de Leche Program." Public Expenditure Tracking Survey. Report to the Public Expenditure Review of Peru.

Jayasuriya R., and Q. Wodon. 2001. "Explaining Country Efficiency in Improving Health and Education Indicators: The Role of Urbanization." Background Paper to *World Development Report 2003*. Washington, D.C.: World Bank.

Jiménez F. 2002. "Perú: Sostenibilidad, Balance Estructural y Propuesta de Regla Fiscal." Seminar on Fiscal Rules, Lima.

Kaufmann, Daniel, Aart Kraay, and Pablo Zoido-Lobatón. 2002. "Governance Matters II: Updated Indicators for 2000/01." Washington, D.C.: World Bank.

Kopits, George. 2002. "Una Vista Panorámica de las Reglas Macro Fiscales." Paper of the Seminar on Fiscal Rules, Lima.

Kopits, George; Juan Pablo Córdoba, Eduardo Ley, and Juan Toro. 2000. "Perú: Racionalización del Sistema Tributario." Fondo Monetario Internacional.

Larrain, F., and J. Sachs. 1991. *Macroeconomics in the Global Economy*. New Jersey: Prentice Hall.

López-Cálix, José R. 2002. "Guatemala: La Macroeconomía del Ciclo Electoral." *Banca Central*, 40, Enero-Abril. Guatemala City.

Ma, J. 2002. "Monitoring Fiscal Risks of Subnational Governments." In H. Polackova and A. Schick, *Government at Risk*. Washington, D.C.: World Bank.

Matsuda, Yasuhiko, and Geoffrey Shepherd. 2000. "Peru's Public Administration and the Delivery of Public Services." Background Paper to the Peru IGR. Washington, D.C.

MED. 2001. "Principales Lineamientos de Política Educativa." Lima.

Moore, Richard. 2002. "Decentralization in the Social Sectors: Prospects for the Decentralization of Health and Education in Peru." Background Paper to the Public Expenditure Review of Peru.

Moore, Richard, and Eugenia Rosales. 2001. "Estudio de Organización, Estructura y Funciones del Ministerio de Educación del Ecuador." Report prepared for the Human Development Network. Washington D.C.: World Bank.

Morón, Eduardo. 2001. "El Debate de la Transparencia." Lima: Universidad del Pacífico.

Mostajo, Rossana. 2002a. ¿"Protección Presupuestaria?–Los Programas Sociales Protegidos en el Perú." Background Paper to the Public Expenditure Review of Peru.

_____. 2002b. "El Sistema Presupuestario en el Perú." Serie: Gestión Pública, Instituto Latinoamericano y del Caribe de Planificación Económica y Social–ILPES.

Oliva, C. 2002. "Fiscal Trends and the Fiscal Sustainability Issue." Background Paper to the Public Expenditure Review of Peru.

Ortiz de Zevallos, Gabriel. 1999. "La Economía Política de las reformas Institucionales en Perú: los Casos de Educación, Salud y Pensiones." Prepared for the Inter-American Development Bank, Documento de Trabajo R-348. Washington, D.C.

Otto, M. James. 2002. "Position of the Peruvian Taxation System as Compared to Mining Taxation Systems in Other Nations." Ministry of Economy and Finance. Report to the Public Expenditure Review of Peru.

Paredes, Carlos, and Jeffrey Sachs. 1991. *Stabilization and Growth in Peru*. Washington D.C.: The Brookings Institution.

PCM. 2002. "The Strategy of Decentralization." Mimeo. Lima.

Perry, G. 2002. "Can Fiscal Rules Help Reduce Macroeconomic Volatility in LAC?" Paper presented at a Seminar in Oaxaca, Mexico.

Reinikka, R., and J. Svensson. 2002. "Assessing Frontline Service Delivery." Draft. World Bank.

Rose-Ackerman, David. 1999. *Corruption and Government: Causes, Consequences and Reform*. Cambridge: Cambridge University Press.

Saavedra, Jaime, Roberto Melzi, and Arturo Miranda. 2001. "El Financiamiento de la Educación Pública en el Perú: El Rol de las Familias." Lima: GRADE.

Schady, N. 2002. "Notes on A Trabajar Program." Mimeo. Washington, D.C.: World Bank.

Schenone, Osvaldo H. 2002. "Exoneraciones y Regímenes Tributarios Especiales en Perú." Background Paper to the Public Expenditure Review of Peru.

Seligson, M. 2002. "The Impact of Corruption on Regime Legitimacy: A Comparison Study of Four Latin American Countries." *Journal of Politics,* 64 :408–33.

Treisman, D, 2000. "The Causes of Corruption: A Cross National Study." *Journal of Public Economics,* 3 :399–458.

Valderrama J. 2002. "Perú: Propuesta de Reforma a las Reglas Fiscales." Paper for the Seminar on Fiscal Rules in Lima.

Winkler, Donald, and Richard Moore. 1996. "Best Practices in Education Decentralization in Latin America." Paper prepared for Seminar on Decentralization in LAC, Caracas, Venezuela.

Wodon, Quentin. 2002. "The Efficiency of Public Spending in Peru." Background Paper to the Public Expenditure Review of Peru.

Wodon, Quentin, and Norman Hicks. 2001. "SIMSIP: A Simulation Tool." Draft. Washington, D.C.: World Bank.

World Bank. 1994. "Peru: Public Expenditure Review." Washington, D.C.

_____. 1999. "Peru: Improving Health Care for the Poor." Washington, D.C.

_____. 2000. "Peru: Policy Notes." Washington, D.C.

_____. 2001a. "Peru: Institutional and Governance Review." Poverty Reduction and Economic Management Unit, Latin America and the Caribbean.

_____. 2001b. *Peruvian Education at a Crossroads: Challenges and Opportunities for the 21st* Century. Washington, D.C.

_____. 2001c. "Voices of the Misgoverned and Misruled: An Empirical Diagnostic Study on Governance, Rule of Law and Corruption for Peru. A Survey." Washington D.C.: World Bank Institute.

World Bank and Inter-American Development Bank. 2001a. "Peru: Country Financial Accountability Assessment." Draft. Washington, D.C.

_____. 2001b. "Peru: Country Procurement Report." Draft. Washington, D.C.

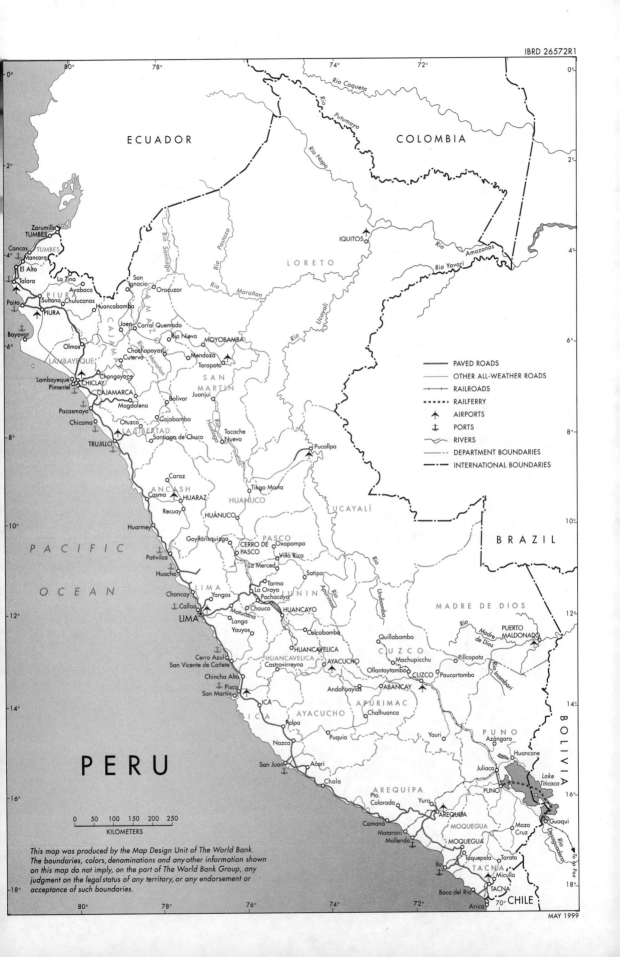